Becoming a Christian in Christendom

Becoming a Christian in Christendom

Radical Discipleship and the Way of the Cross in America's "Christian" Culture

Jason A. Mahn

Fortress Press
Minneapolis

BECOMING A CHRISTIAN IN CHRISTENDOM

Radical Discipleship and the Way of the Cross in America's "Christian" Culture

Cover image: Just Give Me A Sign/Kary Nieuwenhuis/Brotherwolfe/Flicker

Cover design: Laurie Ingram

Library of Congress Cataloging-in-Publication Data

Print ISBN: 978-1-4514-6927-1

eBook ISBN: 978-1-5064-1895-7

The paper used in this publication meets the minimum requirements of American National Standard for Information Sciences — Permanence of Paper for Printed Library Materials, ANSI Z329.48-1984.

Manufactured in the U.S.A.

This book was produced using Pressbooks.com, and PDF rendering was done by PrinceXML.

Contents

"Be not conformed to this world, but be transformed by the renewing of your minds. . ."

—Romans 12:2 (NRSV)

"Where are we? What is the situation in Christendom? It is not difficult to say what the situation is; it is more difficult to change it."

—Søren Kierkegaard, *Judge for Yourself!*

Preface and Acknowledgments

Many, if not most, in the contemporary United States understand themselves to live in a "Christian" country. Some appreciate and want to retain or strengthen this Christian identity. Others take the Christian underpinnings of American culture and politics to prove that we have not yet fully embraced the establishment clause of the American Constitution or what Thomas Jefferson called the "separation of church and state." Surprisingly, some committed Christians also critique this assumed Christian identity of American culture, and do so on Christian grounds. According to them, the infusion of Christianity into mainstream culture and political discourse not only endangers the rights of people of other religions or of no religion; it also imperils the integrity and meaning of Christianity itself. Along with being widely accepted and pervasive, Christianity also becomes compromised or accommodated, according to these Christian critics. At best, a so-called Christian country will promote a compromised "Christian" faith. At worst, the assumed normality and popularity of Christianity may just undercut the relevance and distinctiveness of Christianity itself.

In this book, I join others in arguing against the easy blending of Christian discipleship and mainstream American values. Like other critics arguing on Christian grounds, I believe that Christian capitulations to mainstream North American politics and culture pose particular problems for Christian formation and discipleship. If a person is understood to partake of Christianity by cultural osmosis or by the good luck of having being born in a "Christian" country, what more is to be gained by striving to become deeply and distinctively Christian?

Assuming that Christian discipleship entails standing out—at least to some degree—from what the New Testament calls "the world," what is one to do when that world (or what others refer to as our dominant culture) so readily reabsorbs and repackages Christian distinctiveness, making it more normal, marketable, and mainstream? Put positively, what essential components of Christian discipleship would be better understood and practiced if we considered the faith to be a subculture or even a counterculture that is *within* American culture—but never *of* it? Can Christians once again learn how to "not be conformed to this world" (Rom 12:2)?

While I join other Christian critics of the cultural and political sway of Christianity by asking such difficult questions, I depart from many of them in my description of the particular challenges and opportunities related to Christian faith here and now. Broadly referring to the cultural influence or political power of Christianity as *Christendom*, many Christians now describe North Americans as living in a "post-Christendom" age. By doing so, they suggest that we finally live in a time when Christianity has lost or is quickly losing its political power, its cultural normativity, and its social status. This is good news for these Christian critics insofar as Christians now can more easily practice their faith without the risk of compromising it.

I share with "post-Christendom" writers the hope that would-be Christians will learn to embody their faith without the kickbacks and trappings of accommodated and acculturated Christianity. As the title of this book suggests, however, I believe that we "still" live squarely in Christendom—that is, in a dominant culture that presumes to be Christian or where Christianity remains the cultural norm. We therefore "still" live with the difficult task of learning to become Christian *in* (not after) Christendom. In fact, the challenge of "becoming a Christian in Christendom"—as the religious writer Søren Kierkegaard put it almost 200 years ago—is one that each generation of Christians must work through according to its particular circumstances.

This book addresses the problem of how to live out the Christian faith within a culture that idealizes and privileges that tradition *while also* relativizing it, rendering it redundant and innocuous. By frequently using the phrase "acculturated and accommodated Christianity," I will highlight both the processes and the connection between them. When Christian communities become acculturated, gaining sociocultural power, they typically risk becoming accommodating as well—giving up something of their distinctive shape in the effort to increase or retain their wider "relevance." Beyond diagnosing these dangers, the book also lifts up the witness of ordinary people who do manage to live faithfully in the countercultural tradition called Christianity. I do not write as someone who has become fully Christian, retrospectively rehearsing the path from an acculturated Christianity to more authentic forms. Indeed, I doubt whether that kind of book would be terribly helpful to those looking from the other side. Rather, I write as someone groping my way toward Christianity, able to name particular difficulties and imagine next steps.

I would like to thank a number of people and communities that made this book possible and helped me along the way. Isaac Villegas, pastor of Chapel Hill Mennonite Fellowship in Chapel Hill, North Carolina, listened to early ideas for the book and pointed me to helpful resources. I consider him both pastor and friend, as I do with Becca Stelle, Director of Becoming Church in Washington, D.C., who also oriented me wisely at the start. Ronald Thiemann became a mentor in Lutheran scholarship before he passed away in 2012. He made a number of helpful suggestions while I participated in the Lutheran Academy of Scholars Seminar at Harvard University in 2011; I do wish our friendship would have had time to develop. Stanley Hauerwas also responded to initial ideas and has encouraged me along the way; many will see his influence of what I have written here, and I am thankful for it. Lisa Seiwart read portions of the manuscript and shared her

Master of Sacred Theology thesis on Christian privilege with me at an opportune time.

Paul Martens and David Kramer offered constructive criticisms of my work in bringing Kierkegaard and Yoder together; Lori Brandt Hale did the same for my work with Bonhoeffer, and Carl Hughes with Kierkegaard on Christendom. Dan Morris, my colleague in the Religion Department of Augustana College, Rock Island, Illinois, read the entire book in early draft form and responded in incredibly helpful ways over craft beer at Bent River Brewery (not all in one sitting). David Cunningham of Hope College read the manuscript in what I thought was its almost final form. He recommended ways for me to better say what I wanted to say but hadn't yet said well. This book is much clearer and more compelling because of David's care and wisdom. Finally, Kaity Lindgren spent many hours (and her Starbucks gift cards) doing a final proofread; I thank her for her careful corrections and perceptive suggestions.

Members and participants of the Ekklesia Project, Jesus Radicals, Lutheran Academy of Scholars, Convocation of Teaching Theologians, Søren Kierkegaard Society, and the Vocation of a Lutheran College Conference have been good conversation partners. I also thank the following institutions for inviting me to present on "Christendom" and countercultural Christianity over the past several years: Holden Village (Chelan, Washington), St. Paul Lutheran (Davenport, Iowa), St. Olaf College (Northfield, Minnesota), Trinity Lutheran (Moline, Illinois), Illowa Lutheran Coalition, Baylor University Symposium on Faith and Culture, and the 2014 Interfaith Understanding Conference for ELCA Lutheran Colleges and Universities (Augustana College, Rock Island, Illinois).

I wrote the bulk of the book while on sabbatical from teaching at Augustana. Thank you to Provost Pareena Lawrence for granting the sabbatical and a sabbatical research grant in 2013–14, President Steve Bahls for a Presidential Research Fellowship in 2011, and the selection committee of the William A. Freistadt Grant for Research in Peace Studies to support ethnographic research in Christian intentional communities in 2011–12 and 2013. I did not realize how much I would miss daily contact with Augustana students while stepping away from teaching in order to write; it was all the better, then, that a talented group of undergrads agreed to read and discuss opening chapters in the Fall of 2013—with homemade pie as their only incentive (although my blueberry pie did once win third place in St. John's Lutheran Church pie competition). Thanks to Daniel Anderson, Alex Blust, Gabe Bouzard, Sarah DuRocher, Andrew Ellison, JD Engelhardt, Ally Frueh, Kaity Lindgren, Nik Maggos, Vatina McLaurin, and Maureen Zach for liking the pie and the book—although not without keen criticisms of the latter. Grace Koleczek, Augustana graduate of 2013, became my research partner for an important strand of this project. In the summer of 2013, she and I collaborated in the ethnographies of five religious communities and co-wrote "What Intentional Christian Communities Can Teach the Church" (*Word & World*, Spring 2014), from which I draw in chapter 7. Besides her profound gifts for scholarship and ministry, Grace also bakes, and I don't dare compete with her.

Thank you to the editors of six journals/anthologies for their permission to include within the present book portions of essays that I wrote for them: "Why Interfaith Understanding Is Integral to the Lutheran Tradition" (*Intersections*, Fall 2014); with Grace Koleczek, "What Intentional Christian Communities Can Teach the Church" (*Word & World*, Spring 2014); "Reforming Formation: The Practices of Protestantism in a Secular Age" (*Currents in Theology and Mission*, October 2013); "Called to the Unbidden: Saving Vocation from the Market" (*The Cresset*, Michaelmas 2012); "What Are Churches For? Toward an Ecclesiology of the Cross in a Secular Age" (*Dialog: A Journal of Theology*, Spring 2012); and "Becoming a Christian in Christendom" (*Why Kierkegaard Matters*, Mercer University Press, 2010).

Finally, writing this book has been the excuse that I needed to hang out with and learn from members of Christian communities who take their faith formation and shared practices seriously—but also know how to laugh. While they don't always make it into the footnotes, I've learned as much from members of the following communities as from the writings of professional theologians: New Hope Catholic Worker Farm (LaMotte, Iowa), Rutba House (Durham, North Carolina), the Simple Way (Philadelphia), the Mennonite Worker (Minneapolis), Becoming Church (Washington, D.C.), Christ Community Church (Des Moines, Iowa), Mustard Seed Community Farm (Ames, Iowa), Reba Place Fellowship (Chicago), Micah House (Rock Island, Illinois), and Holden Village (Chelan, Washington).

I dedicate this book to my two sons, Asa and Gabriel, who make me incredibly proud to be a father, and to my own father, William D. Mahn (1943–2015) who was baptized as a child of God, sealed by the Holy Spirit, and marked with the cross of Christ in his childhood home in the spring of 1943.

Introduction: Life in a "Christian" Culture

Near the beginning of his massive *Concluding Unscientific Postscript to the Philosophical Fragments*, the Danish religious author Søren Kierkegaard (1813–1855) makes an interesting observation. He notes that, although he lives in an age in which everything is doubted and nothing taken for granted, one truth is constantly assumed: "Christianity as a given." Or again: "It is assumed that we are all Christians." Christianity is taken for granted; it is so much the normal state of affairs that those questioning their own religious identity and practice—wondering, for example, whether it is right to call themselves Christians—would be met with irritation for making "much ado about nothing." Kierkegaard images one such self-questioning man whose wife might tell him, sweetly but sharply:

> Hubby, darling, where did you ever pick up such a notion? How can you not be Christian? You are Danish, aren't you? Doesn't the geography book say that the predominant religion in Denmark is Lutheran-Christian? You aren't a Jew, are you, or a Mohammedan? What else would you be, then? It is a thousand years since paganism was superseded; so I know you aren't a pagan. Don't you tend to your work in the office as a good civil servant; aren't you a good subject in a Christian nation, in a Lutheran-Christian state? So, of course you are a Christian.[1]

Kierkegaard uses the term *Christendom* to denote this assumed and default religious state—the presupposition that one is automatically a

---

1. Søren Kierkegaard, *Concluding Unscientific Postscript to the Philosophical Fragments*, trans. Howard V. Hong and Edna H. Hong (Princeton, NJ: Princeton University Press, 1992), 1:50–51.

Christian unless one decides *not* to be, and to become something else. This "assumed" state of affairs, this "taking Christianity for granted," might seem at first to be an advantage to Christianity and to Christians; as the default state of affairs, it can easily draw everyone into its orbit. But for Kierkegaard, this situation is much more insidious, and not at all advantageous to Christianity. After all, if almost everyone is assumed to be Christian, what would be the point of digging deeper into one's faith, or of trying to live into more committed and faithful forms of discipleship? Why should we undertake active programs of religious formation if Christianity is merely a state into which one is born, like the water that a fish never notices? And—of great importance to Kierkegaard himself—how can people internalize or inhabit their faith, if determining their religious identity requires nothing more than consulting the local baptismal registry, or looking up "Christians" in a geography or history book? In short, how can people expect to *become* Christians, when their entire culture is already designated as "Christian"?

Faced with these difficulties, Kierkegaard sought to reintroduce a truer form of Christianity into Christendom, that is, into the taken-for-granted "Christian" culture in which he lived. In nineteenth-century Denmark, one officially became Christian by being born on native soil, and subsequently—unless one completed the necessary paperwork to bypass such eventualities—by being baptized as an infant in the Danish Lutheran Church. In a potent image, Kierkegaard likens the state of such Christians to persons so overly spoon-fed that he will have to induce vomiting before they can be fed anything resembling solid spiritual food. He confronts his readers with questions, dislodging their deeply seated assumptions, in order to make room for more thorough Christian formation: to help them "become" Christians in the midst of a culture that already thinks itself Christian. Nor did he exempt himself from this process. To the end, he claimed that he, too, was not (yet) a Christian—only that he was trying to become one.[2]

---

2. Kierkegaard, *The Moment and Late Writings*, trans. Howard V. Hong and Edna H. Hong (Princeton, NJ: Princeton University Press, 1989), 340–43, 212. Elsewhere, Kierkegaard explains his unwillingness to call himself a Christian: "Naturally, it cannot mean that I want to leave

After Christendom?

Certainly, Kierkegaard's "Christian" culture was different from our own. In fact, many would assume that this notion—that Christianity is taken for granted, that it is the assumed state of all people, or that we live in a "Christian society"—has vanished entirely (or is, at the very least, quickly on its way out). A host of recent books confirm this idea that, in the United States (with its legal separation of church and state), as well as in Western Europe, we already live in a *post-Christendom* age—or that we soon will. Religion or seminary students can read about *Worship and Mission after Christendom, Church after Christendom, Faith and Politics after Christendom*, and so on, each announcing the disestablishment or disintegration of "Christian" culture. Interestingly, the authors of these books do not seem particularly bothered by this state of affairs; indeed, perhaps mindful of Kierkegaard's critique, they see the shift to post-Christendom as a positive development. The shift, they argue, can provide "opportunities to recover a more biblical and more Christian way of being God's people in God's world."[3]

And yet, one can legitimately ask whether contemporary society has really moved "beyond Christendom"—that is, whether we are really in so much different a situation than the one described by Kierkegaard. Perhaps, especially, in the Midwest and the Bible belt (the two regions

undecided the question of whether or not I myself am a Christian, am pursuing it, fighting for it, praying about it, and hoping before God that I am that. What I have wanted to *prevent* and want to prevent now is any sort of impression that I am a Christian to any extraordinary degree, a remarkable kind of Christian." Kierkegaard, *The Point of View*, trans. Howard V. Hong and Edna H. Hong (Princeton, NJ: Princeton University Press, 1989), 33. Late in his writing career, he adds this: "I am far short of being a Christian to dare to associate myself with anyone who makes such a claim. Even if I am perhaps a little, indeed, even if it were the case, if I were a bit more than a little ahead of the average among us, I am ahead only in the poetic sense—that is, I am more aware of what Christianity is." Kierkegaard, *For Self-Examination. Judge for Yourself*, trans. Howard V. Hong and Edna H. Hong (Princeton, NJ: Princeton University Press, 1990), 21.

3. Alan Kreider and Eleanor Kreider, *Worship and Mission after Christendom* (Scottdale, PA: Herald, 2011); Stuart Murray, *Church after Christendom* (Milton Keynes, UK: Paternoster, 2004); and Jonathan Bartley, *Faith and Politics after Christendom: The Church as a Movement for Anarchy* (Milton Keynes, UK: Paternoster, 2006). Quotation is from an unnumbered "Series Preface" to the Murray and Bartley volumes. Stanley Hauerwas's *After Christendom?* (Nashville: Abingdon, 1991) is less self-assured that we are, in fact, in a post-Christendom age, as suggested by the question mark in the title.

where I have lived and taught), Christianity remains culturally mainstream. For many people, to be "Christian" means to be "normal." In fact, Christianity can become so subsumed within mainstream American culture that, often, saying "I'm a Christian" becomes indistinguishable from saying that "I'm an American." The word *Christian* becomes a cipher for all perspectives or beliefs that are considered acceptable in dominant society: traditional "family values," self-reliance, moral innocence, patriotism, law-abiding citizenship, good American hard work—the list goes on.

This book seeks to demonstrate that, far from having transcended Kierkegaard's situation or left it behind, we are still living in a culture that takes itself to be Christian and that assumes that being a Christian is the normal state of affairs. In such a culture, it can be difficult to get a handle on what it might mean to practice one's Christianity, to think of it as entailing certain specific kinds of commitments and decisions, or to consider the ways that it might require a person to step away from everyday cultural assumptions. While, at first, it might seem to be an advantage for Christians to live in a "Christian" culture, the opposite is actually the case: because one's Christianity is taken for granted, it will be much more difficult to be intentional, thoughtful, and reflective about one's beliefs and practices. In short, living into one's Christian faith—what I am calling the process of becoming a Christian—is made more difficult by the fact that we continue to live in our own version of cultural Christendom.

Becoming a Christian in a "Christian" culture has certain parallels to other aspects of our lives. For example, it can be difficult for the members of a majority race to think clearly about the category of race, since such persons think of themselves as embodying the "normal" state of affairs, whereas everyone else bears particular marks of their race. Similarly, a person who blends into the majority heterosexual culture may find it difficult to understand that they have one of several sexual orientations, rather than simply being "normal." It can also be difficult for members of the (upper-) middle class to think of themselves, not as merely somewhere in the capacious middle of income-earners, but as inhabiting particular power structures that are afforded to those who are not poor, including the luxury of not having to think in terms of class and privilege at all. People like me—white, straight, relatively affluent—are rather late in thinking about themselves in these terms at all. We have typically assumed that while others may be marked by race, class, and sexual orientation, we lack all these markers; we are just "ordinary" or "normal." So, too, with Christianity in our ostensibly Christian culture: Christians are bound to mistake their own faith as something that is *simply* true, taken for granted, available and acceptable by anyone who is not eccentric. The Christian faith thereby comes to mean anything and everything, but nothing in particular—certainly not anything strange. In such a cultural milieu, it can be difficult to recover Christianity as a scandalous self-revelation of God through Jesus of Nazareth and his call to radical discipleship.

How might we determine that we are still living in a "Christian" culture, in our own new version of Christendom? One might simply cite the number of Americans who believe in God (currently, 86 percent, down from even a few years ago, but much higher than so-called secular European countries) or the 70 percent of Americans whose "religious preference" is Catholic, Protestant, or "nonspecific" Christian.[4] One might also describe how Christianity still gets aligned with governmental authority, for example, by noting its powerful role in Washington across the ideological spectrum (in spite of the common caricature of that city as a "godless" place).[5] In this book, however, I will not attempt to demonstrate this claim by appealing to sociological studies and statistics about the predominance of Christianity in the United States. Rather, I will trace the outlines of our current situation by demonstrating the particular difficulties in which it places us. More specifically, I will show that, in the contemporary setting, those who seek to become Christian tend to see Christian formation and training

4. Gallup, "Religion," accessed August 10, 2015, http://www.gallup.com/poll/1690/religion.aspx.
5. Joshua DuBois, "Joshua Dubois on the Secret Faith of Washington," *Newsweek*, accessed August 10, 2015, http://www.thedailybeast.com/newsweek/2013/04/29/joshua-dubois-on-the-secret-faith-of-washington.html.

in Christian discipleship to be just as needless and redundant as does Kierkegaard's nominal Christian. We do not see the need to explore and deepen our faith, or to make extraordinary commitments on its behalf, because we still allow the tides of culture to carry us along. Even if our contemporary version of "Christian" culture differs from the Christendom of which Kierkegaard spoke, we still face the peculiar challenges of encouraging real discipleship when such efforts are perceived as superfluous. Kierkegaard's *problem* of "becoming a Christian" in such a culture is still with us.

Christianity as Assumed, All-Inclusive, and Normal

Admittedly, most residents of the United States are no longer in the habit (described by Kierkegaard) of assuring themselves that they are Christians simply by noting that it is the predominant religion in this country. Perhaps, too, being a good civil servant or a law-abiding citizen no longer equates to being a good Christian, though this varies; in some regions and among some populations, one senses a near equivalence between "God and Country" or "Cross and Flag." There are even some signs that a significant number of Americans are willing to give up the label *Christian*, increasingly identifying with the "unaffiliated" or as "nones."[6] But in spite of these differences between Kierkegaard's nineteenth-century Denmark and our twenty-first-century setting, the problems that he names are still very much with us. Consider Kierkegaard's imagined character who questions his own commitment to Christianity and the spouse who reassures him. From this vignette, we can extract three important resonances between his time and our own.

Christianity as Assumed

First, Christendom's citizens presume that Christianity is the religion of a person *unless another religious commitment is apparent*. While other

6. "America's Changing Religious Landscape," Pew Research Center: Religion and Public Life, May 12, 2015, accessed August 10, 2015, http://www.pewforum.org/2015/05/12/americas-changing-religious-landscape/.

loyalties (being Jewish, for example, or Muslim—"Mohammedan," in Kierkegaard's language) are typically recognizable as distinct and different, Christians do not typically stand out from the crowd. Mainline and mainstream Christian beliefs and practices in the United States become part of the background for our culture as a whole, abiding as a kind of indistinct "given." According to the recent large-scale National Study of Youth and Religion (NSYR), the religious lives of American Christian teenagers reflect very little of the particular beliefs and historical practices of their professed religious tradition. The researchers, in fact, describe typical teenage believers as relatively unaffected by their beliefs in God (whom they imagine to be a fairly hands-off character), while still receiving some degree of moral affirmation and feeling good about themselves in the process. Better described as "moralistic therapeutic deism,"[7] this conventional faith of American teenagers is only vaguely, conventionally, *almost* Christian. Yet, the researchers conclude that teens adhere to this view, not as an alternative to Christianity, and not because they have rejected Christianity, "but because this is the only 'Christianity' they know."[8] In other words, this watered-down and rather innocuous form of belief *is* functioning for them as Christianity. It is a form of Christianity that requires very little effort or attention in a culture such as ours. It is, as Kierkegaard puts it, "a superficial something that neither wounds nor heals deeply enough."[9] In a cultural situation in which a person is assumed to be Christian unless they explicitly declare themselves otherwise, the predominant faith is very easily homogenized, diluted, and normalized, without much attention to its own more robust historical tradition. As a result, while it is not impossible to stand out from the crowd (religiously speaking), it is difficult to do so, since one's stated religious affiliations simply blend into the overall cultural background. And lest we be tempted to consider this only a teenage

7. Christian Smith with Melinda Lundquist Denton, *Soul Searching: The Religious and Spiritual Lives of American Teenagers* (New York: Oxford University Press, 2005), 118–71.
8. Kendra Creasy Dean, *Almost Christian: What the Faith of Our Teenagers Is Telling the American Church* (New York: Oxford University Press, 2010), 12.
9. Søren Kierkegaard, *Practice in Christianity*, trans. Howard V. Hong and Edna H. Hong (Princeton, NJ: Princeton University Press, 1991), 140.

peer-pressure problem, it should be noted that the NSYR researchers insist that this teenage account of faith accurately reflects the views of the majority of American adults who call themselves Christian.[10] In short, our "Christian" culture is our assumed, default religious state; as a result, it has lost its specific contours and has become relatively homogenous and amorphous. In such circumstances, those who make a genuine attempt to actually become Christian may have to undertake some rather eccentric efforts.

Christianity as All-Inclusive

The reassuring spouse of Kierkegaard's imagined questioner asserts that "it is a thousand years since paganism was superseded; so I know you aren't a pagan." The idea that Christianity surpasses and supplants other historical religions, thereby *superseding* them, is as common today as it was in the nineteenth century—perhaps more so. Historically, the Jewish faith has borne the brunt of such "supersessionistic" sentiments. Particularly after Christianity became the dominant religion of the Roman Empire, Jews came to be seen as those who clung to the old covenant, refusing to submit to the more inclusive promises of God.[11] This way of thinking has led Christians to inflict countless pogroms, defamations, and other forms of persecution upon Jews for more than 1600 years.

Here again, one might imagine that the "supersessionist" mindset would have positive results for its advocates; one's own faith perspective would seem to be bolstered by the claim that it improves upon, and eventually supplants, everything that has come before it. In reality, however, a different process is at work: this account of Christianity can become so all-inclusive—so eager to assimilate not only other religions, but also, all other worldviews—that it begins to lose its own distinctiveness. This is particularly true of Protestantism, which adds an additional layer of supersessionism to a tradition that

10. Smith, *Soul Searching*, 172–92; Dean, *Almost Christian*, 34–37.
11. Note the irony: Nothing excludes those who are deemed exclusionary more forcefully than a tradition that thinks of itself as supremely inclusive. See Diana Eck, *Encountering God: A Spiritual Journey from Bozeman to Banaras* (Boston: Beacon, 2003), 178–90.

already operates with this mindset. Protestant Christianity has often seen itself as seeking to surpass and supplant older, more ritualistic and seemingly restricted forms of faith (mainly Roman Catholicism, but often with imagined links to Judaism). But it has developed this perspective only by calling into question most of Christianity's traditional notions of divine presence and of the church's sacred nature. As Gerald Schlabach has argued, because of its impulse to raise critical questions as to whether any particular place or time can truly disclose the presence of God, Protestantism comes to suffer from its own success. When a movement's entire identity is wrapped up in questioning the relevance of its own institutions, it can quickly render itself superfluous.[12]

As our own religious culture turns to even more inclusive, unspecific depictions of the faith (e.g., "spiritual, but not religious"), Christianity's all-inclusive tendencies will only serve to render it less relevant. Many are still willing to use the term *Christian* to describe themselves, but sometimes, only when they are allowed to clarify what it *does not* mean, that is, what has been left behind. They assure others that they are not too fanatical, not too restrictive, not too ritualistic—in other words, *not too Christian*. Indeed, most of us are better at articulating the unwanted elements of the faith that we have set aside, or that we have subsumed into a new and improved version, than we are at delineating what we actually believe and practice. At worst, these sentiments can constitute "a nostalgic and parasitic attempt to retain the cultural power of Christian symbols without accountable participation in real Christian communities."[13]

Christianity as Normal

If Christianity is assumed to be both assimilated into, and inclusive of, the broader culture, any attempt to be intentional about how one

---

12. Gerald W. Schlabach, *Unlearning Protestantism: Sustaining Christian Community in an Unstable Age* (Grand Rapids, MI: Brazos, 2010), 33. I thank Eric Anglada for pointing me to Schlabach's work.
13. Ibid., 33. Schlabach here characterizes Paul Tillich's method of articulating the Christian faith in broad, universal terms, although the quotation can describe a "Christian culture" that has learned what Tillich called the Protestant Principle all too well.

lives out one's faith begins to seem both irrelevant and redundant. In fact, it becomes difficult even to recognize *anything specifically Christian* about a person's beliefs and practices. In Kierkegaard's words, any form of self-reflection or intentional striving to be true to one's faith will always seem like "much ado about nothing." In our era—and this was already becoming the case in Kierkegaard's era—the problem presented by living in a supposedly Christian culture is not that Christianity becomes "too powerful" or "too political," despite these common impressions. Rather, the problem is that Christianity has come to mean "everything in moderation" or "nothing too much."[14] Christianity has become so normal, so conventional, so much a part of the background of our shared public life, that we hardly ever notice it, ponder it, or intentionally enact it. Why should one undertake deliberate efforts to form the faithful into particular beliefs or practices, or understand one's community to be "called out" from mainstream society,[15] if Christianity is already the norm?

At one time, any talk of a "Christian" culture tended to be associated with overt forms of Christian political empire or nation-states in alignment with church power. In short, Christendom was one in which the church held a dominant and dominating influence over all spheres of life (political, economic, and domestic). This narrow definition of Christendom has led many to believe that it is already far along in the process of giving way to a more secular outlook. But this is too simplistic; it imagines that there is some characteristic called "Christianity" and that this is quantifiable, such that less of it will mean more of an opposite characteristic called "secularism." It also ignores the degree to which more overt forms of Christian dominance can slowly give way to subtle cultural forms. If, however, we take our present-day "Christian" culture, or what might be called neo-Christendom, in the sense that concerns Kierkegaard—as an acculturated and accommodated faith, something that offends no one because it has such little substance[16]—then things become more

---

14. Kierkegaard, *Concluding Unscientific Postscript*, 404.
15. Here, it is worth recalling that the New Testament word for church, *ekklesia*, has its roots in the idea of being called (*kaleo*) out (*ek-*).

complicated. Less Christianity does not necessarily mean more secularism; it may mean a transformation of what is thought to be "Christian." And this, in turn, can actually exacerbate, rather than solve, the problem of becoming a Christian when living in such a cultural milieu.

Kierkegaard himself jumps freely back and forth between these poles. On the one hand, he criticizes such a culture as a state where Christian answers seem everywhere given, where Christians know too much and need to relearn ignorance. On the other hand, he also criticizes "the secularization of everything" where one's "relationship with God is also secularized," which amounts to "sentimental paganism" and only "playing at Christianity."[17] The two are, in some sense, opposite sides of the very same coin. This is well illustrated by the fact that, when Denmark moved from an absolute monarchy to a constitutional monarchy in 1848, the Danish State Church was disestablished and replaced with a "Danish People's Church." But this apparent "secularizing" move did nothing to diminish Christianity's status as "normal"; in fact, it made it rather easier to be "normal." As a result, Kierkegaard's critique only increased.

Of course, adherents of other faith traditions might well wonder why people would complain about their faith being regarded as "normal." From the perspective of a minority faith, subject to various forms of implicit "othering" and explicit persecution, "normality" might seem an outcome devoutly to be wished! The difficulty, however, is that a normal faith perspective can very quickly devolve into a *redundant* one. Why spend much time thinking about one's faith, or deliberately

16. Kierkegaard calls it a "fatuous something that offends neither Greeks nor Jews." *Concluding Unscientific Postscript*, 605.

17. Kierkegaard, *Practice in Christianity*, 91, 95. Compare Kierkegaard, *Christian Discourses. The Crisis and a Crisis in the Life of an Actress*, trans. Howard V. Hong and Edna H. Hong (Princeton, NJ: Princeton University Press, 1997), 11–12; and Kierkegaard, *Sickness unto Death*, trans. Howard V. Hong and Edna H. Hong (Princeton, NJ: Princeton University Press, 1980), 75, where Kierkegaard describes Christendom as veiled paganism. Christendom amounts to the sin of neglect, of omission, of "having taken Christianity's name in vain" (*Sickness unto Death*, 134). Or again, Christendom is a "caricature of true Christianity, or a monstrous amount of misunderstanding, illusion, etc., mixed with a sparing little dose of the true Christianity" (*Point of View*, 80).

accepting the rigors of teaching and formation in that faith, when that faith is already assumed to be present?

The word *redundant* derives from the Latin *redundare*, literally meaning to "overflow, pour-over, or be over-filled." Like water that rises in waves (*undare*), again and again (*re*), redundant measures try to pour themselves into that which is already overflowing. They thus seem pointless, excessive, absurd. What would it mean, after all, to strive to become a Christian if, by living in a particular society, you have already been deemed to be one? On the one hand, the faith is already objectively present; one need only consult the baptismal registries and sociological statistics. It follows that earnest attempts to become Christian seem subjective, idiosyncratic, and frivolous by comparison. On the other hand, the very charge of redundancy and excess signifies that, in our so-called Christian culture, the appropriate posture is to not-stand-out, to fit in, to be nothing-too-much. Those who "pour themselves out" in Christian discipleship run the risk of being seen as *too* Christian; after all, the normal and normative form of Christianity is not one of excess. If becoming a Christian in a "Christian" culture is, as Kierkegaard asserts, a problem of *redundancy*, this means that the culture that creates this problem is not monolithic or domineering. Ironically, its particularly invasive power is to dissolve differences and level distinctions, including those that would distinguish Christianity itself.

How This Book Unfolds

Part 1 of this book takes a deeper look into the forms that our so-called "Christian" culture (or neo-Christendom) take today, especially as these forms relate to other kinds of majority consciousness within a world that thinks of itself as increasingly secular. At one time, Christendom meant expanding borders and the political triumph of a Christian empire or nation; America's Christendom, as I will argue in chapter 1, is more about a loss of borders, of meaning, and of identity. In chapter 2, I examine certain parallels between religion and race— comparing the nominal, acculturated forms of Christianity to the experience of being white in the United States. This suggests that certain elements of a "Christian" culture not only do harm to others (as white supremacy has hurt so many racial minorities, or as patriarchy and paternalism have hurt so many women), but also, leads to the erasure of Christianity itself. In fact, one of the worst symptoms of Christian majority consciousness is the inability to see or know or own one's faith tradition—just as white privilege allows white people to avoid considering themselves truthfully.

Part 2 focuses on three important theological critiques of Christian culture. The first of these, in chapter 3, examines the tendency of Christianity to become a purveyor of solace and comfort—a kind of "feel good" Christianity. This chapter returns to Kierkegaard and examines his critique of nineteenth-century Danish Christianity along these lines. In chapter 4, I turn to Christian culture's tendency to make easy alliances with the state, most clearly illustrated by the rise and fall of "German Christians" under Nazism. Dietrich Bonhoeffer finds ways to resist that particularly dangerous form of Christian accommodation; I argue that his work and witness remain relevant to contemporary America despite—or precisely because of—our legal separation of church and state. Chapter 5 focuses on Christianity's role as a "chaplain" to the prevailing cultural winds, reinforcing certain cultural trends and placating anyone who seems concerned about them. Mennonite theologians and other critics of "Constantinian" alliances prove to be valuable resources for identifying this prevalent problem of giving Christian legitimacy to dominant culture. The writings of these theologians provide resources for contemporary thinking about such matters. Together, they also help us understand that the problems of a so-called Christian culture are not alleviated by the process of secularization; indeed, that process can actually aggravate its woes.

At the end of this section (and the midpoint of the book), I pause to observe that these three distinctive (although overlapping) Christian critiques of "Christian" culture arise from two different sets of concerns. The first of these trace back to Martin Luther and those in his wake (Kierkegaard, Bonhoeffer, and other "theologians of the cross") who resist Christianity's capitulation to a normal and nice culture by underscoring the *strangeness*, or even the *scandal*, of an all-powerful God who is fully revealed in the suffering and death of Jesus. The second group comprises critics of the church's collusion with power politics, symbolized by the conversion of the Roman Emperor Constantine in the early fourth century. Many of these writers trace their roots to (or have been strongly influenced by) the writers of the Radical Reformation, including John Howard Yoder, Stanley Hauerwas, and intentional communities that have been grouped under the heading of "the new monasticism." Naming these two groups enables me to more explicitly compare, contrast, and integrate their perspectives throughout the second half of the book.

In part 3, then, I make use of these resources to address particular issues and difficulties related to Christian identity and community in contemporary American culture. These issues involve money, politics, war, and religion—that is, all the topics that we are told not to bring up in polite conversation. Chapter 6, "Economy: Free Grace in a Culture of Cheap," examines our so-called Christian culture in terms of the increasingly expansive marketing, privatization, and economization of what were once shared, public goods—including the theological goods of faith and grace. While Kierkegaard, and especially, Bonhoeffer explicitly name and resist this cheapening of grace, I will argue that Luther himself offers particularly important resources for understanding the exact sense in which grace is free—that is, in helping us to understand the difference between claiming that something is *free*, and the idea that it *costs nothing*.

Chapter 7, "Politics: Getting Radical and Staying Ordinary," turns to the critiques of Christianity's easy accommodation to the politics of its age. Much of this resistance is rooted in perspectives emerging from the Radical Reformation, but is now practiced by many residents of Catholic Worker Houses, urban anarchist Christian gatherings, New Monastic communities, and other "radical" intentional Christian communities. Among the many gifts such writers and activists offer to mainline and mainstream Christians is that of inhabiting trust and community within a dominant culture of strangers and suspicion produced by political liberalism.

In chapter 8, "War: Subversions of the Cross," I bring the Radical Reformation's critique of the church's collusion with power politics alongside Luther's theology of the cross, with its emphasis on God's self-revelation in and with the victims of violence. Writers from various peace church traditions provide an invaluable critique of the ways most Christians have avoided the hard saying of Jesus in which he tells his followers, "Love your enemies, do good to those who hate you" (Luke 6:27; Matt 5:44). At the same time, Luther's theology of the cross, especially as reworked by Kierkegaard, Bonhoeffer, and feminist and liberationist theologians, corrects a one-sided emphasis on the historical Jesus and noncreedal Christianity as alone able to resist the Christianization of war and the militarization of Christianity. Together, radical politics and cruciform theology point forward to a more self-reflective and faithful discipleship.

Chapter 9, "Religion: Guests in the House of Israel," considers Christian particularity—and even Christian uniqueness—in relation to other religious traditions. If Christians believe that God is fully revealed in the cross of Christ, how do they relate to those whom they love and respect, but who do not see God there—who see God elsewhere, or not at all? Alternatively, can Christians acknowledge the truthfulness and integrity of Muslims, Jews, Buddhists, secular humanists, and others without thereby sliding into a vague relativism that too often gets affirmed within a nominally Christian culture? My goal in this chapter is to distinguish Christian particularity and peculiarity from Christian triumphalism and supersessionism. By recognizing themselves as "guests in the house of Israel," Christians have the opportunity to hold fast to their own robust religious identity *and* to remain open to religious others. Indeed, the chapter argues that Christian distinctiveness may be found in that very process of taking itself out of the center—in its "eccentricity."

Finally, the concluding chapter that makes up part 4 moves more decisively from the *problem* of living in America's new Christendom to the ways one might work *through* it, even if not fully *out* of it. It returns to central themes of the book with particular focus on the relationship between the communal, formative function of church, on the one hand, and the personal (not private) responsibility of "single, existing individuals" to choose Christianity, on the other. Can personal intentionality and decisive volition be made compatible with communal formation and even something like *submission* to the body of Christ?

Throughout the book, I write as both a theologian and as a would-be Christian. On some days, I feel very much like Kierkegaard's imagined "seeker," wondering whether I can or should call myself a Christian. Does it matter that I was baptized as a baby, regularly attend St. John's Lutheran Church in Rock Island, Illinois, and teach Christian theology at a small church-related college? Or are these just the ways that I participate in our so-called Christian culture? On other days, I do want to call myself a Christian, but doing so carries a double risk: I may hypocritically fail to meet my own standard, or I may be committing myself to the painful process of actually becoming what I profess to be. In either case, I still often find myself wondering whether the label *Christian* is accurate, helpful, or even meaningful. Regardless of these quandaries, I remain convinced of three things. First, I am called to faithful Christian discipleship and full-bodied participation in the Christian community called church, as a way of resisting the segregating, isolating, relativizing, and violent ways of the supposedly "Christian" culture in which I live. Second, this more authentically Christian way is not something that I have achieved, nor that I will ever achieve; it is still "ahead" of me, and Kierkegaard would suggest that it will *always* be ahead of me. Third, and finally, if I am to move forward, to make progress in this way, I will need to attend carefully to the host of barriers to this new form of life—barriers that are, at least in part, a product of our newest form of Christendom.

While I hope that the book may be helpful to others faced with the challenge of its title, I should note that I hope to offer a theological analysis, rather than a devotional tract. Kierkegaard again provides a helpful analogue. Much of his work was an attempt to move his readers from a merely *objective* grasp of Christianity to the task of *becoming* passionately invested in the Christian faith. Yet, he always refused to relegate this process to the realm of personal opinion, emotional enthusiasm, or the kinds of reactions sought by motivational speakers. Quite the contrary, he wanted to give careful definition to the Christian life by offering thick descriptions of the particular moods and passions, the vulnerabilities and virtues, that Christians do (or should) display. In other words, he sought to render the interior landscape of the Christian life in clear and concrete terms, asking his reader to consider them with care—even though they might otherwise be dismissed as private opinions or mere emotions. I'm no Kierkegaard, but I do hope to join him in trying to think carefully about the concrete shape of Christian formation and discipleship. I also hope that the present book participates, in a small way, in the countercultural tradition called Christianity that it seeks to promote.

PART I

PROBLEMS

1

Christendom, Then and Now

In this chapter, I describe in greater detail the particular "Christian" culture prevalent in the United States in the early twenty-first century. Because the rise of that culture parallels the loss of conventional, inherited Christian forms, the shift may appear to get us out of the problems of Christendom. However, in most cases, an older, more obvious form of Christendom is simply replaced by a newer, more ironic, and even "secular" form. The new cultural mindset still regards itself as Christian; as a result, it presents the same dangers (albeit in different ways) as the more obviously Christian culture it has replaced.

Two Scenarios

I begin with two scenarios—one fictional, and the other, real.

Modeling for Christ

Along Interstate 75, heading into Atlanta from Macon, Georgia, drivers can see—tucked in between billboards for Waffle House and various car dealerships—an enormous sign adorned by a 30-foot blond with a sweeping neckline, her perfect mouth smiling over the eight-lane freeway. The billboard advertises "Models for Christ" (MFC), a Christian modeling agency for those "seeking to honor God as they navigate the unique opportunities and challenges within the fashion industry." When they arrive home, drivers can peruse the organization's website, where they will learn that MFC seeks to connect models with opportunities to share God's love with others in the industry, as well as offering "industry-relevant Bible studies" and "leadership discipleship training."

The website is linked to that of Christian Talent Network, a for-profit company commissioned "to help you find your way safely into the many possibilities available for you in the exciting world of modeling and TV commercials." Counsel is available from experienced mentors "who have experienced the many challenges in the industry and seen God guide them safely to success." Their services include agency referrals; composite, portfolio, and head shot photography; international guidance and connections for modeling and TV work; and "work referrals to Christ-honoring photo, TV and film productions."

The company offers a number of testimonials (both about God's power and about the worth of the company) from born-again models and actors, almost all of whom follow a script in which they have fallen into sin and despair, and then, found themselves saved by Christ. They speak of eating disorders, conspicuous materialism, consumerism, promiscuousness, shame, self-glorification, and self-loathing; they have fallen into the temptations both of idolizing the profession and of becoming an idol to others. They then speak of the guidance and security they have found in Jesus and that they hope to offer to new recruits.

What is unclear in all of this is exactly what the designation "Christian" means for a particular model's work in the fashion industry. It seems to be something fairly general, about not falling into the celebrity lifestyle of excess. Jeremy, who became a model after entering a national underwear modeling contest his senior year of college ("My granddad took a couple of pictures of me and sent them in with my entry form, not really thinking I had a chance . . ."), now decides which fashions he will or will not model by asking whether the job "is truly part of God's redemptive work." As one might suspect, however, his notion of "redemptive" is fairly capacious. His advice to beginning Christian models is this: "Don't think that you have to be part of the 'party' scene to be successful. Treat modeling as a business, and be known for your character with your agents and the clients. When working, look for ways to bless the other models and clients by serving and doing your best." Another model, Laura, commends Christian acceptance and self-confidence in the midst of an industry that preys on insecurity: "If God didn't make you a certain height or weight, you need to do the best with what He's given you. Find out what you look good in and work with that." Finally, there's Rachel, a former Playboy model—a position that she now calls "a playmate and spokesperson of lies"—who has converted to become a spokesperson for Jesus, "crowned with His beauty." While "modeling for Christ," she tells of being tempted to shoot a hair advertisement for a client who wanted a silhouette of her back "with a shaded hint of other areas to be exposed." Refusing to do the shot, she risks forfeiting the job. But God makes a way out of no way; according to Rachel, "I took a stand for my beliefs and kept the job—Praise God! And I praise Him for MFC!"

Golfing with Jesus

Meet Dr. Thomas More, who, "in these dread latter days of the old violent beloved U.S.A. and of the Christ-forgetting Christ-haunted death-dealing Western world," comes to himself in a grove of young pine trees somewhere on the outskirts of Paradise Estates, Louisiana. Recently out of a mental institution where he both practiced his own psychiatry and was treated as a patient, Tom now wonders whether his brooding despair is caused by the seemingly normal surrounding community. "People look and smile and are nice and the abyss yawns," he says. "The niceness is terrifying."

Indeed, everything in Paradise Estates appears rather nice and normal and nonthreatening to all but Tom, whose acute sense of alienation and impending doom may be healthier than the widespread obliviousness to the fact that anything is wrong. Life in Paradise Estates is seen as "an oasis of concord in a troubled land." Amidst violent national conflict between white and black, right and left, residents of this gated community live and let live. Some go to church while others go birdwatching. Some attend American Civil Liberties Union meetings, lobbying for poor and disadvantaged youth, while others support an anti-communist organization. And yet, all "play golf, ski in the same bayou, and give 'Christmas gifs' to the same waiters at the club."

In order to register the malaise that no one else seems to notice, Tom invents an Ontological Lapsometer, a kind of stethoscope of the human spirit, which can detect a person's alienation from her- or himself. But in a society that gives equal credit to birdwatchers and churchgoers—and in which Christianity has become indistinguishable from patriotism, market economics, and mainstream American culture—the factors working to conceal such spiritual lapses are immense. In fact, based on the names of organizations such as the American Christian Proctological Society or the Kaydettes corps of Christian baton-twirlers, Christianity would seem exceedingly important, second only to that which it qualifies. The same might be said of Louisiana's leading faith community, the American Catholic Church (ACC), "which emphasizes property rights and the integrity of neighborhoods." Saint Pius XII, Paradise Estates' parish church, has retained the Latin mass and plays The Star-Spangled Banner at the elevation of the Host. In preparation for Property Rights Sunday, a major feast day in the ACC, the congregation hangs a blue banner beside the crucifix that depicts Christ holding the American Home with a picket fence in his two hands. Jesus makes other appearances as well: the golf pro at the country club decides to host a "golfarama" outing—a week of golf on a Caribbean island with the Greatest Pro of Them All, where religious revivals conducted by members of the old Billy Graham team would punctuate premier rounds of golf. At last, one can attend to one's piety while also working on one's putting.

Of course, combining so many cultural forms with religious traditions and moral precepts does lead to certain discrepancies. For example, as Tom gets sucked further into an apocalypse-sized plot, he comes across leftist students driving nails into golf balls and filling Coke bottles with gasoline as they prepare for a "nonviolent demonstration for peace and freedom in Ecuador." When Tom asks how their preparations could possibly fit with their professed pacifism, their leader—a famous scholar from Harvard—explains: "We practice creative nonviolence violence, that is, violence in the service of nonviolence. It is a matter of intention." Another crack in the full enculturation of religion can be glimpsed in the private school in town, which is "founded on religious and patriotic principles and to keep Negroes out."

Despite such discrepancies, what is thought to be the best of America and the best of Christianity form an alliance that manages to withstand the misgivings of misanthropes such as Tom. Tom himself finally settles down, confesses his sin (or at least, the sin of not feeling sorry for his sins), and returns to St. Pius XII. On one particular Sunday, the service ends by asking for the reunion of Christianity and the United States. After Mass, a "rowdy but likable lot" of children shoot off firecrackers and cry out: "Hurray for Jesus Christ! Hurray for the United States!"

Christian Culture, Real and Imagined

Readers of Walker Percy will quickly recognize the second scenario, which can be found in his 1971 novel, *Love in the Ruins*.[1] On the contrary, Models for Christ provides the sort of material that makes Percy's fictionalized account work so well as a parody of the real thing[2]—just as "Buddy Christ," the smiling, winking, thumbs-up Jesus designed to

1. Walker Percy, *Love in the Ruins: The Adventures of a Bad Catholic at a Time Near the End of the World* (New York: Avon Books, 1971). Quotations and direct references above are from pages 3, 5, 12, 19, 43, 165, 173, 185, 207, 269, and 377.
2. "Life Portraits," and "Become a Model," Models for Christ, accessed August 10, 2015, http://www.modelsforchrist.com/. Compare also "Christian Modeling Agencies: Does modeling conflict with Christian values?," accessed August 10, 2015, http://www.modelmanagement.com/modeling-advice/christian-modeling-agencies/.

replace the "wholly depressing" crucifix in the satirical film *Dogma*, really does reflect trends in (usually Protestant) church marketing.[3]

However believable or exaggerated either of these accounts may sound, both reveal the ways that Christianity has become, or is becoming, combined and allied with cultural forms that would otherwise seem irrelevant or even hostile to it. Both accounts describe the *acculturation* of Christianity into the dominant social ethos. They presuppose that Christianity can meld into other social forms (advertising, baton-twirling, or being a good golfer) without noticeable change on either side. They also describe the *accommodation* that accompanies this cultural melding. Christianity goes from being a distinctive and discernible subculture in its own right to becoming little more than a cipher, an empty adjective that can be added to nearly any aspect of mainstream culture. This is what it means to live, not in a Christian culture, but in a *"Christian"* culture—with the quotation marks firmly in place. This term—along with *Christendom* as I am using it here—marks the collective failure to observe and consider Christianity on its own terms, that is, as a network of local human communities sharing common, distinctive, and sometimes countercultural practices, beliefs, and social forms that do not always cohere with all aspects of mainstream American culture. Indeed, some aspects of Christianity would seem to be quite foreign to that culture insofar as Christianity calls disciples to follow a God scandalously made known through a Palestinian Jew, who undergoes persecution and execution by "the establishment" and implores his followers to accompany him. Can such a faith perspective really acquiesce to whatever ethos the dominant culture transmits? Is it really possible to use the qualifier *Christian* to legitimize the nation, the market, or spirit of the times?

Many of us could name times when this temptation to acculturate and accommodate the Christian faith to a nation or ideology has quickly gotten ugly. Take, for example, the "German Christians" in the

---

3. *Dogma*, DVD, directed by Kevin Smith (1999; Sony Pictures Home Entertainment, 2008). See also James B. Twitchell, *Shopping for God: How Christianity Went from In Your Heart to In Your Face* (New York: Simon & Schuster, 2007).

1930s, who linked their fidelity to Jesus as Lord with allegiance to Hitler as *Führer*. There, a theological account of the Christian church was wedded to a set of political ambitions to restore Germany to a *Volk*—not simply a nation, but a people who share the same loyalties, bloodlines, and language. Or, closer to home, think of the way descriptions of the United States as a Christian nation often dovetail with appeals to tighten national borders and the scapegoating of recent immigrants. A clear example of packaging God with Country can be found in the Tea Party, whose "15 Non-negotiable core beliefs" include the requirement of English as the country's core language and the "encouragement" of traditional family values. The fifth core belief professes that gun ownership is sacred—not a matter of constitutional rights, or as a necessity, given the perceived threat of governmental encroachment, but as *sacred*. How long until Jesus is depicted with a semi-automatic in his wounded hands, guarding the land of the free?[4]

Or finally, consider the monumental impact on church history when, in the year 312, the Roman Emperor Constantine converted to Christianity, followed by another emperor, Theodosius, declaring it Rome's official religion in the year 380. Over the course of the fourth century, Christianity went from being an oft-persecuted religion *under* Roman rule to becoming the official religion *of* the Roman Empire.[5] This "Constantinian shift" can sound like a good thing for Christians, and certainly, fewer of them were killed once adherence to the Christian faith became permitted, and then, sanctioned. But when Christianity becomes the religion *of* empire, it becomes more difficult to distinguish between its own ways (being willing to die rather than kill, as Christian martyrs were trained) and the ways of Rome (being willing to kill rather than die, as Roman soldiers were trained). Practicing Christians who happen to live within the empire now

---

4. The list of Tea Party commitments (but no such image of Jesus) can be found at: "About Us," Tea Party, accessed August 10, 2015, http://www.teaparty.org/about-us/.

5. Church historians clarify that this "Constantinian shift" actually begins around the year 200 and takes more than 200 years to unfold. John Howard Yoder, *The Royal Priesthood: Essays Ecclesiastical and Ecumenical,* ed. Michael G. Cartwright (Scottdale, PA: Herald, 1998), 53–64. For even more historical nuance, see Peter J. Leithart, *Defending Constantine: The Twilight of an Empire and the Dawn of Christendom* (Downers Grove, IL: InterVarsity, 2010).

become professed "Christian" Romans—with emphasis on the Roman. In the process, Christianity becomes something easy to ascribe to, but difficult to describe as distinctive or to carry out with any real risk vis-à-vis the dominant culture.[6]

Of course, Christian Nazis or America's Christian Far Right can become red herrings in depicting the dangers of a so-called "Christian" culture. Modeling for Christ seems much more innocuous, as does Walker Percy's depiction of the Homeowner's Christ or Kevin Smith's Buddy Christ. From another angle, however, the very innocuousness of more subtle forms of Christendom is part of what makes them so dangerous. Early Christian supporters of Nazism did not think of it as a dangerous betrayal of their faith; for many, the connections between Christian belief and a strengthened German state seemed benign and banal.[7] We may feel the same way about, say, pledging allegiance to "one nation under God," placing the American flag behind the altar, or calling on voters to elect the most "Christian" candidate. But are contemporary American Christians any more discriminating than the German Christians of the 1930s or the Roman Christians of the fourth century? Perhaps the most significant danger of Christendom lies precisely in its ability to look so innocent.

All of this cultural accommodation can, however, nudge us toward an equal and opposite mistake. If Christianity's acculturations also dilute, compromise, or accommodate Christianity itself, the alternative would seem to be to keep the Christian faith pure by keeping it *spiritual*—a matter of personal conviction, and so, divorced from politics, culture, or any other public form. But this move contributes to

---

6. Readers familiar with H. Richard Niebuhr's *Christ and Culture* will know that his book has defined much of the debate about Christianity and social and cultural forms since its first publication in 1951 (now published through New York: HarperCollins, 2001). In Niebuhr's terms, the present book could be seen as pushing toward his "Christ against Culture" or "Christ and Culture in Paradox" models of Christian identity and community. Its larger goal, however, is to help readers rethink the terms of the debate, as do, for example, Craig A. Carter in *Rethinking Christ and Culture: A Post-Christendom Perspective* (Grand Rapids, MI: Brazos, 2006); Rodney Clapp in *A Peculiar People: The Church as Culture in a Post-Christian Society* (Downers Grove, IL: IVP Academic, 1996), 58–75; and David S. Cunningham, *Christian Ethics: The End of the Law* (London and New York: Routledge, 2008), 106–9.

7. See Hannah Arendt, *Eichmann in Jerusalem: A Report on the Banality of Evil* (Harmondsworth, UK: Penguin, 1977).

the same problem. By removing overtly political action and language from all conversations about faith and the church, we can unwittingly endorse the status quo—leaving unquestioned whatever political arrangements currently reign. If, in order to depoliticize Christianity, we find ourselves spiritualizing and privatizing it, this does not prevent it from being accommodated to culture. In fact, by depriving the faith of its distinctive social shape, it can become so empty of real content that it can be attached to just about anything else without having to make any adjustments whatsoever.

Whatever else, quests for a "pure" and "spiritual" Christianity risk betraying the central claim of the Christian faith, a claim that God enters history through a covenant with God's people and through the life, death, and resurrection of Jesus of Nazareth, who calls followers not to some free-floating spiritual realm, but to the way of the cross, a life of radical discipleship.[8] Similarly, specific Christian practices—including, for example, active peacemaking, the forgiveness of sin, and a commitment to the poor and marginalized—end up being set aside when "personal" beliefs must be checked at the door of the public square.

As noted in the Introduction, the word *Christendom* is traditionally used to refer to Christian-majority countries or countries in which certain elements of Christianity play a dominant role. Today, such lands tend to be found in Africa and the Global South.[9] In a more historical sense, *Christendom* typically designates the medieval and early modern period of Western Europe, when Pope and Emperor kept church and empire allied and dominant within their cultures. It can also refer to the post-Reformation rise of established state churches, such as German or Scandinavian Lutheran bodies or Catholic France, Italy, and Spain, where national citizenship and church membership largely matched. Finally, the word is sometimes used to describe a consensual "civil religion," as espoused especially in the United States almost since its founding, whereby a plethora of Christian denomi-

---

8. Compare Clapp, *A Peculiar People*, 33–43.

9. Philip Jenkins, *The Next Christendom: The Coming of Global Christianity* (Oxford: Oxford University Press, 2007).

nations—though officially decoupled from the state—nonetheless imagine themselves as nominally unified and as sustaining civility and upholding American "Judeo-Christian" culture.

This last version of Christendom—more tacit and cultural, less institutionalized—is the primary target of my descriptions and critiques in this book. But I will also make the case that America's newest form of Christendom might even circumvent the implicit ecumenical and interreligious ties of American churches and synagogues. Our own culture no longer functions to stitch together one "sacred canopy" that houses the ethical-religious ethos of the United States as a whole. Instead, it would seem to legitimize a sense of togetherness that is so thin that it allows us to remain largely *disconnected* from one another—venerating the right of individuals and affinity groups to decide what is helpful, true, or moral for themselves. Even with its quotation marks in place, can "Christian" culture or the term *Christendom* be used to designate so individualist and dissolute a culture as ours?

Christendom's Tenacity and Its "Very Ironic Advantage"

Many writers believe we are beyond the problem of Christendom in any form—or, at the very least, that we no longer live in a Christian culture (with or without the scare quotes). As noted in the Introduction, the authors of these books—while using the word *Christendom* in various ways and disagreeing over the nature of its consequences—largely agree that the political disestablishment and cultural diminishment of Christianity is a godsend for authentic Christian community and discipleship. According to these authors, present-day Christians can now be Christian without compromise, since they no longer need worry about being influenced by the state or by ecclesial-cultural conventions. Instead, they can undertake an authentic discipleship that entails personal commitment and intentional choices—freed from the powers of culture as a whole.

Often, such "authentic disciples" are also portrayed as having been freed from the rituals and hierarchy of the institutional church, which is portrayed as having been beholden to these same cultural forces. Not only in books, but also in Christian communities, many folks calling themselves *missional* or *emerging* or *emergent* Christians experiment with creative, mobile, and transient forms of Christian life that are also interpersonal, noninstitutional, and social-media savvy. If "Christendom" or "Christian culture" was a mighty fortress, these new disciples seem quite satisfied to pitch their tents among its ruins—replacing a sanctuary's hard pews with coffee shop-style couches and throw rugs, adding yoga practice to the anointing of the sick, or preaching and posting sermons that look and feel more like TED Talks.

I share with post-Christendom authors and emerging church movements their deep concerns about established or "inherited" churches that are fading away, as well as their hope for a revitalized Christianity that may take unexpected forms. Where I part company with them, however, is in their assumption that Christendom has practically vanished, that we have become a secular society, and that this, in turn, will allow the emergence of more faithful Christian "networks." In other words, they assume a zero-sum game between Christendom and the secular world, where the advance of the latter necessitates the retreat of the former. With this assumption comes a fairly robust optimism that—*by the very momentum of Western political and cultural history*—Christianity is or soon will be freed from the dangerous politico-cultural entrapments. Whatever other sensibilities these authors might share with Kierkegaard,[10] he strongly resisted the notion that anything related to the Christian faith happens simply "as a matter of course."[11] In fact, as noted in the Introduction, he saw the presumed *ease* of becoming a (nominal) Christian to be part and parcel of the *problem* of Christendom—a problem that makes it so difficult to become a Christian in something more than name. In this sense, the claim that secularism has displaced Christendom turns out to be

10. Kyle A. Roberts, *Emerging Prophet: Kierkegaard and the Postmodern People of God* (Eugene, OR: Cascade, 2013).

11. Kierkegaard, *Concluding Unscientific Postscript to Philosophical Fragments*, trans. Howard V. Hong and Edna H. Hong (Princeton, NJ: Princeton University Press, 1992), 1:46–49, 129–88, 610–16.

something of a Trojan horse. What appears to be an act of liberation turns out to be a way of reinforcing our captivity—and perhaps, even helping us to like it. In Rodney Clapp's terms, Weber's "iron cage" may have mutated into a "liberal cage," where our own freedom of choice is actually what keeps us locked up.[12] This may, in fact, constitute the newest, most ironic form of Christendom.

If the difficult and needed task is "to become a Christian in Christendom" (as Kierkegaard would put it), then we ought not make that task "easier" (and so, ironically, increasingly difficult) by presupposing that Christianity now carries little social or political power. Kierkegaard's humorous attempt to cut through the irony was to claim to be helpful by making things more difficult—precisely because other writers already have a corner on the market of making things easier! In fact, he wants to put a positive cast on the very *difficulty* of becoming an authentic Christian in an inauthentic Christian culture. Such a setting, he believes, is the opportune setting for true Christian discipleship. This is its "very ironic advantage."[13]

Clearly, frequent allusions to our so-called "post-Christendom" or even "post-Christian" age can inadvertently obscure both the difficulty and the possibility of becoming Christian. As Ron Adams and Isaac Villegas argue, "to proclaim Christendom's death prematurely only serves to mask all the ways we benefit from the institutional prominence of cultural Christianity as it shapes our society." For these authors, the issue is not *how Christian* our society remains, but whether, in assuming that we live in a post-Christendom culture, we are helping or hurting the cause of Christian mission and discipleship. Claims about the demise of Christian culture may not only be premature; they may actually mask the institutional prominence of a form of Christianity that has been accommodated to every other aspect of culture, thus making it all too easy to "pass" as a Christian.[14] Put

---

12. Clapp, *A Peculiar People*, 67. Compare Stanley Hauerwas, "The Democratic Policing of Christianity," in *Dispatches from the Front: Theological Engagements with the Secular* (Durham, NC: Duke University Press, 1994), 91–106.
13. Kierkegaard, *Concluding Unscientific Postscript*, 186, 606.
14. Ron Adams and Isaac Villegas, "Post-Christendom or neo-Christendom?," *The Mennonite*, accessed August 10, 2015, https://themennonite.org/feature/post-christendom-neo-christendom/. See

positively, these authors insist that our culture still regards itself as "Christian" in order to force us to face the problem of acculturated and accommodated Christianity. Only through this process, they believe, can we truly hear the calling to renewed discipleship and community.

Can Secularism Save?

As I have suggested, many authors see things differently. They welcome the upsurge of secular culture, with its emphasis on individual mobility, authenticity, and freedom of choice—not only because it seems inevitable, but because they believe it promises a sure antidote to the problems of Christendom. Once the churches have been thoroughly disestablished, and once individuals have been thoroughly liberated from clerical-ritualistic-cultural traditions—so the argument goes—then we can all freely choose the traditions to which we want to "belong." When this happens (and many so-called emergent or emerging church spokespersons assume the time is near), then Christians will find themselves without cultural-political power, but also, without the ideological temptations of "the establishment." The tradeoff seems propitious.

Consider a few representative examples from the authors to whom I refer. In her recent book, *Christianity After Religion: The End of Church and the Birth of a New Spiritual Awakening*, Diana Butler Bass describes the colossal shift in American religious life since the 1960s away from older forms of institutional power, unreflective ritualism, and by-the-book belief. The growing alternative is a spirit-led and experientially varied revival of religiosity.[15] Unlike an earlier generation that bemoaned this shift toward "individual spiritual questing" as entailing the tragic loss of community and civic togetherness,[16] Bass seems to celebrate it. She

also Isaac S. Villegas, "Christendom Isn't Dead," *Mennonite World Review*, June 11, 2012, accessed August 10, 2015, http://www.mennoworld.org/archived/2012/6/11/christendom-isnt-dead/. The Post-Christendom language that Adams and Villegas critique is from Stuart Murray, *The Naked Anabaptist: The Bare Essentials of a Radical Faith* (Scottdale, PA: Herald, 2010), 71–91.

15. Diana Butler Bass, *Christianity After Religion: The End of Church and the Birth of a New Spiritual Awakening* (New York: HarperCollins, 2012). See also Harvey Cox, *The Future of Faith* (San Francisco: HarperOne, 2009); and Brian McLaren, *A New Kind of Christianity* (San Francisco: HarperOne, 2010).

16. Robert N. Bellah et al., *Habits of the Heart: Individualism and Commitment in American Life* (Berkeley, CA: University of California Press, 1985).

15

honors those who call themselves "Christian, but not religious" and celebrates their place in a choice-based, privatized, and secularized society, which is "driven by preference and desire instead of custom and obligation."[17] In Bass's reading, religion-as-institution should happily give way to the more interpersonal (and often virtual) togetherness that has been forged by each individual's uncharted spiritual path.

Similarly, for Phyllis Tickle, the Western world's new way of being Christian and being church emerges primarily over and against "established churches and their governing bodies"—or, again, against those "inherited" churches filled with members who cling to traditional religious forms. Such traditionalists are, she says, "like those who have fallen heir to Grandpa's old home place and who still like things just the way he had them"; they see no need to "change the furniture."[18] Far from simply rearranging rooms, however, the "great emergence" as described by Tickle amounts to a giant rummage sale, in which the church cleans out its attic, basement, and much of the rest of the house. She sees this process as something that needs to happen in roughly 500-year intervals; previous housecleanings are associated with the Great Reformation, the Great Schism, Gregory the Great, and the great emergence of Christianity itself.[19] Tickle's metaphor is telling: the church that now requires such a thoroughgoing purge is not a group of real people, but an impersonal structure—a house with cluttered attic and all. In contrast, her candidates for the most promising new forms of Christian identity decidedly resist becoming institutionalized, ritualized, uniform, authoritarian, or otherwise too "churchy." The choice appears to be between buoying individual freedom and creativity, on the one hand, and clinging to impersonal wooden social conventions, on the other. On those terms, who wouldn't choose as she does?

Bass's and Tickle's appeals also welcome the advent of secularism—again, with an institutionalized Christendom as its

---

17. Bass, *Christianity After Religion*, 40–41.
18. Phyllis Tickle, *The Great Emergence* (Grand Rapids, MI: Baker, 2008), 135–40.
19. Ibid., 19–31.

negative foil. In fact, they and other proponents of emerging/ emergent Christianity carry forward the vision first announced in 1965 with Harvey Cox's *The Secular City*. Cox unambiguously described the baggage of Christendom and secular society as diametrically opposed and mutually exclusive. More surprisingly, he explicitly *celebrated* secularity as authentic Christianity's first and truest form. Cox assumed that the inevitable currents of secularism were flowing in his direction. He awaited in America the liberation that he believed had already been secured in Europe:

> Increasingly, the process of secularization in Europe has alleviated Kierkegaard's problem [that is, of becoming a Christian in Christendom]. Marxism of various kinds, existentialism in its different forms, the passionate humanism of Camus, and a kind of "what-the-hellism" associated with *la dolce vita* ["the sweet life"] have increasingly presented Europeans with genuine, live options to Christian faith. More and more, "being a Christian" is a conscious choice rather than a matter or birth and inertia. The change can hardly be viewed as unfortunate.[20]

As with Bass and Tickle, individual choice for Cox confers authenticity on faith and practice. As opposed to a previous era, in which a Christian culture provided the church with the power to acculturate and indoctrinate, we are now freed for genuine, responsible faith by a "secular" culture.

Cox anticipates the newer forms of "emergent" Christianity in other ways as well. Both he and Bass link Christendom to idolatry, which they understand as the confinement of God to a parochial place—usually the nation-state, but also, including the institutional church. Cox thus describes the process in which God is liberated from confinement to a particular space—beginning with the Jewish recognition that Yahweh could not be "localized," even in the Ark of the Covenant. This movement was renewed by Jesus's promise to destroy the Temple, and so, resist the temptation to confine God to that particular location. And now, in our own age of mobility, God is fully revealed as a universal, spiritual, hyper-mobilizing event, above and beyond all borders. By

20. Harvey Cox, *The Secular City: Secularization and Urbanization in Theological Perspective* (New York: Macmillan, 1965), 91.

comparison, the institutional church can only appear restricting—in Cox's words, a "patriarchal, agricultural, prescientific relic."[21] Bass and Tickle are similarly captivated by virtual spaces, notions of "liquid church," and networks of "performativity"—all of which are seen as preventing God from idolatrously being boxed in to any particular location.

These writers are not alone in assuming that the problem of Christian culture is a problem of structure and of sealed borders, or that the solution is to let in some air (or clean out the attic) by welcoming the inevitable secularization of society. For example, the premier Canadian contextual theologian, Douglas John Hall, considers Christendom's erosion to be no less inevitable than does Bass or Cox. Strangely, however—given that assumed inevitability—he also calls on Christian churches to disestablish themselves. Finally, he too assumes that "cultural" Christianity tends to confine God to one's own understanding, church, culture, or nation. At the same time, Hall is more nuanced in his descriptions of the "Christendom" that he and others want us to get past. A closer look at his complex work will help us better understand the issues surrounding the current conversation.

In his short book, *The End of Christendom and the Future of Christianity*, Hall asks a simple question that congregations must consider, but—for the most part—have avoided: "What are churches *for*?"[22] The question seems important in our current historical circumstances, described by one author as the "awkwardly intermediate stage" between a past Christian culture (in which mainline churches had considerable influence) and a less-established church of the future.[23] Hall describes how an earlier model of Christendom had a clear but pernicious mission—namely, to increase its influence by converting individuals and controlling more territory. Overtly imperialistic forms of this mission enjoyed a close relationship with political conquest, first

---

21. Ibid., 56–59, 220.
22. Douglas John Hall, *The End of Christendom and the Future of Christianity* (Harrisburg, PA: Trinity, 1997), 23.
23. George Lindbeck, *The Nature of Doctrine* (Philadelphia: Westminster, 1984), 134, as cited in Hall, *The End of Christendom*, 53.

through the northern expansion of the Holy Roman Empire,[24] and later, through the European colonization of India, the Americas, and much of Africa. The violence that accompanied these campaigns was sometimes curtailed by the Christian missions that went before and after them; however, those same activities also legitimated the conquests.

Today, according to Hall, we face another form of Christian imperialism—one that is yet more pernicious because more subtle. Mainline churchgoers declared that the twentieth century would become "The Christian Century" (a popular journal still bears that name). The social order was to be "Christianized" by engendering social support systems or by subsuming them under the label of Christianity. Even though such a "conquest" might well be seen as preferable to the earlier imperial version, it is no less triumphalistic or utopian. In both cases, the goal was "to turn the whole world, if possible, into church."[25] Church has seemed to exist for spreading itself—either outward, into new territories, or down into the soul of society.[26]

Hall's account thus focuses both on the issues of indoctrination and institutionalization (Weber's "iron cage") and on Christianity's capitulation to our modern-day preferences, needs, and freedoms (Clapp's "liberal cage"). But for all the complexity and nuance of this diagnosis, his proposed solution sometimes seems inadequate by comparison. Focusing almost exclusively on how institutional churches should respond to these circumstances, he calls on them to "disestablish themselves" (often followed by an exclamation mark).[27]

---

24. See James Carroll, *Constantine's Sword: The Church and the Jews* (Boston: Houghton Mifflin, 2001), 171, 177, 191–94.
25. Hall, *The End of Christendom*, 17. That Hall sees (neo-)Christendom in both forms puts him ahead of Cornel West, whose otherwise compelling portrayal of "Constantinian" versus "Prophetic" Christianity unfortunately praises prophetic/social gospel versions of Christianity as being entirely part of the solution—never complicit in the problem—of hegemonic Christianity. Cornel West, *Democracy Matters: Winning the Fight Against Imperialism* (New York: Penguin, 2004), 146–55.
26. These directions of Christian expansionism might be put in temporal terms as well, as conservative Christians wax nostalgic over some privileged Christian past (the Middle Ages, the religion of the American founders, or pre-1960s America), while liberal or progressive Christians sometimes look to a future civilization as the triumph of Christianity. See Charles Taylor, *A Secular Age* (Cambridge, MA: Harvard University Press, 2007), 745.
27. Besides *The End of Christendom*, Hall calls for disestablishment in *The Reality of the Gospel and the Unreality of the Churches* (Minneapolis: Augsburg Fortress Press, 1975); *Has the Church a Future?*

Rather than cling to models of Christian culture that are inevitably fading away, churches should *willingly* embrace the processes of disestablishment and secularization. Hence, his solution largely parallels that of Cox, Bass, and Tickle: Christians should embrace the cultural move toward secularism as providing an opportunity for real witness, individual choice, and deep commitment. But given the complex entanglements that Hall so clearly describes, can the problem really be solved by simply swimming along with the secular tide? Can one *choose* one's way out of Christendom? What if individual, unencumbered choice entails the very thing that the newest form of Christendom holds sacrosanct?

Borders of Belonging

Previous versions of Christendom were focused on geographical space—both in a literal sense (expansionist military and missionary movements), and as a controlling metaphor for the church's cultural power. In contrast, the language of Christianity's "redundancy" (as suggested by Kierkegaard) is more interested in the atmosphere within the space that it occupies. The problem is not that Christian culture is too "big" (geographically or otherwise), but that its presence is thin and dissipated. It is all-encompassing everywhere, but so sparse and vacuous as to be irrelevant. Thus, rather than being concerned (as is Hall) about Christianity's attempt to push its borders outward in order to gain more territory or downward to capture more souls, Kierkegaard worries about the loss of borders altogether.[28] In a culture that believes itself to be Christian, it can be difficult for any given person to see what "being a Christian" might look like. The distinctiveness of the faith has been "captured" by the surrounding culture, making any effort at

(Louisville: Westminster John Knox, 1980); *Confessing the Faith* (Minneapolis: Fortress Press, 1996), 201–340; *The Cross in Our Context: Jesus and the Suffering of the World* (Minneapolis: Fortress Press, 2003), 157–78; and *Bound and Free: A Theologian's Journey* (Minneapolis: Fortress Press, 2005), 83–86.

28. This may help us understand why some Christian thinkers have called for the reassertion of the "borders of baptism." Michael Budde, *The Borders of Baptism: Identities, Allegiances, and the Church* (Eugene, OR: Cascade, 2011). It should be noted that such borders are transnational, truly *catholic*, and so, distinguish particular practices and allegiances from those of mainstream society. They are a different sort of border than those that all too handily distinguish groups of people according to their national citizenship, class, race, or gender.

true discipleship redundant, and diluting the faith into something that everyone can accept (i.e., the "moralistic therapeutic deism" of which Smith and his colleagues speak).[29]

In this light, Hall's proposals for churches to disestablish themselves and "rediscover the possibilities of littleness"[30] inadvertently perpetuate the all-too-popular assumption that the best form of Christianity is that with the least impact. It resembles the description offered in the Introduction, to the effect that we want to be seen as "religious, but not *that* religious"; we want our faith to be innocuous and small-to-mid-sized, as though we were comparing responsible ownership of a Honda Accord to those who hog the road with SUVs.[31] Ironically, however, our current "Christian" culture is underwritten by our tendencies in this very direction. We are expected to don Christianity lightly, to be privately spiritual (and not too publicly religious), to be nice to one another. This is the borderless and "thin" version of Christianity that marks our culture. It has little use for more robust accounts of a God made flesh, or for those who want to live out that belief in ways that will be noticed.

In chapter 5, I will turn to the work of Stanley Hauerwas and others influenced by Anabaptist or Mennonite accounts of the church as important resources for addressing these questions by pointing us toward different starting points. Like Hall, Hauerwas believes that contemporary Christians are living in an "awkwardly intermediate stage" between a definitively Christian culture and a future era in which churches are completely disestablished.[32] For Hauerwas, however, this transition is necessarily marked by various ironic

---

29. Christian Smith with Melinda Lundquist Denton, *Soul Searching: The Religious and Spiritual Lives of American Teenagers* (New York: Oxford University Press, 2005), 118–71.

30. Hall, *The End of Christendom*, 66.

31. Kierkegaard describes human sagacity in terms of understanding "moderation, the middle way, the medium size, this is the truth." Kierkegaard, *For Self-Examination. Judge for Yourself*, trans. Howard V. Hong and Edna H. Hong (Princeton, NJ: Princeton University Press, 1990), 161. Many today also assume that any religion with determinate content should be suspected of "fanaticism," just as charges of "sectarianism" have been used from the late nineteenth century to dismiss religions that are ill-fitted for cultural assimilation. See Brad S. Gregory, *The Unintended Reformation: How a Religious Revolution Secularized Society* (Cambridge, MA: Harvard University Press, 2012), 356.

32. Hauerwas, *After Christendom? How the Church Is to Behave if Freedom, Justice, and a Christian Nation Are Bad Ideas* (Nashville: Abingdon 1991). According to Hauerwas in *God, Medicine and Suffering*

reversals. One of his books on this topic is titled *After Christendom?* (note the question mark); there, he notes that proposals to reduce the church's "establishment" influence tend to presume its continued social and cultural power. In other words, "You do not need an established church when you think everyone more or less believes what you believe." This is similar to Kierkegaard's claim about the redundancy and "thinness" of Christianity in our culture; it sweeps almost everything under a nominally Christian canopy, which means that the church has no distinctive social shape or discernible set of visible practices to give it an identity. Thus, the *withdrawal* of Christianity into the private sphere and into individual beliefs is precisely what allows it to remain in a culturally powerful position. Or *vice versa*: the only way that a nominally Christian culture can continue its past program of *expansionism* is by *quarantining* Christian belief, making it a matter of private concern to certain individuals.

Admittedly, Hauerwas welcomes secularism in ways that parallel (other) post-Christendom writers. While addressing the relationship between church and academy, he notes that "secular universities may be more hospitable to Christian knowledges than many universities that are allegedly Christian."[33] Similarly, Hauerwas begins his recent *War and the American Difference* by asserting that, as a Christian, he would prefer that the nation were more secular and that Christianity were less "American." "In short," writes Hauerwas, "the great difficulty is how to keep America, in the proper sense, secular."[34]

But for all these similarities with Bass, Tickle, Cox, or Hall, Hauerwas also refuses to allow new forms of Christendom to make use of their own leading tactic—forwarding the cause of secularism by celebrating individual religious preferences and choices. It would be better, he thinks, to live under something like the parish system in the Church of England, where one's individual "preferences" about where to go to

(Grand Rapids, MI: Eerdmans, 1990), 76n40, he planned for the subtitle of *After Christendom* to be: "Christians Living in Awkward Times."

33. Hauerwas, *The State of the University: Academic Knowledges and the Knowledge of God* (Malden, MA: Blackwell, 2007), 8.

34. Hauerwas, *War and the American Difference: Theological Reflections on Violence and National Identity* (Grand Rapids, MI: Baker, 2011), 6–7.

church are bypassed by a system that essentially tells one where to go. Others would find this parish system a remnant of older forms of Christendom that are fading and should fade away. But for Hauerwas, this holdover of an older form of Christendom might just foster more faithful discipleship than an American neo-Christendom that depends so heavily on choice. Hauerwas explains:

> More people may go to church in America than in England, but the church to which they go, exactly because it is a church of their choice, lacks the ability to resist accommodation to economic and political powers. The voluntary character of the church, enshrined in the language of "joining the church," turns out to be a perfect Constantinian strategy.[35]

In other words: because we Americans "choose" a particular church, rather than being born into one, we will end up making those choices for reasons that have more to do with our surrounding culture than with particular Christian beliefs and practices. Unpacking this claim will need to wait for subsequent chapters; for now, we need only note that our freedom to reject or accept certain elements of Christianity not only reduces our capacity to *undergo* formational processes, but may also perpetuate the most damaging features of America's neo-Christendom.

These claims also mark the work of the other authors whom we will explore more deeply in part 2 of this book. Each of them critiques the impersonal structures of established churches, welcomes something like disestablishment and secularity, and encourages intentional and personal formation and discipleship. Yet, they do not think that any of this can happen simply because individuals make their own "authentic" choices, as though they were buying jeans that fit really well. For these authors, the assumption that one can "decide" to be Christian, apart from being engrafted into the social body of Christ, is itself a supreme example of accommodated and acculturated Christianity. One cannot make a "leap of faith" from sheer willpower, as though it were more manageable if one managed to get a running

---

35. Ibid., 156.

start.[36] Rather than assuming that secularization and individualization have solved the problem of living in a nominally Christian culture,[37] these authors will suggest that secularism itself is simply a new form of ostensibly "Christian" culture.

Christendom's Nots and Nones

Meanwhile, we tend to define ourselves by what we are not. Christianity is *not* Islam; our religion is *not* fanatical or political; our God is *not* bloodthirsty or legalistic or sectarian. Such contrasts can be useful, but they also have a liability. Christianity itself can become little more than a "not," perhaps synonymous with the category "none of the above" on a questionnaire. Unlike older forms of Christian culture that enforced their claims with the sword, our current version maintains its hold on us by leaving each of us autonomous, able to select (or not) any religious or spiritual identity of our own choosing. This means that almost anything can become Christian—baton twirlers, golfing groups, modeling agencies—albeit in name only.

And maybe not even in that. In attempting to determine contemporary Christianity's degree of cultural density (or the lack thereof—what I have called its "thinness"), perhaps the ultimate test is whether even those who describe themselves as "religiously unaffiliated" still somehow belong within this ostensibly Christian culture. These individuals identify themselves as belonging to no religious tradition. They are sometimes referred to as "nones," meaning that, on forms that ask for religious preference, they check the box marked "none." A recent survey by the Pew Foundation finds their numbers increasing quite dramatically—up from 16.1 percent in 2007 to 22.8 percent in 2014—totaling 56 million religiously unaffiliated adults in the United States today. "Nones" include not only self-described atheists and agnostics (7 percent in 2014, up from 4 percent in 2007), but also, those who do not embrace these terms, but still describe their own religious outlook as "nothing in particular." The

36. Kierkegaard, *Concluding Unscientific Postscript*, 365–66.
37. As does Cox, *Secular City*, 91, when he speaks of "solving Kierkegaard's problem."

rising number of "nones" and corresponding drop in Christian affiliation are spread throughout the American "religious landscape," affecting every major demographic group in the country, coast to coast. The religiously unaffiliated are more numerous than either Catholics or mainline Protestants; among religious groups, they are now second in numbers only to evangelical Protestants.[38]

How is my account of "Christian" culture and America's new Christendom affected by these changes in America's religious landscape? At the very least, it suggests that fewer people are willing to identify themselves with the label *Christian*. Whereas Americans in past decades typically continued to identify with the Christian denominations in which they were raised (even if they stopped going to church, or otherwise practicing their faith, years ago), they now more accurately describe themselves as having left Christianity.[39] As such, they contribute less to the cultural confusions between Christianity's specific character, on the one hand, and our personal opinions and preferences, on the other. The unaffiliated thereby seem to identify their own views more accurately than do those who describe themselves as Christian, but for whom this claim has very little impact on their lives. Those who describe themselves as unaffiliated are also less inclined to view religion's declining influence on American culture as a bad thing.[40] They cling less to civic religion and other traces of the Christian establishment in our culture. There may even be a few among the 56 million religiously unaffiliated who check that box for the same reasons as Kierkegaard's imagined seeker questions whether he can be called Christian. That is, perhaps they too

38. "America's Changing Religious Landscape," Pew Research Center: Religion and Public Life, May 12, 2015, accessed August 10, 2015, http://www.pewforum.org/2015/05/12/americas-changing-religious-landscape. See also Michael Lipka, "A Closer Look at America's Rapidly Growing Religious 'Nones,'" Pew Research Center, May 13, 2015, accessed August 10, 2015, http://www.pewresearch.org/fact-tank/2015/05/13/a-closer-look-at-americas-rapidly-growing-religious-nones/.

39. "In 2007, 38% of people who said they seldom or never attend religious services described themselves as religiously unaffiliated. In 2012, 49% of infrequent attenders eschew any religious affiliation." "'Nones' on the Rise," Pew Research Center: Religion and Public Life, October 9, 2012, accessed August 10, 2015, http://www.pewforum.org/2012/10/09/nones-on-the-rise. I will use the smaller study from 2012 when data are not yet available from 2014.

40. Ibid.

see the appeal of Christianity, but worry that they are not sufficiently attentive to its beliefs and practices to call themselves Christians.

But while the rise of the religiously unaffiliated may mean fewer nominal Christians and a less nominally Christian culture, an alternative interpretation is possible. This trend may have the result of further extending the power of a so-called "Christian" culture, even though this power remains hidden to view. Note, for example, that of those who identify as religiously unaffiliated, a relatively small percentage also identify as atheist or agnostic. This suggests that many of them may still be more beholden to cultural Christianity than they realize.[41] Note also that the majority of the unaffiliated still describe themselves either as a religious person (18 percent) or as "spiritual but not religious" (37 percent); in other words, less than half of "nones" have abandoned the language of religion and spirituality altogether. Nearly two-thirds of them say they believe in God.[42] In 2014, a notable 30 percent of the unaffiliated affirmed that religion was either "very" or "somewhat" important to them.[43] It seems that many of these individuals still continue to "believe without belonging." And while the shape of their belief (and the character of the God in whom they believe) is not entirely Christian, they still seem to make use of residually Christian categories in describing their views with respect to religion. Some might even remain ready to don some elements of the Christian faith again—however loosely and periodically—when cultural or family expectations demand: a church baptism, wedding, or funeral; a moment of tragedy when prayer seems appropriate; or when a church's vacation bible school program could save them a week of summer daycare expenses. For many, religion in a quasi-Christian sense remains an important component of social capital, even if they mainly participate only "vicariously," through the "surrogacy" of others.[44]

---

41. Avoiding both definitive belief and resolute disbelief, they hover in the margins with an "ironist's faith." See Charles Taylor, *Varieties of Religion Today: William James Revisited* (Cambridge, MA: Harvard University Press, 2002), 56–60; Peter E. Gordon, "The Place of the Sacred in the Absence of God: Charles Taylor's *A Secular Age*," *Journal of the History of Ideas* 69.4 (Oct. 2008): 655.
42. "'Nones' on the Rise."
43. "America's Changing Religious Landscape."

Still, among the religiously unaffiliated, we can find some of the sharpest critics of Christendom. People in this group are much more likely than is the general public "to say that churches and other religious organizations are too concerned with money and power, too focused on rules, and too involved in politics." And yet, curiously, a solid majority of the unaffiliated continue to think that religion is good for society, with 78 percent saying religious organizations bring people together and help strengthen community bonds, and 77 percent saying religious organizations play an important role in aiding the disenfranchised.[45]

I want to suggest that this ambiguity—this irony of associating religion with the betterment of society, and yet, holding it at arm's length—may function as one more marker of the nominally Christian culture or newest form of Christendom that I have been describing. For Americans in the present moment, there is very little difference between identifying with Christianity (as our culture conceives it) and identifying with nothing at all. "Nones" may simply more honestly affirm what nominal Christians also know (but about which they are less self-aware): namely, that they can more easily explain what they are *not* than what they *are*. Both groups—nominal Christians and "nones"—participate in a kind of majority consciousness. Like being white in American society, some are blissfully unaware of the privileges that they enjoy by identifying with this majority group, while others may be more aware of it (and feel more uncomfortable about it). We have heard of the category of "white privilege," but might it also be the case that many Americans participate in a kind of "Christian privilege"? It is to this question that the following chapter turns.

---

44. Grace Davie, "Debate," in *Praying for England: Priestly Presence in Contemporary Culture*, ed. Sam Wells and Sarah Coakley (London: Continuum, 2008), 154–55. *Social capital* is a term popularized by Robert D. Putnam in "Bowling Alone: America's Declining Social Capital," *Journal of Democracy* 6.1 (Jan. 1995): 65–78; the term refers to features of social organization that facilitate social trust and cooperation for mutual benefit.

45. "'Nones' on the Rise."

2

Unpacking Christian Privilege

Part of what it means to live in a "Christian" culture is that we end up accepting a formal system of customs and rituals that script our lives before we fully consent to them. We may need to embrace the free and authentic commitments of individuals in order to move ourselves and others beyond the entrapments of Christendom. But the last chapter also suggested that a second danger is equally pressing: if a primary "script" of the newest forms of Christendom is that we determine our own future direction for ourselves—that each of us gets to author our own lives—then simply choosing whether or not to be Christian may be just as culturally determined and accommodating. We want to be able to choose, in order to avoid an easy alliance with our culture; but what if the very act of choosing ends up being culturally normal and normative?[1]

Indeed, nothing now seems more passively consumed and

---

1. I am helped here by Charles Taylor's analysis of authenticity in his *Ethics of Authenticity* (Cambridge, MA: Harvard University Press, 1991). In this book, Taylor explicitly retrieves authentic choice as meaningful and powerful expression of individual integrity. At the same time, we are sometimes tempted to assign to the fact of choice itself ultimate value and meaning. When choice per se becomes overly privileged, then authenticity is undercut, precipitating a slide toward empty relativism.

conventional—you might say "scripted"—than the idea that each person's task is to express her or his own unique, authentic self. This irony sets up something of a rat race for authentic individuality. We sense that inherited forms of church create a drag on our unhampered freedom—only to discover just how widespread that sentiment is, and to find ourselves "conforming" to rituals of nonconformity. Indeed, churches that describe themselves as nondenominational and seeker-sensitive are quick to seize on this irony and can even help fashion it; by rejecting the empty rituals of traditional denominations, one is free to join a larger, livelier church—where, soon enough, one will be doing the same things that everyone else does. It is as if we have all read a copy of the *Off the Beaten Path* travel guide, and so, get all the more bothered by those terribly conventional tourists who are now blocking our view of Stonehenge.

Because this newer, ironic form of Christendom is emerging no less quickly than the church meant to combat it, the present book considers the positive elements of (what may at least seem to be) more passive and scripted processes of formation. It also seeks to raise questions about and de-emphasize the centrality of the seemingly unencumbered, individual "choices" that we think we are making. Note, however, that neither these diagnoses of neo-Christendom, nor the attempt to retrieve the idea of communal formation, can eliminate the older problem of rote repetition or the importance of personal commitment. If our supposedly "Christian" culture were exhaustively defined by one of the two extremes—*either* our unreflective repetition of canned rituals, *or* uncritical faith in free-floating individual choices—then our path forward would be fairly straightforward. But in this awkward moment of its shifting forms, deeply entranced as we are in what James Baldwin called the "schizophrenia in the mind of Christendom,"[2] our neo-Christendom remains tenacious and manifold enough to require both responses simultaneously—even as they pull in opposing directions.

Let me offer a brief personal example to illustrate this dilemma. My

2. James Baldwin, *The Fire Next Time* (New York: Vintage, 1993), 47.

spouse, Laura, grew up in the Christian Church (Disciples of Christ) tradition and is now an ordained minister in a Disciples church. Her tradition practices believer's baptism; they understand baptism to follow from an adult's (or older child's) free decision to acknowledge God's grace, become a Christian, and commit to the church. I grew up and identify with the Lutheran church, which (like many mainline Protestant and Catholic traditions) typically baptizes infants out of the conviction that God calls that child to God's grace regardless of the child's awareness or decision. Since the start of our marriage, we have mainly appreciated these different theological sensibilities and ecclesial practices. But when our firstborn child, Asa, was born ten years ago, we needed to face some big questions. Should we allow Asa to be baptized as a baby—as was customary in my extended family, and meaningful (that is, theologically significant) to me? Or should we wait until he was older and let Asa decide for himself, which was customary in Laura's family, and which avoided the threat of triviality, artificiality, and empty custom? On the one hand, if we allowed him to be baptized without his understanding and choice, this might risk bypassing and perhaps then undercutting the significance of his own religious commitment. On the other hand, if we waited until Asa expressed the desire to be baptized as a "believer," we would risk making his life of faith dependent on his own decision and accomplishment, rather than on the unbounded graces of God—a God who, we both believed, had claimed Asa before he was free to acknowledge this reality.

These brief reflections on whether to have Asa baptized only clumsily gesture toward the real problem facing him, his parents, and anyone else who might hear a call to discipleship: How might one respond to that call in an intentional and decisive way, yet without putting more faith in the power of one's choice than in the power of the One who calls us? Or, put another way: How might one come to know oneself as always already called and claimed, without allowing that marvelous gift to obscure one's own role of responding?

The complicated response that I am here imagining requires two different sets of resources for spotting the snares of "Christian" culture and becoming a Christian in Christendom. If America's new Christendom is not only a monolithic, dominating force from which one seeks deliverance, but also, a set of loosely knit and deeply seated cultural assumptions that privilege individual choice (even the choice to reject Christianity), then the way "out" of Christendom must first involve seeing something that is otherwise hidden, before and beyond the volitional choice to be done with it. In this sense, both the problem and any "authentic" response parallel problems and responses related to other forms of majority consciousness and unrecognized privilege. I turn here to problems and possibilities related to racial reconciliation and white privilege in order to gain some perspective on the problems and possibilities of becoming a Christian in Christendom.

Invisible Knapsacks

Today's American Christians—and their close cousins, who identify themselves as "nones"—face an abiding tension. As suggested in chapter 1, they are fairly certain and often vocal about what they are not; they are not fanatical, fundamentalist, missionary, indoctrinated, extremist, violent, sectarian, superstitious, subservient, sacrosanct, or otherwise *too* religious. But this leads to a curious ambiguity, and perhaps a quiet anxiety, about who they *are*—that is, they find it difficult to offer a positive account of their own identity. They might regret this lack of clarity, but they also reap a number of unacknowledged benefits from it. They can thus be fruitfully compared to other majority identities and dominant cultural groups, in that they are often carriers of unearned privilege. Being a member of a majority group allows people to ignore questions about their own identity—how it shapes them and how it confers certain advantages, both before and beyond the choices made by individual members of that group.

In *White Like Me: Reflections on Race from a Privileged Son*, Tim Wise offers a critique of the claim that we live in a post-racial society—especially insofar as this claim is used to suggest that we have overcome our differences, or to minimize problems of inequality and systemic injustice. Many today at least contend that they are now *colorblind*, that they take no notice of another person's race. Yet, from Wise's perspective, the refusal to see another person's color is akin to a failure to "see the *consequences* of color."[3] The assertion of "colorblindness" results in an automatic privileging of the norm (which, with respect to race in the United States, means "white"). If we hope to come to terms with the privilege embedded in "whiteness" (and the accompanying marginalization of everyone else), we need *more* color-consciousness, not less. This is especially true with respect to the ways that color continues to divide us.[4]

But if color-consciousness is what is needed, it is also difficult to come by, especially when it comes to a white person's awareness of whiteness, with all the hidden benefits that that assumed lack of color conveys. Wise asks: "What does it mean to be white in a nation created for the benefit of people like you?"[5] It is a hard enough question for white people such as me to respond to. But the deeper problem is that the question often does not even register. Wise explains:

> We don't often ask this question, mostly because we don't have to. Being a member of the majority, the dominant group, allows one to ignore how race shapes one's life. For those of us called white, whiteness simply is. Whiteness becomes, for us, the unspoken, uninterrogated norm, taken for granted, much as water can be taken for granted by a fish.[6]

Perhaps then the most detrimental effect of white privilege is a certain obliviousness about that privilege. Wise connects such naiveté to the inability of upper-middle-class white people to understand why anyone would have grievances with the United States. He notices that black and brown folks often did not have to ask the "Why do they

3. Tim Wise, *White Like Me: Reflections on Race from a Privileged Son*, rev. ed. (Berkeley, CA: Soft Skull Press/Counterpoint, 2011), 67. I thank Paul Croll for recommending Wise's work to me.
4. Ibid., 253–54. See also Ellis Cose, *Color-Blind: Seeing Beyond Race in a Race-Obsessed World* (New York: HarperCollins, 1997), who claims that colorblindness "is not a racial equalizer but a silencer—a way of squashing questions about the continuing racial stratifications of the society and a way of feeling good about the fact that the world of elites remains so predominantly white" (210). A documentary film featuring Tim Wise is also helpful: *White Like Me*, Media Education Foundation, 2013, accessed August 10, 2015, https://www.youtube.com/watch?v=NynTIaCM988.
5. Wise, *White Like Me*, 2.
6. Ibid.

hate us?" question following the terrorist attacks of 9/11. It is white people, and especially upper-middle-class, straight, employed, able-bodied white people, who have more difficulty recognizing the systemic injustices built into an exploitative economy and an interventionist foreign policy, and who thus wonder "why anyone would hate us?" It is also they (or we—including me) who have substantial difficulties looking at ourselves from the outside-in, perhaps to the degree that we believe our security depends on the same cultural-military-industrial complex. We might thus recognize the "monochromatic nature of the naiveté"—but again, it is often more easily recognized by those at the margins.

In fact, Wise draws on his own Jewish background, and on his own firsthand experiences of being marginalized in that respect, to help him see, by contrast, his own otherwise-hidden privileged position as a white male.[7] In this respect, his work parallels that of Peggy McIntosh—an earlier prophetic voice on white privilege—who, drawing on her own experiences of disadvantage as a female, considers the ways she is overly or unduly advantaged as a white person. Coming to terms with such privilege helps McIntosh dismantle a central myth that Americans typically tell of themselves:

> It seems to me that obliviousness about white advantage, like obliviousness about male advantage, is kept strongly inculturated in the United States so as to maintain the myth of meritocracy, the myth that democratic choice is equally available to all. Keeping most people unaware that freedom of confident action is there for just a small number of people props up those in power and serves to keep power in the hands of the same groups that have most of it already.[8]

While most people deplore active forms of overt racism and white supremacy, many of them continue to overlook racism's systemic or embedded forms. In fact, these forms are often obscured most dramatically for the members of a majority or dominant racial group,

7. Ibid., 63.
8. Peggy McIntosh, "White Privilege: Unpacking the Invisible Knapsack," *Peace and Freedom*, July/ August 1989, 12 (as excerpted from Peggy McIntosh, working paper: "White Privilege and Male Privilege: A Personal Account of Coming to See Correspondence through Work in Women's Studies").

who simply are not confronted with these systemic issues on a regular basis.

Wise points out that, in the United States today, being white is not seen as belonging to one particular race among others. To be white is to participate in a comprehensive worldview that becomes so overarching and all-consuming that it denies the legitimacy of everything (and everyone) else:

> The ability of whites to deny nonwhite reality, to not even comprehend that there *is* a nonwhite reality (or several different ones), indicates how pervasive white privilege is in this society. Whiteness determines the frame through which the nation will come to view itself and the events that take place within it. It allows the dominant perspective to [attain] the status of unquestioned and unquestionable truth.[9]

We may express indignation about the more overt forms of white supremacy in our culture, but this more hidden form is very widespread. In fact, coupled with the myth of meritocracy and claims about equal opportunity, it may become something close to an initiation into "the American way of life." It thus becomes exceedingly difficult for a majority or dominant culture to recognize itself as anything other than "normal."

Understanding this, both Wise and McIntosh write in personal and even confessional ways about their own struggles to see themselves and others accurately and justly. McIntosh admits that, "For me, white privilege has turned out to be a tricky subject. The pressure to avoid it is great."[10] In her now famous phrasing, coming to terms with it is as elusive as "unpacking an invisible knapsack." How does one start to interrogate—how does one "unpack"—a set of assumptions so pervasive and normative that they merely appear (if at all) as merely the way things are? Wise also comments on the "invisible" nature of the situation: "Privilege sometimes costs us the clarity of vision needed to see what we're doing, and how even in our resistance, we sometimes play the collaborator."[11]

9. Wise, *White Like Me*, 212.
10. McIntosh, "White Privilege," 11.

Wise frames an example of the problem by narrating a story involving an "Undoing Racism" workshop. There, black participants were asked what they liked about being black and white participants about being white. The former had an easy time comprising their list; African Americans appreciated their strong families, camaraderie, music, culture, rhythms, customs, skin color, and the perseverance of their ancestors. White attendees, by contrast, had a much harder time naming what they liked about themselves. In fact, they largely failed the assignment. Their lists largely comprised what they liked about *not* being a person of color: whites do *not* get followed around in stores on suspicion of shoplifting; they do *not* feel out of place in colleges or most professions; they do *not* have to overcome prejudice and stereotypes on a daily basis.[12] They defined whiteness by what it is *not*.

This suggests that life in a majority culture involves a kind of Faustian bargain. One maintains the aura of the normality of the dominant group only by suppressing all the particular customs, traditions, music, culture, style, and ethos that belong to a particular tradition. Wise summarizes the problem with language that is commiserating, but hardly consoling:

> To define yourself by what you're not is a pathetic and heartbreaking thing. It is to stand bare before a culture that has stolen your birthright, or rather, convinced you to give it up; and the costs are formidable, beginning with the emptiness whites often feel when confronted by multiculturalism and the connectedness of people of color to their heritages. That emptiness gets filled up by privilege and ultimately forces us to become dependent on it, forcing me to wonder just how healthy the arrangement is in the long run, despite the advantage it provides.[13]

This suggests, notably, that white supremacy is also damaging to *whites*—in other words, that institutionalized, embedded racism not only does real and lasting damage to its victims, but also, produces certain pathologies among those who, by virtue of their membership in a majority or dominant race, are not among its most direct and obvious

11. Wise, *White Like Me*, 124.
12. Ibid., 178–79.
13. Ibid., 180.

victims. This claim is central to Wise's argument; so much so, in fact, that he believes that when whites get involved in matters of racial justice, they should admit that their reasons for doing so are, in some ways, not wholly altruistic. For example, he meets a white student who wonders whether she will be misunderstood and mistrusted by black activists if she were to participate in racial reconciliation. He answers that the desire to do reconciliation work cannot be based only on the desire to help members of marginalized races, or even to meet with their approval. Operating with these motives alone would be a recipe for paternalism. Just as significant is that, unless the members of a dominant cultural group engage in such work, they cannot fully know—much less appreciate—their own identity. Privilege has its benefits, but they are fleeting and ephemeral. Its costs, both to oneself and to others, are huge. Wise thus emphasizes that his own fight against racism is motivated in part by the realization that "racism is a sickness in *my* community, and it damages me."[14]

I have undertaken this excursion in the problem of white privilege because of how well it aligns with the experience of being identified as a Christian in the United States today. To paraphrase Wise's claim, we might say that, for those of us called Christian, Christianity simply is. Christian becomes, for us, the unspoken, uninterrogated norm, taken for granted, much as water can be taken for granted by a fish.[15] This helps us understand why mainline and mainstream Christians find it easier to describe what they are not than what they are. Like the members of a majority race, they have a difficult time in even knowing their own identity, much less appreciating it. In the cultural landscape in which we dwell, whites can imagine that the specificities of race don't really apply to them. Christians are in a similar situation. Unlike those who practice faiths that mark them as distinctive or different (Jews, Muslims, and members of certain marginalized Christian groups), members of the dominant or majority faith—a not-too-specific cultural Christianity—can imagine that their lives are, in Chris Haw's

14. Ibid., 182.
15. Compare the phrasing in Wise, *White Like Me*, 2, as quoted earlier in this chapter.

words, "unencumbered by the hassle of old-fashioned custom and dogma."[16]

Becoming Christian: Interested, Involved, Imaginative

A culture in which certain generic forms of "Christianity" are the norm (and one in which whiteness is also the norm) presents challenges for defining the identity of that majority group. Like being white, being Christian means knowing about what one is *not*, but having relatively little clarity about (and love for) that which makes one unique—what some writers have called the distinct social and ethical *shape* of Christianity. While there are, of course, dangers in too closely aligning religious privilege with racial privilege,[17] it can still be instructive to compare the two. I will here name here three helpful connections.

Becoming Interested

Recall Wise's comment that he is motivated in part to interrogate white privilege because racism "is a sickness in *my* community, and it damages me." While this may seem a bit jarring in its apparent self-interestedness, it does provide an important insight for those who wish to come to terms with Christian privilege. Such "privilege"—or, more exactly, the assumed normativity of Christian identity in our culture—is seen as wholly compatible with, and thus, helps to underwrite, other dominant identities: being Western, law-abiding, "family-oriented," putatively capable of wielding violent power responsibly, and so forth. While these associations seem to have

16. Chris Haw, *From Willow Creek to Sacred Heart: Rekindling My Love for Catholicism* (Notre Dame, IN: Ave Maria, 2012), 127–28.

17. The analogy between white privilege and Christian triumphalism breaks down in key places. For example, I wonder whether Christians who swim in their faith like fish in water, and so, do not notice that through which they are looking, would be as negligent as the white person oblivious to white privilege. In many ways, any Christianity worth its salt *should* become a lens through which all else is seen; perhaps the inability to turn the lens on itself, to see it fully and directly—despite the theologian's particular imperative to seek to understand one's faith—remains testament that Christianity or any other "religion" is more like a way of encountering the world than a reified thing capable of being interrogated. See Wilfred Cantwell Smith, *The Meaning and End of Religion* (Minneapolis: Fortress Press, 1991), 119–53. McIntosh also attends to the "difficulties and angers surrounding the task of finding parallels" between racism, sexism, and heterosexism; see "White Privilege," 12.

certain advantages, lending the Christian faith whatever cultural power it still has, they also lead many people to hold a negative view of the word *Christian* and anything it modifies. These associations can also confuse Christians about their own identity.

Recall our discussion in chapter 1 of the "Constantinian shift," when Christianity became first legalized and then institutionalized with the Roman Empire. Such *acculturation* ended many forms of Roman persecution against Christians, and allowed Christianity to flourish. But it also meant that Christianity quickly became *accommodated*, beholden to the empire that had adopted it. Critics of this shift see it, too, as a Faustian bargain that exacts a heavy price. Christianity became protected from persecution by agreeing to sanction the Roman way of life—including the violent persecution of (different) religious communities. Christians thereby attenuated or wholly surrendered their faithful allegiance to Jesus and handed it (or at least, some of it) over to Caesar. In the process, they also lost many of their distinctive, countercultural practices, including the practice of nonviolence.

Like white *supremacy*, "official" Christianity has often been merciless in its claims to normativity. Sometimes, it has imposed its creeds on others as the equivalent of a loyalty oath or a pledge of allegiance; it has frequently forced Jews and other non-Christians to bow before the cross. But like white *privilege*, the ensuing "Christian" culture has itself become compromised, vacated of its specificity, thus resulting in a merely nominal Christianity that has often been indistinguishable from the empire or nation-state within which it operates. Not only did Christians gain too much power (using it to dominate those persons who were not sanctioned and protected, as the long history of anti-Jewish violence demonstrates), they also set aside the particular power of their distinctive, countercultural practices. Or again: they allowed their faith to become a shapeless "spiritual" identity that easily aligned with, and even sanctioned, their now more primary allegiances to empire or nation.

Then as now, Christianity loses its distinctive identity when it becomes the normative identity of a culture. Roman Christians—a distinctive (and persecuted) minority—quickly became Romans who happen to be Christian, easily merging this identity with other identities as soldiers, workers, or civil servants—all of whom helped to support and undergird the empire. Similarly, American Christians often become Americans who happen to be Christian, not allowing this latter identity to come into conflict with the ways that they support and undergird the state. And so, just as white privilege is a sickness that not only victimizes nonwhites, but also, damages white people, so too with Christian privilege. It not only has persecuted non-Christians, but also, has done damage to the Christian faith as a whole. And just as whites need to recognize that coming to terms with privilege is in their own interest, Christians need to grapple with their own privilege so that they can see Christianity as worthy and good in its own right—rather than something defined primarily by what it is not,[18] or worse, as something about which they should feel guilty.

Of course, much depends on how Christians "spend" the cultural capital that accompanies the specificity that they might come to reclaim. Will it be used to renew fidelity to the tradition, including its works of mercy for those outside the tradition? Or will it simply serve to bolster its own status, and thus risk entrenching itself in the next form of cultural Christianity? The tension brings us to a second connection between racial privilege and religious privilege.

Becoming Involved

White privilege and Christian privilege both call for new forms of responsibility—forms that go beyond discrete choices and avowed intentions of individuals. One does not need to make a conscious decision to become a bigot or supremacist in order to benefit from white privilege. Similarly, one does not need to be overtly triumphalistic or condemning of other faiths in order to gain the

---

18. James Baldwin puts the analogous racial matter thus: "It is a terrible paradox, but those who believed that they could control and define Black people divested themselves of the power to control and define themselves." Baldwin, "On Being White . . . And Other Lies," *Essence*, April 1984, accessed August 10, 2015, http://www.cwsworkshop.org/pdfs/CARC/Family_Herstories/2_On_Being_White.PDF.

advantages of identifying (or passing) as a Christian in a majority Christian culture. These forms of privilege depend only on quiet compliance, which is made all the easier by the fact that we often do not realize that we are complying. Inversely, it will likely require deliberate effort to avoid benefiting from institutionalized racism or from cultural Christianity, and even more, to unpack or dismantle their assumptions. This recalls the messages of theologians such as Douglas John Hall and of many emerging church leaders: disestablishing churches and disowning cultural power requires effort and intention. And yet, once one finds protection and sanction in cultural Christianity or benefits from white privilege, it will also take more than simple effort and intention, simple refusal or repudiation, to set aside all the advantageous contents of those invisible knapsacks.

The need for action beyond explicit disavowal helps explain why the essays by (white) white-privilege theorists are typically self-reflective. Christians might even call them *confessional*, in the double sense that Augustine intended in the title of his work: both negative (a confession of sin and failure) and positive (a confession of faith and trust).[19] White-privilege theorists admit that, "even in our resistance, we sometimes play the collaborator."[20] They also recognize that the work to dismantle white privilege only becomes available and influential because they have amassed the social capital that such privilege confers.[21] It thus remains an open question whether, in McIntosh's words, we will, in fact, make the right choice and "use unearned advantage to weaken hidden systems of advantage."[22] Yet, it should be clear that *if* those who benefit from unearned power and privilege

---

19. Augustine's *Confessions* is addressed as a prayer to the God in whom he now believes and trusts, but it is also a confession of a long history of sin and failures—beginning with the infant craving for his mother's milk and continuing post-conversion—which kept (and still keep) him from fully participating in the life of God. Saint Augustine, *Confessions*, trans. Henry Chadwick (New York: Oxford University Press, 1991).

20. Wise, *White Like Me*, 124.

21. Thus one of the undeserved privileges that Peggy McIntosh owns up to is this: "If I want to, I can be pretty sure of finding a publisher for this piece on white privilege" ("White Privilege," 11). Similarly, Tim Wise begins a lecture on white privilege with the poignant reminder that one of the reasons he gets to speak and others listen is because he is white. Wise, *On White Privilege: Racism, White Denial and the Costs of Inequality*. DVD. Media Education Foundation, 2008.

22. McIntosh, "White Privilege," 125.

choose to divest themselves from it, the "choice" to do so will be more complexly self-involved than is true of most choices if, by that, we mean straightforward decisions or selections. The same goes for "authentic" attempts at becoming Christian in Christendom. Indeed, if by "authentic" or "earnest," we mean mere declarations or resolutions that we will work from a purity of heart, unencumbered by our complicities in hidden injustice, then we may only be in denial about the depth of our predicament. Truthful efforts at becoming Christian in a nominally Christian culture must acknowledge *both* the urgency of pushing past that culture, *and* the inconvenient truth that, in doing so, we often draw from Christianity's cultural power. Extricating ourselves from the current morass will require us to own up to the ways in which we continue to benefit from Christianity's cultural dominance, even as we seek to move beyond it. We cannot simply return to an early, pre-Constantinian Christianity, acting as though present-day cultural Christianity confers no social or material protection. Doing so would be as disingenuous as attempting to escape white privilege by claiming that we live in a post-racial world where we no longer see color.

Becoming Imaginative

Becoming a Christian in a nominally Christian culture has another similarity to coming to terms with white privilege: both depend upon a *new way of seeing.* Many years ago, James Baldwin observed that being white means you never have to think about it, whereas black and brown and red people are "endlessly defined by those who do not dare define, or even confront themselves."[23] Unlearning such learned ignorance requires work of the moral imagination—re-visioning the whole of culture, both in its dominant and marginalized aspects, from the perspective of those who sit at the "underside of history." White, mainstream Christians need to be able to reimagine the whole of Christian culture by being in solidarity with the poor and the oppressed and learning to see things as they see them.

23. Baldwin, "On Being White," 3.

One primary way to do so would be by learning from liberation theologians, those who think about God from the vantage point of the poor and marginalized and summon affluent and mainstream North Americans to see from their point of view. These include theologians from base communities in Latin America, black liberation theologians, *mujeristas* (Latina women), many feminists, womanists (black women in America), and others. Despite much diversity in their approaches to theology, hope, and struggles for justice, these prophetic Christians underscore the New Testament's central proclamation of God's special, surprising good news to the poor (see Luke 6:20–26). Those who are not poor or black or brown are not loved by God any less, but receiving that love and grace and distinguishing them from unearned privilege (and from cheap grace) requires that they be in solidarity with those whose sociocultural marginality enables them to see from a particular angle. When God's grace, the gift of God's own self, is imagined from a position of privilege, it is difficult to distinguish from unearned privilege itself—that is, it is difficult even to see. When, by contrast, grace is conceived and received alongside those who do not inherit social privilege, it can be known for what it is: God's surprising adoption of those whom others forget or reject.

The task of reimagining Christianity apart from our cultural Christendom, and grace apart from privilege, need not entail abandoning the theological vision of figures who are considered "mainstream" or who have become the namesakes of "mainline" denominations. Within my own tradition, for example, Martin Luther's ecclesial and cultural protests begin a theological trajectory (including the epistemological privilege of the poor and marginalized) that liberationists pick up and carry forward (and also, surpass).[24] For example, something as seemingly mundane as Luther's account of the sacraments offers a way of seeing certain fundamental elements of

---

24. See Walter Altman, *Luther and Liberation: A Latin American Perspective*, trans. Thia Cooper, 2nd ed. (Minneapolis: Fortress Press, 2016); Paul Chung, Ulrich Duchrow, and Craig L. Nelson, eds., *Liberating Lutheran Theology: Freedom for Justice and Solidarity in a Global Context* (Minneapolis: Fortress Press, 2011); and Jason Mahn, ed., *Radical Lutherans/Lutheran Radicals* (Eugene, OR: Cascade, forthcoming).

our world as able to reveal God and make God present to us: water, bread, wine, neighbor love, daily tasks, and joys. Such a vision of God's presence in the world resists the treatment of religion as a "merely spiritual" perspective that is assumed to be compatible with, and is sometimes used to christen, any and every social form. In fact, Luther underscores the New Testament claim that God inhabits those places where we would *least* expect to find the divine: in a stable, among the poor, and in suffering, death, and the cross. Recognizing the presence of God in these places requires us to face our own prejudices, including our desperate, sinful attempts to avoid the scandal of the cross. Thus, Luther claims that coming to know God requires attending to the seemingly God-forsaken. Just as white privilege remains an invisible knapsack of hidden benefits until we learn to unpack it, so too do the truths of Christianity remain veiled among the forgotten and oppressed until we learn to see God hidden there. At the same time, Luther (and many others) insist that this "work" of human faith is but another result of God's grace, God's self-giving and self-revealing. As a result, the work of *becoming imaginative* might be considered a "point of contact" between humanity's efforts and the gifts of a transcendent God.[25]

Christian Difference

The comparison I am here offering between white privilege and Christian privilege also requires recognizing a significant difference. Both require a critical lens through which we learn to become attentive, get involved, and learn to see differently. But what kind of critical lens is needed? White privilege theory—like many approaches that have grown out of modern sociology—tends to presuppose the principles of the Enlightenment. It suggests that a good analysis involves bracketing particular biases and perspectives handed down from authorities, questioning everything anew, and coming to know truth *for oneself*. In Immanuel Kant's famous terms, to be enlightened

---

25. Garrett Green: *Imagining God: Theology and the Religious Imagination* (San Francisco: Harper & Row, 1989).

is to be "released from [one's] self-incurred tutelage"; the power of that liberation is seen as coming from within.[26] No tutors are allowed; every framing story that has been handed down to us must be called into question. It follows that to believe or belong simply because others have done so is to be less than fully enlightened—less than fully rational, almost less than human.

In contrast, the process of becoming a Christian does involve believing and belonging—often in emulation of what others have done. The church is meant to be a place of belonging; it should be radically communitarian, the very body of Christ. Of course, this is not to say that Christians are merely an "affinity group," in which like-minded (or similarly complexioned!) people come together with only a vague sense of who they are. "Church" should, rather, name those who have undergone the difficult process of Christian formation by which they come to see themselves as distinguishable from the wider culture, and to see that culture as the theatre of God's strange grace—often hidden under opposite signs. Such work depends upon both community and imagination; it requires a hermeneutic of trust, and not just one of suspicion. In other words, if Christians hope to see themselves, God, and the neighbor truthfully, they cannot simply step away from all the authorities, stories, and practices that define the Christian life. Instead, they need to be willing to embody their particular traditions and worldviews more fully. This does not mean blindly accepting everything handed down, of course; nor does it mean seeking to "belong" out of a need for comfort and solace. But it does mean raising questions about certain assumptions of Enlightenment culture (becoming skeptical of the skeptics), including its claim that we should live only according to those stories that each of us writes for ourselves.[27] It also means allowing our imaginations to become

26. Kant, "What is Enlightenment?" in *On History*, trans. Lewis White Beck (New York: Macmillan, 1963), 3.

27. I am here paraphrasing one of Stanley Hauerwas's many descriptions of Enlightenment rationality in general, and of American appeals to freedom in particular. For examples, see Stanley Hauerwas and Jean Vanier, *Living Gently in a Violent World: The Prophetic Witness of Weakness* (Downers Grove, IL: IVP, 2008), 83; Hauerwas, *God, Medicine, and Suffering* (Grand Rapids, MI: Eerdmans, 1990), 53, 108, 125; and Hauerwas, *War and the American Difference* (Grand Rapids, MI: Baker, 2011), 17.

engrafted into God's story, in which each of us is neither the sole author nor the main protagonist, but rather, characters within a larger story, organs within the body of Christ. It means setting aside the *privilege* that comes with participating in a nominally Christian culture, and replacing it with the true *gift* of participating in genuine Christian community.

Religion, Race, and Repentance

Of course, the above reflections on race provide more than just an arbitrary metaphor for Christian culture. At least in our place and time, Christianity and white privilege are closely linked. The dominant, generic form of Christianity in American culture has been an Anglo-Saxon Protestant version—which is to say, *white* Christianity. Nowhere is this clearer than in contemporary "Christian" discussion about immigration. For example, those who wish to exclude migrant workers of certain ethnicities from legal status as American citizens often try to paint them as non-Christian—even though most come from specifically Christian backgrounds. And of course, given the fact that so many white Anglo-Saxon Protestants trace their own roots to immigrant families of the past, new racial categories have to be invented and maneuvered in order to hypothesize a distinction that does not actually exist. Those who guard the so-called family values of our "Christian nation" often end up policing the borders between white and nonwhite.

Policing those borders sometimes takes the shape of heinous crimes. As I write this, many are mourning the murder of nine black church members in Emanuel African Methodist Episcopal Church in Charleston, South Carolina when they were attending a prayer meeting on June 17, 2015. The shooter was a white supremacist and declared a war on race before sitting through an hour of the meeting, and then, committing the atrocity. Such a crime is easy to rack up to a young and troubled lone shooter; but the tragedy actually reveals a more systemic form of white supremacy woven into certain forms of cultural Christianity that have always resisted the transformation demanded by the gospel. Tragically, Americans typically imagine racial segregation as natural; they base their assessments on sociological assumptions about racial belonging, rather than recognizing the church as a single body of Christ and allowing this claim to determine Christian identity in more primary and subversive ways. Church shootings and overt racial hatred thus expose a problem that is less dramatic, yet actually runs much deeper—namely, that whites tend to identify with whites (and to treat nonwhites as "other"), rather than stressing the racially diverse nature of the one body of Christ.[28]

This particular form of Christian culture's obliviousness—the systemic failure of white, upper-middle-class Christians to *see* nonwhite bodies—accepts and extends many other disparities in the United States, as Mary McClintock Fulkerson has argued.[29] Unlike the glaring racist acts—including murder—by self-proclaimed white supremacists, the white privilege and white obliviousness evident on Sunday morning are typically subtle and reflexive, rather than overt and intentional, registered only in the movement of bodies, perusal of eyes, and small turns of phrase.[30] In a multiracial church that McClintock Fulkerson attended, assumptions of white Christian supremacy came to surface when a preacher from Liberia visited and the number of black participants outnumbered white participants, followed by the complaint among some white members that the church was getting "too black."[31] Such a comment might seem egregious, but the fact that most white Christians never voice that complaint may have more to do with the fact that, given the deep racial segregation between one congregation and the next, the question never even has the opportunity to arise. The sanctuaries and gathering halls in most white churches remain governed by "white space"—an implicit bodily sense of ownership of space that gives free and

---

28. "Black minister: Black churches were safe spaces, affirmations of humanity" (Interview with Willie James Jennings), MPR News, June 19, 2015, accessed August 10, 2015, http://www.mprnews.org/story/2015/06/19/bcst-history-ame-church.
29. Mary McClintock Fulkerson, "A Place to Appear: Ecclesiology as if Bodies Mattered," *Theology Today* 64 (2007): 159–71.
30. Ibid., 165.
31. Ibid., 164.

comfortable movement to whites while demanding other bodies to conform.[32] It is only when such spaces get disrupted that deeply seated assumptions about the normality of white Christianity come to the fore.

Fortunately, some of the same church communities that are questioning present-day cultural Christianity and hoping to restore more faithful forms of discipleship are also attending to the realities of white privilege and *de facto* segregation, which is nowhere more apparent than on Sunday morning. Negotiating among these concerns can be difficult work. Exploring the twelve "marks" or practices of a group of intentional Christian communities called New Monasticism, Chris Rice suggests that the most difficult of these practices entails "lament for racial divisions within the church and . . . the active pursuit of a just reconciliation." With the help of Spencer Perkins, a black leader at Antioch (an interracial Christian community in Jackson, Mississippi), Rice has learned firsthand that Christians attracted to these neo-monastic communities are likely to come from places of privilege. Fewer people of color come to live in communities such as Antioch, or to Sojourners in Washington, D.C., or Reba Fellowship in Chicago. This disparity, Rice suggests, stems from the fact that the willingness to explore "downward mobility" requires one to have begun in a position of privilege from which one can descend. By contrast, a call for the renunciation of material comfort and social power is hardly audible to those who benefit from neither. And so, two groups—divided by lines of race and class—have found it difficult to achieve true reconciliation, despite the fact that both are committed to restorative justice. As Rice puts it: "Moving from power, you carry more guilt and are more interested in gaining relationship and trust; moving from the margins, you carry more interest in changing the status quo and addressing issues of power, without which you believe you cannot trust."[33]

32. Ibid., 167.
33. Chris Rice, "Lament for Racial Divisions within the Church and Our Communities Combined with an Active Pursuit of a Just Reconciliation," in *School(s) for Conversion: 12 Marks of a New Monasticism*, ed. the Rutba House (Eugene, OR: Cascade, 2005), 66.

It is to the credit of such intentional communities that they are aware of the deep challenges of racial reconciliation, as well as the failure of North American churches (including their own communities) to respond to them adequately. According to Rice, it is only by "proclaiming what is not" that would-be Christians learn to hope, to become humble, and "to resist certainty, self-congratulation, and the pride which so easily besets self-proclaimed 'radical disciples.'"[34] McClintock Fulkerson even suggests that we need to find ways to interrupt and transgress the church's assumptions about race, noting that "unless our habituations into the proprieties of dominant groups are transgressed in some way by 'others,' our well-meaning obliviousness and its accompanying unintended consequences will continue."[35]

In a similar way, Michael Budde takes racial reconciliation and deep inclusivity to be one of the failures of the church as a whole. His comments arise from his involvement with the Ekklesia Project, a network of church leaders and laity who want the church to become a visible alternative to cultural Christianity. The church's racial failures are not lost on this group. Although its members want the church to become countercultural, Budde admits that in the area of race, "the Church has done *worse* than the American empire that so many of us criticize—we're more segregated than the public schools, than residential neighborhoods, than places of employment, than the military, than almost any other social force outside the Ku Klux Klan."[36] That is a piece of news most Christians remain hesitant to face. The difficulty arises, in part, because facing the structural and unintended powers of segregation—and making the "whiteness" of many Christian communities visible—must also entail questioning many other elements of the church's relationship with the wider culture. But if indeed Budde and others are right (and I think they are) when they discern that racism and white privilege have contributed mightily to

34. Ibid., 67.
35. McClintock Fulkerson, "A Place to Appear," 171.
36. Michael L. Budde, *The Borders of Baptism: Identities, Allegiances, and the Church* (Eugene, OR: Cascade, 2011), 113.

the church's cultural captivity,[37] then confronting this reality will be an essential part of becoming a Christian in America's new Christendom. Such self-examination promises to be rather painful. As Toni Morrison reminds us, "Anything dead coming back to life hurts."[38]

I should add here, however, that fixating on the pain of such rebirth can lead us to avoid cultivating the capabilities that we need to embody Christian discipleship—especially among relatively affluent and socially privileged people like me. Recall that, as Tim Wise notes, part of the reason that whites need to come to terms with white privilege is that they, too, are damaged by it. Social and material privilege seems like a desirable thing, but it is actually the false consolation prize for those who have lost a more robust understanding and appreciation of themselves. To see privilege for what it is, and to renounce it (at least to some degree), is the first step toward reclaiming a particular identity. The same can be said of Christian privilege and a more robust Christian identity. Christians ought to "disestablish themselves," to take up a more marginal place in society—if not literally, then at least symbolically, and if not permanently, then at least periodically. They should do so, not merely out of solidarity with those whom the culture deems "less fortunate," but also, because Christian privilege also damages the privileged. They desperately need something of more consequence, more substance, and more orientation toward community than is possible in a generic cultural Christianity. They need to see themselves as the loved and graced body of Christ that they are, eccentrically called out from the privileged, nondescript normal.

This emphasis on working from need rather than self-sacrifice was brought home to me in a conversation I had with my friend Isaac Villegas, a Mennonite pastor in Chapel Hill, North Carolina who (along with Jonathan Wilson-Hartgrove) gave name to the New Monasticism movement. At the end of a long weekend with members of an intentional Christian community called Rutba House, I asked Isaac whether he thought such communities largely attracted people

37. Ibid., 117.
38. Toni Morrison, *Beloved: A Novel* (New York: Knopf, 1987), 42.

who—again, like me—have had things all-too-easy and now needed the discipline (and possibly the pain) of renunciation. "Honestly," Isaac replied, "I think we come to these communities because otherwise we'd be lonely. We need them." Isaac insists that a decade ago when he helped form Rutba House, he needed a community that was deeper and more diverse than the homogeneous affinity groups of like-minded people that pass for "church communities" today. Admittedly, it will be painful to undergo the ongoing disciplines necessary to become one part of a corporate body that resembles the corporeal body of Christ. But Isaac and others assure those who are nervous about the pain (as well as those who romanticize and seek it out) that the joy of Christian community alone must provide the true motivation and reward.

Toward Specifying Today's Christendom

Earlier in this chapter, I noted that, if today's nominally Christian culture were defined by only one of two extremes—*either* our unreflective repetition of canned rituals, *or* uncritical faith in free-floating individual choices—then we would have a clearer sense of how to respond. No such luck: we actually need to respond to both of these extremes simultaneously. We need two different sets of resources for spotting the snares of Christendom and becoming a Christian in the midst of it. We need theological negotiations, such as those by "anti-Constantinian" theologians and a central strand of Dietrich Bonhoeffer's work, that describe the church's Constantinian "fall" in vivid terms, thereby forcing us to intentionally, courageously choose between inauthentic acculturation and faithful discipleship. We also need resources, such as those offered by Søren Kierkegaard and a different stand in Bonhoeffer, that highlight just how thoroughly accommodated Christianity is, and thus encourage us in a kind of constant vigilance and new way of seeing, along with a renewed reception (however "passive" it seems) for God's in-breaking grace.

The primary problem driving the next three chapters is whether these diagnoses of Christendom, Constantinianism, and "Christian" culture remain relevant to the contemporary United States, despite its ostensible secularization. In these chapters, I will attempt to show that past critics of Christendom are still relevant—perhaps increasingly relevant—to the politics and culture of "secular" North American society. In retrieving these resources, I will continue to show that, in three important areas of life, secularism has done little to alleviate the problem of acculturated and accommodated Christianity. In fact, as we will see, secularism actually makes things worse so long as it hides the damage that is done by a nominally Christian culture, making it even harder to detect and to treat.

PART II

RESOURCES

3

Purveyors of Comfort and Kierkegaard's
Call to Discipleship

In part 2 of this book, I more closely analyze three temptations among Christians who live in America's new Christendom, and consider what it would mean to rethink these tendencies from the perspective of a deeper, broader Christian worldview. I will suggest that the "Christian" culture in which we live today encourages us to tolerate and maintain that culture in various ways. Specifically, we are tempted to function as purveyors of comfort, as upstanding patriotic citizens, and as "chaplains" to culture, providing an aura of divine sanction to whatever we were going to do anyway. At the same time, I will suggest that the Christian faith commands an enormous range of resources that can help us resist these temptations, such that the faith can become something very different: a call to discipleship, a prophetic critique of the worst tendencies of the nation-state, and an active witness to the ways that Christians sometimes are called to act in countercultural ways.

To make this case, I will employ the work of leading critics of

Christendom (Søren Kierkegaard, Dietrich Bonhoeffer, and a host of twentieth-century "anti-Constantinian" theologians), showing how their diagnoses and prognoses remain relevant to the United States in the twenty-first century. To underscore this relevance, I pair their critiques with contemporary sociological and historical accounts of secularization. This allows us to raise questions about the widespread assumption, introduced in chapter 1, that the shift from established Christendom to a secular culture is a zero-sum game (i.e., that a more secular landscape will necessarily eclipse the Christian elements in our culture). Indeed, we will discover the flaws inherent in the claim that Western culture is, by its own momentum, moving from Christian hegemony to a purely secular society. I will suggest that both our contemporary "Christian" culture or neo-Christendom (as diagnosed by the theologians that I cite) and our growing "secular" culture (as described by some prominent theorists) can more easily accommodate, bear, and conceal one another than the standard narrative suggests. Far from making our task easier, then, the rising tide of secularism actually functions as a particularly complex manifestation of religious accommodation and acculturation—adding even more challenges to the work of becoming a Christian in Christendom.

Purveyors of Comfort

Why do people go to church? For all sorts of good reasons, of course. Historically, church has been a place where people receive the sacraments—seven in the Catholic Church (baptism, confirmation, the Eucharist, penance, anointing of the sick, holy orders, and marriage), and typically, two in Protestant denominations (baptism and the Eucharist or the Lord's Supper). From the fifth century until the rise of modern science (and for many Christians, continuing until today), receiving the sacraments was thought to provide protection against hostile spiritual powers (Sin, Death, and the Devil). Each sacrament provided tangible, earthly signs (water, oil, bread, wine) that reassured Christians that they were reconciled with God, were in God's good graces, or that even brought that state about. Seen in this way, the church has almost always been a place of reassurance and comfort for wayward and weary souls. We call the worship space a sanctuary (from the Latin *sanctuarium*) because it keeps sanctified people and holy elements safe from harm. Christians cross themselves or are blessed with the sign of the cross in order to mark and guard them as they begin worship. The benediction at the end of the service bestows God's blessings and peace, literally, with a good word (*bene–diction*) of comfort and inspiration as worshippers are sent out into the wider world. Finally, Christians participate in all of this as a way of securing (or at least testifying to) their *salvation*, which (from the Latin *salus*, meaning *health*) is all about safety and well-being, both spiritual and physical.

Thus for most of Christian history, the church's worship and the proclamation of salvation itself have comforted countless Christians with the gospel, with God's good news, with that "balm in Gilead" that makes "the wounded whole," as the African American spiritual has it. *Yet, this was only half the story.* Besides giving comfort to the sin-sick soul, the church has also been about the business of reforming desires so that Christians would come to want the highest good, which is nothing less than friendship with God, according to the most important medieval theologian Thomas Aquinas.[1] In other words, the church not only sought to satisfy the wants and needs of those who came through its doors, but also, to instruct such seekers as to what *truly* comforted, what was *really* worth having. Such "instruction" entailed a thorough re-formation of desire—the prolonged and often painful process of weaning oneself from immediate wants and needs (food, drink, sex, entertainment, and even human love) so that they ceased to be one's final ends; would-be Christians needed to learn to love these more limited goods only insofar as *through them* they loved and enjoyed God.[2] These two primary functions of Christian

---

1. Thomas Aquinas, "Questions on Love and Charity," trans. the Fathers of the English Dominican Province. *Other Selves: Philosophers on Friendship*, ed. Michael Pakaluk (Indianapolis: Hackett, 1991), 172.
2. St. Augustine thus distinguishes between the use (*uti*) by which everything (and everyone) other than God must be loved (these things are "used" in order to love God through them), and the

practice—"satisfying" desires and *reshaping* them—could not be pulled apart. It was only through the painful process of being reshaped and reformed that a Christian could come to enjoy the healing and grace being offered.[3]

Much of this has changed in subtle but significant ways, maybe especially in the United States over the course of the last century. If the bulk of the Christian tradition thought that human happiness (or *eudaimonia*, closely linked with the virtues) was achievable when desires were schooled until Christians wanted what was worth wanting, with the rise of psychoanalysis, and more generally, the triumph of a therapeutic culture, Westerners now interpret such *askesis*, or formation, as forms of unwanted and unneeded repression. Freud (and most of us since) now link happiness with fulfilling *my* desire, not the reshaping of it; we want freedom in the plain negative sense of being free to pursue happiness, however one defines it.[4] Contemporary Christians thus increasingly speak of what is most spiritually meaningful or authentic in terms of what fulfills one "personally." Christianity, in short, has become a kind of "psychotherapeutic faith," one that leaves it up to individuals to experiment with what makes them happy and then try to "get" it as best they can.[5]

Those who declare themselves "spiritual but not religious" are just one obvious example. According to sociologist of religion Wade Clark Roof, an almost altogether new kind of religiosity began with the baby boomers and now dominates the religious "marketplace," one that emphasizes seeking rather than believing or belonging (and even less, being schooled, disciplined, or formed). It focuses on developing the

enjoyment (*frui*) with which God is loved as a final end and highest good. Saint Augustine, *On Christian Doctrine*, trans. R. P. H. Green (Oxford: Oxford University Press, 1997), 1:22–27.

3. Talal Asad, *Genealogies of Religion: Discipline and Reasons of Power in Christianity and Islam* (Baltimore: The Johns Hopkins University Press, 1993), 125–67.

4. Philip Rieff, *The Triumph of the Therapeutic: Uses of Faith After Freud* (New York: Harper & Row, 1966), 1–27, 87–90.

5. Ibid., 89. See also my "Choking on Christian Authenticity: Some Theological Predicaments in Light of Pharmacology, Hollywood Film, and Post-Freudian Therapeutics," *The Other Journal: An Intersection of Theology and Culture* (Dec. 3, 2007), accessed August 10, 2015, http://www.theother journal.com/2007/12/03/choking-on-christian-authenticity-some-theological-predicaments-in-light-of-pharmacology-hollywood-film-and-post-freudian-therapeutics.

kind of faith that a person finds fulfilling and that responds to a person's need, often by offering comfort and security.[6] Millennials have largely followed suit. The "moralistic therapeutic deism" which many of them mistake for Christianity offers a God who, beyond everything else, just wants them to be happy—and this happiness largely consists of letting them have what they want.[7]

Add to this the late-capitalist precipitous rise of a consumerist society in the latter half of the twentieth century, and you come to the now-prevalent idea that churches must attract members by appealing to their individual wants and needs, and by never asking too much of them. The idea that one could only find true happiness insofar as one's desires were reformed within the entire church body is no longer congenial to American Christianity; rather, "most of us imagine an autonomous self existing independently, entirely outside any tradition and community, and then perhaps choosing one."[8] Churches have not gone away, but they have adapted accordingly. Megachurches and seeker-sensitive churches try to meet the needs and fulfill the desires of their members (and potential members), often using extensive market research to discern those yearnings. They offer various ministries that cater to individual interests and needs (youth ministry, singles ministry, parent ministry, sports ministry, outdoor ministry, and so on) and deliver services geared toward a host of life topics (psychological health, financial security, marital intimacy, leadership, addiction, and so forth). While these churches obviously do a whole lot of good, serving individuals and offering them a place to belong, they seem particularly prone to packaging the gospel in ways that make it attractive in "the religious marketplace," typically by making belonging as immediately satisfying and painless as possible. Indeed, almost every church today thinks of evangelism in terms of *attracting*

6. Wade Clark Roof, *A Generation of Seekers: The Religion of the Baby Boom Generation* (San Francisco: HarperCollins, 1993).
7. Christian Smith with Melinda Lundquist Denton, *Soul Searching: The Religious and Spiritual Lives of American Teenagers* (New York: Oxford University Press, 2005), 118–71.
8. Robert N. Bellah et al., *Habits of the Heart: Individualism and Commitment in American Life* (New York: Harper & Row, 1985), 65.

new members, often by offering ways to be healthy, happy, and comfortable, spiritually and otherwise.

It would be too easy—and a bit uncharitable—to blame contemporary Christian churches for selling out. The gospel is, quite literally, good news; to proclaim it as such and hope that people take comfort under its wings constitutes a primary part of the mission to which Christians are called (see Mark 16:15). Still, the American consumerist and therapeutic context leads many to emphasize the "demand" side of Christianity at the expense of preserving what is actually "supplied" (along with the gospel's own "demands"). By catering to unreformed need, churches risk losing their ability to teach the distinction (and maybe, even to distinguish) between deep Christian joy and a peace that passes all understanding (Phil 4:7), on the one side, and mere comfort, contentment, and ease, on the other. What is more, in a cultural landscape that promises instant gratification, in which the average human attention span is now less than that of a goldfish,[9] where Americans have become okay with being called "consumers," and when church-growth experts link the survival of the church with savvy marketing and messaging, the pressure to flatten the Christian message, making it shiny but shallow, is quite immense.

I am trying here to suggest that present-day cultural Christianity has come to function as a purveyor of comfort, rather than as encouraging genuine discipleship, which brings deeper joy, but also, asks a good deal more of one. Cultural Christianity has strayed from earlier Christianities in this regard, offering comfort and satisfaction but not calling us to discipleship. Rather than catalogue further examples to support this, in this chapter, I turn to Søren Kierkegaard's critique of nineteenth-century Denmark's "brand" of Christendom, a brand that anticipates our own. But first, we turn to contemporary accounts of secularism to show how secularism enables—and does not reverse—this trend toward "feel good" Christianity.

---

9. Kevin McSpadden, "You Now Have a Shorter Attention Span Than a Goldfish," *Time*, May 14, 2015, accessed August 10, 2015, http://time.com/3858309/attention-spans-goldfish.

Cultural Christianity and/or Secularism

Over the last forty years, scholars have argued about whether contemporary Western society is becoming secularized (or how quickly this is occurring, or how extensively). Most have rejected or revised the secularism theory of the 1960s, including one of its strongest early proponents, Peter Berger.[10] The standard theory posits that as the modern age advances in enlightened thinking and technological control, including urbanization, industrialization, and democra-tization, the need for and presence of religion gradually but irreversibly diminishes. Charles Taylor names this way of thinking a "subtraction story"; it understands religious belief to function as an overleaf or "cloak"[11] of superstition, which necessarily drops out as humanity becomes more enlightened, self-guided, or simply "secular."[12] Berger now admits that he originally conflated two phenomena that are related but distinct: the *secularization* of religion and its *pluralization*. The forces of modernity do not necessarily manifest themselves as a wholly secular society (if this means the *loss* of religious commitments), but they do tend to diversify a culture's worldviews, values, and religious beliefs.[13]

For his part, Taylor offers his own complex story about how the absence of any one widely held faith perspective becomes, in late modern Europeans and North Americans, not merely one option among many, but the default position. He describes secularism as a proliferation of spiritual options, coupled with the "disembedding" of the modern self from any encircling meaningful cosmos or community (other than the associations that a person freely enters). This not only results in a wide range of religious choices (including demurral about or rejection of religious belief), it also creates a shift in culture, in

---

10. Peter Berger, "Secularism in Retreat," *The National Interest* (Winter 1996/97): 4.
11. Enlightenment philosopher Immanuel Kant writes explicitly of the "cloak" of "holy tradition" that should give way to a religion entirely bounded by the limits of reason alone. Kant, *Religion within the Bounds of Bare Reason*, trans. Werner S. Pluhar (Indianapolis: Hackett, 2009), 135.
12. Charles Taylor, *A Secular Age* (Cambridge, MA: Belknap Press/Harvard University Press, 2007), 22ff.
13. Charles Matthews, "An Interview with Peter Berger," *The Hedgehog Review* 8.1–2 (Spring/Summer 2006): 152–53.

which unbelief shifts quickly from "wholly inconceivable" to "the default option."[14]

Other scholars take up a more functionalist view of religion, arguing that it is neither waning nor waxing, but simply being changed in form, becoming more diffuse and decentralized.[15] According to this account, every event of disestablishment or disappearance of organized religion is countered by new forms emerging in other places (the churches of the Global South, for example), or in other ways (Facebook as the new "communion of saints").[16] In this view, religion is not being *replaced* by modern secular life; it is merely being *re-placed* (that is, relocated or repositioned) within the contemporary landscape. At the same time, many of those studying secularization argue that these kinds of significant changes in form and location suggest a deeper change in the very nature of religious faith.[17] Even those who "still" believe do so in a markedly different way than when they had only one "option." Religion has become personalized, privatized, therapeutic, and rendered *optional*. This is highly significant for the issues raised in this book, since anything that is a matter of opinion or personal preference is easily appropriated by other forces in culture; in other words, it "fails to resist co-option."[18]

14. Taylor, *A Secular Age*, 437. Sociological confirmation of this theory of secularization in America can be found in the latest Pew Research findings. American adults polled in 2014 were four times more likely to have moved from a religious tradition to unaffiliation, than the other way around. See "America's Changing Religious Landscape," Pew Research Center: Religion and Public Life, May 12, 2015, accessed August 10, 2015, http://www.pewforum.org/2015/05/12/americas-changing-religious-landscape.

15. Conrad Oswalt, *Secular Steeples: Popular Culture and the Religious Imagination* (Harrisburg, PA: Trinity, 2003), 1–38.

16. See Philip Jenkins, *The Next Christendom: The Coming of Global Christianity* (Oxford: Oxford University Press, 2002), and Bruce David Forbes and Jeffrey H. Mahan, eds., *Religion and Popular Culture in America* (Berkeley, CA: University of California Press, 2005), especially part 3: "Popular Culture as Religion."

17. In fact, "religion" as a category (which presupposes various "options") arises alongside the modern nation-state (and the secularized society it offers) as a supposed antidote to the so-called wars of religion that followed the fissure of medieval Christendom during the Reformation. See William Cavanaugh, *The Myth of Religious Violence: Secular Ideology and the Roots of Modern Conflict* (Oxford: Oxford University Press, 2009), 57–122. The most helpful secularization theorists track a change in the different *ways* religious beliefs are now held by individuals and communities. Those more bound to quantitative sociology will also account for "a decline not only in the prevalence of religious beliefs but also in the saliency of these beliefs." See Eva M. Hamberg, "Christendom in Decline: The Swedish Case," *The Decline of Christendom in Western Europe, 1750-2000*, ed. Hugh McLeod and Werner Ustorf Astor (Cambridge: Cambridge University Press, 2003), 47.

That last comment (by Steve Bruce, whom Berger refers to as a "heroic upholder" of the old secularization theory[19]) suggests that a thoroughly secularized faith is easily assimilated into the overarching civil religion or ethos of a nation or culture. This claim parallels my own argument in this and the following chapters. Before developing it, I should admit first that, especially as a story revised and rendered complex, secularism certainly seems to characterize our place and time in ways that differ markedly from earlier forms of nominally Christian culture, especially those signified by the word *Christendom*—a word employed regularly by Kierkegaard. To the degree that we associate the label *Christendom* with a unified, hegemonic, and official Christian civilization or state, the process of secularization would seem to entail its loss—almost by definition. Christendom and secularism seem mutually exclusive, with the rise of the second constituting the collapse of the first. This assumption is common in the work of recent authors such as Harvey Cox, who—as we noted in chapter 1—argues that Kierkegaard's worries about Christendom no longer trouble those who live in the present-day "secular city."[20] In fact, many writers suggest that whatever remnants of Christianity remain in our culture, they too will pass; they will eventually be overcome by technological advances, more instrumentalist views of human rationality, and the continuing relativization of religion. This suggests that, if we are still concerned about the entrapments of cultural Christianity, we won't be bothered for long. I will argue exactly the opposite case.

Kierkegaard's Attack

The story of Kierkegaard the person is rather boring. He was born and died in Denmark, living the whole of his adult years in Copenhagen (minus two trips to Berlin) during Denmark's Golden Age, when liberal and democratic movements arose (1830s), when Denmark peacefully

---

18. Steve Bruce, "Secularization and the Impotence of Individualized Religion," *The Hedgehog Review* 8.1–2 (Spring/Summer 2006): 44.
19. Matthews, "Peter Berger," 152.
20. Harvey Cox, *The Secular City: Secularization and Urbanization in Theological Perspective* (New York: Macmillan, 1965), 91.

transitioned from a monarchy to a constitutional monarchy (1848–49), and when the Danish Lutheran State Church became the People's Church, albeit still a *de facto* state church (1848).[21] He did make his story a bit more lively by falling for "a girl"—*literally* a girl: Regine Olsen was fourteen when the twenty-four-year-old Kierkegaard met her. He became engaged to her three years later, only to break off the engagement thirteen months after that. Although she eventually married another, she remained Kierkegaard's one true love, the reader in whose image he envisioned his wider audience, and his sole beneficiary. Aside from brooding over her and a one-year polemical bout with a popular Danish newspaper, Kierkegaard spent most of his days standing at his desk, writing literary, philosophical, and religious works at a quill-breaking pace—then circling Copenhagen by foot, sometimes ducking into the Royal Theatre during intermission to make it seem as though he was up to even less.[22]

From 1851 until his death in 1855, Kierkegaard secluded himself almost entirely, writing less and publishing nothing—that is, until his final year, when he unleashed a series of pamphlets mounting a direct "attack on Christendom." The confrontation was occasioned by the death of Bishop Jacob Mynster, who was a friend of Kierkegaard's father and a minister to the family. Hans Martensen, Mynster's successor, declared the deceased to be "a witness to the truth"; Kierkegaard regarded this as intentional nonsense at best.[23] For many years, Kierkegaard had been urging the Danish church *either* rigorously to strive to embody the high standard of New Testament Christianity, *or* to admit its shortcomings and complacency, humbly drawing on

---

21. Sylvia Walsh, *Kierkegaard: Thinking Christianly in an Existential Mode* (Oxford: Oxford University Press, 2009), 23.
22. Two fine, long biographies of Kierkegaard are available: Alastair Hannay, *Kierkegaard: A Biography* (Cambridge: Cambridge University Press, 2001) and Joakim Garff, *Søren Kierkegaard: A Biography*, trans. Bruce H. Kirmmse (Princeton, NJ: Princeton University Press, 2005). For a short introduction, see Gordon D. Marino, "Making Faith Possible" (Review of *Kierkegaard's Writings*, ed. Howard Hong), in *The Atlantic Monthly*, July 1993, 109–13; reprinted as Marino, "Søren Kierkegaard: Biography and Significance," accessed August 10, 2015, http://www.stolaf.edu/collections/kierkegaard/about/kierkegaard.html.
23. If he were writing today, he might have called it *bullshit*—in a quite technical sense of the term. See Harry G. Frankfurt, *On Bullshit* (Princeton, NJ: Princeton University Press, 2005); Kierkegaard, *The Moment and Late Writings*, trans. Howard V. Hong and Edna H. Hong (Princeton, NJ: Princeton University Press, 1989), 3–8, 19–27.

God's grace. (Even better than choosing either option, he believed, would be to do both.) When Martensen declared that the church, symbolized by its bishop, already embodied the ideal, Kierkegaard took it as an obfuscation of his own lifelong mission of making Christian ideals pronounced.[24] It made the gift and task of the gospel a bit of empty chatter.

While there are few remarkable developments in Kierkegaard's life, his massive literary production, including twenty-five volumes translated into English and thousands of pages of journals, has a life story of its own, marked by a complex personality and a series of emotional upheavals. Kierkegaard came to see great continuity of purpose in his various works that were written under various pseudonyms and from different points of view. Working in concert, the "aesthetic writings" would depict the dead-ends of a life lived merely for pleasure; "ethical" musings would introduce meaning, principles, and purpose, but also, fail to capture life at its most passionate and profound. Finally, Kierkegaard's explicitly "religious writings," many devotional in character and published under his own name, would depict the life of authentic, obedient discipleship—providing a somewhat unexpected culmination to his literary output.[25] Despite this coherence that Kierkegaard retrospectively comes to find in (or assign to) his multifaceted authorship, his work also includes reversals and reconsiderations that have all the contingencies and convolutions of a life lived forward.

The Indirect Attack

The year 1848 marks a key turning point, not just for Kierkegaard, but for his country and for the whole of Europe. As noted above, Denmark experienced a peaceful political transition that ended its absolute monarchy and its official state church. But this did not signal for Kierkegaard an end to Christendom or to "established Christianity."

---

24. Compare Frankfurt, *On Bullshit*, 18.
25. Kierkegaard, *The Point of View: On My Work as an Author. The Point of View for My Work as an Author. Armed Neutrality*, trans. Howard V. Hong and Edna H. Hong (Princeton, NJ: Princeton University Press, 1989), 33–37.

He continued to treat the new "Danish People's Church" and Bishop Mynster as though they were officially endorsed by the state;[26] he also believed that a nominally Christian culture would only be reinforced by Denmark's half-turn toward representative democracy. He predicted that this transition would lead to a "turn toward the religious,"[27] but that emphatically did not mean that cultural Christianity would simply go away quietly; indeed, it would fight back fiercely and thereby precipitate a momentous battle with genuine Christianity or what Kierkegaard calls "the Christianity of the New Testament." For Kierkegaard, then, the term *Christendom* is not limited to a kind of unified, hegemonic, and official Christian civilization; he did not think that it had been much altered by the removal of official alignments between the nation of Denmark and the Lutheran Church. In fact, he argued that the decoupling of those two bodies signaled an *upsurge* in the "delusion" of established Christianity.

At about the same time, Kierkegaard begins to develop a more specifically theological critique.[28] It begins to appear in his *Practice in Christianity*, where he provides an account of the transitions from early Christianity to the present age.[29] In its first phase, he contrasts the "militant church" with the "church triumphant." The first term does not mean "military," but rather, suggests the era when Christianity stood defiantly against the beliefs and practices of the Roman Empire and where persecution and martyrdom were therefore perennial dangers. The second term gestures toward medieval Christendom, where Christian belief was rewarded with cultural status and enjoyed political support. According to Kierkegaard, early Christianity and the later "official" Christian culture resemble one another no more than a circle resembles a square. The early church can be discerned only

---

26. Walsh, *Kierkegaard: Thinking Christianly*, 23.
27. Kierkegaard, *Søren Kierkegaard's Journal and Papers*, trans. Howard V. Hong and Edna H. Hong (Bloomington: Indiana University Press, 1968), 6:6255.
28. The indirect attack and Kierkegaard's middle authorship are represented primarily by the two books, *Sickness unto Death* and *Practice in Christianity*, written under the pseudonym Anti-Climacus, whom Kierkegaard describes as a Christian of "an extraordinarily high level." Kierkegaard, *Søren Kierkegaard's Journal and Papers*, 6:6255.
29. Kierkegaard, *Practice in Christianity*, trans. Howard V. Hong and Edna H. Hong (Princeton, NJ: Princeton University Press, 1991), 201–32.

inversely—by being hated by "the world." In contrast, medieval Christendom's Christians gain favor, honor, and esteem in "the world"—in fact, Kierkegaard adds, that "world" is now thought to be identical with Christianity.[30] The militant church and the church triumphant are binary inversions or polar opposites of one another; they would seem to establish endpoints of a political-religious spectrum.

But Kierkegaard then introduces a third category, the church of "indifference," which complicates the picture by introducing "another *kind* of opposition."[31] Here, church and world do not blend into one another as they do in the church triumphant. The world as a whole does not necessarily applaud outward demonstrations of religiousness. But neither do the two stand in opposition to one another, as they did in Christianity's earliest years. Rather, in the "church of indifference," Christians now face the "peculiar difficulty" of being met with apathetic acquiescence; the world *simply doesn't care* whether someone is earnestly Christian. The problem of maintaining religious identity against indifference is then exacerbated by the fact that this new "established Christendom," as Kierkegaard here calls it, treats all concrete manifestations of faith as shallow and smug. Real Christians, according to this perspective, would never show themselves as such; their piety is too lofty for that.[32] In this era, martyrdom and persecution are just as unimaginable as they were in the church triumphant, since this would presuppose that faith is recognizable, that it might actually do something that mattered, and that anyone would care enough to persecute it. In the age of "the church indifferent," the truest sign of one's earnest Christianity is the ability to don the faith loosely, with an air of ironic detachment, and thereby, blend into the rest of the (nominally) Christian crowd.

Kierkegaard wants real embodiments of the church militant to manifest themselves in moments of suffering; this is what should follow from the injunctions of the New Testament, which call

30. Ibid., 212–13.
31. Ibid., 214–15, my emphasis.
32. Ibid., 217.

Christians to the work of "denying [themselves], renouncing the world, [and] dying to the world."[33] But how does one induce such conflict between authentic Christianity and the ways of the world, if one lives in the era of "the church indifferent"? How does one stand up to mere yawns of acceptance and acquiescence? Eventually, Kierkegaard came to regard his earlier use of pseudonyms and indirection as essentially unable to call Christians out from the safe havens that had been created by a culture that allowed, but didn't care about, their faith. He would have to confront them directly under his own name, call them names, make fun of their pastors, offend them into conversion.[34] At the same time, he knew that the one true offense was Christ crucified—a stumbling block to the Jews and foolishness to the Greeks (1 Cor 1:23). By raising up Christ in all his scandalous particularity, Kierkegaard sought to force a choice between merely being offended, and becoming a true Christian who takes no offense at Jesus (Matt 1:6; 7:23). His goal was to undermine the middle ground of acculturated and accommodated Christians.

The Single Individual *contra* Christendom

As one element of his effort to "offend" his readers into intentional discipleship, Kierkegaard constantly carps at the crowd, with all its "chatter" and what we now call "group-think"—whether in the form of the press, the public, the state, or the church. Over and against these masses and this "mass mentality," he repeatedly valorizes individual responsibility, commitment, and passionate faith. He urges that each of us, alone out on "70,000 fathoms of water," should make our own leap; we should not try to lean on the assurances of reason or the props of church and state.[35] This single individual, who appropriates Christianity as a thinking, willing person or "subject," stands

---

33. Kierkegaard, *The Moment*, 36.
34. David McCracken, *The Scandal of the Gospels: Jesus, Story, and Offense* (Oxford: Oxford University Press, 1994), 43.
35. Kierkegaard, *Concluding Unscientific Postscript to the Philosophical Fragments*, trans. Howard V. Hong and Edna H. Hong (Princeton, NJ: Princeton University Press, 1992), 1:204.

throughout Kierkegaard's writings as a foil for (and antidote to) a merely cultural Christianity.

Accordingly, Kierkegaard treats *Christendom* as a rhetorical trope that overlaps with others, including "the crowd," "leveling," "the established order," "the present age," and "the spiritless." As such, *Christendom* broadly signals any number of situations in which "spiritless" persons (or better: spiritless so-called "persons") are easily mistaken for faithful disciples. The task of becoming a Christian, not to mention an authentic human being, entails becoming passionately engaged in one's destiny. Infinitely worse off than those who try to do so and fail, from Kierkegaard's standpoint, are those who never take it up in the first place. Worse off still are those who conceal their lack of resolve with the presumption that, by living in a nominally "Christian" culture, they have already become Christians. Kierkegaard's critique, then, is not limited to his own time and place. This is so because he targets not only the ways in which nominal Christianity has come to underwrite political expediencies, from Constantine's era to his own, nor even the particular cultural assumptions and social structures that explicitly paint themselves as Christian. Rather, Kierkegaard concerns himself with the pervasive empty chatter or lip service given to faith, God, Jesus, or religion that ostensibly mark their importance but actually enable so-called individuals to comfortably fit into what is deemed normal, and thus, to avoid the dangerous task of actually becoming a Christian.

To many, it is this emphasis on personal appropriation and individual commitment that seems to suggest that to get beyond Christendom, one must get beyond community as such, even and especially the community called church. It also then would seem that Kierkegaard's problem of Christendom is bypassed by an individualist culture such as ours. This so-called champion of inwardness and the single individual would seem to welcome secularism, in Charles Taylor's sense of the dis-embedding of the individual from a shared cosmos. Could Kierkegaard and Taylor rather be resisting the emergence of a similar kind of self?

The Secular/Spiritless Self

Charles Taylor focuses his massive philosophical analysis of Western secularism on the making of the secular subject and its unique experience of the world. According to Taylor, what Max Weber called the process of disenchantment (*Entzauberung*, literally "de-magic-ation") is related to the emergence of a "detached" or "buffered" self in the late medieval period. This new kind of "radically reflexive"[36] self seeks to protect itself against powers that impinge on it from without—not only against the influence of other persons, but against impersonal, "magical" powers that, in earlier times, enchanted the world and could possess individuals, for good or ill. This "buffered" self comes into being and is shaped by the forces of modernity; it is not simply discovered once the cloak of religion falls away, as subtraction theories would have it. With the innovation of the buffered self, a number of new options arise—including that of retreating inwardly in self-protection, of radical disengagement from the wider world. According to Taylor, a person need not carry out this disengagement constantly, or even frequently, for the world to change in momentous ways. The very fact that it is now *possible* to disengage—the mere fact that I have the option of being "myself" apart from you, God, and the rest of the objective world—marks the inception of secularism.[37]

Taylor's "Buffered Selves" and Kierkegaard's "Christendom"

As we have seen, for Kierkegaard, the problem of Christendom includes the fact that apathetic, spiritless persons, with backing from the church, can mask their lack of spiritual resolve through the mutual pretense that we are all already Christian. Cultural Christians, like Taylor's "buffered selves," have become invulnerable, immune from failure, protected by the unspoken assumption that they are just like everyone else. In this light, there seems to be very little difference between Taylor's description of the secular citizen and Kierkegaard's

36. Charles Taylor, *Sources of the Self* (Cambridge, MA: Harvard University Press, 1987), 127–58.
37. Taylor, *Secular Age*, 29–41.

so-called Christian of Christendom. At any rate, their relationship cannot be one of mutual exclusivity—a zero-sum game in which more of one creates less of the other. Rather, these two accounts name similar sorts of selves—disengaged, self-protective, uncommitted to anything definite. Both of them underwrite the capacity of persons to disengage; the two can thus work rather well in tandem, each account bearing and concealing the other.

But again, some will be quick to object that, insofar as this is the problem, Kierkegaard is surely part of it. After all, he is a known proponent of inwardness and subjectivity. How can this view fail to advance the turn toward modern individualism? Here, much depends on how we read Kierkegaard's praise of subjectivity and his defense of "inwardness" and "subjective truth." In our current cultural milieu, surrounded by the secularism that Taylor describes and fully in the grip of the philosophical assumptions of the modern age, we tend to read Kierkegaard's language of "inwardness" as a private, sequestered space. Here, in this space, we imagine that we can live as private, well-buffered selves, with our own individual opinions and beliefs—including our "own personal Jesus," as the Depeche Mode song has it. In our era, the language of "subjective truth" seems to imply that truth (and everything else, including one's relation to God) is relative, atomistic, self-enclosed. It is whatever we want it to be.

This, however, was not Kierkegaard's view. In fact, as Edward Mooney reminds us, for Kierkegaard, subjectivity is almost the reverse of our present-day account:

> One has more or less subjectivity as one has (or takes) more or less responsibility for one's life, or is more or less affectively and morally responsive to others and one's ideals, or is more or less subject to passions and the heart. Subjectivity for Kierkegaard is an openness to be affected by (subject to, responsive to) deeply moral, religious, and aesthetic pulls, initiatives, invitations, pleas, calls, demands.[38]

Kierkegaardian subjectivity entails openness and responsiveness to the

---

38. Edward Mooney, *On Søren Kierkegaard: Dialogue, Polemics, Lost Intimacy, and Time* (Aldershot, UK: Ashgate, 2007), 63.

call of others.[39] True subjects are "subject" to others: available, porous, responsive, vulnerable. Indeed, Kierkegaard reverses common assumptions related to self and other, subjectivity and objectivity: "Most people are subjective toward themselves and objective toward all others, frightfully objective sometimes—but the task is precisely to be objective toward oneself and subjective toward all others."[40] In other words, we need to look at *ourselves* with an objective eye, not allowing ourselves to fall into the self-delusions and easy acquittals to which we are so prone. With respect to others, however, we should be acting as subjects: attentive, available, truly "present" to the other. This is, obviously, a very different kind of "inwardness" than the "buffered self" of modernity.

It should be clear that the problems of cultural Christianity are neither solved nor circumvented by the emergence of secularism and the autonomous self. Rather, that "modern self" is quite central to Kierkegaard's critique of Christendom. The heart of Taylor's description of the emergence of secularism—the production of a self that can abstract itself from the great cosmic order—parallels Kierkegaard's critique of the spiritlessness of the crowd: a loss of the capacity for devotion to something greater than oneself, as well as an unwillingness to suffer for that same greater good.

Taylor's "Authenticity" and Kierkegaard's "Spiritlessness"

Taylor mentions a compelling irony that marks the emergence of secularity—namely, that it often follows (and sometimes accompanies) the democratization of religious practices and an increase in religious fervor.[41] In other words, an increase of attention to religion can

---

39. Recent comparisons with Levinas have made this clear. See J. Aaron Simmons and David Wood, eds., *Kierkegaard and Levinas: Ethics, Politics, and Religion* (Bloomington: Indiana University Press, 2008); and Merold Westphal, *Levinas and Kierkegaard in Dialogue* (Bloomington: Indiana University Press, 2008).

40. Kierkegaard, *Søren Kierkegaard's Journal and Papers*, 4:4542.

41. For example, he traces how the late medieval turn from a realist worldview to the nominalist insistence on God's unfettered willpower, along with the new status nominalism affords to individuals as more than instantiations of the universal, seek to restore the transcendence of God and enrich the common person's devotional life, but ironically, end up sowing the seeds for the privatization of belief and the instrumentalization of reason, as well as God's effective removal

sometimes pave the way for an increase in secularism. Consider the examples of the Protestant Reformation and of some twentieth-century defenses of Christianity. Both of these movements embraced an "affirmation of ordinary life" that sought to affirm, defend, and extend belief in God. Yet, in doing so, they also introduced the possibility of an "exclusive humanism," where worldly goods become ends in themselves, and where human flourishing becomes the only worthy goal.[42]

Clearly, at least some of the roots of the emergence of secularism have theological aspects.[43] This notion is corroborated when Taylor writes about the "Age of Mobilization" (roughly 1800 to 1950).[44] This historical period allows for a proliferation of spiritual options, from religious to anti-religious to nonreligious, into which individuals must be "mobilized," and which together provide only relative, nonbinding possibilities. Here, we see secularism as providing the soil in which spiritual options can grow, and this has two important results. First, it makes unbelief the starting point for the emergence of religious life. Second, it leads to the development of wider cultural sensibilities, in which the "Judeo-Christian tradition" becomes the preferred religious terminology for identifying what unifies people, despite the plurality of their chosen affinity groups. In the American context, this means that the "right" to have a number of faiths (or no faith at all) becomes the first article of civil religion's creed. In fact, this very plurality of options (and the freedom to disengage from any one of them) confirms, for many people, that America is God's chosen nation. Once again, secularism and cultural Christianity—now in a thoroughly disestablished but widespread cultural form—go hand in hand.

Finally, Taylor describes the most recent form of "secular Christendom," which builds on but goes beyond the Reformation's

from the cosmos, except as the initial designer of a disenchanted order. Taylor, *A Secular Age*, 92–99; 221–32. Brad Gregory focuses even more on the theological roots of secularism, especially in the theology of the Reformation. See his *The Unintended Reformation: How a Religious Revolution Secularized Society* (Cambridge, MA: Harvard University Press, 2012).
42. Taylor, *A Secular Age*, 19, 230–33, 305–6, 369–70, 650.
43. The *locus classicus* on this point is Michael J. Buckley, *At the Origins of Modern Atheism* (New Haven: Yale University Press, 1987). See Taylor, *A Secular Age*, 225, 293–95.
44. Taylor, *A Secular Age*, 123–72.

affirmation of ordinary life and the growth of American civil religion. This analysis focuses on cultural assumptions from the 1960s to the present, which Taylor calls our Age of Authenticity.[45] Despite widespread instances of glib expressivism and therapeutic language in our culture (all promising to "help you find yourself, realize yourself, release your true self, and so on"),[46] the Age of Authenticity is not simply spiritual consumerism at its thinnest. Rather, according to Taylor, it has deep roots in the Romantic critique of the disciplined self and of a rigid moral order, with Schiller's *Letters on the Aesthetic Education of Humanity* as perhaps its early manifesto. Nonetheless, in our Age of Authenticity, Christianity—among a host of other meditational techniques, pilgrimages, and practices—becomes a spiritual practice by which individuals seek self-fulfillment, harmony, balance, or centeredness. They find meaning in personal depth and originality, rather than in any shared social order—especially when that order connotes moralism and conformity.

Christianity, if and when it thrives in this age, becomes a path toward personal fulfillment and a sign of the individual's spiritual depth. The Age of Authenticity produces individuals who are decidedly "spiritual, but not religious," whether they use that designation or not.[47] Such persons are concerned with personal flourishing and uniqueness over against what they perceive as the moral strictures, rote collectivism, and empty rituals of traditional religious worship. Thus, to the extent that they still make use of Christian language or apply the label *Christian* to themselves, they do so in ways that are thoroughly accommodated to the culture of authenticity in which they live. If the "buffered self" withdraws from the surrounding cosmos and cultural milieu, the "authentic self" withdraws from the church and other organized religious forms in particular. As a result, the present

---

45. See also Charles Taylor, *Ethics of Authenticity* (Cambridge, MA: Harvard University Press, 1991), and chapter 2, footnote 1 above.
46. Taylor, *A Secular Age*, 475.
47. Researchers from the National Study of Youth and Religion find that younger generations do not describe themselves as "spiritual but not religious"; indeed, many have never heard that term and most cannot make sense of it. Still, their own "Christian" commitments largely follow the model of personal spirituality coupled with ambivalence, at best, about corporate formation, communal worship, and theological education. Christian Smith, *Soul Searching*, 118–71.

forms of our secular age begin to look very much like the cultural Christianity that some writers seem to think has been replaced.

It can be difficult to get our minds around the notion that a movement so dedicated to individualism can be so thoroughly tapped into collective consciousness and a shared religious worldview. Admittedly, if that collective worldview were to be defined as it was in previous eras (i.e., the era of the church triumphant), then these two categories would indeed be mutually exclusive. This explains why Taylor writes of a precipitous "retreat of Christendom" over the last several decades, whereby the above move toward personal fulfillment makes it "less and less common for people to be drawn into or kept within a faith by some strong political or group identity, or by the sense that they are sustaining a socially essential ethic."[48] Similarly, Kyle Roberts sometimes suggests that individual authenticity provides sure passage from "Christendom," as Kierkegaard defines and confronts it.[49] Both these analyses are correct; however, the categories with which they operate are more fluid than the writers sometimes acknowledge. For example, individual spiritual "questers" are not without a sense of belonging to one another—however one-dimensional that sense of belonging might sometimes be. Taylor, in fact, writes of a "space of fashion," where individual expressions of meaning intersect and clump together in the contemporary era. For example, my supposedly "individual choice" about the way I might wear my hat (or my cross?) might express a certain form of cockiness, but only because it draws on a common language of style that has developed across a broader group. I gain my "own" sense of style only through a unique play of imitation and parody with the rest of society. Kierkegaard calls "spiritless" this inability to *truly* be an individual because one is busy "aping others."[50] His term still applies to those who mimic others' alleged individuality.

---

48. Taylor, *Secular Age*, 515–20.
49. Kyle A. Roberts, *Emerging Prophet: Kierkegaard and the Postmodern People of God* (Eugene, OR: Cascade, 2013), 146. In this first paragraph of his concluding chapter, Roberts mentions *authenticity* four times in three sentences, pitting the search for a deeper authenticity against "the trappings of static forms of institutional religion."
50. Kierkegaard, *Sickness unto Death*, 101.

Of course, in the Age of Authenticity, people share *senses* and *feelings*, rather than actions—and so, to be sure, we are far away from "Christendom" as a political body or shared mission. But I would suggest that the shared feelings and meanings that permeate our individual quests for authenticity and individuality are perfectly capable of co-opting Christianity (or being co-opted by it). Nor are these shared feelings less consequential; consider, for example, the communal sense of being "one nation, under God" during the days following September 11, 2001. Our emotions can sustain a prolonged impression that we are unified as a free nation of free individuals—unlike (so the impression goes) those against whom we are fighting. Certainly, in a consumerist culture such as ours, authentic Christianity is prone to be manufactured and marketed as "cool"—and as a way to find personal fulfillment. That the rate of "religious switching" is at an all-time high indicates that Americans increasingly shop for churches they find attractive, reversing ecclesial commitments almost as readily as they return jeans that they thought looked good in the dressing room.[51] Nineteenth-century Denmark packaged authenticity differently, but Kierkegaard foresaw the dangers of making Christianity attractive, something that directly fulfills one's desires. Much of his resistance falls under the category of aestheticism.

Kierkegaard's Critique of the "Purveyors of Comfort"

I have offered accounts of secularism and of "Christian" culture in this chapter so that I can present a particular aspect of Kierkegaard's critique that is especially important to the kind of cultural Christianity

---

51. See "America's Changing Religious Landscape." According to the Pew Research study, switching religions is now common: 34 percent of American adults have a religious identity (Catholic, Protestant, Jewish, "none," etc.) that is different from the one in which they were raised. This number does not include switches among the three major subsets of Protestantism; the total goes up to 42 percent if you distinguish mainline, evangelical, and historically black Protestantisms. What is more, people are four times more likely to move from religious affiliation to nonaffiliation than the other way around. In other words, the group that has experienced the largest gains through religious switching is the "nones." For church marketing in relation to dominance of religious switching, see James B. Twitchell, *Shopping for God: How Christianity Went from In Your Heart to In Your Face* (New York: Simon & Schuster, 2007).

that we face in the United States today. I am referring to the worldview described at the outset of this chapter, wherein people find ultimate meaning in personal pleasure—and where religious faith is focused on being true to yourself, finding fulfillment, and allowing others to do the same. In such a cultural milieu, one of Christianity's chief functions is to provide "comfort"—whether in terms of salving wounds, mitigating grief, or simply making people feel good. The ultimate goal is to maximize personal happiness and minimize struggle and suffering.

This is precisely the kind of life, and the use of the Christian faith, that Kierkegaard exposes in his writings. He refers to these seekers of comfort (and avoiders of the struggle of reforming desire) as "aesthetes." Aesthetes try to carefully control how they spend their time, their energies, and even their affections. In ways that easily lead to manipulation and control, they work to get as much enjoyment as possible out of their passions—including, but not limited to, physical or erotic relationships—while being as invulnerable as possible by avoiding heartache, loss, rigorous training, and suffering. Rather than lambaste this worldview from without, Kierkegaard writes through the voices of pseudonymous "authors" who adopt it as their own. This allows him to show how the pursuit of pleasure and comfort breaks down under its own weight.[52] Kierkegaard makes three important arguments against this kind of life—and against a church that caters to it.

One central problem with following one's immediate passions is that they are *never passionate enough* so long as they avidly avoid suffering

---

52. Kierkegaard, *Either/Or*, trans. Howard V. Hong and Edna H. Hong (Princeton, NJ: Princeton University Press, 1987). The first volume of *Either/Or* has Kierkegaard inventing an imaginary editor, Victor Eremita, who finds and publishes the collected papers of a young aesthete, whom Kierkegaard through Eremita calls "A." The end of the book describes the carefully executed conquest by Johannes, a seducer, of a reticent younger woman named Cordelia (1:301–445)—but also, the way that erotic passion dissipates as soon as it is consummated because, in Johannes's words, "to love is beautiful only as long as resistance is possible; as soon as it ceases, to love is weakness and habit" (1:445). It also juxtaposes such questing with a methodical "rotation of crops"—necessary attempts by hedonists to stave off inevitable boredom (281–300), as well as with descriptions of "the unhappiest one" (1:217–30) and of a poet as "an unhappy person who conceals profound anguish in his heart but whose lips are so formed that as sighs and cries pass over them they sound like beautiful music" (1:19).

or *pathos* itself. For Kierkegaard, passion must include suffering. Kierkegaard lionizes suffering in many ways, focusing especially on the suffering of Christ in his indirect attack and—in his final, direct attack on Christendom—on the Christian's necessary "suffering at the hands of the world" that follows from "denying myself, renouncing the world, [and] dying to the world."[53] Throughout his writings, Kierkegaard links faith to passion and passion to suffering. Indeed, in the context of his early exploration of the particular "fear and trembling" of Abraham, this father of faith, Kierkegaard asserts that "the highest passion in a person is faith."[54] Such a juxtaposition of fear, trembling, and suffering with passion and faith seem strange to many of us. Kierkegaard may have been morose, but it may also be that our aversion to affliction stems from the ubiquity of our "liberal, sanitized Christianity that doesn't quite know what to do with suffering."[55]

For Kierkegaard, and for those of us who live in the nominally Christian culture of the present age, this portrait of aesthetic desire can appear very similar to—indeed, nearly indistinguishable from—determinate Christian faith. After all, both are about passion. The Christian is simply the more passionate lover, and faith is the highest passion. Moreover, both the aesthete and the person of faith are also at home in the world. Both would enjoy a special hot meal cooked by a loving spouse, such that a Christian disciple can hardly be distinguished from those who strive for creature comforts.[56] We cannot simply look at people and their actions, and thereby garner the information that we would need to line up all the therapeutic,

---

53. Kierkegaard, *The Moment*, 36.

54. Kierkegaard, *Fear and Trembling* (with *Repetition*), trans. Howard V. Hong and Edna H. Hong (Princeton, NJ: Princeton University Press, 1983), 121, 122.

55. Taylor, *A Secular Age*, 318; I am here helped by George Connell's analysis in "Suffering and Enchantment: Placing Kierkegaard in Charles Taylor's *A Secular Age*," *Søren Kierkegaard Newsletter* 57 (May 2011): 19–23, accessed August 10, 2015, http://wp.stolaf.edu/kierkegaard/files/2014/03/Newsletter57.pdf. Dorothee Soelle and Douglas John Hall insightfully compare contemporary forms of Christendom with apathy, the inability to suffer, and/or the sentimentalization of suffering and concomitant inability to be in solidarity with those who suffer involuntarily. See Douglas John Hall, *The Cross in Our Context: Jesus and the Suffering World* (Minneapolis: Fortress Press, 2003), 137–55; Dorothee Soelle, *Suffering*, trans. Everett R. Kalin (Philadelphia: Fortress Press, 1975), 33–59; and Soelle, *The Strength of the Weak: Toward a Christian Feminist Identity*, trans. Robert and Rita Kimber (Philadelphia: Westminster, 1984), 24–30.

56. Kierkegaard, *Fear and Trembling*, 37–38.

consumerist, hypocritical, inauthentic Christians on one side of the communion rail and all the genuine Christians on the other. How then does one tell them apart?

Answering this question brings us to a second way in which Kierkegaard might resist and reverse Christian fixation with "comfort," both in his day and in our own. For him, differentiating between true Christian discipleship and mere religious posturing and parroting has little to do with applying a particular orthodox standard (Christians are those who confess the creeds), or evangelical standard (Christians are those who have accepted Jesus Christ as their personal Lord and Savior), or even ethical or ecclesial standards (Christians are those who visit the imprisoned or show up for church).[57] Such discernment does, however, depend on whether the walk and the talk of an alleged Christian would allow *any* such standard to be applied. Kierkegaard's earliest comments on the hidden interiority of faith are not designed to be wielded by nominal Christians simply as *cover* for their lack of personal appropriation of the faith, or as a *demonstration* that they have already become Christians. As Kierkegaard moved closer to his final attack, it was this very relativism—this endless aesthetic desire to find whatever "feels" good to the individual—that he took to characterize Denmark's culturally accommodated Christians. Without *any* objective standard ("New Testament Christianity"), and without an original paradigm (Christ as the pattern for discipleship), each novel performance of religion *seems* authentic, but we have no standard against which to measure its degree of genuineness. It can be called neither faithful nor disloyal, neither virtuous nor sinful, since such labels require something to measure it against. In Kierkegaard's harsh terms, those who only seek out comfort live "a life that is so immersed in triviality and silly aping of 'the others' that it can barely be called sin, a life that is too spiritless to be called sin and is worthy only, as Scripture says, of being 'spewed

---

57. John Howard Yoder will insist on the last standard, however, and this distinguishes his critique of established Christendom/Constantinianism, which I explore in chapters 5 and 7.

out.'"[58] Compared to such lukewarm "playing at Christianity," the self-conscious sinner or resolute apostate can appear closer to truth.

In our particular Age of Authenticity, our various forms of cultural Christianity often allow us to talk about (and claim belief in) some kind of religious faith, yet without needing "to think of anything specific."[59] Socially acceptable (and sometimes politically required) tropes about God, prayer, Jesus, grace, heaven, and so forth amount to what Kierkegaard called "the chatter of the crowd" and what we might call "B.S."[60] The use of such terminology is meant "to convey a certain impression" about oneself, to try out opinions to hear how they sound and see how others react, all without becoming committed to them.

Similarly, with respect to their actions, culturally accommodated Christians can largely do whatever they like. Convinced that true Christians will not show themselves as such, no one can judge them based on what they do. This may help to explain why Americans who do not attend church still tend to call themselves Christians, or why occasional appeals to a moralistic, therapeutic, deistic God seems impossible to differentiate from, say, the Ignatian Prayer of Examen or praise of God through Christ in the presence of the Spirit.[61] Throughout his writings, Kierkegaard resists this slide toward empty chatter and gesturing at Christianity by insisting on *the very fact of* Christian standards and definition. Despite his talk about subjectivity and personal appropriation of Christianity, it needs to be identifiable by its beliefs and practices, and these require some kind of standard. While the standards that Kierkegaard lifts up vary and are not always determinate, each of them circles around one that is particularly particular and scandalously absolute—Jesus, the object of faith and the possibility of offense.

Third and finally, then, Kierkegaard distinguishes every beautiful, alluring, immediate object of ostensibly passionate desire from

---

58. Kierkegaard, *Sickness unto Death*, 101, quoting Rev 3:16.
59. Kierkegaard, *Judge for Yourself!*, 135; *For Self-Examination*, 74.
60. See footnote 23 above.
61. "America's Changing Religious Landscape"; Dean, *Almost Christian*, 179–82; Catherine Mowry LaCugna, *God for Us: The Trinity and Christian Life* (New York: HarperCollins, 1991), 112–17.

Jesus—the "object" of faith—whose scandalous suffering and un-substitutable particularity seems to shout "Away, away O unhallowed ones" (quoting Virgil's *Aeneid*) in the same breath that he utters "Come to me, all you who labor and are burdened and I will give you rest" (Matt 11:28).[62] According to Kierkegaard, we cannot fully digest either the idea that this single Palestinian Jew fully discloses God (a theology "from below"), or the claim that God incarnates this one individual without reserve (a theology "from above"). He seems to revel in the intellectual paradox and affective scandal that faces those who are initially drawn to Christ, then made hesitant when they notice the cross that towers behind him. Christ certainly draws all to himself—but only by simultaneously "thrusting them away" by virtue of his abasement, suffering, and death.[63] Like rigorous religious formation that fulfills only as it reshapes all desire, Jesus himself attracts individuals by "stirring them all against himself."[64]

Jesus certainly heals and provides salvation, but, according to Kierkegaard, he also ineluctably introduces the possibility of offense, opening his disciples to ridicule and suffering of their own. Much of the conundrum amounts to what Kierkegaard calls the scandal of particularity:

> When in sickness I go to a physician, he may find it necessary to prescribe a very painful treatment—there is no self-contradiction in my submitting to it. No, but if on the other hand I suddenly find myself in trouble, an object of persecution, because, because I have gone to *that* physician: well, then there is self-contradiction. The physician has perhaps announced that he can help me with regard to the illness from which I suffer, and perhaps he can really do that—but there is an "*aber*" [but] that I had not thought of at all. The fact that I get involved with this physician, attach myself to him—that is what makes me an object of persecution; here is the possibility of offense.[65]

Kierkegaard distinguishes the treatments any doctor prescribes from the suffering that ensues from coming to *this particular* Physician.

62. Kierkegaard, *Practice in Christianity*, 23, 381n3.
63. Ibid., 153.
64. Ibid., 171.
65. Ibid., 115.

"Getting involved" with or "attaching oneself" to Christ is abhorrent to those outside this faith commitment. Why?

The first and primary answer has to do with the incommensurability of Christ, this scandal of particularity. But he also points to another inextricable factor: the desperate and sinful attempt to make everything commensurable, which Kierkegaard calls "the calamity of Christendom."[66] Christian formation looks so peculiar because it involves the *unconditional* love of a *particular* Physician. Such excessive love challenges attempts by acculturated Christians to mediate all differences, to secure themselves against the pain of formation and interruptions from without. Kierkegaard makes Christianity strange by emphasizing the scandal of the gospel in the face of the many attempts—then and now—to hem in God's scandalously unbounded love for particular persons in all their frailty and sinfulness.

For all the present-day chatter about the culturally central nature of Christianity, such leveling essentially subordinates the actual person—Jesus the Savior—to the salvation that one can get out of him. Cast as the immediate object of Christian desire, as the answer to (unreformed) hopes and dreams, Jesus, in turn, gets associated with success, triumph, and glory. As a way of resisting this account of Christianity as the purveyor of comfort, Kierkegaard emphasizes again and again that no one comes to Jesus except by the way of the cross. Without going the "roundabout way"[67] through lowliness, the Christian would be drawn "naturally" to faith, and that faith then would become ultimately indistinguishable from other limited and exchangeable goods. The direct path of our desire for comfort obliterates the value of faith. And because Kierkegaard assumes that "there is only one thing to which no one ever felt naturally drawn, and that is to suffering and abasement,"[68] he emphasizes Christ's suffering in order that no one be merely "enticed" to come to him.[69]

While Kierkegaard never mentions the document by name, his

---

66. Ibid., 35.
67. Ibid., 238.
68. Ibid., 167.
69. Ibid., 153.

repeated resistance to aesthetic desire by lifting up the wounds of Jesus circles around Luther's early Heidelberg Disputation of 1518. There, Luther juxtaposes "theologians of glory" with "theologians of the cross." The latter come to know God only through the suffering and cross of Jesus. Even there, Christians only glimpse a God who remains hidden even in the self-disclosure, a God who "is hidden in his suffering."[70] No one is drawn "naturally" to that God, as we are to "virtue, godliness, wisdom, justice, goodness"[71] and other aspirations. By distinguishing such gods, Kierkegaard joins Luther in resisting an account of Christianity that turns it into something that merely purveys comfort to those who cannot imagine—because they have not been re-formed—something infinitely more happy.

Spiritual Nourishment

Perhaps it is the case—both in nineteenth-century Denmark and contemporary America—that the most tenacious forms of established cultural Christianity do not come from blending that faith with political empires, formal universal ethics, or even particular political philosophies—as many contemporary critics would have it. Perhaps the newest and knottiest form of Christendom blends faith with longing, taste, and personal preference, making Christianity one option among many for seeking comfort and self-fulfillment, useful to those who happen to feel drawn to it. This is accompanied by a shared general sense that forging a connection between the individual spirit and the Spirit of God requires a radical disengagement from any form of religious discipline or morality that might bind us to one another. If that is the case, then becoming a Christian in Christendom today will necessary entail more than retrieving an authentic church from beneath the corruptions of history. Rather, it will entail something like the deconstruction of aestheticism from within, allowing the widespread attraction to inwardness, depth, originality, and

---

70. Martin Luther, Heidelberg Disputation (1518), in *Martin Luther's Basic Theological Writings*, ed. Timothy F. Lull, 2nd ed. (Minneapolis: Fortress Press, 2005), 57 (thesis 20).
71. Ibid., 57 (thesis 19).

authenticity to come to grief so that a more porous, responsive, and vulnerable self might emerge. Kierkegaard understood his entire corpus as enacting something like this deconstruction, forcing bad food out of the mouths of overstuffed Christians so that they might feed again on something that would provide genuine spiritual nourishment. While the paths for becoming Christian in our present cultural moment will differ, we need to begin by discerning all the entrapments of cultural Christianity, including those that are hidden under the label of "the secular."

4

Upstanding Patriotic Citizens and Bonhoeffer's Faithful Resistance

The forms of Christian culture that dominated past periods of history—in which the church was closely allied with the empire or the nation-state—are much less obvious in our so-called secular world. The nominally Christian culture of the present day is more likely to make itself known through less explicit channels, quietly accommodating Christianity to the social, cultural, and economic structures that we desire. By blanketing these structures with broadly approved forms of religious faith, we lend an aura of respectability to whatever beliefs and practices we had already adopted as our own.

This tendency also applies to our political lives, as we will see in the present chapter. However, when we examine other cultures and other periods of history, here again, we often find much more explicit and obvious forms of "Christian" politics, that is, visible and definitive alliances between church and state. For example, in the historical period that we will attend to here—Germany under National Socialism—Christian beliefs and practices were co-opted by the state in forthright, obvious ways. This was an alliance of church and state in which we almost immediately recognize a twentieth-century version of what previous eras called Christendom. More recently, we have tended to think of such easily alliances of political and religious powers as something that only occurs "over there," in "the Muslim world."

Within our own culture and in our own era, however, we find it much more difficult to recognize the too-easy alignment of religion and politics. The legal disestablishment of religion in the United States—our "separation of church and state"—is assumed to be an adequate bulwark against ideological forms of cultural Christianity at home. We further assume that the rise of secularism (together with the decreasing authority of the church) will provide any antidote that may be needed against Christian capitulations to nationalism, nativism, and militarism. My goal in this chapter is to show that we in the United States are not as well inoculated against these particular maladies as we believe.

I begin by examining the political accommodation of the church in Nazi Germany, followed by an account of the resistance to that form of Christendom in the work of the theologian and pastor Dietrich Bonhoeffer. In his late writings, Bonhoeffer notably wrote about the possibility of a "religionless Christianity," and about the need for forms of faith that are suitable to a "world come of age." Bonhoeffer's comments are sometimes used (especially by "secular" and "death of God" theologians) to suggest that the best way to overcome the "synchronization" of church and state is to do away with church as institution altogether—or, at the very least, to make sure that it remains completely outside the realm of politics. The operative assumption here is that a politicized Christianity is too Christian, and the solution to be less so. By juxtaposing the Nazification of the church with Bonhoeffer's plea for a religionless Christianity, I intend to demonstrate why so many students of this era have concluded the politicization of faith is only properly solved by abandoning it altogether.

But this is not the entire story. Much happened in the decade between the rise of German nationalist Christianity and Bonhoeffer's final musings, and the rest of this chapter will explore those events. Our investigations will suggest that the tendency to describe Christians as "upstanding patriotic citizens" is not simply the work of a powerful nation-state that can enforce its claims through violence. It is certainly the case that nation-states have explicitly co-opted Christian language, but it is also the case that Christians have permitted and even encouraged them to do so. Sometimes, they have done this through active invitations, lauding the idea of a "Christian nation"; but they have also done so in less explicit ways, by turning inward, and thus, becoming relativized and rendered politically irrelevant, thereby sanctioning politics of the status quo. Thus, before turning back to Nazi Germany and to Dietrich Bonhoeffer, I will offer a few reflections on how this more implicit process takes place in our own cultural setting.

American Christians as Upstanding Patriotic Citizens

Most of us know, and many of us identify with, American Christians who are sometimes called "God and Country" folks. These are Christians who are also upstanding citizens and American patriots, and for whom both commitments (to God and to Country) are closely brought together. Often symbolized by a cross or Bible draped in the American flag, these overlapping commitments reinforce one another, sometimes even merging into one. Both commitments are commendable, of course. Dietrich Bonhoeffer, as we will soon see, loved his German nation so much that he voluntarily suffered with compatriots during World War II in preparation for Germany's restoration afterward. Certainly, he loved the God revealed in Jesus no less. But problems arise when God and Country are loved with the *same kind* of love, or worse, when they constitute two sides of a *single object* of love, so that religious faith and loyalty to nation become nearly indistinguishable. Bonhoeffer strategically resisted that blending in his own setting. We should learn to do so in our own.

The merging and blending of nationalism with religious devotion can sometime be obvious, as with Christians who proclaim the United

States to be God's chosen nation or when "The Battle Hymn of the Republic" gets sung within a church service. Usually, though, the coupling is only indirectly implied. When an American refers to how "we" must battle against "Iraqi Muslims," for example, the pairing connotes, without having to explicitly define the "we," both a national identity (American) and a religious one (presumably "Christian" or "Judeo-Christian"). Such allusions, when frequent, have the power to blend religious and national communities, subtly making America Christian and Christianity American even without direct avowals. Aware of such dangers, some critics of state–church alliances vigorously interrogate seemingly harmless pronouns such as "we."[1]

Beyond the indirection and ambiguity with which it is expressed, the blending of Christianity with nationalism and patriotism remains a complex and paradoxical phenomenon. Particular accommodations in the contemporary United States are so complex that spatial models, which otherwise might track how "far" church and state are kept apart or how "closely" they come together, quickly become unhelpful. It may even be the case that the very "separation" of church and state that most Americans endorse can be used as evidence for how "we" are a Christian country—especially in contrast to "Islamic nations" who do not enjoy such separation. Let me unpack this complexity by rehearsing a very short history of America's religious self-understanding.

As is well known, early Puritans explicitly regarded America as the new Israel, the Promised Land, a place to reinvigorate their community and covenant of faith apart from religious persecutions in England. In John Winthrop's evocative (and biblical) imagery, the new American colony was a "city upon a hill" (Matt 5:14), to which the rest of the world could look for inspiration.[2] Being set apart in this way was not

1. Stanley Hauerwas, for example, typically tells a "Lone Ranger and Tonto" joke to underscore the difference between the "American we" and the "Christian we." Accessed August 10, 2015, http://www.theworkofthepeople.com/lone-ranger-and-tonto.
2. John Winthrop, "A Model of Christian Charity" (1630), accessed August 10, 2015, http://religiousfreedom.lib.virginia.edu/sacred/charity.html, as cited by William T. Cavanaugh, *Migrations of the Holy: God, State, and the Political Meaning of the Church* (Grand Rapids, MI: Eerdmans, 2011), 90.

all about position and prestige. Puritans knew that with God's special election also came God's special judgment; as it was for ancient Israel, they expected the church of the "new world" to be held to a higher standard.[3] By identifying the American colony with a new Israel, Puritans strove for a theocracy (literally, to be "ruled by God") through which God would govern both politically and ecclesiastically. Church and state were very "close."

That near identity between political rule and ecclesial rule gets clearly pulled apart with the First Amendment to the Constitution, with its disestablishment of any one official religion, along with its guarantee that citizens can freely worship the God of their choosing or no God at all. From 1775 to 1791, the nation transitioned from maintaining religious establishments in most of the colonies to an official disestablishment at the national level and in most of the states. Founded on Enlightenment ideals, what Thomas Jefferson and others called the legal "separation of church and state" would seem to decouple, once and for all, lingering desires for a "Christian nation." Some commend this aspiration to pry politics and theology apart, but think that the job has been left half done. According to them, we Americans must become more "enlightened," that is, more vigilant about creating the secular state that we say we want to live in.[4] Others want to blow harder on the religious embers that they presume were glowing at the time of the nation's founding. According to them, the practice of a politics devoid of religious values—what Richard John Neuhaus calls our "naked public square"—not only robs Christians of their public voice, but also encourages open hostility toward religion, ironically breaking the First Amendment's "free exercise" clause.[5]

Answers to the question of whether the United States is or is not a Christian nation, and whether it should or should not be, have shifted over the country's two and a half centuries. Often, those with strong

---

3. Cavanaugh, *Migrations of the Holy*, 89–90.
4. Mark Lilla, *The Stillborn God: Religion, Politics, and the Modern West* (New York: Vintage/Random House, 2008).
5. Richard John Neuhaus, *The Naked Public Square: Religion and Democracy in America*, 2nd ed. (Grand Rapids, MI: Eerdmans, 1986).

prescriptions project them back onto *descriptions* of the nation's origin. According to a recent book by Stephen Green, it was probably early-nineteenth-century Christians who first rewrote eighteenth-century American history to include the idea of its founding as a Christian nation.[6] Again in the 1950s, there were introduced a number of measures—from adding "one nation under God" to the Pledge of Allegiance to making "In God We Trust" the national motto—that convinced many that the country essentially is—and originally was—Christian.[7] Today, the vast majority of Americans believe that America used to be Christian, but are divided about whether it remains so. Thirty-five percent believe America is and has always been a Christian nation. (This percentage has declined since 2010, when 42 percent said the same.) Another 45 percent today think that we *were* a Christian nation, but that we are no longer, while only 14 percent of us think that we were never a Christian nation.[8]

It would be easy to assume from all this that two impulses predictably spar with one another and never themselves come to terms. In one corner stands the legal separation of church and state, as enshrined in the First Amendment's disestablishment of religion and its promise of free exercise. In the opposing corner stand America's "original" Christian values, which help create "We the People" before and after the Constitution, and which characterize God's chosen people. In other words, those who want to keep church and state "apart" seem to be battling those who want to bring them "together."

But it is exactly here that spatial metaphors and zero-sum logics break down. As political theologian William Cavanaugh has demonstrated, the official decoupling of Christian church bodies with the United States government through the official disestablishment of religion can have the ironic effect of recoupling "God" and "America"

---

6. Stephen K. Green, *Inventing a Christian America: The Myth of the Religious Founding* (Oxford: Oxford University Press, 2015), 199–241.

7. Mark Edwards, "Was America Founded as a Christian Nation?" *CNN*, July 4, 2015, accessed August 10, 2015, http://www.cnn.com/2015/07/02/living/america-christian-nation/.

8. Daniel Cox and Joanna Piacenza, "Is America a Christian Nation? Majority of Americans Don't Think So," Public Religion Research Institute, July 2, 2015, accessed August 10, 2015, http://publicreligion.org/2015/07/is-america-a-christian-nation-nearly-half-of-americans-no-longer-think-so/#.VjIq_GyFPZ4.

as broader, vaguer, and more capacious ideals. Rather than being *replaced* by the separation of church and state, the theocratic desires of the Puritans have been *re-placed*, that is, repositioned and recombined into America itself as God's chosen nation. Cavanaugh describes this as a "migration of the holy." In the case of the eighteenth century, Cavanaugh traces it thus:

> With the shift from Puritan theocracy to the disestablishment of the church in the First Amendment, the theme of the new Israel became an important one in nascent American nationalism. The relationship between God and America was increasingly direct. . . . The new Israel was identified not with any church or churches in their manifold diversity, but with America as such. . . . The primary difference is that the location of chosenness moved beyond the confines of ecclesiastical structures and embraced the new nation as a whole. America, as the new Israel, became itself a kind of metachurch.[9]

This decoupling of church and state and the concomitant recoupling of God and America can lead to all sorts of paradoxes. Among them is the fact that religious tolerance, the worthy desire to leave it up to each individual's conscience to decide whether and how to worship, can become the very thing that marks America as so godly. Freedom itself becomes holy, and Americans come to "worship our freedom to worship God."[10] Secularism itself can become proof that America is blessed by God, or even become the blessing itself. And whereas the theocratic dream of the American church as the new Israel also held it to a higher standard (we would stand as one nation *under* God), when America itself becomes God, there can be little to keep it from uncritically blessing itself.

If these ironic reversals remain possibilities—if America can become God's chosen nation *exactly because* it separates church and state—then the awareness of this danger and resistance to it depends on something other than straightforward efforts to keep the church out of politics, given that that very de-politicization can invite the sacralization of the nation itself. One of the reasons I find Bonhoeffer so helpful is because

9. Cavanaugh, *Migrations of the Holy*, 91.
10. Ibid., 96.

he not only saw the dangers of manifest idolatry—of the temptation of the church to link up with (or "synchronize" with) the powers of a militarized government, although he also spotted this danger more clearly and sooner than most, but also understood that the de-politicizing of church was also a danger. It could lead to a situation where the church turns inward, giving up its prophetic voice of standing under God's judgment, together with the nation. Early in his career, Bonhoeffer even looks across the Atlantic and considers whether America's freedom of religion can become a God in itself. We turn now to his life and writings, hoping to find in his critical, confessional perspective a way with which to view ourselves.

From Ideological to Religionless Faith

I begin by juxtaposing two parts of the story of Nazi Germany. The first of these describes the clear and explicit ways that Christianity was co-opted by the German state in order to fulfill its political goals. The second part of the story examines Bonhoeffer's late writings, showing why they are sometimes taken to provide the obvious solution to a form of Christianity that has accommodated itself into the service of the state.

Hitler as Lord

On February 16, 1933, Adolf Hitler, the newly elected Chancellor of Germany, gave a speech in Stuttgart that heartened many Christians: "Today Christians and no international atheists stand at the head of Germany. I speak not just of Christianity; no, I also pledge that I never will tie myself to parties who want to destroy Christianity. . . . We want to fill our culture again with the Christian spirit, not just theoretically."[11] By April, most leaders of Protestant churches were in favor of "synchronizing" church and state. In May, "New Guiding

---

11. Ernst Christian Helmreich, *The German Churches under Hitler: Background, Struggle, and Epilogue* (Detroit: Wayne State University Press, 1979), 128–29, as quoted in Mark Nation, Anthony G. Siegrist, and Daniel P. Umbel, *Bonhoeffer the Assassin? Challenging the Myth, Recovering His Call to Peacemaking* (Grand Rapids, MI: Baker, 2013), 39.

Principles of the German Churches" redesignated the Protestant Church as a fellowship of German Christians of Aryan race only. After church elections of July 23, about two-thirds of the elected delegates were "German Christians"—those willing to swear allegiance to Hitler and work toward the harmonization of German politics and Christian beliefs and practices.

In September, Ludwig Müller was unanimously elected Reich Bishop; at the same synod meeting, it was decided that only those who were Aryan and who proclaimed unconditional support for National Socialism could serve as clergy. Such "Aryan clauses," as they came to be known, prohibited people of Jewish descent, regardless of baptism and their religious affiliation, from holding public office. Since pastors were legally considered state officials, the Aryan clauses effectively prohibited converts from Judaism to Christianity and the spouses of Jews from serving as church leaders. In the end, the large majority of Protestant Church bodies simply integrated the racist ideology of National Socialism into their own ecclesial structures, thus becoming known as "German Christian" churches.

In hindsight, these attempts to align the Christian faith with allegiance to Hitler and racial purity seem incredibly brazen and clearly idolatrous. But while it is easy for us to see the racist intent of such prohibitions, it is often harder to recognize that the church's willingness to go along with such poisonous claims was motivated by its desire to ingratiate itself with the political authorities of the day. We need to recognize the church's actions, not merely as a blindness to its own racism, but as a particularly grave example of Christian capitulation to the state.[12] Apparently, however, the horrific nature of the German Church's actions were not obvious then; if it had been, then resisting it would have been straightforward and simple. In reality, that resistance required a monumental effort: a handful of dissenters had to reconsider and rearticulate fundamental Christian

---

12. Nationalist churches continue a trend conceived by the Reformation principle, *cuius regio, eius religio* ("whose realm, his religion"), born by the "Peace" of Westphalia (1648), developed through the nation-state's awkward transition from empires and other pre-national states, and seasoned by World War I.

assumptions about the relationship between the church and proper political authority, about Christianity's relationship to contemporary Judaism, and about the presence of Christ in a suffering world. In fact, so much had to be rearticulated that, at the end of his life, one of those dissenters had to reconsider how the very language of *religion* and *God* function—and whether they should be scrapped altogether.

As If There Were No God

While imprisoned for resisting the Nazis (and the German Christians who sided with them), Dietrich Bonhoeffer gave new thought to the meaning of Christianity for what he called "a world come of age."[13] Writing from Tegel prison to his friend Eberhard Bethge, Bonhoeffer explains his recent ruminations:

> What keeps gnawing at me is the question, what is Christianity, or who is Christ actually for us today? The age where we could tell people that with words—whether with theological or with pious words—is past, as is the age of inwardness and of conscience, and that means the age of religion altogether. We are approaching a completely religionless age; people as they are now simply cannot be religious anymore.[14]

In his last flurry of letters, Bonhoeffer also famously declared that "the foundations are being pulled out from under all that 'Christianity' has previously been for us"; that we "cannot be honest unless we recognize that we have to live in the world—'*esti deus non daretur*' [as if there were no God]"; that modern people are quite capable of managing life on their own, without the "working hypothesis" of God; and that the task before the theologian is to work toward the "nonreligious interpretation" of biblical and theological concepts.[15] While Bonhoeffer does outline a book on these themes,[16] he mostly

---

13. Bonhoeffer, *Letters and Papers from Prison*, trans. Isabel Best et al. (Minneapolis: Fortress Press, 2009), 426, 450, 457.
14. Ibid., 362.
15. Ibid., 362–63, 425–26, 478, 475. Bonhoeffer first uses the phrase *as if there were no God* in reference to Grotius (via Bonhoeffer's reading of Dilthey), who "sets up natural law as an international law, which is valid *esti deus non daretur*, 'as if there were no God.'" Bonhoeffer, *Letters and Papers from Prison*, 476.
16. Ibid., 499–504.

has half-hunches and a batch of intertwined questions: "What kind of situation emerges for us, for the church? How can Christ become Lord of the religionless as well? Is there such a thing as a religionless Christianity?"; "How do we speak . . . in a 'worldly' way about 'God'?"; and finally: "What does a church, a congregation, a sermon, a liturgy, a Christian life, mean in a religionless world? How do we talk about God—without religion, that is without the temporally conditioned presuppositions of metaphysics, the inner life, and so on?"[17]

Given these ruminations, we can easily understand why Bonhoeffer has been understood as an advocate for the secularization of Western societies, ranging from the so-called "death of God" theologies of the 1960s to contemporary "post-Christendom" or "emergent" theologies that see our new secular age as a boon to Christianity. When, for example, Harvey Cox announced in 1965 that the process of secularization has alleviated Kierkegaard's worries about Christendom, he drew positively from Bonhoeffer's late reflections on the possibility of a "religionless Christianity." In the last chapter of *The Secular City*, Cox echoes Bonhoeffer's question of how to "speak in a secular fashion of God." He highlights the impasse of Christians who are compelled both to speak of God and to do so with the awareness that the word means so little to modern secular people.[18] Many other commentators have taken this route, reading Bonhoeffer as advocating secularism because it provides the optimum means of escape from our nominally Christian culture. To these readers, Bonhoeffer offers a form of Christianity that is still believable in an age that is "post-Christendom" or even "post-Christian."

This, I want to argue, is not only a misreading of Bonhoeffer's theology, it is also far too optimistic in claiming that such an approach can overcome the new forms of Christendom in which we remain

17. Ibid., 363–64.
18. Harvey Cox, *The Secular City: Secularization and Urbanization in Theological Perspective* (New York: Macmillan, 1965), 241. See also Cox, "Beyond Bonhoeffer? The Future of Religionless Christianity," in *The Secular City Debate*, ed. Daniel Callahan (New York: Macmillan, 1966), 205–14. Compare Bass's use of Bonhoeffer in Diana Butler Bass, *Christianity After Religion* (New York: HarperOne, 2012), 9, 215. The best accounting of *The Secular City* may be Cox's own: "The Secular City 25 Years Later," *The Christian Century*, November 7, 1990, 1025–29, accessed August 10, 2015, http://www.religion-online.org/showarticle.asp?title=206.

deeply mired. If we examine Bonhoeffer's claims more carefully, we will discover that his concern about the word *religion* is actually a critique of a particularly *modern* way of life—not a critique of every historical expression of faith. Likewise, his use of the word *religionless* is not meant to describe a pristine, natural, "secular" state—something that is "left over" once the accoutrements of custom and dogma fall to the floor (as "subtraction theories" of secularism would have it).[19] For Bonhoeffer, as we will see, to live in a "religionless" way entails the reconstitution and revitalization of some of the deepest roots of Christianity. It is no accident that Bonhoeffer's most extended reflections on reconstructing faith in a world come of age culminate in a hope founded on faith in redemption. In his words, "only the suffering God can help."[20]

In any case, Bonhoeffer would not think of present-day secularism as providing an adequate response to his provocative call for the church to become more "worldly." In fact, Bonhoeffer's writings offer a number of careful distinctions between the forms of "worldly Christianity" for which he calls, on the one hand, and the culturally accommodated forms of Christianity in which we find ourselves ensnared. Before exploring this, the following brief biography will help contextualize his work in his life.

Bonhoeffer's One Wild and Precious Life[21]

Dietrich Bonhoeffer was born in 1906 to an upper-class family in Breslau, Germany. His decision to enter seminary and become a Lutheran pastor surprised his family, who were only quietly religious.

---

19. Certain phrasings by Bonhoeffer are misleading when isolated in this regard. On the one hand, he is critical of Bultmann for too easily distinguishing portions of the biblical story that invite demythologization from its essential, timeless truth. On the other hand, he also aligns his quest for a nonreligious biblical and theological interpretation with that of his teacher, Adolf von Harnack, who, following Troeltsch, seeks to distill a "kernel" of Christianity from its historical "husk." In my reading, Bonhoeffer's particular refashioning of Christianity avoids the timeless essentializing of liberal historicists insofar as the "essence" he rediscovers is not a timeless truth, but the God who reveals Godself in the historically contingent suffering of Jesus. To shed religious "baggage" thus gets one closer to a God scandalously revealed and confessed.
20. Bonhoeffer, *Letters and Papers from Prison*, 479.
21. The language is from Mary Oliver's poem, "The Summer Day," *New and Selected Poems*, Vol. 1 (Boston: Beacon, 1992).

Two days after Hitler became Chancellor, the twenty-six-year-old Bonhoeffer was cut off from a radio broadcast while criticizing Germany's "leadership principle" on religious grounds. Within the next ten years, Bonhoeffer and the country he loved would undergo tremendous upheavals. Having first upheld the Christian's duty to go to war when necessary,[22] Bonhoeffer met the French pacifist Jean Lasserre in New York while doing postdoctoral work at Union Theological Seminary (1930–31). The radical French pacifist rubs off on the more traditional "two kingdoms" German Lutheran—one who believed that Christians should follow Christ in church matters, but their commander-in-chief when it comes to "national security." Bonhoeffer becomes a Christian pacifist (or practices a "peace ethic") in his own right, emphasizing later (in his best-known work, *Discipleship*) that Christ calls his followers to the dangerous way of the cross.[23] They, like Jesus, must accept their own suffering and death over a life secured by the expulsion and deaths of others.

Also in New York, Bonhoeffer was influenced by his black friends at Abyssinian Baptist Church in Harlem, where Bonhoeffer taught Sunday school and formed a love for African American spirituals. From them, he learned to see God and history from the margins—a lesson that he brought back to Germany and applied to his persecuted Jewish "brothers and sisters in Christ," as he would eventually call them.

During a two-year position as a pastor in England (1933–35), Bonhoeffer began to understand more fully the important role of the worldwide Christian church for critiquing German nationalism. He then returned to Germany, teaching briefly in Berlin, where he was denounced as a "pacifist and enemy of the state."[24] He accepted the call to head an underground, illegal seminary for the Confessing Church, located first in Zingst, and later, in Finkenwalde, in northern Germany. There, he wrote *Discipleship* (that most famous book), and later, *Life*

---

22. Dietrich Bonhoeffer, *Barcelona, Berlin, New York: 1928–1931*, trans. Douglas W. Scott (Minneapolis: Fortress Press, 2008), 367–72.

23. This work, the German title of which is simply "Discipleship" (*Nachfolge*), was first translated into English as *The Cost of Discipleship* (1937).

24. As quoted in Eberhard Bethge, *Dietrich Bonhoeffer: A Biography*, ed. Victoria J. Barnett, rev. ed. (Minneapolis: Fortress Press, 2000), 511–12.

Together, an account of the communal life and shared practices at Finkenwalde. When the Gestapo closed down the seminary in 1937 and arrested twenty-seven pastors and former students, Bonhoeffer took his teaching and mentoring further underground, meeting with small cells of resisting Christians—even as many more enlisted in the German Army, turned inward in self-protection, or disappeared altogether.

In 1938, Bonhoeffer's brother-in-law, Hans von Dohnanyi, introduced him to a group whose goals included seeking to aid Jewish escapees, alerting international contacts of SS crimes against humanity, and working inside the German military intelligence office (the *Abwehr*) in order to overthrow and assassinate Hitler. With a world war imminent and Bonhoeffer's leadership uncertain, Bonhoeffer once again left for New York in June 1939, but returned to Germany only a few days later, on the last scheduled steamer to cross the Atlantic. As he explained to Reinhold Niebuhr at Union Seminary:

> I have come to the conclusion that I made a mistake in coming to America. I must live through this difficult period in our national history with the people of Germany. I will have no right to participate in the reconstruction of Christian life in Germany after the war if I do not share the trials of this time with my people.[25]

When Bonhoeffer returned to Germany, he became officially involved in the *Abwehr* in order to avoid conscription and to aid resistance to Hitler. Even when it became clear that his decision to return to Germany and to take part in the resistance would cost him his life, Bonhoeffer stood by it.[26]

Bonhoeffer's work in the *Abwehr* enabled him to help Jews escape Germany and to continue to develop international contacts that he believed would prove helpful in postwar reconstruction—all under the cover that he was gathering information for Nazi Germany. The extent to which Bonhoeffer condoned plots by *Abwehr* agents (including Dohnanyi) to kill Hitler remains a matter of debate (largely between differing Christian theological traditions, both of which want to claim

---

25. Ibid., 655.
26. Bonhoeffer, *Letters and Papers from Prison*, 236.

Bonhoeffer as one of their own).[27] In any case, Bonhoeffer clearly entered the messy world of counter-intelligence and conspiracy; he was aware that neither he nor the church could do so innocently, but that they must cling to God's mercy and promise of forgiveness. Far worse would be to retreat from politics in order to remain "pure" (as he eventually accused his own Confessing Church of doing), or to justify one's actions by way of abstract ethical or quasi-religious principles.

Just three months after becoming engaged to Maria von Wedermeyer, the daughter of family friends and co-conspirators, Bonhoeffer's subversive work in the *Abwehr* was discovered. He spent a year and a half in the Tegel political prison, where sympathetic guards helped him smuggle letters to his family and best friend, Eberhard Bethge. A failed attempt on Hitler's life (on July 20, 1944) led to the arrest of some 7000 additional people and the slapdash execution of 4500—Bonhoeffer among them.[28] The last letter that he was able to send asks his parents to "take complete charge of my things and . . . give away whatever anyone might need without giving it second thought."[29] He was moved to the Flossenbürg concentration camp. On April 8, 1945, the SS led him naked to his execution, three weeks before Hitler would commit suicide and a month before the war's end.[30]

As this short biography suggests, Bonhoeffer was sufficiently opposed to the accommodation of Christianity to the German state that, in order to keep those two entities apart, he was willing to insert between them his very life. But throughout that life, he also worked

---

27. See Larry Rasmussen, *Dietrich Bonhoeffer: Reality and Resistance* (Louisville: Westminster John Knox, 2005) for the traditional understanding of Bonhoeffer as involved in the plot to kill Hitler. Nation, Siegrist, and Umbel challenge that received reading in *Bonhoeffer the Assassin?*, 209–33, as does Stanley Hauerwas in *Performing the Faith: Bonhoeffer and the Practice of Nonviolence* (Grand Rapids, MI: Brazos, 2004), 32–54. I return to realist versus pacifist interpretations of Bonhoeffer and the threat of war in chapter 8.

28. Nation, Siegrist, and Umbel, *Bonhoeffer the Assassin?*, 87. This way of putting the matter is less enthralling—but perhaps also truer to historical facts—than typical proclamations that Bonhoeffer was executed after his involvement in a plot to kill Hitler was discovered. See pages 71–97, which draw substantially on Sabine Dramm, *Dietrich Bonhoeffer and the Resistance*, trans. Margaret Kohl (Minneapolis: Fortress Press, 2009).

29. Bonhoeffer, *Letters and Papers from Prison*, 552–53.

30. For accounts of Bonhoeffer's life, see Bethge, *Dietrich Bonhoeffer*; Charles Marsh, *Strange Glory: A Life of Dietrich Bonhoeffer* (New York: Knopf, 2014); and the DVD by Martin Doblmeier, *Bonhoeffer: Pastor, Pacifist, Nazi Resister* (2004).

and reworked important theological themes concerning the relationship between church and state, about Christianity and secularism, and—most centrally—the meaning of Jesus in a tumultuous time. As we have seen above, certain elements of those writings have been taken to argue in favor of a less "Christian," more "secularized" culture. As we will see, however, this is too simplistic a reading of Bonhoeffer's complex theology.

One Lord and Two Kingdoms

The best-known dissent from the church's easy "synchronization" with German politics was the Barmen Declaration. This 1934 statement brought about the formation of the Confessing Church as a visible form of opposition to the "German Christian" accommodation of, and subordination to, the Nazi state. The Barmen Declaration emphasized that Jesus Christ alone is Lord—explicitly employing the German word *Führer*, and thereby undercutting the authority of anyone else who sought to usurp that name. The Declaration takes the proclamation of the Lordship of Christ as its one foundation, presenting a certain kind of challenge (implicitly and sometimes explicitly) to Lutheran distinctions between different "orders of creation." These distinctions are often summarized as the Lutheran doctrine of the "two kingdoms"—the kingdom of church and kingdom of "the world." According to the authors of the Barmen Declaration, including the important Swiss Reformed theologian Karl Barth, such distinctions too easily allow allegiance to Christ to be merged with other allegiances.

Barth and others argued that the language of distinguishable "realms" or "kingdoms" (through which God reigns in different ways) functions to offer the German state a divine rubber stamp to do what it will.[31] Bonhoeffer, too, criticizes particular uses of "two kingdoms" to justify theologically actions of the state that should be recognized as theologically untenable. Early on, he prefers to speak of "orders of

31. For overlapping concerns, see Ernst Troeltsch, *The Social Teachings of Christianity*, trans. Olive Wyon (Louisville: Westminster John Knox, 1992), 2:569–76; and Reinhold Niebuhr, *The Nature and Destiny of Man* (Louisville: Westminster John Knox, 1964), 2:184–98.

preservation" (i.e., sinful orders, which God nonetheless "preserves" to bring about limited justice), rather than the traditional language of "orders of creation." Later, he writes of "divine mandates" (which might be revised or interrupted by God's command). His goal with each is to prevent blanket claims about divine justifications of the messy realities of political history. Still, Bonhoeffer does not reject the idea that God can and does work through political realities—even ambiguous ones—to sustain relative order and provide the grounds for God's redemption. For him, the central mistake of Nazi-supporting German Christians was not that they obeyed the authority of Jesus, on the one hand, and political authorities, on the other hand; rather, they did not carefully enough *distinguish* the two, which led to their *uncritical* support of the latter.

There is thus a subtle difference between the Barmen Declaration's critique of Christian nationalism (based on the exclusive lordship of Jesus) and Bonhoeffer's critique (based on a more nuanced account of the "two kingdoms" distinction). Bonhoeffer's approach here is consonant with his initial responses to the Aryan clauses described earlier in this chapter (which were promulgated about one year before the Barmen Declaration was authored). Some theologians had excused the Aryan clauses by minimizing the number of people they would affect or by assuming that they would not be carefully enforced. But Bonhoeffer recognized that the damage done by these clauses was not dependent only on the number of people they would affect; they were flawed because they claimed for the state the right to decide who is and is not Jewish and, by implication, who is and is not Christian. In other words, the law defined Judaism genetically and racially (which was being established by the rising "science" of eugenics), rather than religiously. In so doing, it positioned, as the alternative to Judaism, not the Christian faith (as the church had done for most of its history), but instead, a newly constructed racial identity: the Aryan race. For Bonhoeffer, the Aryan clauses overstepped a clear division of responsibilities and freedoms between "church" and "state," inherited from Lutheran claims about the "two kingdoms." Bonhoeffer argued that only Christians can decide whether converts from Judaism are Christians. The state should stay out of the church's business.

Thus, while later Confessing Church members suspected that a "two kingdoms" perspective would too easily lead to collusions of church and state, for Bonhoeffer—as for the early Luther—the primary purpose of this language was to *prevent* the association of the promised Reign of God with any other reign. (Keep in mind that the German phrase for what is known, in English, as the "Reign of God" or the "Kingdom of God" is *das Reich Gottes*; the easy elision of this into *das dritte Reich*—the Third Reich—was present even at the level of vocabulary.)

Bonhoeffer's approach can seem much more politically conservative. For example, his April 1933 essay "The Church and the Jewish Question" readily admits that "Without doubt, the Church of the Reformation has no right to address the state directly in its specifically political actions . . . but must rather affirm the state to be God's order of preservation in a godless world."[32] Nevertheless, he goes on to assert that, *based on the same division of spheres,* "the church cannot allow its actions toward its members to be prescribed by the state"[33]—which is exactly what the state was doing when determining who was or was not a Jew. From the perspective of the church, a "baptized Jew" is a Christian, and the state may not prescribe his or her role within the church. This may appear to be a rather slim claim against the powers of the state, but it can easily lead to a protest just as determined as that declared in Barmen.[34]

In fact, what appears to be a more conservative political position actually enables Bonhoeffer to go beyond the mere *proclamation* of Jesus as Lord, envisioning action as well as words. Here, already he considers the possibility that Christians will be called "not just to bandage the victims under the wheel [of the state], but to jam the

---

32. Bonhoeffer, *No Rusty Swords: Letters, Lectures, and Notes, 1928-1936* (New York: Harper & Row, 1965), 222.
33. Ibid., 227.
34. Barmen's language describes the church as being *in statu confessionis* (in a "confessional status"); that is, present-day events have demanded that the church state its claims in a clear and forthright manner.

spokes of the wheel."[35] The legitimacy of such direct political protest—a significant detail, given Bonhoeffer's eventual direct resistance—is determined by the state's failure to allow the church to be the church. The state must allow the church to carry out the work that the church is called to do.[36]

Of course, there are a number of ambiguities and theological tensions in Bonhoeffer's early response to Nazi anti-Semitism, not least important of which is the fact that Bonhoeffer seems protective here exclusively of Jewish converts to Christianity ("baptized Jews") and even perpetuates a theological version of anti-Judaism, or supersessionism, in his efforts to resist Germany's anti-Semitic laws.[37] Despite this, Bonhoeffer finds leverage against the Aryan clauses in the very distinction (between the "two kingdoms") that others, including Barth, assumed was the source of the problem. Perhaps this subtle difference also informs the way Bonhoeffer eventually distances himself from Barth's political theology and the unintended results of the Barmen Declaration, which Bonhoeffer eventually describes as

---

35. Ibid., 225. I have altered the translation (normally: "put a spoke in the wheel itself") following Lori Brandt Hale's helpful suggestion.

36. This, we should note, does assess the grounds for political dissent in ways that Luther would not or could not. For Luther, the church might resist the state only if the latter directly encroaches on Christian understandings and receptions of God's grace and justification. Bonhoeffer imagines that the state might fail at its own mission by failing to provide enough stability and freedom to its subjects and that that failure would subsequently affect the stability of the church. This extends Luther's dialectical, critical understanding of the two spheres.

37. Take, for example, passages that perpetuate a version of the "deicide" charge mounted by Christians against Jews: "The church of Christ has never lost sight of the thought that the 'chosen people,' who nailed the redeemer of the world to the cross, must bear the curse for its action through a long history of suffering." Or one that sees the worth of Judaism only insofar as it is engrafted into and so superseded by Christianity: "The history of the suffering of this people, loved and punished by God, stands under the sign of the final home-coming of the people of Israel to its God. And this home-coming happens in the conversion of Israel to its God." Bonhoeffer No Rusty Swords, 226. Still, Bonhoeffer can be read as subtly critiquing the very theological anti-Judaism that he otherwise uses against secular anti-Semitism: "This consciousness on the part of the church of the curse that bears down upon his people, raises it far above any cheap moralizing; instead, as it looks at the rejected people, it humbly recognizes itself as a church continually unfaithful to its Lord and looks full of hope to those of the people of Israel who have come home . . . and knows itself to be bound to them in brotherhood." Ibid., 227. Bonhoeffer also later criticizes himself for not having defended Jews *as Jews* in the early 1930s. For a generous assessment from a Jewish point of view of Bonhoeffer's supersessionistic (anti-Jewish) theology, and how it nonetheless provided the grounds for its own overcoming and his political resistance, see Richard L. Rubenstein, "Was Dietrich Bonhoeffer a Righteous Gentile?" *New English Review*, April 2011, accessed August 10, 2015, http://www.newenglishreview.org/custpage.cfm/frm/86357/sec_id/86357.

encouraging Christians "to entrench ourselves persistently behind the 'faith of the church,' and evade the honest question as to what we ourselves really believe."[38] While this failure was egregious and obvious in the case of the German Christians, Bonhoeffer also perceives it in the tragic eventualities within his own Confessing Church.[39] He wants to find ways of avoiding any self-enclosed, self-protective version of church—whether flagrant or more subtle. This is why, in his late writings, he calls his fellow Christians to immerse themselves fully in the "secular" world.

Bonhoeffer's goal was to recognize that God and Christ have a place in the world, but not to allow this claim to provide a blanket justification for everything that is undertaken within that world. Bonhoeffer develops his theological response by creatively reworking the claim that in Christ, God becomes incarnate and dwells among us.

A Hidden, Manifest God

Far from abandoning religious institutions of traditional Christian theology in his final days, Bonhoeffer's language attempts to witness to, and to participate in, the Incarnation—God's presence among us. By advocating "religionless" Christianity, and by calling Christians to behave "as if there were no God," his goal is not to promote atheism, but to find new ways of making God known in an ostensibly godless world. As we noted above, Bonhoeffer retains some elements of Luther's distinction between the two kingdoms. In addition, he appropriates (and radicalizes) Luther's understanding of the sacraments, which Bonhoeffer describes as making God present in the *saeculum*—in the "ordinary time" between Christ's first coming and final return. Given Bonhoeffer's attention to the secular order, we here return to the work of Charles Taylor, whose account of "the secular" was examined in the previous chapter.

---

38. Bonhoeffer, *Letters and Papers from Prison*, 502.
39. See, especially, the section on "Guilt, Justification, Renewal" in Bonhoeffer, *Ethics*, trans. Reinhard Krauss et al. (Minneapolis: Fortress Press, 2005), 134–45, as well as discussions by Matthew D. Kirkpatrick, *Attacks on Christendom in a World Come of Age: Kierkegaard, Bonhoeffer, and the Question of "Religionless Christianity"* (Eugene, OR: Pickwick/Wipf & Stock, 2011), 195–96.

Excarnation according to Taylor

According to Taylor, we who live in the contemporary West live in an "immanent frame"—a closed worldview that makes secular humanism the norm and treats encounters with transcendence as private and thoroughly optional.[40] Much of this can be traced back to Protestantism and other reform movements in the late medieval and early modern West. Such reforms, designed to ferret out "papist" idolization of the material world, often ended up marginalizing religious belief altogether. According to Taylor, these reform movements tend to raise questions about the very cornerstone of Christianity—namely, faith in a God who becomes incarnate in a human being and dwells in the material world. Taylor thus takes the Reformation as an "engine of disenchantment," which culminates in "excarnation"—the disembodying of religious life, which is less and less carried out in public, bodily forms. In the contemporary scene, religion is much more a matter of the mind and the will, rather than being enacted by the material body.[41]

Is Bonhoeffer the Lutheran theologian and defender of Reformation theology complicit in such excarnation? Certainly, one recognizes traditional understandings of the "doctrine" of the two kingdoms in Taylor's description of how a neutral, secular space must be created in place of the monastery to hold the religious flourishing and democratization of priests and saints in the Reformation era. But we have seen above that Bonhoeffer's own account of this theology seeks to prevent the appropriation of "two kingdoms" language as a means of uncritically baptizing wholly autonomous decisions of the state. Bonhoeffer also portrays church in robust, communitarian terms, as a visible reality integrally related to (but extending beyond) those specific locations where the sacraments are distributed and the Word of God is preached.[42] Thus, *if* Luther inadvertently participates in

---

40. Charles Taylor, *A Secular Age* (Cambridge, MA: Harvard University Press, 2007), 552–57.
41. Ibid., 77, 554, 771.
42. Bonhoeffer, *Sanctorum Communio: A Theological Study of the Sociology of the Church*, trans. Reinhard Krauss and Nancy Lukens (Minneapolis: Fortress Press, 1998), 58–106.

excarnation—Taylor's "disenchantment of the world"—then Bonhoeffer's reformulation seeks to set up a bulwark against that process.

Incarnation according to Luther

I would argue that, rightly understood, Luther's sacramental theology actually *resists* the excarnation that Taylor describes. In this sense, Bonhoeffer seeks not so much to counter the Lutheran tradition, but to extend and deepen it. Both theologians resist the disenchantment or secularization of the world not by reserving some special place or time for God's "transcendence," but by witnessing to a God who is *thoroughly* worldly, or transcendent in and through God's radical immanence. In both accounts, God is so thoroughly worldly, so deeply present in the secular world, that any account of God's removal does not look closely enough. Taylor's account of disenchantment seeks to explain the wholesale separation of the "spiritual" realm of God from this "material," bodily realm. But Luther never participates in this kind of separation; the world that we see and touch is the very place that God abides. Yes, Luther argues against confusing the different ways God works (law and gospel), and the different realms in which God rules (kingdom of God, kingdom of the world). But this should not be taken as implying a dualistic account of the spiritual and material realms.

Indeed, Luther explicitly argues against the sacramental theologies of other reformers precisely to avoid such a dualistic account that would divorce spirit from flesh, or God from the world. Writing against Zwingli in 1528, Luther refuses to separate Christ (the second member of the Trinity) from Jesus of Nazareth (who has—or rather, *is*—a body, before his resurrection and ascension and remaining so afterward). Our access to God does not require calling down some pure spiritual presence through a ritual of "remembering." Such an account, Luther believes, is rooted in a reading of the gospels that essentially "applies all the texts concerning the passion only to the human nature [of Jesus] and completely excludes them from the divine nature."[43] By contrast, for Luther,

Wherever you place God for me, you must also place the humanity for me. They simply will not let themselves be separated and divided from each other. [Christ] has become one person and does not separate the humanity from himself as Master Jack takes off his coat and lays it aside when he goes to bed.[44]

According to Luther, we have God only in the form of Christ—and Christ only in the form of the bodily Jesus. In this light, Luther's sacramental writings seem to mitigate against Taylor's modern and postmodern engines of disenchantment, rather than to fuel them.[45]

This analysis suggests a possible flaw in Taylor's account. He mourns the absence of the transcendent in our immanent frame; in our present era, he believes, no particular place, thing, time, or person necessarily points beyond itself. But might this perceived absence of transcendence inadvertently overlook the possibility that God manifests Godself, not only in explicit ways, but also "in, with, and under"[46] our so-called secular world, if only we had eyes to see? Moreover, could the eyesight needed to see such hidden forms of transcendence—to see God incarnate in the secular world—also remind us that God can be made manifest in the lowliest, most unlikely places? Might that transcendence be made known in, for example, the cross and in other places of abandonment and anguish?

43. Martin Luther, "Confession Concerning Christ's Supper—From Part I (1528)," in *Martin Luther's Basic Theological Writings*, ed. Timothy F. Lull, 2nd ed. (Minneapolis: Fortress Press, 2005), 263.

44. Ibid., 267.

45. Admittedly, Taylor himself mentions what might be called the "Lutheran exception" as he otherwise traces our excarnate, disenchanted world back to the late medieval reform movements. Taylor, *Secular Age*, 75. Bradley Gregory does the same in *The Unintended Reformation: How a Religious Revolution Secularized Society* (Cambridge, MA: Harvard University Press, 2012), 42. Gregory also helpfully notes that transcendence is lost not by contemporary Western captivity within an immanent frame, but by the very denial that God can and does incarnate the material world. The sacramental worldview—which is Luther's and Bonhoeffer's worldview—considers God's immanent presence in the created world to be the very sign and means of God's transcendence. In Gregory's words, "Not despite but *because* God is radically other than his creation, it is claimed, God can and does manifest himself in and through it, as he wills." Gregory, *Unintended Reformation*, 32. On not pitting God's transcendence against God's immanence, see also William Placher, *The Domestication of Transcendence: How Modern Thinking about God Went Wrong* (Louisville: Westminster John Knox, 1996).

46. This Lutheran understanding that Christ is really present "in, with, and under" the elements of a sacrament goes back to the Formula of Concord (1577), Article X, in *The Book of Concord: The Confessions of the Evangelical Lutheran Church*, trans Charles Arand, et. al. (Minneapolis: Augsburg Fortress Press, 2000).

Radical Incarnational Worldliness according to Bonhoeffer

Bonhoeffer's own christological commitments to "worldliness" arise from the same sacramental tradition, which informs his theological writings from beginning to end. In his 1933 Christology lectures, for example, he emphasizes Christ's incarnational solidarity with humanity as it is—even in suffering, death, and sin. Later in his *Ethics* manuscript, too, he writes of the call to a worldliness patterned on the self-emptying of Jesus—offering this perspective as a contrast to the temptation to turn inward:

> The church can only defend its own space by fighting, not for space, but for the salvation of the world. Otherwise the church becomes a "religious society" that fights for its own interest and this has ceased to be the church of God in the world. So the first task given to those who belong to the church of God is not to be something for themselves, for example, by creating a religious organization or leading a pious life, but to be witnesses of Jesus Christ to the world.[47]

Ironically, the church only properly preserves its own identity when it divests itself, giving away its property and participating in the worldly tasks of the broader community. In Bonhoeffer's famous phrasing, "The church is church only when it is there for others."[48] Many of his descriptions of the different orders of preservation—work, marriage, government, and church, as well as the "worldly" callings within them—are thoroughly christological. If Christ takes the form of bread broken, water poured out, and the word proclaimed within the church, then Christ also hides within (and is revealed by) broken bodies, abandoned neighborhoods, and acts of solidarity in churchless, "godless" places. We are called more deeply into the godless world, not simply as a means of curbing sin and sustaining order (as some accounts of Lutheran vocation would have it), but to become, with Christ, an incarnating and sanctifying presence in that world. This is the church's true vocation.

Bonhoeffer's incarnational commitments and sacramental logic

47. Bonhoeffer, *Ethics*, 64.
48. Bonhoeffer, *Letters and Papers from Prison*, 382.

enable him to give an account of secularism that distinguishes a particularly *Christian* form of worldliness from more "pious," less faithful forms. We turn now to those explicit accounts.

God's Seculum

For Bonhoeffer, the easy accommodation of church and state is not only a temptation to idolatry and an appeasement of the state's evil actions. It is also a means of consigning church to a "sanctuary"—a safe haven—that inadvertently limits and controls the wildness of God's willingness, through Jesus, to reach out into the godless world. To get at this second problem, spatial thinking can get one only so far; accounts of the "proper boundaries" of church and state, of the "two kingdoms," or even of Christ's "two natures" all tempt us toward ahistorical, timeless categories. Bonhoeffer thus goes beyond the mere policing of proper borders among distinct realms and asks a question that is fundamentally more interested in relationship and in the presence of God among us. Bonhoeffer's key question is this: "Who is Christ actually for us today?"[49]

Through his account of developments within Western political and intellectual history, Bonhoeffer attempts to discern God's will within the vicissitudes of history, yet without equating the two—without allowing his theological account to baptize every action of the secular world. He does this by keeping an eye on the way God chooses to be revealed, not in history's victors, but in its victims and collateral damage. He hopes to find a third way, neither describing a static deadlock between ultimate and penultimate realms, nor perpetuating a myth of historical conquest as divinely sanctioned. His own schematic accounts of secularism remain open to the possibility that God works in mysterious ways—even through the fragmentation or pluralization of a unified body of Christ. This claim, however, presents him with a problem: How can one recognize God and church in secular, fragmented, and pluralized society, without sliding into an empty

49. Ibid., 362.

relativism in which everything becomes divine? Or, employing the language that we have used elsewhere in this book: How does one step out of an earlier form of cultural Christianity (a Christendom in which church was merged with empire) without landing squarely in another form of cultural Christianity, in which the term *Christian* has become so devoid of meaning that it can be applied to everything? Bonhoeffer's account of "a world come of age," his advocacy of a "religionless Christianity," and his call for Christians to live "as if there were no God" offer an attempt to find a way forward.

Like Charles Taylor, Bradley Gregory, and other recent theorists who make use of theological categories to explore the process of secularization, Bonhoeffer sees Christianity—and even the biblical God—as contributing to this process.[50] *Because* God is a God of covenant-making and promise-keeping, history need not be dressed up to promote particular empires or nations, nor return to timeless, mythological foundations. Rather, God chooses ordinary time and "secular" history—in all its messiness and apparent godlessness—as the true mode of God's own activity.

In light of the political context in which Bonhoeffer made such claims (probably in 1941), such an account of historiography is deeply countercultural (which also means, in Bonhoeffer's era, deeply counter-Nazi). He roots Christian history in an earlier history of God's covenant-making and promises to the Jewish people, even claiming that "driving out the Jew(s) from the West must result in driving out Christ with them, for Jesus Christ was a Jew."[51] Even less subtly, Bonhoeffer sees every effort "to connect with an indigenous Germanic pre-Christian past"—as Nazi ideology so graphically did—as entailing a mythologization of history: a romantic denial of the meaning of Western history and God's *historical* involvement in the world.

Bonhoeffer accepts that the unity of the church was shattered by the Reformation.[52] But this is not all bad, according to Bonhoeffer. In the

---

50. Taylor, *A Secular Age*, 92–99, 221–32; Gregory, *The Unintended Reformation*; Mark C. Taylor, *After God* (Chicago: University of Chicago Press, 2007), 153; Bonhoeffer, *Ethics*, 104.
51. Bonhoeffer, *Ethics*, 105.
52. Ibid., 111.

splitting of Europe's medieval Christendom into contending states and various confessional churches, Bonhoeffer sees not only the *result* of the Reformation's intensifications (like other accounts of secularism), but also the *source* of a deeper unity—and the *means* for church revitalization by way of public confession. For this hidden unity to be recognized, however, the "secular" world must be understood in constitutive, tensive relation to the realm of the church or the kingdom of God. Moreover, particular church bodies must understand themselves as parts of the broader body of Christ, confessing their guilt for its brokenness. Neither of these has occurred, and as a result, two different, less hopeful forms of secularism have emerged instead.

The Godless Christendom of Europe

Immediately after imaging the possibility of a deeper sense of church unity as disclosed through the shared confession of guilt, Bonhoeffer notes that, instead, "the great process of secularization very quickly set in all along the line, at the end of which we stand today."[53] Clearly, this is not the secularism that Bonhoeffer calls Christians to embrace in his final musing about a religionless Christianity. It arises, instead, from a "*misunderstood* Lutheran doctrine of the two kingdoms."[54] That misunderstanding essentially entails too clean a break between the two kingdoms, to the point where neither can hold the other in check; this can result in the secular government being given divine sanction, or at least, being made its own supreme end. And so, this particular forms of secularization (which follows in the wake of the French Revolution) issues in two unfortunate results. First, society becomes radically disenchanted; government, reason, economy, and culture each claim their own autonomy. Second, because church and state lose their reciprocal accountability, the otherwise thoroughly secularized state simultaneously becomes deified; it is, for a world that places no authority in the church, the only remaining bearer of ultimate value and hope. A newer, paradoxical form of Christian culture then

---

53. Bonhoeffer, *Ethics*, 113.
54. Ibid., 114, my emphasis.

ensues: the new secular realms claim the right to autonomy, "but in this autonomy underst[and] themselves to be *not at all at odds* with Christianity."[55] We experience the same ironic reversal today, when our thoroughly spiritualized, individualized, and depoliticized forms of "Christian" culture enable the state to demand our ultimate allegiance.

According to Bonhoeffer, European culture easily transfigures into "the *cult* of ratio, and the *divinization* of nature, [and] *faith* in progress."[56] In other words, the problem with the secular world as it emerges from the "misunderstood" doctrine of two kingdoms is that *it is not secular enough.* Divorced from the very realm (the "kingdom of God") that could keep it in check, it is bound to claim for itself *supreme* autonomy. It essentially becomes like God[57]—and so, becomes an anti-God, a "hopeless godlessness dressed up in religious Christian finery."[58]

This apparent godlessness actually becomes a key ingredient in the establishment of a pseudo-Christian culture. In describing the "Western godlessness" that emerges in the wake of the French Revolution, Bonhoeffer observes that

it is different from the atheism of particularly Greek, Indian, Chinese, and Western thinkers. It is not the theoretical denial of the existence of a God. . . . Particularly in Germany, and also in Anglo-Saxon countries, *this godlessness is emphatically Christian.* In every possible Christianity—nationalist, socialist, rationalist, or mystical—it turns against the living God of the Bible, against Christ.[59]

This last sentence reminds us that the "Christianity" of such secular, Western godlessness is closer to what Bonhoeffer will, in his late writings from prison, refer to as "religious" Christianity—that is, a quintessentially *modern* form of Christianity, in which "believers" posit

---

55. Ibid., my emphasis.
56. Ibid., 115, my emphasis.
57. See Bonhoeffer, *Creation and Fall, Temptation: Two Biblical Studies,* trans. John C. Fletcher (New York: Touchstone, 1997). In the manuscript we have been considering, Bonhoeffer adds the marginal note "a strange repetition to the biblical Fall!" beside his description of the French Revolution, where he describes what he calls "the basic law of history"—"that the desire for absolute freedom leads people into deepest servitude. The master of the machine becomes its slave; the machine becomes an enemy of the human being. What is created turns against its creator. . . ." Bonhoeffer, *Ethics,* 122.
58. Bonhoeffer, *Ethics,* 124.
59. Ibid., 122.

an interventionist, deistic God. This divine power (which is invoked primarily to save us from danger and erase our moral failings) only functions to justify our own quests for invulnerability, our manipulation of nature, and our lack of empathy for those who suffer when we cannot (or will not) ameliorate their condition.[60] In those later writings, Bonhoeffer distinguishes this false "religious" Christianity from a more promising "religionless" or secular one; similarly, in these earlier accounts, he sets this "pious godlessness"—or what we might call Europe's godless yet still nominally Christian culture—beside a more "promising godlessness" that would be fully worth retrieving.

This "promising godlessness" is also "peculiarly Western." It appears antichurch and antireligious, but Bonhoeffer makes clear that it is to be preferred over "pious godlessness." In fact, it entails "protest against pious godlessness insofar as that has spoiled the churches"; it thereby has the potential to preserve "the heritage of a genuine faith in God and of a genuine church."[61] Does this mean that a Christian should leave a church that has become thoroughly acculturated and accommodated? He seems to realize that this may be the more faithful path; and here, he is retracing questions that troubled him since the rise of the Confessing Church in 1933, that is, whether a Christian is obligated to leave a church that has accommodated itself to Nazism.[62] And yet, he is also aware that departing from the church can place a person in the sway of new forms of secularism, which themselves can be used by the state in order to create similarly troubling forms of cultural Christianity. To state the driving question again: How might one fully claim the inherent worth and capabilities of individuals in

---

60. Jeffrey C. Pugh, *Religionless Christianity: Dietrich Bonhoeffer in Troubled Times* (London: T&T Clark, 2008), 45–68. Pugh helpfully connects "religious" Christianity, "pious" godlessness, and the interventionist God of modern deism.

61. Bonhoeffer, *Ethics*, 124.

62. Ibid., 125n100. Bonhoeffer wonders whether Christians should leave an accommodated church as early as 1933, soon before the July church elections, where two-thirds of the elected delegates were German Christians: "There is no doubt in my mind that the victory will go to German Christians, and this will very quickly bring into view the contours of the new church, and the question will be whether we can even support it as the church." Bonhoeffer, *Berlin: 1932-1933*, trans. Isabel Best and David Higgins (Minneapolis: Fortress Press, 1996), 140, as cited in Nation, Siegrist, and Umbel, *Bonhoeffer the Assassin?*, 41.

a world come of age, allowing them to question and to critique the church's accommodations to culture, without glorifying and ratifying individual choice and authenticity as the latest compulsory creed?

Earlier chapters of this book have associated that difficult question with a paradoxical version of Christendom to which America is particularly prone. Interestingly, immediately after introducing the ambiguous relation between pious and promising godlessness, Bonhoeffer takes up this question himself. "At this point," he writes, "we must consider the special development in the Anglo-Saxon countries, especially America."[63]

The Glorification of Tolerance in the United States

Bonhoeffer underscores the differing attitudes toward church and state in Europe, with its roots in an anti-ecclesial French Revolution, and in America, where religious dissidents played a founding role and where democracy is "regarded as the Christian form of the state."[64] Still, Bonhoeffer admits that, despite the powerful claims of American civil religion, secularization is no less rampant in the United States. He suggests that, whereas Europe's secularization occurs through too hard a division between the two kingdoms (leading to the glorification of any and every political form), America's version of this process actually results from an *insufficient* distinction between the two kingdoms. In other words, America, in spite of its separation of church and state, errs by allowing a "complete collapse of the church into the world."[65] American churches mobilize volunteers to improve neighborhoods or lobby for political reform, but in doing so, they become almost indistinguishable from other like-minded special-interest groups. Although Bonhoeffer does not rank the dangers of European versus American forms of pious godlessness, he does state that, in America, "the godlessness remains concealed," and thus suggests a particular danger here. While one experiences less enmity toward the church

63. Bonhoeffer, *Ethics*, 125.
64. Ibid., 126–27.
65. Ibid., 127; compare Bonhoeffer, *No Rusty Swords*, 107–8.

in the United States, this also means a withdrawal of "the blessing of suffering and of the rebirth that might follow from it."[66]

Bonhoeffer's account of American religiosity has resonances in the contemporary setting. Nearly every sociologist tracking and theorizing secularism today remarks on "the American exception": the disarming fact that despite (or because of) the "establishment" clause of the First Amendment (which prohibits a state church), professed Christian commitments and public Christian practices and influence are more pronounced in the United States than in any other Western industrialized nation.

Bonhoeffer underscores this point; indeed, it made an impact on him during his first visit to New York in 1930–31. There, he wrote "Protestantism without Reformation," in which he first traced the paradox of the American churches' significant sociopolitical influence—as well as its newer, odder forms of "Christian" culture—despite (or because of) legal disestablishment. He recounts how Anglo-Saxon America was settled by religious dissidents who escaped religious persecution in Europe after protesting against earlier forms of Christendom. But when dissent becomes a virtue in and of itself, the result is extreme denominationalism. Because different interest groups are served by different denominations, by individual congregations within a denomination, and sometimes, even by particular programs within a congregation, Christians increasingly self-select into narrower and narrower ecclesial bodies. Each of these groups has less and less contact with other groups, which it regards with a rather thin form of indifference, or, at the most, a vague appreciation that "there are other options out there." Bonhoeffer perceives that "for American Christianity the concept of *tolerance* becomes the basic principle of everything Christian," and again, that "any intolerance is in itself unchristian."[67] That correlation of "Christian" with tolerance (and intolerance with unchristian) disturbs Bonhoeffer—but not, of course, because he wants the church to be xenophobic and narrow-minded.

66. Bonhoeffer, *Ethics*, 127.
67. Bonhoeffer, *No Rusty Swords*, 103.

(His critiques of German nationalism would later make that point very clear.) Rather, he is disturbed by the way that the increasingly divided American churches allow for a certain kind of freedom *from* other Christians—and *from* non-Christians with whom they should stand in solidarity. This new form of freedom easily displaces the primary Christian calling, which is to be free *for* others, responsible to the whole body of Christ and to the world Christ loves, which may often require protesting against that world. If our encounter with others is limited to merely tolerating them or appreciating them from afar, we never have the opportunity to stand in solidarity with them.

An additional result of this process, as Bonhoeffer notes, is that this "tolerance" (as "the basic principle of everything Christian") then gets woven back into accounts of the American political order, which also enshrines the virtues of tolerance. American democracy absorbs and institutionalizes this religiously sanctioned account of tolerance; as a result, Bonhoeffer notes, "in America democracy can be extolled as *the* form of the Christian state."[68] In Europe, democracy and Christianity pull in opposite directions;[69] but in America, "freedom from interference" is at the heart of both American democracy and American Christianity, and thus becomes the very thing making the United States a "Christian nation." If Bonhoeffer were making these observations today, we can only suppose that his impressions would have intensified; since his day, the choice to belong to this or that religious group (or none at all) has become even more thoroughly coupled with accounts of American democracy; and this has only been compounded by the rise of church marketing and the increasing commercialization of all society, including the church.

Bonhoeffer for Here and Now

Do Bonhoeffer's critiques of America's peculiar form of religious nationalism have anything to do with the one that was already on the rise in Germany, and to which he fell victim a decade later? Yes and

---

68. Ibid., 108.
69. Ibid.

no. Admittedly, Hitler and his henchmen are more easily recognized as part of the European "pious godlessness" that Bonhoeffer describes—a demonic revolt from God that essentially replaces God, while the protesting church is sidelined. At the same time, Bonhoeffer would also later come to criticize the ambivalence and protective stance of the Confessing Church, which was tempted to retreat into the protection of an interior faith, and therefore, to avoid active protest as the secular government continued to churn out victims. In this light, Bonhoeffer's last critique of the church—*his own* church—parallels his earlier critique of Christianity on the other side of the Atlantic. By finding God only among the safety of the likeminded, both the American church and the Confessing Church risked turning in on themselves, keeping their protests calm and quiet, perhaps more sanctimonious than saintly. In both cases, the problem is not that the church was too worldly; rather, it was not nearly worldly *enough*.

To put this matter another way: with its seminaries closed down and its members entering the German Army, the Confessing Church was tempted to fall into what Bonhoeffer earlier had designated as a particularly "American" form of Christendom. Confusing holiness with purity, these churches were able to remain true only to themselves—giving up on their ecumenical ties and wider callings to social responsibility. Needless to say, this analogy can only be taken so far. After all, the Confessing Church grew out of a direct political protest, a clear *Nein* to all attempts to nationalize Christianity and to "Christianize" Germany. Still, we have much to learn from Bonhoeffer's bifocal attention, *both* to the ways that nation-states can become deified by applying Christian language to themselves, *and* to how churches permit them to do so by turning inward, and thus, becoming relativized and depoliticized. Only by keeping both these elements in focus will we be able to forge a path toward becoming true Christians in a nominally Christian culture.

It is difficult to sum up Bonhoeffer's diverse writings. Their various contexts spanned a highly volatile decade, both in European politics and in the Christian church. However, from the above analyses, we can highlight four overlapping themes and interpretative "keys" in his work—two that arise from his account of Luther's "two kingdoms," and two that arise from his reflections on the person of Christ. First, Bonhoeffer insists that a two kingdoms approach to political theology—while badly needing reconstruction—nevertheless enables Christians to see God at work in seemingly godless places, including within the political order. Second, such discernment (for those with eyes to see) need not justify and sanctify every historical development, whether it be Hitler's rise to power or Germany's eventual defeat. Rather, Christians believe that God is at work "under the form of the opposite"—whether by *sustaining* whatever order and justice is available in messy circumstances, or by empowering *resistance* to unjust, unsustainable, and unchristian ideologies.

Third, Bonhoeffer stresses that the world and the judgment of the world are christological motifs. The bodily, earthly, ambivalent, and fallen political world is part of the material order, which is the very place that Christians come to know God in Christ, and to serve God and neighbor by becoming the body of Christ. To be sure, God is also found in the church, but only when it incarnates Christ's own form, which lowers itself within the world and for the sake of the world. Finally, this christological foundation for the church's worldly engagement need not privilege all secular forms, any more than Bonhoeffer's retrieval of the "two kingdoms" would justify every political authority. Rather, Bonhoeffer's christological bearings enable him to give an account of secularization that distinguishes two kinds of godlessness: those that truly disclose Christ, on the one hand, and on the other, those that become pious, constrict truth to tolerance, and otherwise evolve into new and more elusive forms of Christendom.

The "religious" version of Christianity that Bonhoeffer critiques with his pen—and which he resists with his life—designates a faith accommodated to deeply modernist, individualist assumptions. Likewise, his consent to a world come of age and proposal for "religionless" Christianity entail the careful, critical reconstruction of certain opportunities afforded to those who live in a nominally

Christian culture. Bonhoeffer's "religionless" Christianity is, oddly enough, deeply incarnational and Christocentric. He critiques the church for not being Christocentric or incarnational enough—which also means that it is not worldly or secular enough.

One might say that throughout his writings Bonhoeffer sees worldliness and authentic Christianity as intrinsically connected—based on the incarnational, radically kenotic (or "self-emptying") nature of God as disclosed through the incarnation, death, and resurrection of Christ. This means that Bonhoeffer's call for *religionless* Christianity is also a call to an *unaccommodated* Christianity, whereas a "religious" Christianity is almost synonymous with the so-called "Christian" culture in which we live. Read in this light, Bonhoeffer's final musings on a world come of age should be read as imperatives rather than indicatives. Christians need not, in fact should not, merely settle into the historically accidental processes of secularism where they happen to find themselves, resigned to embracing a "post-Christendom" world. Rather, Christians are called, in the name of Jesus, to work diligently against the sacralization of nation-states—against the glorification of abstractions such as "freedom," "patriotism" and "political necessities"—and maybe, even against the church itself, particularly when it chooses to close in on itself. Christians forge such resistance in order that God may be seen where God chooses to be revealed—in godless places and godless people, including the "collateral damage" of war and all those whose lives seem forgettable and ungrievable.

5

Church as Chaplain and Contemporary
Critics of Constantine

The previous chapter dealt with the ways that allegiance to God and to the nation can meld almost into one. While the idolatry of pro-Nazi "German Christians" seems easy enough to spot, Bonhoeffer also shows how democracy, tolerance, "America," and even the separation of church and state also can risk becoming idols. In this chapter we move to wider developments that are more subtle and difficult to diagnose. I will follow leading critics in designating these developments as *Constantinian*, a pejorative term that is shorthand for those movements and broader transitions in church history (including, but not limited to, the "conversion" of Constantine in the fourth century), through which the church gives up its distinctive socio-cultural-political form, and becomes spiritualized, otherworldly, and privatized. It is thus made compatible with any and every dominant way of life. Because this accommodation includes capitulation to a culture's prevailing way of seeing and knowing (for example, writing history from the perspective of its victors), Constantinianism also involves the loss of Christianity's unique way of making sense of history and the cosmos itself.

Critics of Constantinianism typically associate the early church with pacifism and peacemaking, and its compromise with the endorsement of war and Christian participation in it. Not surprisingly, then, critiques of Constantinianism have gotten sharper and louder in the decade since America's military presence in Afghanistan and Iraq. These critiques often identify America as an empire, which, in theological quarters, associates it with Rome, the empire under which, and by whose authority, Jesus was put to death. The suggestion is that America, like Rome, is incapable of mediating the peace of Christ, and fails miserably when it tries. But for Christians in America to be accused of Constantinianism, they need not explicitly invoke Jesus's name when acting politically or militarily. Instead, they need only fail at standing apart from history as successful empires and prosperous nation-states have written it. They quietly, seemingly harmlessly *forget* that Jesus was an outsider to the dominions of this world (and to their war-making), and that he called disciples to the margins of sociopolitical power (to suffering and the cross rather than to a security purchased with violence).

Thus, beyond the risk of idolatry, of misplaced devotion to a political leader, nation, or symbol alongside devotion to God, Christians also risk passively accepting Western history as the only and ultimate reality, conforming to these worldly ways with a "realism" that they presume to be necessary. An accommodated, Constantinian church is best recognized not by what its members do wrongly (sometimes nothing much), but rather, by what they fail to do and what they fail to be (often quite a bit). To diagnose Constantinianism, one needs to focus on our having made "peace" with non-Christian politics. Most relevant here (but incredibly difficult to spot) is the fact that most of "we Christians have no fundamental quarrel with the powers-that-be."[1]

---

1. Stanley Hauerwas and William H. Willimon, *Resident Aliens: A Provocative Cristian Assessment of Culture and Ministry for People Who Know That Something Is Wrong* (Nashville: Abingdon, 1989), 33.

By focusing on how thoroughly Christianity becomes accommodated to dominant culture, critics of Constantinianism contribute invaluable resources for working our way out of America's newest Christendom, not least of which is their diagnosis of just how unproblematic a thoroughly accommodated church can appear. I will call such critics "anti-Constantinians," knowing full well that this defines them by what they oppose. Anti-Constantinians ask troubling questions about whether history as we know it entails the deepest reality, whether it should be written by its winners, and whether Christians should even try out for that team. They often write revisionist histories of the early church that enable us to gain some epistemological leverage against widespread assumptions about the church's power, relevance, normalcy, and its need to work through nonecclesial agencies (governmental and nongovernmental) in order to effect real change in the world. Before holding up a number of theological resources for becoming a Christian in Christendom, I need to describe what I mean by "church as chaplain" and why that might be a problem.

Chaplains to Culture, Then and Now

In a 1526 tract called "Whether Soldiers, Too, Can be Saved," Martin Luther assured the prince's soldiers that when "being a soldier, going to war, stabbing and killing, [and even] robbing and burning" are required by military necessity, then Christians ought to do these things and not have a guilty conscience when they do.[2] According to Luther, it is only their impersonal offices or professional positions that wield the sword or pull the hangman's switch. Soldiers as individuals can be fully Christian, just as capable of receiving salvation and doing good and needed work as the priest who presides over Mass.

Luther alleviated the troubled consciences of soldiers soon after accusing peasant rebels (who held no official "office") of "cloaking" their own violence in the name of Christ.[3] This can make him appear

2. Martin Luther, "Whether Soldiers, Too, Can be Saved" (1526), trans. Charles M. Jacobs, in *Luther's Works* (American Edition), vol. 46, ed. Robert C. Schultz (Philadelphia: Fortress Press, 1967), 95.
3. Martin Luther, "Against the Robbing and Murdering Hordes of Peasants" (1525), trans. Charles M.

more than a little beholden to established political powers, if not altogether hypocritical. It was only *certain* consciences—those of persons acting with governmental *authority*—that Luther was willing to comfort. But while some might wish he had offered comparable Christian assurance to the rebelling peasants, the most incisive critiques of Luther ask whether *any* conscience should be alleviated or *any* violent act justified on Christian grounds. Recall that Bonhoeffer preferred to speak of "orders of preservation" and of "mandates" rather than created orders and eternal laws in order to emphasize that no vocation or office—no matter how officially sanctioned or seemingly necessary—should be occupied without asking troubling questions about how one should follow Christ from within it. Even when he acted as something of a chaplain to those involved in a conspiracy plot to kill Hitler, he refused to justify their actions as "right," and much less as "Christian." By his estimation, the conspirators (and Bonhoeffer himself) were indefensibly sinful, fully thrown on the grace and forgiveness of God.[4] Kierkegaard says something similar when thinking through the depiction in Genesis 22 of Abraham's willingness to kill Isaac at the summoning of God. Abraham's actions remain unjustifiable, according to any moral or human accounting. One ought not to call them "necessary" or "ethical" or even "understandable," although they may very well be faithful.[5]

Christians from outside the magisterial (mainline) Protestant tradition will raise other critical questions about the desire to offer comfort to the troubled consciences of those holding all-too-worldly vocations. Stanley Hauerwas insists that to understand any and all necessary work as compatible with Christian vocation would force one into idolatry.[6] Such critiques of vocation often arise from the Radical

---

Jacobs, in *Luther's Works* (American Edition), vol. 46, ed. Robert C. Schultz (Philadelphia: Fortress Press, 1967), 50–51.

4. Dietrich Bonhoeffer, *Ethics*, trans. Reinhard Krauss et al. (Minneapolis: Fortress Press, 2005), 131, 274.

5. Søren Kierkegaard, *Fear and Trembling* (with *Repetition*), trans. Howard V. Hong and Edna H. Hong (Princeton, NJ: Princeton University Press, 1983), 54–67.

6. Stanley Hauerwas, "Work as Co-Creation: A Critique of a Remarkably Bad Idea," in *Co-Creation and Capitalism: John Paul II's Laborem Exercens*, ed. J. W. Houck and O. F. Williams (Lanham, MD: University Press of America, 1983), 48.

Reformation or Anabaptist tradition. For many contemporary neo-Mennonites, Christians ought to restore the New Testament's usage of *vocation*, which means to call persons into a radically new and spirit-driven Christian community that is set apart from the dominant order. For them, the magisterial Reformation's use of vocation, by contrast, functions only to "divine rubber stamp" the ways of the world.[7]

Should a contemporary Christian pastor or Christian community comfort those who feel that the primary arc of their lives is un-Christian or sub-Christian? Certainly, there are moments when we would expect nothing less. A hospital chaplain comforts the dying; she hears words of confession and fears related to meaninglessness, and then, speaks words of promise that give hope to the ill and their families. College chaplains do the same for students as they navigate responsible (or not) adult lives apart from their parents and home communities. Military chaplains, too, may actually help give voice to the struggles that introspective Christians, Jews, Muslims, and others have with who they are, what they are doing, and whom they are ultimately serving. The question here is not whether chaplains are needed and useful (they certainly are), but whether *the church as a whole* has come to think of itself as something like a chaplain to the whole dominant culture. Comparing mainline Western Protestant and Catholic churches to the grassroots "base" religious communities in Latin America, Johann Baptist Metz finds that the church in prosperous countries

> has become here a form of bourgeois religion in which "Christian values" arch over a bourgeois identity without really affecting it in terms of a possible transformation or a promised fulfillment. Under the cloak of a merely believed-in (but not lived) faith. . . . Christianity easily becomes the religious alibi for bourgeois innocence and the guarantee of a good conscience in a situation that really requires us to make the experience of guilt and failure in regard to these poor churches the very foundation of our everyday consciousness.[8]

7. John Howard Yoder, *The Priestly Kingdom: Social Ethics as Gospel* (Notre Dame, IN: University of Notre Dame Press, 2008), 210n9.

8. Johann Baptist Metz, *The Emergent Church: The Future of Christianity in a Postbourgeois World*, trans. Peter Mann (New York: Crossroad, 1981), 76–77.

Is the (Western) church as a whole capable of raising critical questions about our economies, politics, military strategies, and other central undertakings, distinguishing them from the calling of Christians to discipleship and stoking the consciences of those who feel pulled between each? Or does it primarily function as a "religious alibi," guarantee a good conscience, and otherwise put a "divine rubber stamp" on the ways of the world, thus allowing things to run all too smoothly?

It is usually non-Christians who ask such critical, suspicious questions about how Christianity functions. Karl Marx was a master of suspicion for doing exactly this; his main critique of Christianity was that, regardless of professed motives, it actually operates to appease poor Christians, comforting them with thoughts of afterlife, ensuring that they do not rise up and try to change the way the dominant society/economy works. Many deep critiques of religion as ideological—especially those proffered by certain "masters of suspicion" (Feuerbach, Marx, Nietzsche, Freud—and Karl Barth, too)—can be acknowledged by faithful Christians and used to purify their faith. Christians can learn from non-Christians to ask: *How does faith function? What are the real "operative motives" behind such faith? Who benefits?*[9] Anti-Constantinians join them in questioning whether and how Christianity has come to function as justification (and the church as chaplain) for comfortable lives.

A similar focus on religion's function has come to characterize recent secularization theory.[10] While earlier, grand narratives assumed that "religion" was inevitably, *quantifiably* decreasing in the enlightened, industrialized West, the revised theory sees it changing in *qualitative* form or in terms of its *function*. Charles Taylor describes this in terms of the rise of the ironist's faith—of believing but not believing, or wanting to believe but not being quite able to do so.[11]

9. Merold Westphal, *Suspicion and Faith: The Religious Uses of Modern Atheism* (New York: Fordham University Press, 1998), 10–17, 25–29.
10. David Martin, *On Secularization: Toward a Revised General Theory* (Aldershot, UK: Ashgate, 2005), 24–25.
11. Charles Taylor, *Varieties of Religion Today: William James Revisited* (Cambridge, MA: Harvard

Peter Berger writes of the new "vulnerability" with which religion is maintained intuitionally and in an individual's consciousness, given the pluralization of options.[12]

Grace Davie's work is most important in this context. She writes of how religion for many today entails "believing without belonging," and thus, becomes "vicarious" or a form of "surrogacy"—something that benefits almost every corner of society, but mainly at second hand.[13] Religion functions differently when people believe in it without belonging to a church. People are glad that churches exist, if only to have somewhere to turn during life's major transitions (births, deaths, weddings, baptisms) or national tragedies (9/11, mass shootings, political assassinations). Most of us vicariously benefit from churches in these ways and during these pivotal moments.[14] Churches and church leaders are thus increasingly regarded as the chaplains of society as a whole, places and people that are there when you need them, but let you do what you want when you don't. Indeed, in Western Europe and increasingly in the United States, church has become something of the public face of whole nations or "the Western world" even—and especially—when few show up on a typical Sunday.[15] At first glance, it would seem that the findings of other secularism theorists pull in an opposite direction when they argue for an increasingly individualized and privatized faith, one designed to fulfill the immediate longings of individuals but by no means bind us together.[16] But really, Christianity can serve as the chief chaplain of the whole public only after the church has been thoroughly privatized, has lost its own distinctive cultural-political form. Both the contraction

University Press, 2002), 56–60; Peter E. Gordon, "The Place of the Sacred in the Absence of God: Charles Taylor's *A Secular Age*," *Journal of the History of Ideas* 69.4 (Oct. 2008): 655.

12. Charles Matthews, "An Interview with Peter Berger," *The Hedgehog Review* 8.1–2 (Spring/Summer 2006): 153.

13. Grace Davie, "Debate," in *Praying for England: Priestly Presence in Contemporary Culture*, ed. Sam Wells and Sarah Coakley (London: Continuum, 2008), 154–55.

14. Grace Davie, "Vicarious Religion: A Methodological Challenge," in *Everyday Religion: Observing Modern Religious Lives*, ed. Nancy T. Ammerman (New York: Oxford University Press, 2006), 21–37.

15. Compare Philip Jenkins, *God's Continent: Christianity, Islam, and Europe's Religious Crisis* (Oxford: Oxford University Press, 2007), 69, who argues that even in secular Europe, Christianity thusly "continues as a ghostly presence."

16. Steve Bruce, "Secularization and the Impotence of Individualized Religion," *The Hedgehog Review* 8.1–2 (Spring/Summer 2006): 42–44.

(privatization) and the extension (cultural chaplaincy) of Christianity are signified by "the Constantinian shift."

Much of this theory on the secularizing of religion confirms what chapter 3 also argued, namely, that Christianity now largely dispenses comfort, rather than calling disciples. It also verifies what I am arguing here: less and less frequently is the church understood (and governed) as an *alternative* to dominant society, as a distinctive culture from which one can question the "necessity" of the ways of the world. Instead, it increasingly functions to implicitly or explicitly *endorse* dominant culture, including assumptions about the beneficence of free market capitalism, the necessity of war, and the primacy of individualism.

Constantinian Shifts and Their Critics

According to its critics, Constantinianism names the transition first encountered in the early fourth century when the church was able to set aside its status as a minority, persecuted subculture under Roman rule, and to become the permitted (and, later, the official) religion of the now *Holy* Roman Empire.[17] In terms of how we remember this history, the name "Constantine" brings along with it a host of historically contingent, but mutually reinforcing assumptions that have been taken as "history" or "truth" or simply "the way things are." One such assumption is that the church becomes effective and Christian "ideals" become realizable only as Christians take the reins of history by baptizing emperors, utilizing soldiers, or otherwise implementing their vision through the powers of this world.

Pre-Constantinian Christians could visibly see that their ethic was different in kind from the powers that ruled the wider world. What "worked" for them would not necessarily work for the Roman Empire, and *vice versa*. The difference in ethics or politics was clear to both sides. After the shift, the church could no longer be identified by distinctive practices and ethics, given the fact that now even soldiers

17. John Howard Yoder, *Christian Attitudes to War, Peace, and Revolution*, ed. Theodore J. Koontz and Andy Alexis-Baker (Grand Rapids, MI: Brazos, 2011), 57–65, 69–74; Yoder, *Priestly Kingdom*, 135–41.

who kill their enemies, rather than loving them and turning the other cheek, are considered Christian. At the same time, God's will becomes almost directly discernible from the spread of Christianity throughout Rome, and then, to previously "unbelieving" lands. Proponents of the shift—including those for whom Constantine became something close to a second messiah—will say that a Rome that is Christian (even in compromised form) is better than a thoroughly pagan, merciless empire. Nevertheless, this shift does not simply change the *degree* and *range* of the faith; it changes the *quality* and *function* of Christianity. After Constantine, the church ceases to witness to a different way of life. Instead, it works to *legitimize* or *justify* the "way things have to be" if Christians are to remain on the winning side of history.

This is what it means for Christianity to become a kind of chaplaincy to culture: the faith now functions to ease the consciences of those whose hands must get dirty in the name of political responsibility. As a result, Christianity comes to underwrite empire building, political expedience, baptism by the sword, swearing of oaths, devotion to national security, and a host of other undertakings that early Christians would have considered thoroughly incompatible with discipleship.

Constantinian Christianity encourages the assumption that Christianity amounts to a mere spiritual ideal—one that can be (or needs to be) actualized through non-Christian means. Thus, the Constantinian shift is not just a troubling form of accommodation of the church to culture; it actually suggests that the faith itself doesn't amount to much until it becomes allied with an empire or other major cultural force. It suggests that the church needs to be allied with a political force, rather than seeing it as itself a distinctive politic: a culture unto itself, a way of ruling (by serving). In other words, there is really no "enculturation" of Christianity without first "deculturing" it—marginalizing or forgetting the features that make it a culture unto itself. "Constantine," then, must first *take away* the politics of the church, in order to engraft an alien politics upon it.

This is a point made repeatedly by John Howard Yoder and Stanley

Hauerwas, two of the best-known anti-Constantinian writers of the late twentieth and twenty-first centuries. They attend primarily to the church's distinctive sociopolitical practices (peacemaking, forgiveness, reconciliation, table fellowship, sharing resources, befriending strangers, dying well) and to the way embodying this ethic will bear witness to real alternatives in front of the watching, wider world. As Hauerwas likes to say, the first political or social task of the church *is to be the church*, and thus, to witness to the possibility of a countercultural way of life, rather than to try to directly transform the world through nonecclesial means.[18] It follows that, despite my categorization of "anti-Constantinianism," these critics are "pro-" something as well. Their important critical leverage depends on a positive description of what Jesus and early, faithful Christians positively are. In fact, only with such a thick description of a true and visible church, and lives that witness to its inhabitability, can the omission or absence of such a countercultural community be seen in the first place.

I will now analyze some of the more influential anti-Constantinian figures, often representing or influenced by Anabaptism (Hauerwas and Yoder), but also, including groups and movements (the Ekklesia Project and neo-monasticism) that seek to embody a less compromised, more intentional church. At risk of stretching groupings too far, I will also point to some theological movements and cultural critics (African American cultural criticism, liberation theology, feminist theology) that are anti-Constantinian in deep and important ways, but who critique the "sectarian" impulses of other anti-Constantinians, as well as push back against what they take to be exclusive attention to state-sponsored violence while largely ignoring violence against the poor, people of color, and women, which is sometimes perpetuated by church members themselves.[19]

---

18. Hauerwas and Willimon, *Resident Aliens*, 38; Compare Hauerwas, *Vision and Virtue: Essays in Christian Ethical Reflection* (Notre Dame, IN: University of Notre Dame Press, 1981), 6; and Hauerwas, *The Peaceable Kingdom: A Primer in Christian Ethics* (Notre Dame, IN: University of Notre Dame Press, 1983), 99.

19. Such liberationists and feminists typically critique anti-Constantinians (sometimes called "witness theologians," "postliberals," or "radical ecclesiologists"—i.e., those who clearly emphasize the church as a visible, inhabitable alternative to dominant politics and culture) for failing to attend to the structural sins inhabited by the church itself: sexual violence, patriarchy,

Thickly Describing Discipleship

John Howard Yoder wrote his best-known work, *The Politics of Jesus*, at an opportune time. Published in 1972, the book built on and gave voice to discontent with America's involvement in an unpopular war as it reconstructed Jesus not as a spiritual, apolitical leader of people's hearts, but as concerned with issues of power, privilege, economic disparities, and war—both sanctioned and unsanctioned. In Yoder's reading, Jesus and the early church join the Israelites in exhibiting a distinctive social arrangement—an "ethic" or "culture" or "politic"—which is recognizable and inhabitable and which provides a real alternative to the power politics, hierarchical structures, and sanctioned violence perpetuated by empires and modern-day nation-

white privilege, capitulations to global markets at the expense of Christian solidarity with the global poor, etc. By including what can look like anti-anti-Constantinian voices in a chapter about anti-Constantinians, I am aware that I risk making the category too broad to be helpful. I will accept this risk largely because, first, I am convinced that many liberationists and feminists share much more with "postliberals" or "witness" theologians than either side sometimes assumes, given the reciprocal caricatures of each. This is directly and convincingly argued by Karen V. Guth, in *Christian Ethics at the Boundary: Feminisms and Theologies of Public Life* (Minneapolis: Fortress Press, 2015), 113–51. Second, to include the self-critical ("anti-anti-Constantinian") critique, especially as it attends to violence against women, minorities, and the people of "developing countries" within the critique of Constantinianism is especially important, now that John Howard Yoder, arguably the most influential critique of Constantinian arrangements, has been shown to have committed egregious sexual violence against women he knew throughout much of his career. Over thirty years after Yoder was first accused of sexual misconduct and almost twenty years since his death in 1997, his abusive behavior is still being investigated, lamented, and negotiated within Mennonite communities. See David Cramer, Jenny Howell, Paul Martens, and Jonathan Tran, "Theology and Misconduct: The Case of John Howard Yoder," *Christian Century*, August 20, 2014, 20–23. It is already painfully clear that Yoder violated numerous women with whom he worked, usually in a position of authority. Rachel Waltner Goossen, "'Defanging the Beast': Mennonite Reponses to John Howard Yoder's Sexual Abuse," *Mennonite Quarterly Review* 89.1 (Jan. 2015): 7–80; see also Guth, *Christian Ethics*, 21–22n36, which also gives bibliographic information with the original reporting of the offenses. That Yoder horrifically failed to live up to the Christian pacifism he professed is clear. There are other bad ironies as well: one of Yoder's primary objections to the Constantinian arrangement was that it covers over its own tracks, that the church justifies its endorsement of empire as necessary and inevitable while occluding alternative options and the New Testament peace witness itself. And yet, Yoder seems to have done exactly this, both covering over the extent and perversion of his own violence and justifying it to himself and to others (including the victims). By focusing on the way Christians as a whole often accommodate themselves to the violent "peace of Rome," and then, justify that accommodation as necessary, given the workings of the world, I draw insights from Yoder and others while remaining aware that Yoder perpetuated a number of the very Constantinian self-justifications that he diagnosed. There are whole books written on this tragedy and its effect on Christian pacifism and neo-Mennonite theology, not to mention Yoder's more immediate victims. I can only here add that an anti-Constantinian church or an anti-Constantinian Christian must perpetually critique itself/himself/herself in order to be fully anti-Constantinian. In this sense, the anti-anti-Constantinians fully belong to the theological tradition I am recounting.

states. Because the life and death of Jesus provide a pattern of radical service, forgiveness, and active peacemaking to the powers of church and state, disciples of the crucified one will inevitably find their community countercultural and politically subversive.

As I have already indicated, the real tragedy of the Constantinian shift is not that Christianity becomes dominant or mainstream (*acculturated* to empire or powerful nation-states), but that it ceases to have a *distinctive* ethos and politics (and thus, *accommodated* in many ways). Once soldiers or hangmen (or the rich, for that matter[20]) are baptized without requiring their conversion, Christianity becomes not a way of life but a doctrine to believe. Most disconcerting, once the church and nation share borders—as with the Holy Roman Empire or state–church arrangements, but also, according to popular sentiments about a "Christian America"—then a "real church" must be posited above and beyond historically visible churches. In other words, in order to preserve any meaning to "the true church" or "the elect," Constantinian churches need to posit a difference between the visible and invisible church. The "real" church becomes invisible to the extent that the "actual" church becomes compromised.

This means that the only way to gain any real leverage against a Constantinian account of the church is to offer a thick description of "the politics of Jesus" and that of the early church, reclaiming both as inhabitable and otherwise "realistic." Only by paying careful attention to the history of Christianity, and by taking into account the best biblical scholarship, can we begin to understand the early followers of Jesus in sufficient detail. This, in turn, allows us to begin to see *exactly what is lost* when the church is rendered invisible, and thus, made to accommodate other social forms. Without a visible church, past or present, we have no means of marking its absorption into "Christian" culture and its disappearance into the hidden church.[21]

---

20. Nicholas M. Healy, *Hauerwas: A (Very) Critical Introduction* (Grand Rapids, MI: Eerdmans, 2014), 93–94n12.

21. This narrative simplifies things considerably and has been criticized for doing so. Peter J. Leithart, in *Defending Constantine: The Twilight of an Empire and the Dawn of Christendom* (Downers Grove, IL: InterVarsity, 2010), 303–6, 316–21, accuses Yoder's anti-Constantinian Fall narrative as falling victim to the same "monological" historical ideology as the Constantinianism it opposes. See also

The Mennonite Challenge

Radical reformers and their heirs assume that membership within the dissident grassroots political community called church (*ekklesia*) entails being different, "called out" (*ek-klesia*) from the ways of the world. This shared vocation is exhibited by voluntary church membership, nonviolent resistance, the church's power to excommunicate and reconcile estranged members, meal fellowship, rule by consensus, and other visible marks.[22] Yoder retrieves these social practices from Jesus and the early church as recounted in the gospels, Acts, and other early Christian literature.

By emphasizing again and again just how possible, inhabitable, or "realistic" New Testament and early Christian forms of faith and community were, Yoder tries to cut off the reoccurring critique of those who charge him with being a "sectarian."[23] Often, these critics say they appreciate the critique of accommodated Christianity, but then mediate and dilute the critique and vision with a healthy dose of modern-day "realism." They are happy that some Christians (call them radicals or pacifists or Mennonites[24]) remind the rest of us what an ideal Christian community should look like, prophetically calling us to an "impossible ideal." Yet, these critics also underscore that such

---

Alex Sider, *To See History Doxologically: History and Holiness in John Howard Yoder's Ecclesiology* (Grand Rapids, MI: Eerdmans, 2011), 97–132. Yoder is aware of this difficulty and responds by noting that Constantine's "conversion" has already been thoroughly mythologized; one can respond to it only by using the "conscious anachronism and oversimplification of reaching back to the New Testament to state an alternative"—not as proof text or prescription but as "provocative paradigm." Yoder, *Priestly Kingdom*, 155.

22. John Howard Yoder, *Body Politics: Five Practices of the Christian Community Before the Watching World* (Scottdale, PA: Herald, 1992), 14–46.

23. Critics often charge Yoder, Hauerwas, and other "witness" theologians with being "sectarian." The most famous charge is by James Gustafson, "The Sectarian Temptation: Reflections on Theology, the Church, and the University," in the *Proceedings of the Catholic Theological Society* 40 (1985): 83–94. Sectarianism as a category is employed in an allegedly neutral, sociological way to define radical Christian communities, but (as in the work of Ernst Troeltsch, where it originated) functions to sideline as much as to define. Yoder, *For the Nations: Essays Evangelical and Public* (Grand Rapids, MI: Eerdmans, 1997), 3; Yoder, *Christian Attitudes to War*, 298, 300.

24. Yoder is nervous that this latter term characterizes his position as narrowly cultural and denominational. He insists that Mennonite theology and ecclesiology entails "a vision of unlimited catholicity because, in contrast to both sectarian and 'established' views, it prescribes no particular institutional requisites for entering the movement whose shape it calls 'restoration.'" Yoder, *Priestly Kingdom*, 4. I use "Mennonite" here simply to mark the importance of a particular, visible community of worshippers from which and to which Yoder frequently writes.

a vision *is* idealistic, sectarian, and naïve if and when it is assumed to be fully realizable. The counterargument hangs on the ability to show how Jesus, his disciples, and early Christians *actually* shared resources, ate with one another, befriended strangers, refused to honor Caesar as Lord, and (most important to pacifist anti-Constantinians) participated in church, *rather than* participating in the Roman military.

Given the charge that such radical forms of discipleship participate in a form of "sectarian withdrawal," readers are often surprised to see just how frequently and emphatically Jesus's way of the cross is portrayed as a public, practical, passable path—one that is open to all Christians.[25] Certainly, loving enemies, forswearing oaths, and forgiving trespasses will prove to be less *efficient*, especially in the short term, than unflinching retaliation, uncritical patriotism, and unforgiving revenge. But to consider only short-term gains or to reduce relevance to efficiency misses the prudence and usefulness of movements such as the civil rights movement or of the role of martyrs in religious resistance groups. Discipleship sometimes requires a choice for faithfulness and witness at the cost of forfeiting practical results. Yet, to judge the value of an action exclusively by results, to assume that a Christian should act as if she could control history, and to pit effectiveness and faithfulness against one another in a zero-sum game[26] is, in each case, to fall for the too-easy opposition of "real" and "ideal."

A Mainstream Response

A number of recent, popular biblical scholars have given their own

---

25. Yoder and Hauerwas differ by way of emphasis on this point. Both authors emphasize that for the church to be relevant to the world, it must first be itself, performing possibilities that would otherwise go unrealized. Yoder, however, also consistently emphasizes the universality and communicability of the church's witness for the whole world, whereas Hauerwas underscores the incommensurability between the politics of church and alternative politics, perhaps sensing that the work of translation and relevance inevitably obviate the church's particularity and sidestep ways that relevance and faithfulness do sometimes collide. Yoder accounts for the difference by writing in *For the Nations* (note the title) that Hauerwas "maximizes the provocative edge of the dissenting posture with titles like *Against the Nations . . .* or *Resident Aliens*." Yoder, *For the Nations*, 3n6.

26. Yoder, *For the Nations*, 28.

descriptions of the early Christian counterculture. Some of these scholars continue to read Christian history as the conflict between the religion of empire and the Judeo-Christian tradition, but do so with nuanced historical-critical scholarship. They attend to the differences between various empires (Babylonian, Assyrian, Roman, American) and how Israelites, and then Jews and Christians, variously resist them to "come out" as God's people.[27] Others seem to radicalize the already radical (deeply rooted) historical reconstructions of other anti-Constantinians. They locate the "original" turn or "fall" more deeply in the transition from archaic/agrarian cultures to urban societies. Jesus, an itinerant rabbi, calls disciples to a way of life on the land and off the grid, a life that resists powers-that-be, then and now.[28] Eco-feminists bring feminism and ecology together to criticize the mutually enforcing hierarchies of patriarchy and human exploitation of nonhumans. They tell their own stories of having fallen from more egalitarian relationships between humans and nonhumans. Through such stories (which they admit are more imaginative and provocative than historically certain), they both gain critical leverage against patriarchy/human domination over nature and begin to imagine what inhabiting a more faithful human community and sustainable ecological practices might look like.[29]

Even mainstream biblical scholars writing for popular audiences have questioned deep assumptions of contemporary Christians by revisiting the politics of Jesus as they butt up against the dominant politics of Rome and of America. In a book devoted to explicating the events surrounding the last week of Jesus's life, authors Marcus Borg and John Dominic Crossan portray Jesus as a "political Lord and Savior"

---

27. Wes Howard-Brook, "Come Out, My People": God's Call out of Empire in the Bible and Beyond (Maryknoll, NY: Orbis, 2010).

28. Ched Meyers, Binding the Strong Man: A Political Reading of Mark's Story of Jesus, 20th anniversary ed. (Maryknoll, NY: Orbis, 2008). Meyers's work joins other anarcho-primitivists, those who critique the origins and "progress" of civilization itself. Others include Vernard Eller, Christian Anarchy (Grand Rapids, MI: Eerdmans, 1987); and Jacques Ellul, Anarchy and Christianity, trans. G. Bromiley (Grand Rapids, MI: Eerdmans, 1988); see also Ched Meyers, "Anarcho-Primitivism and the Bible," in Encyclopedia of Religion and Nature, ed. Bron Taylor (London: Continuum, 2005), 56–58.

29. Rosemary Radford Ruether, Sexism and God-Talk: Toward a Feminist Theology, 10th anniversary ed. (Boston: Beacon, 1993), 72–92; Ruether, Gaia and God: An Ecofeminist Theology of Earth Healing (New York: HarperCollins, 1992), 173–201.

above and beyond the "personal Lord and Savior" he is normally confessed to be.[30] Depicting Jesus as such enables one to rethink the central characters and conflict that culminates in Jesus's death. The conflict is not primarily "religious," that is, about Jesus and his disciples versus "the Jews" who don't "believe" in him. Rather, Jesus dies because the political powers of Rome and select Jewish leaders who are in cahoots with the empire understand Jesus's lordship as subverting their own.[31]

Many mainstream Christians remain unconvinced. To live at the margins of empire and to embody an alternative to its forms of domination and control of history—these strategies may have seemed possible for fishermen or underground house churches in the ancient Mediterranean world. In today's interconnected world, the vision seems starry-eyed or disingenuous. It does not help matters that, despite the wide diversity of anti-Constantinian New Testament scholars and early church historians, images of radical discipleship remain associated primarily with Anabaptist communities, which tend to evoke images of Pennsylvania women in bonnets, horse-drawn buggies, and Indiana farmboys in overalls. Such assumptions about "ethnic isolation, Germanic folkways, [and] the simplicity of immigrant village culture" all contribute to making the vision of radical Christian discipleship seem anachronistic and idealistic.[32] We are glad disciples are around *and* that we are not one of them. We appreciate an unusually radical perspective on discipleship, as long as it remains just that. We value historical accounts of early Christian radicals and martyrs as long as they are ancient history—an era from which we have emerged, one worth remembering but not reverting to. Retrieving pre-Constantinian models of discipleship and church in a secular or post-secular age remains rife with such equivocations.

---

30. Marcus J. Borg and John Dominic Crossan, *The Last Week: What the Gospels Really Teach about Jesus's Final Days in Jerusalem* (New York: HarperOne, 2006), 215.
31. See also John Dominic Crossan, *God and Empire: Jesus Against Rome, Then and Now* (New York: HarperCollins, 2007).
32. Yoder, *Priestly Kingdom*, 4.

Church Politics and Identity Politics

The biblical scholars, historians, and theologians referenced above disagree on exactly when and how the dominant reading of church history displaced the story of scripture and of the early church as the lens through which to understand what Christianity is all about. Yet, they agree that there was a "fall" sometime in the past and that getting out from behind Constantine's wake requires subtle and imaginative revisioning. Other anti-Constantinians attend more fully to recent developments, tracing how the Constantinian shift has reproduced itself again and again in the modern world. Stanley Hauerwas is certainly the most provocative among them.

What makes Hauerwas so intriguing (and to some, so maddening) is his ability to see latent, noncausal associations between a number of our contemporary problems, including: modern apologetics or rational defenses of Christianity, especially when based on ostensibly universal, Enlightenment reason; the desire to control history through war; America's avoidance of suffering, finitude, and death; the assumed universality of modern ethics, which is purchased by forfeiting Christianity's particular stories and practices; and finally, the ascendency of individualism and the political liberalism that presupposes it. In various ways, Hauerwas associates each of these characteristics of modernity with the forfeiture of the church as the primary site and meaning of Christian salvation. But because of the underlying connections he unearths between contemporary American culture, modern philosophy, liberal theology, and political realism, Hauerwas ends up with a capacious and malleable understanding of contemporary Constantinianism. I focus on three dimensions of his anti-Constantinianism and its often under-acknowledged relationship to that of other critics, including feminists, liberation theologians, and black cultural critics.

Civil Religion as Explaining, Christianity as Re-Storying

Hauerwas writes of coming to pacifism slowly, only vaguely aware that declaring himself a pacifist "might have some serious consequences."[33] Since that time, he no less than Yoder has been chiefly preoccupied with resisting the idealization and marginalization of Christian nonviolence. But while Yoder and other neo-Mennonites have largely staked their case on the inhabitability and effectiveness of New Testament Christianity and Mennonite polity,[34] Hauerwas typically works from the other end. By this, I mean that, in response to charges of sectarianism, Hauerwas largely admits that the true church consists of the dedicated, however few they may be; he only questions why so-called "sects" should be seen as inferior to churches that posit an invisible "elect" somewhere in their midst.[35] More importantly, rather than show how Christianity can be made compatible with non-Christian political forms, Hauerwas beguilingly shows that our ostensibly nonreligious politics and economics always already function as civil religion for us. The problem for him is not really that the nonviolent ways of Jesus and early Christians are taken to be too unrealistic to be practical. The problem is that the ways of the world have been sanctified and deified, too sacred for us to replace. Hauerwas thus largely works to demythologize the ways that dominant powers, especially the military and political liberalism, function as our leading religion.

For example, in his pacifist response to 9/11, Hauerwas asserts that war has become America's leading theodicy—its explanation of otherwise incomprehensible suffering and death. In the immediate wake of the terrorist attacks, Americans "desperately want to 'explain' what happened." We use the "normalizing discourse" of war, knowing that phrases such as "we are at war" offer "magical words necessary to reclaim the everyday."[36] In other words, because America treated

33. Stanley Hauerwas, "September 11, 2001: A Pacifist Response," in *Performing the Faith: Bonhoeffer and the Practice of Nonviolence* (Grand Rapids, MI: Brazos, 2004), 203.
34. Indeed, Harold Bender, a pioneer in the political theology of neo-Mennonites, argued that democracy is founded on nothing less than the Free Church model. Harold S. Bender, *The Anabaptist Vision* (Scottdale, PA: Herald, 1944), 3–4, as cited in Paul Martens, *The Heterodox Yoder* (Eugene, OR: Cascade, 2012), 11–12.
35. Stanley Hauerwas, *Christian Existence Today: Essays on Church, World, and Living in Between*, Reissue ed. (Eugene, OR: Wipf & Stock, 2010), 7.
36. Hauerwas, "September 11, 2001," 202.

the 9/11 attacks as an act of war and answered them with more war, victims did not have to die as victims; they got transfigured into meaningful heroes.[37] In *God, Medicine, and Suffering*, Hauerwas reads America's sometimes automatic reversion to interventionist and experimental medicine (seeking to cure rather than to care) in times of crisis and the vow to "fight" every disease and "fix" every problem—even the problem of death itself—as another instance of our inability to suffer without creating explanations or asserting that we are in control. Seemingly nonreligious actions such as fighting terrorists or fighting diseases have become our culture's dominant religion—that in which we put our ultimate trust and through which we make our lives meaningful. According to Hauerwas, Christianity's vision and virtues should include coping with tragedy, enduring pain, abiding in silence, trusting God, remaining patient, and knowing how to die well. These get sidelined not because they are impractically religious, but because things such as war and medicine already justify the way things are and need to be.

The final sentence above indicates why Hauerwas would see war and medicine, as well as liberalism's evocation of self-protection, as recapitulating a kind of Constantinianism. Chief components of the Constantinian shift include the idea that God is on the side of history's victors and that Christians must assume control of history and their own lives. This puts tremendous pressure on Christians to enforce (even with force) whatever change they wish to see in the world, and to be autonomous and effective, even if this means ceasing to witness to the God revealed in a particular story. In short, when the church comes to serve as a chaplain to society, it ceases to witness to another way of life and largely functions to justify the way things are. Such rationalizations of suffering end up defending a God whose omnipotence and omnibenevolence remain entirely abstract and

---

37. Ibid., 203. Feminist theorist Judith Butler leans on the theorist of religion, Talal Asad, to make a similar point about how language of "war" always already frames our moral evaluations, making some instances of violence understandable and others utterly incomprehensible, and thus, deserving of unrestrained retaliation. See Judith Butler, *Frames of War: When Is Life Grievable?* (London: Verso, 2009), 152–57. I return to Butler in chapter 8.

theoretical; indeed, rational defenses for such an all-powerful, unilateral deity often only justify the unilateral, controlling, autonomous acts of those who "believe" in "Him."[38] Liberation theologians, those who lift up God's preferential option for the poor, also critique such cultural-political self-justifications. Gustavo Gutiérrez suggests that many first-world Christians have a "barter conception of religion"[39] or an instrumental faith, that is, a faith "that reduces God to a means or instrument for achieving our own human purposes with professedly divine power and sanction."[40]

James Baldwin, the African American writer and social critic, also traces the (fallen) function of contemporary religion back to our inability to accept finitude and fragility:

> Perhaps the whole root of our trouble, the human trouble, is that we will sacrifice all the beauty of our loves, will imprison ourselves in totems, taboos, crosses, blood sacrifices, steeples, mosques, races, armies, flags, nations, in order to deny the fact of death, which is the only fact we have.[41]

Baldwin's own version of the Constantinian shift attends to the way white North Americans "have forgotten that the religion that is now identified with their virtue and their power—'God is on our side' . . . —came out of a rocky piece of ground in what is known as the Middle East before color was invented."[42] Baldwin also agrees that the needed liberation essentially entails the demythologizing of America's civil religion. If and when this happens (and Baldwin thinks it is inevitable), "Western nations will be forced to reexamine themselves and release themselves from many things that are now taken to be sacred, and to discard nearly all the assumptions that have been used to justify their lives and their anguish and their crimes so long."[43]

---

38. Stanley Hauerwas, *God, Medicine, and Suffering*, 39–58; compare Metz, *The Emergent Church*, 26–27.
39. Gustavo Gutiérrez, *On Job: God-Talk and the Suffering of the Innocent* (Maryknoll, NY: Orbis, 1991), 1.
40. Westphal, *Suspicion and Faith*, 6. See also Dorothee Soelle's discussion of Eckhart's resistance to this "business spirit" of religion in *Suffering*, trans. Everett R. Kalin (Philadelphia: Fortress Press, 1975), 96.
41. James Baldwin, *The Fire Next Time* (New York: Vintage, 1993), 91.
42. Ibid., 44.
43. Ibid., 44–45.

Elisabeth Schüssler Fiorenza, a leading feminist biblical scholar, uses careful historical reconstruction—attending to the *facts* of female leadership in early Christian communities—to mount her own demythologization of the seemingly normal, if not sacrosanct, patriarchy of the contemporary church and of critical biblical scholarship.[44] African American philosopher and cultural critic Cornel West also closely links what he calls the "amnesia" of "American Constantinian Christians" to their "sponsorship" of American imperial ends.[45] Without a firm grasp on Christian history (and with an almost willful misremembering of America's checkered past, especially when it comes to race), everyday American Christians are left vulnerable to the manipulation of corporations and politicians who invoke their faith in support of the status quo. Writes West, "The very notion that the prophetic legacy of the grand victim of the Roman empire—Jesus Christ—requires critique of and resistance to American imperial power hardly occurs to them."[46]

Hauerwas might say that, without embodying the original, properly political nature of church, Christianity becomes little more than a cipher and cover for other political agendas, some good, many distinctly unchristian. He, like Schüssler Fiorenza and West, thinks that remembering and retelling Christian history (or in Hauerwas's terms: "the Christian story") provides resistance to the Constantinian story that things are the way God means them to be. In his sermon immediately following the attacks on 9/11, Hauerwas dramatically juxtaposes the two stories:

> Christians are not called to be heroes or shoppers. We are called to be holy. We do not think holiness is an individual achievement, but rather a set of practices to sustain a people who refuse to have their lives determined by the fear and denial of death. We believe by so living we offer our non-Christian brothers and sisters an alternative to all politics based on the denial of death. Christians are acutely aware that we seldom

44. Elisabeth Schüssler Fiorenza, *In Memory of Her: A Feminist Theological Reconstruction of Christian Origins*, 10th anniversary ed. (New York: Crossroad, 1994).
45. Cornel West, *Democracy Matters: Winning the Fight Against Imperialism* (New York: Penguin, 2004), 145–72.
46. Ibid., 151.

are faithful to the gifts God has given us, but we hope the confession of our sins is a sign of hope in a world without hope. This means pacifists do have a response to September 11, 2001. Our response is to continue living in a manner that witnesses to our belief that the world was not changed on September 11, 2001. The world was changed during the celebration of Passover in A.D. 33.[47]

The idea that Christians should "merely" continue to witness to Jesus's death and resurrection when others are moved to swift retaliation as a way to keep Americans from dying in vain will be difficult for many contemporary Christians to accept. Such waiting and abiding introduces us to a second characteristic of Hauerwas's anti-Constantinianism.

Undergoing Formation

A second characteristic of Hauerwas's creative construal of contemporary Constantinianism relates to the "passive virtues" (being patient, abiding in suffering, hoping, witnessing) that I have already introduced. While most Christians believe that they are called to act decisively to change the world for the better, Hauerwas argues that Christians must first learn to *be acted on*, to *undergo* formation, and otherwise *submit themselves* to the discipline necessary to become the people they are called to be.

Of course, Hauerwas no less than Yoder emphasizes that Christianity is primarily about ethics (actions) over beliefs and doctrines (understandings). He thinks the two cannot really be separated; it is ingenuous to assume "that if we get our 'beliefs' right, we will then know how to act right."[48] Yoder typically associates this emphasis on action and ethics with the "voluntarism" of his Free Church tradition, often emphasizing the necessity of the free decisions of adult individuals for church membership, and critical of infant baptism on the same grounds. By contrast, Hauerwas, who has called himself a "high church Mennonite," is more interested in the formative

47. Hauerwas, "September 11, 2001," 208–9; compare Hauerwas and Willimon, *Resident Aliens*, 28–29.
48. Stanley Hauerwas, *Sanctify Them with the Truth: Holiness Exemplified* (Edinburgh: T&T Clark, 1998), 157.

processes and practices of the church as a whole, to which individuals submit themselves. Recall from chapter 1 that he even admits to preferring older forms of Christendom over an American neo-Christendom that depends so heavily on the free choices of individuals: "The voluntary character of the [American] church, enshrined in the language of 'joining the church,' turns out to be a perfect Constantinian strategy."[49] Because we Americans choose to belong to a particular church of our choice (and often change our choice again and again to fit changing desires and needs), we end up avoiding the long, difficult process of being formed into a people who know what (and Who) to desire in the first place.

If virtue formation is already passive, requiring one to *be* schooled and *undergo* formation, Hauerwas emphasizes the most passive among the virtues. This connects to his somewhat different take on Constantinianism, which Hauerwas links to a loss of the Christian's capacity to be vulnerable and to suffer, to mourn, and to die well—as well as the capacity to care patiently for all who undergo these experiences. The association of "peaceableness" (a central virtue for Hauerwas) with patiently abiding, even in the midst of tremendous pain, also explains why Hauerwas repeatedly asserts that pacifism is not a *strategy* to rid the world of violence, but rather, names the acquired *dispositions* that are necessary to live faithfully in a violent world.[50] Strategies are engineered and implemented, the quicker the better. The practices of bending and submitting, of being formed and corrected, provide Christians with an alternative to (and prophetic critique of) America's neo-Christendom. Some recent Christian communities have tried to "argue" for this by displaying it.

The Ekklesia Project is an ecumenical network of Christians dedicated to becoming "church-centered," that is, committed "to the Church as Christ's gathered Body, whose true heart is communal worship and whose true freedom is disciplined service."[51] Their language of discipline and formation, including "fraternal correction"

---

49. Stanley Hauerwas, *War and the American Difference: Theological Reflections on Violence and National Identity* (Grand Rapids, MI: Baker, 2011), 156.
50. Hauerwas, "September 11, 2001," 203.

(cf. Matt 18:15–18; 1 Thess 5:14) can sound repressive, but members lift up those dispositions exactly as a prophetic critique of the "communities and practices that have minimized or diluted the church's obligation to be a 'light to the nations' (cf. Isa 49:6) and a foretaste of the promised Kingdom of God."[52] In short, the Ekklesia Project believes that only by submitting to the formative and corrective processes of the church can Christians properly resist the equally authoritarian (and, in practice, much more formative) powers of consumerism, militarism, and secular liberalism today.

New Monasticism, one name for a loosely knit collective of intentional religious communities that has gained mainstream exposure and interest over the past decade, also lifts up seemingly antiquated practices that they trace back to the early church and St. Benedict's Rule.[53] Among the twelve marks of neo-monasticism, many rub up against our dominant culture's preference for individual empowerment and decision-making. The new monastics vow "humble submission to Christ's body, the Church"; they follow Benedictine practices of "intentional formation in the way of Christ and the Rule of the Community along the lines of the old novitiate"; they explicate Matthew 18 in confronting one another for mutual correction and restoration to the life of the community; and they commit to a *disciplined* contemplative life, the central prayer of which practices dying well by repeating Jesus's final words on the cross: "Into thy hands I commend my spirit."[54]

These communities (and communities of communities) try to embody church as an organic, collective body (Rom 12:4–4; 1 Cor 12:24–26; Eph 4:11–16). Each member wins her or his fullest freedom

---

51. Ekklesia Project, "Who We Are." Accessed August 10, 2015, http://www.ekklesiaproject.org/about-us/who-we-are.

52. Ekklesia Project, "Dedication and Invitation." Accessed August 10, 2015, http://www.ekklesiaproject.org/about-us/who-we-are/declaration-and-invitation.

53. For one account of this lineage, see Jonathan Wilson-Hartgrove, *New Monasticism: What It Has to Say to Today's Church* (Grand Rapids, MI: Brazos, 2008), 41–56. For the founding vision, see the Rutba House, ed., *School(s) for Conversion: 12 Marks of a New Monasticism* (Eugene, OR: Cascade, 2005).

54. See essays by Ivan Kauffman, David Janzen, Fred Bahnson, and Jonathan Wilson-Hartgrove in Rutba House, ed., *School(s) for Conversion*. The titles of chapters are quoted here; Wilson-Hartgrove's reference to the prayer of contemplatives is from page 168.

not by protecting it from the incursions of others, but by finding it resurrected in the body of the whole. Balancing calls for collective submission, discipline, and undergoing formation against recourse to individual decisions, protections, and rights is no simple matter, and I will return to this issue in chapter 7. For now, it is clear that the passive dispositions heralded by Hauerwas and others correlate to a final characteristic of anti-Constantinianism: their full-bodied understandings of church.

Church as Counterculture

In the sermon he delivers immediately after 9/11, Hauerwas directly confronts predictable allegations that anti-Constantinian pacifists have no large-scale alternatives to war in the wake of such tragedies, and therefore, can be dismissed as idealist and impractical. Hauerwas characteristically responds by conceding the point, and then, overturning the weighted categories: "Such questions assume that pacifists must have a foreign policy. I have something better—a church constituted by people who would rather die than kill."[55] For him (as for Yoder, the Ekklesia Project, and others, including a number of feminist theologians),[56] the church does not simply weigh in on political matters from partisan points of view or inspire and mobilize its parishioners for advocacy work or other political activities. Rather, the church *is a* political body or *polis* in its own right. Cornel West calls this Hauerwas's "prophetic ecclesiasticism," a name that suggests that prophetic Christianity (West's alternative to Constantinian Christianity) must first be inhabited in Christian quarters and on Christianity's own grounds for it to be truly prophetic, able to call into question all that passes as normal and necessary.[57] Indeed, "absent a countercommunity

---

55. Hauerwas, "September 11, 2001," 207.
56. See the helpful discussion of how deep sensibilities by "witness" (or anti-Constantinian) theologians converge with those of feminists in Guth, *Christian Ethics*, 136–49.
57. West, *Democracy Matters*, 161. While positioning his own project of retrieval close to that of Hauerwas and sharing many critiques of Constantinianism, West goes on to critique Hauerwas for "unduly downplay[ing] the prophetic Christian commitment to justice and our role as citizen to make America more free and democratic" (162). Compare Daniel A. Morris, *Virtue and Irony in American Democracy: Revisiting Dewey and Niebuhr* (Lanham, MD: Lexington, 2015), 221–24.

to challenge America" (which for Hauerwas *is* the church), politics as we know it quickly becomes despairingly cynical in its "realism."[58]

In their own ways, Hauerwas, Yoder, "postliberal theologians," new monastic communities, and the Ekklesia Project all make the "ecclesial turn," insisting that the first social task of the church is simply to be the church, a community set apart from dominant politics in order to witness to a different way of being together. Constantinianism from this perspective is, first of all, a *de-politicizing* of the early church, making it compatible with the politics of empires and nation-states. Feminist theologians and theorists also frequently criticize "liberal political ideology" for fashioning a dualism between a so-called private sphere (which allegedly houses "religion," often associated with "the feminine") and the political or public sphere composed of institutions and collectives (to which males have more access).[59] Feminists respond by insisting that "the personal is the political." For (other) anti-Constantinians, such a solution involves the willingness to embody church as a real alternative—a counterculture—to other associations and politics.

However, if robust understandings of and commitments to a visible, embodied, witnessing church entail the most central component of some anti-Constantinians, it is also at this very place where others part ways. Some Christian theologians (many also feminist or liberationist) critique the ecclesial turn for positioning the true church almost exclusively over-and-against state-sponsored violence, relatively unconcerned with the "internal violence of trauma or the pervasive forms of systemic violence within the church and in society at large."[60] Whereas someone like Hauerwas pits formation in and by the church against formation by the state and marketplace, feminists often expose the way the Christian tradition itself can be (and has been) deeply

---

58. Hauerwas, "September 11, 2001," 207. Yoder too laments how easily and even understandably Christians resign themselves to a less painful and less transformative realism. John Howard Yoder, *The Royal Priesthood: Essays Ecclesiastical and Ecumenical* (Scottdale, PA: Herald, 1998), 350.

59. Beverly Wildung Harrison, *Making the Connections: Essays in Feminist Social Ethics*, ed. Carol S. Robb (Boston: Beacon, 1985), 27–28; Guth, *Christian Ethics*, 78–80. For the effect of this on national security, see Sharon D. Welch, *A Feminist Ethic of Risk*, rev. ed. (Minneapolis: Fortress Press, 2000).

60. Guth, *Christian Ethics*, 43. Needless to say, this critique has become most pertinent and pressing in light of Yoder's violence against women. See footnote 19 above.

malformative. Rather than retrieving the centrality of church, they often thus position themselves at "the margins of ecclesial power."[61] These feminist and liberationist anti-Constantinians expose and resist systemic violence no less than self-described pacifists, but they include therein ecological violence, first-world exploitation of the poor, domestic violence, and child abuse, and argue that these widespread forms of violence have been justified as necessary and normal just as often (and perhaps more so—maybe *especially* by the church itself), than has the violence of war.

One might designate the broader charge as proffering "overidealized ecclesiologies,"[62] accounts of the church and church life that fail to represent the "confusingly messy realities of ordinary church life."[63] Hauerwas believes that the myths of liberalism and individualism can only be critiqued by a more compelling story, and that the answer to being formed by the market or the state is to be formed more determinatively by the church. It is understandable, then, that he wants to make that alternative story of church as compelling as possible, just as Yoder admits to oversimplifying Constantine's conversion in attempting to put forth a "provocative paradigm."[64] Still, Gloria Albrecht charges that such understandings of the church as an alternative *polis* with alternative formative processes tend to reproduce a monolithic political body, a "singular cultural-linguistic tradition" or "false universal" by which individual differences and freedoms are washed out.[65] Such strong churches render the individual too passive; the disciplined Christian undergoes full formation, but loses her appeal to personal experience and self-determination in the process.

While these critiques of an overly idealized ecclesiology often miss key components of Hauerwas's writings,[66] I find them useful for

---

61. Ibid., 58,
62. Ibid., 28. Compare Nicholas M. Healy, "Practices and the New Ecclesiology: Misplaced Concreteness?" *International Journal of Systematic Theology* 5.3 (2003): 287–308; and Healy, *Hauerwas*, 73–99.
63. Healy, *Hauerwas*, 98.
64. Yoder, *Priestly Kingdom*, 155.
65. Gloria H. Albrecht, *The Character of Communities: Toward an Ethic of Liberation for the Church* (Nashville: Abingdon, 1995), 64, 76–77, 90.

indicating an oddity of Hauerwas's understanding of church—namely, that he wants to save it from a neoliberal, all-too-American form of Christendom only to restore what can look like an older, equally hegemonic form. Hauerwas even confesses his "lingering longing" for an older, ostensibly more churchy, form of Christendom.[67] Christian feminists and other "anti-anti-Constantinians"[68] can help purify the anti-Constantinian posture, which, at best, is a way of critically interrogating *any* grand narrative or vision of reality that people take as simply or obviously true, including any story about the church's "original" innocence.[69]

Finding Our Way Out of Constantine's Trap

Throughout this chapter, I have presented the Constantinian *turn* or *fall* as essentially a *trap*: what looks like gaining valuable cultural influence turns out to be a loss of Christianity's distinctive cultural-political form. As the faith moves from the margins of empire to help control its reins, it exchanges its prophetic, dissenting, minority voice for the role of chaplaincy, one that largely explains and justifies why things are as they are. Christians now seem to discern the will of God directly from historical (missionary, military) events; yet, they lose every glimpse of God's way with the world exactly where it should be

---

66. To take one example, Albrecht charges the theology of Hauerwas with assuming a "God who is in absolute control over history," but such a God belongs squarely to the Constantinian accommodation that both Yoder and Hauerwas continually critique, and that Hauerwas likens to the projection of bureaucratic, Enlightenment reason. See Hauerwas, *God, Medicine, and Suffering*, 39–58.

67. Stanley Hauerwas, *A Better Hope: Resources for a Church Confronting Capitalism, Democracy, and Postmodernity* (Grand Rapids, MI: Brazos, 2000), 227n39. See Hauerwas's counter-critique of feminist critiques of his work in Stanley Hauerwas, "Failure of Communication *or* A Case of Uncomprehending Feminism," *Scottish Journal of Theology* 50.2 (1997): 228–39.

68. See footnote 19 above.

69. Compare Sider, *To See History Doxologically*, 97–132. "Constantinianism is not a problem. It is totalizing discourse. This is to say a number of things, among which is that the resources one has by which to see oneself out of Constantinianism will themselves likely be implicated in Constantinianism. It is also to acknowledge an ambiguous distinction between the narrative one tells about Constantinianism . . . and the architectonic discourse that conditions the possibility of the narratives themselves (Constantinianism as episteme)" (120). Anti-Constantinians with a radical ecclesiology certainly acknowledge that even the most faithful, embodied church is composed of sinful members. They remain suspicious, however, of the way that that concession is often used to justify the abandoning of a distinctively Christian ethics in favor of political realism. I return to this issue in chapter 8.

most apparent: in the visible church, the very body of Christ. Among other things, the rather complex nature of this trap means that the relationship between the old problem of Christendom and any secularism that would seem to solve it turns out to be rather complex as well.

Pro-Secular Anti-Constantinians: Separating Church from State

It would not be surprising if the modern process of secularization might be seen as alleviating some forms of cultural Christianity. At the very least, there is something to be said for the process of social differentiation—separating out, from church control, the increasingly autonomous social spheres of state, science, and the market.[70] Such disentangling of church from other sectors can help liberate the church to be itself. In Yoder's terms:

> From the perspective of the church of believers, there is a certain sense in which we can with gratitude accept the "secularization" that characterizes the modern age. To the extent that this means Christian faith is being disentangled from a particular civilization, a particular part of the world, a particular social structure, and especially to the extent to which it is being disentangled from identification with the total membership of any one social group or nation, this development "clears the decks" for a restatement of what it means for the church to be in but not of the world.[71]

Some legal measures, such as the disestablishment of religion in the United States, and some empirical processes, such as social differentiation, can prove helpful for occasioning Christian faithfulness. For example, "a great originality of the great American system is disestablishment. The exercise of religion is constitutionally defended against infringement by governmental authority and the establishment of religion is removed from the purview of the federal government."[72] There are positive elements in disestablishment,

---

70. Martin, *On Secularization*, 20.
71. John Howard Yoder, *Revolutionary Christianity: The 1966 South American Lectures* (Eugene, OR: Cascade, 2011), 11.
72. Yoder, *Priestly Kingdom*, 177.

including participatory democracy and the freedom of religious adherence,[73] the freedom of churches to acquire the "dignity of dissent" in a culture with allowances for public protest,[74] and the freedom of Christians to commend unpopular social stances occasioned by participatory government and made visible by the freedom of the press.[75] The "Christian case for democracy" can be considered "one of the prophetic ministries of a servant people in a world we do not control."[76]

Hauerwas, too, accepts that a secular, thoroughly demythologized state might allow the church to be the church in ways that a sanctified civil religion simply does not. For example, Hauerwas examines practices that would appear to make religion more publicly visible, such as prayer in public schools. While this practice might, at first, seem to be a means of preserving a more robust Christian identity, Hauerwas is more concerned that prayer will become conflated with patriotism and civic duty. In other words, governmental support of public prayer might be the very thing that effaces any distinctive elements of Christian identity.[77] Cornel West's appeal is even more urgent, given his attention to the racialized hate crimes that have been permitted and sanctioned when church and state blend together. To take just one example: for over one hundred years, black worship without white supervision constituted a crime punishable by torture or death in the United States. Clearly, the "doctrine of the separation of church and state is precious to the prophetic black church."[78]

These "pro-secular" sentiments could have been penned by Harvey Cox or leaders of the emerging church[79]—except that they see secularization as happening as a matter of course, whereas for many anti-Constantinians, it is something that must be actively fought for and maintained, and on distinctively Christian grounds. Christians

---

73. Ibid., 151–71.
74. Ibid., 167.
75. Ibid., 98.
76. Ibid., 166.
77. Stanley Hauerwas, "A Christian Critique of Christian America (1986)," in *The Hauerwas Reader*, ed. John Berkman and Michael Cartwright (Durham, NC: Duke University Press, 2001), 459–80.
78. Cornel West, *Prophetic Fragments* (Grand Rapids, MI: Eerdmans, 1988), 23.
79. See the discussion in chapter 1 above.

need to work hard at "secularization" in order to keep their country from using God to justify its own actions.

Post-Secular Anti-Constantinians: Expelling the Myth of Progress

In spite of certain positive features of the secularization of society and American disestablishment of religion, both can have drawbacks. They can easily come to be seen as exhibiting God's providence in the American historical context, and thereby help to reinforce an even more tenacious form of Constantinianism. Thus, even if the Constantinian coupling of church and state is mitigated by their legal separation, this may not address the deepest difficulties of living in an ostensibly Christian culture. Perhaps "this apparent step forward [is] on a more fundamental level a step sideways: i.e. an avoidance of the problem on its deeper level by means of a reformulation on the surface."[80]

As it turns out, the problem that other cultures faced (in binding church and state together) is also present in contemporary America, which may very well exhibit the "newest metamorphosis of the old dragon of religious establishment."[81] We are easily tempted to sacralize democracy over monarchy or even theocracy as the "one righteous social order which glorifies God by its very existence and thus will also be used for God's global purposes."[82] The real work of freeing ourselves from Constantine's trap, then, involves exposing its fundamental flaw. This means finding ways to stop thinking of Christianity as a chaplaincy that helps us make peace with the way the real world really works, and instead, envisioning the faith as prophetically witnessing to the particular politics of Jesus. If it does not make this shift, the church will continue to function as a chaplain, long after it ceases to be the official religion of a nation or empire.

The goal here must be to call the church back to its proper form and purpose, rather than to write off religion as such as inherently

---

80. Yoder, *Priestly Kingdom*, 177.
81. Ibid., 178.
82. Ibid., 159.

functioning to support the status quo. Secularization offers historical-critical tools to see through the myth of a "Christian society" and to raise up the role of informed choice in the decision to become a Christian (or not). As such, we can welcome secularization in general and Enlightenment thinking in particular insofar as they might occasion the revitalization of a believer's church. But we must also remain aware that accounts of secularization can become just as ideological as the religious myths they are meant to expose. As we have seen, the name "Constantine" names the deeply seated assumption that God is directing history through civic authorities; Christians, if they are to be responsible and effective, are encouraged to join this work, even when it overshadows or displaces their prior calling to embody the church's alternative practices. *Secularization can be grafted into this same story, repeating the same logic.* So, for example, immediately after admitting that "the assumption that we live in a Christian world no longer holds," Yoder notes that

> [t]he predominant theological response to this development has been to face the fact without evaluating it. Apart from a few clericalists and monarchists who are still working to restore the past, most thinkers simply make their peace with the new situation [of secularization] as they had with the old, assuming that the total process is of God's doing.[83]

This means that the ostensibly fundamental shift from medieval Christendom to modern secularism may entail only a changing of the emperor's clothes. Underneath, deeper assumptions remain, which are perhaps now better disguised. Just as the medieval church assumed that God was moving history through the expanding empire, now others assume that God is moving history through the secularization of society (and—often more violently—through the spread of democracy throughout the world). In either case, the church has adapted itself "to a new situation that it assumes to be providential, always a half-step behind in the effort to conform, being made by history instead of making history."[84] The intricacy of Constantine's trap is witnessed by

83. Yoder, *Royal Priesthood*, 55.
84. Ibid.

"the fact that it survives even as the situations which brought it forth no longer obtain."[85]

When the contemporary church functions as chaplain—when it not only identifies with extra-ecclesial powers, but also, justifies them, defends them, and ordains them as the necessary vehicle for God's rule of history—then there is little left for the church as church to do, especially if that involves calling political powers into question. In this sense, the progressive secularization of Christendom not only repeats it in various keys, but actually "heightens" the basic error. At least the Holy Roman Empire and medieval Europe gave bishops certain powers over an emperor or prince; they could threaten excommunication, and at times, call leaders to be Christian in more than just name. This moral and legislative autonomy is partly sacrificed already with the neo-Christendom of Protestant state churches and continues thereafter to decline: "Evidently, each further shift, as the church seeks to hang on to a status slipping from her hold, decreases even further the capacity to be concretely critical."[86] A wholly acculturated faith is also a fully accommodated one.

The persistence of Constantine's trap also makes it difficult to imagine what a successful disavowal of Constantine would look like. It seems like all "efforts to renew Christian thought regarding power and society remain the captives of the fallen system they mean to reject."[87] Given this complexity of neo-Christendom, it would also seem that one cannot simply will one's way out of it. If the "free church" model for Christian community is to contribute to a solution, then it must designate more than the lack of coercion, more than the official uncoupling of state–church communions, more even than an endorsement of believer's baptism. Coming to belong to such a community will entail as much imagination, surrender, and confession of sin as knowledge and willpower. One cannot *simply* sign up for it.

Typical dialogue between Anabaptists and Mainliners especially Lutherans, often turns on exactly this point. Anabaptist radicals insist

---

85. Yoder, *Priestly Kingdom*, 141.
86. Ibid., 144.
87. Ibid.

that Jesus's Sermon on the Mount, with its command to love and pray for enemies, to turn the other cheek, to give to all who take from you, and to otherwise "be perfect, as your heavenly Father is perfect" (Matt 5:48), describes a social ethic that is difficult, but inhabitable within the sanctified life and by the grace of God. Lutherans focus not on the thick descriptiveness, but on the performance or function of those very texts. Radical scriptural callings to discipleship also reveal just how sinful even (and especially) the best of us remain, driving each of us back to God's grace. One side implores Christians to become more particularly, faithfully Christian. The other side is quick to confess all the ways that even our most faithful, authentic choices remain bound to fallen powers.

Throughout the rest of this book, I will work back and forth between "Mennonite" or "Anabaptist" anti-Constantinian perspectives (which include Yoder, Hauerwas, and the pacifist Bonhoeffer) and that of theologians of the cross (which includes Luther, Kierkegaard, and a different side of Bonhoeffer). Before proceeding to part 3, I want to highlight some of the clear but complementary differences between those "camps."

Concluding Heuristic Postscript to Part Two

In part 2 of this book, I have described three theological resources for resisting Christendom. While the insights and commendations of Kierkegaard, Bonhoeffer, and critics of Constantinianism overlap considerably, categorizing them as Anabaptist and Lutheran, or as anti-Constantinian and theologies of the cross, can be useful for tracking the ways that they complement one another, and sometimes, reciprocally check and correct one another. Would-be disciples need *both* sets of resources for becoming Christian in Christendom.

Indeed, given their shared critiques of Christendom, the most important difference between them is not between vigilance about sin and execution of discipleship, as some realist versus pacifist debates about sanctioned violence would have it. The Lutherans Kierkegaard and Bonhoeffer do continually underscore sin, but never at the expense of discipleship, as their incisive critiques of "cheap grace" make clear. The more meaningful difference lies in different understandings of the one Christians are called to follow and what that following entails. Do would-be Christians follow Jesus the Palestinian Jew, whose own human life and radical politics provide a pattern for the early church, and then, also for later Christians, as Yoder and Bonhoeffer insist? Or does discipleship also include a beholding, an interminable witness, before one whose suffering and death fully disclose the very power of God, as theologians of the cross such as Kierkegaard and a second "side" of Bonhoeffer also insist? We might name this as a difference between the typically "low Christology" (emphasis on the human Jesus as an example and pattern of discipleship) of anti-Constantinians and the "high Christology" (emphasis on the incarnation and cross of Christ through whom God is fully revealed, which reverses normal associations of God with unilateral power) of theologians of the cross.

Along with the different emphases that various critics of Christendom place on Jesus and the God revealed in him, there follow a number of other differences, if only by way of emphasis:

- Anti-Constantinians resist Christian accommodation by showcasing the *real possibility*, *inhabitability*, and *repeatability* of Christian discipleship by lifting up Jesus's example and that of the early church. Theologians of the cross resist Christian accommodation by underscoring the intellectual *paradox* and the affective *scandal of particularity* of God's full revelation in Bethlehem and Golgotha. The first contests the necessity of accommodation by witnessing to the concrete and practical pattern of authentic discipleship. The second challenges efforts to make Christianity comprehensible and palatable by lifting up its most incomprehensible and off-putting conviction: that God and God's power are fully revealed in a dead Palestinian Jew.

- While both groups witness to a countercultural way of life, the site and posture of this witness differ. Anti-Constantinians who have made the "ecclesial turn" lift up the church as the primary way that God's way of peace and hope is embodied in the world. Theologians of the cross typically witness to the particularity and peculiarity of Christianity through a christological anthropology rather than a radical ecclesiology. That is, they depict the reversal of expectations and desires that single individuals "experience" as they stand before God in Christ on the cross. Different postures correspond: Whereas anti-Constantinians tend to highlight the similarity between Jesus, his disciples, and the visible church but maximize the church's difference from "the world," theologians of the cross blur any stark boundary between Christians and non-Christians (all are revealed as sinful), but maximize the difference between all human expectations, convictions, and desires and their cataclysmic reversals at the foot of the cross.

• Because anti-Constantinians argue for the real possibility of radical, communal discipleship, and thus need to lift up moments in church history when the church acted more faithfully, they often seek to *restore* the church to its early form, even if it is creatively and imaginatively retrieved. They are rightly called "restorationists" in this regard. Theologians of the cross want to perpetually *reform* the church (and individuals therein) rather than to restore it and them; at best, this is done by critiquing Christianity's own temptations toward ideology and idolatry. To take one central example, theologians of the cross seek to reform the way "free grace" easily becomes cheapened within the very Reformation churches that most loudly proclaim it. Corresponding to this difference between restorationist and reforming churches is the position they assume within the church catholic. One acts as a prophetic voice, calling other Christians to be more determinatively Christian. The other acts as leaven from within a church that is called always to be reforming itself.

• Anti-Constantinians lift up the peace ethic or pacifism of Jesus, the early church, and other witnessing communities over and against what they take to be the primary compromise (or most obvious compromise) of Christendoms then and now—namely, the assumption that one can "believe" in Christianity while wholly belonging to an empire or nation-state that kills enemies and criminals, inside and outside its borders. These Christian critics of Christendom are absolutely invaluable for reconsidering all-too-handy distinctions between a Christian's public duties and his or her private religious life. Mainline Protestants and Catholics should not sidestep this critique by appealing to necessary vocations, but extend it by becoming theologians of the cross. God's power—the power at the heart of the universe—is fully revealed in light of Christ's cross as the power of weakness, of servanthood and suffering love. When Christians of all stripes witness to this fact, they call into question not only the compatibility of Christianity and war, but also, a host of other latent or manifest forms of violent unilateral action that our "Christian culture" has mistaken as power.

These are only ideal types, and I list them for their heuristic value. Some figures whom I have introduced in part 2 clearly belong on one or the other "side." Yoder (with his inhabitable ethic) and Kierkegaard (who underscores the cross's necessary scandal) are divergent examples, and yet, their critiques of Christendom also share much, including a retrieval of New Testament Christianity and criticisms of infant baptism. Other figures such as Hauerwas and (especially) Bonhoeffer seem to be securely positioned in one camp, but fit just as neatly into the other when it comes to a different issue. Indeed, because Bonhoeffer distinctively brings together the high Christology and posture of repentance of theologians of the cross with a call to discipleship and a peace ethic patterned after Jesus and the Sermon on the Mount, which he shares with anti-Constantinians, his life and writings are uniquely positioned to bring various critics of Christendom together. I *divide* these resources here only to clearly define what I want to employ *together*. We turn now to part 3, drawing on both "Lutheran" and "Radical" sources to think through particular Christian capitulations to the market, politics, war, and religion.

PART III

CONTOURS

6

ECONOMY: Free Grace in a Culture of Cheap

In this chapter, we turn to the first of several concrete issues related to America's new Christendom and the task of becoming Christian within it. In particular, we will explore the problem and possibility of realizing and valuing the free grace of God in a culture where almost anything and everything can be bought and sold.

The market has, in many ways, become America's God. We decide what work to do, where to live, whether to marry, get a divorce, have children, or retire after consulting market forecasters. Religion is affected as well, as we "pick and choose religious moments as our schedules and checkbooks allow."[1] The processes of commodification, commercialization, and monetization have crept into all areas of our lives. Public goods and services (parks, education, sidewalks, police protection, access to clean water, etc.) used to be shared and free for the user, and public obligations (waiting in line at the airport, jury duty, going to jail if you break a law) used to be (more) equitable,

---

1. Norman Wirzba, *The Paradise of God: Renewing Religion in an Ecological Age* (Oxford: Oxford University Press, 2003), 90.

whether you had money or not. Now, almost everything can be bought and sold. Those who can purchase private education, neighborhood security, or fast passes through airports or gridlocked highways do so, leaving others stuck with shoddier goods and a good deal of resentment.

While this may not seem like a theological issue, this chapter will argue that both the problem and answer depend on theology—on how we think about God and creation and salvation, God's gifts to us, or don't. When Christians are able to understand grace and life as priceless gifts, they may be able to resist the encroachment of the market and temptations to worship it. They might also find themselves called to countercultural (counter-consumerist) discipleship, given that an incalculable gift calls forth an immeasurable response, and because "authentic expressions of peace, gratitude, and joy . . . tend to be found in dispositions and acts that define themselves in opposition to conventional economic goals."[2] Alternatively, American Christians might mistake grace for something they deserve, either because they have earned it or (more commonly today) by virtue of being born in a prosperous country with a number of freedoms and advantages—grace being among them. The gifts of grace and of creation itself can quickly become privileges, while American Christianity becomes the invisible dispenser of such benefits.

I will try to show that one predominant stronghold of such acculturated and accommodated Christianity arises with subtle slippage from Martin Luther's doctrine of "free grace" (read: immeasurable, priceless grace) to what Bonhoeffer calls "cheap grace"—grace as latitude and license, grace as privilege, grace as having the carefully calculated value of absolutely nothing. The trick will be to value grace, to appreciate it with gratitude and respond to it in discipleship, without that valuation quantifying, commodifying, and so, cheapening it. In what follows, I want to read the Christian "doctrine" of grace differently than the standard reception, showing that an understanding of free grace shared by Luther, Kierkegaard, and

---

2. Ibid., 158.

Bonhoeffer might help resist the economization and desacralization of creation, and so also the cultural entrapments of Christendom.[3] Before revisiting sixteenth-century Saxony, nineteenth-century Copenhagen, and early-twentieth-century Germany, I turn to appraise the economic-cultural milieu of twenty-first-century North America.

Cheapening Gifts and Giftedness

In his book, *What Money Can't Buy: The Moral Limits of Markets*, American political philosopher Michael Sandel points to hundreds of cases where encroachments of "the market" on goods that used to be priceless corrode civic values and cohesion in the United States. Some of the market's expansions are irksome but perhaps morally inconsequential: the trend toward monetizing gifts through those once-tacky gift cards, the scalping of campsite tickets for Yosemite National Park, or the corporate renaming of professional baseball parks. Others are ethically alarming: the sale of the right to immigrate, cash to female drug addicts if they undergo sterilization, or the rise of the viatical industry, through which a terminally ill person sells his or her life insurance to a third party who then makes money when the terminal person dies—the sooner the death, the bigger the profit.[4] One of Sandel's primary objections to the expansion of market forces into the civic realm is that putting a price on public goods or "incentivizing" consumers to choose the right thing to do (lose weight, stop smoking, give blood, care about the environment) does not simply add external motivations to internal ones, but actually corrodes the latter. We no longer do what is good because it is good or right or helpful to those in

---

3. I am not interested in saving Luther or Lutherans from their complicity in the desacralization of God's world or the deification of the present order—including all that which is increasingly ordered by the Invisible Hand of the Market. It turns out that, for all the ways in which Luther might be retrieved and reconceived as helping us become true followers of a crucified Christ within Christendom, his theology also helped create the very conditions of Christendom that now confront us. This is especially true of desacralization by the expansion of the market. See Brad S. Gregory, *The Unintended Reformation: How a Religious Revolution Secularized Society* (Cambridge, MA: Harvard University Press, 2012), 235–97.

4. Michael J. Sandel, *What Money Can't Buy: The Moral Limits of Markets* (New York: Farrar, Straus & Giroux, 2012), 35–37, 62–65, 136–49.

need. We do it because we are paid. And when those payments cease to be worth our effort, we stop doing it altogether.[5]

While shared goods presently sell off at surprising rates, Sandel's concerns are not new. Some twenty years ago, Larry Rasmussen foresaw how the market beguiles us into believing that obligation to others is fulfilled through calculated self-interest.[6] Some two centuries before that, Adam Smith, the very person who first surmised that purely self-serving desires could lead to social benefits,[7] also insisted that capitalism could help humans flourish only so long as nonmarket civic virtues restricted the domain and curbed the temperament of economic exchange.[8] If Sandel and Rasmussen are right, that time is passing or has passed. According to Wendell Berry, "a state of virtually total economy" has been imposed upon us, "in which it is the destiny of every creature (humans not excepted) to have a price and to be sold."[9]

A similar trend hits closer to home for those of us involved in teaching and learning. In her book, *Not for Profit: Why Democracy Needs the Humanities*, Martha Nussbaum documents the particular corrosion that worldwide pursuits of profitability have on humanistic education and its promise to educate for citizenship and democracy.[10] When education becomes primarily for economic growth, we lose the dispositions that are at the center of humanistic education and that are necessary for human flourishing.[11]

According to Sandel, Rasmussen, and Nussbaum, the expanding encroachment of the market cheapens our ability to give gifts to one

---

5. Ibid., 84–91.
6. Larry Rasmussen, *Moral Fragments and Moral Community: A Proposal for Church and Society* (Minneapolis: Augsburg Fortress Press, 1993), 61–76.
7. Adam Smith describes the theory that competition directs self-interest toward socially desirable ends in *The Wealth of Nations* (New York: Modern Library, 1937), Book I, Chapter 7.
8. Adam Smith, *The Theory of Moral Sentiments* (Oxford: Clarendon, 1976), as discussed in Rasmussen, *Moral Fragments*, 41–45.
9. Wendell Berry, *Life Is a Miracle: An Essay Against Modern Superstition* (New York: Counterpoint, 2000), 132. According to Johann Baptist Metz, "the permeation of the whole of life by exchange and competition" necessitates that first-world Christians need to struggle to resist their own "ingrained ideals of always having more." Metz, *The Emergent Church: The Future of Christianity in a Postbourgeois World*, trans. Peter Mann (New York: Crossroad, 1981), 12.
10. Martha Nussbaum, *Not for Profit: Why Democracy Needs the Humanities* (Princeton, NJ: Princeton University Press, 2010).
11. I have tried to address this and related questions in my "Called to the Unbidden: Saving Vocation from the Market," *The Cresset* (Michaelmas 2012): 6–17.

another, whether that be through our participation in civic life, in democracy, or by ethical action in general. But there is more. The economization or marketization of nearly every sector of life also cheapens our sense of *giftedness*—what makes human individuals peculiar, special, and capable of offering such gifts in the first place. In "The Case Against Perfection," Sandel inquires into Americans' shared ill ease with breakthroughs in genetic engineering (think "designer babies") and performance-enhancing drugs ("doping"). The two most common explanations revolve around issues of autonomy and fairness. Yet, autonomy and fairness turn out for Sandel to be *almost the exact opposite* of why he thinks we are—or should be—concerned with the drive to engineer the perfect person. For Sandel, the problem with doping and biotechnology and even helicopter parenting is not the loss of agency, but the drive toward *hyperagency*; we are becoming too autonomous, too responsible for our own fates, and so, are losing our "openness to the unbidden."[12] We are losing our ability to mourn tragedy and honor good luck, in short, our appreciation for life's giftedness. It is at this point that Sandel almost gets theological, as his allusion to "gift" suggests. Asking, "What would be lost if biotechnology dissolved our sense of giftedness?" Sandel responds:

> From a religious standpoint the answer is clear: To believe that our talents and powers are wholly our own doing is to misunderstand our place in creation, to confuse our role with God's. Religion is not the only source of reasons to care about giftedness, however. The moral stakes can also be described in secular terms. If bioengineering made the myth of the "self-made man" come true, it would be difficult to view our talents as gifts for which we are indebted, rather than as achievements for which we are responsible.[13]

Even the nonreligious should view their talents as gifts for which they are grateful and responsive, even if they remain agnostic about any Giver of those gifts and the Recipient of their thanksgiving.

---

12. Michael J. Sandel, "The Case Against Perfection," *The Atlantic Monthly*, 293.3 (April 2004): 51–62, accessed August 10, 2015, http://www.theatlantic.com/magazine/archive/2004/04/the-case-against-perfection/302927/.

13. Ibid.

Leaving theological overtones aside for the moment, Sandel critiques what others have called our meritocratic society—the prevailing assumption that we should form culture and a political economy in such a way that each person gets recognized and compensated according to her or his "output"—no more and no less. Meritocracies seem fairer and more egalitarian than the traditionalist cultures they replace, where a queen or man of genteel status, for example, was owed honor simply by nature of her or his standing at birth. If Sandel is right, however, meritocracies slowly corrode capabilities to mourn the simple bad luck of tragedy, to experience awe over a sense of unbidden giftedness, or to be radically grateful for all that we did not and cannot earn. Others critics suggest that meritocratic cultures necessarily develop economies that maximize opportunities for the talented at the expense of devaluing and exploiting those seemingly stuck in the places the upwardly mobile so readily abandon.[14] Political economies that are devoted to maximizing opportunities and democratizing access to those opportunities can help level unjust privilege, but they almost always do so by purchasing deracinated ways of life at the expense of farmers, craftsmen, family businesses, and fidelity to extended families and home communities—not to mention the well-being of the land and its nonhuman creatures.[15]

Here, the fairness argument returns, but now the inequity is between the whole system that promotes access to "opportunities" and the people and places that suffer from it. Meritocracies and the free market economies that sustain them often stockpile national wealth at the cost of its health. They free many for mobility by indenturing others (human and nonhuman) to increasingly meaningless, piecemeal, and unsustainable work.

But gifts, giftedness, gratitude, and being gracious are not

14. Jeremy Beer, "Wendell Berry and the Traditionalist Critique of Meritocracy," in *Wendell Berry: Life and Work*, ed. Jason Peters (Lexington, KY: University of Kentucky Press, 2007), 212–29.
15. Readers of Wendell Berry will see his imprint here. Newcomers to his work might begin with his first classic, *The Unsettling of America: Culture and Agriculture* (San Francisco: Sierra Club, 1977), or with the essay collections, *What Are People For?* (New York: North Point/Farrar, Straus & Giroux, 1990), and *Sex, Economy, Freedom and Community: Eight Essays* (New York: Pantheon, 1993).

cheapened by virtue of any and every economy. *Particular* trends in *particular* economic systems cheapen the gifts and tasks of would-be Christians. We have begun to examine the way gifts and giftedness (including the gift of creation, grace, and being graced) might be overlooked in contemporary American culture. We now turn to how they might be retrieved but thoroughly cheapened.

Gnostic, Privileged, "Christian" Consumers

In the United States, consumer spending counts for about 70 percent of the nation's gross domestic product. Mainstream media increasingly call us "consumers" rather than "citizens," thereby subtly reifying our primary public identities as those who buy. Many, if not most, implicitly accept that our duty as consumers is to find the best deal possible, which means buying cheaply made goods cheaper and cheaper, at the cost of the quality of those products, our care of them, living wages, and a sustainable economy.

It was not until the 1960s that buying goods "on discount," and then, erecting entire "discount stores" began to dominate the general merchandise sector. Before then, independent, freestanding retailers who knew their customers and employed knowledgeable salespersons formed the center of economic and social life, together with the craftsmen and craftswomen who supplied those goods. With the rise of discounting, however, the benefits and wages of employees—and the services they offer to those of us shopping—were cut back to sell products more cheaply. The discounting formula soon became a mantra for business: "Sell it cheap, buy it cheaper, and convince consumers that low price trumps all." We are now willing to trade quality for cost under the guise of "value."[16]

One need not be Marxist to see how easily such developments (not *into* a free market economy, but *within* it) lead to many forms of alienation. The gap between rich and poor is immense and widening. In 2008, 80 percent of income went to the top 1 percent of earners.[17]

---

16. Ellen Ruppel Shell, *Cheap: The High Cost of Discount Culture* (New York: Penguin, 2009), 39, 42, 51.
17. Ibid., 49.

In 2012, the average CEO made 380 times the salary of his own average employee.[18] Centralized capital through the rise of multinational corporations has led to the de-skilling of labor, making workers (who are now even referred to as "human capital") less valuable and more replaceable. This leads to loss of job security and a disinvestment of workers from the means and materials of their work—not to mention its meaningfulness. It also unglues those relationships otherwise cemented between buyer and seller, employer and employee, and producer and consumer.[19] Many of us, even in typically white-collar professions, increasingly feel like moveable parts.

The endless quest for cheaper goods also ineluctably creates the endless quest for cheaper labor, sending many United States manufacturing jobs to "right to work" states or, more commonly, overseas. This curtails the participation in and power of labor unions to improve the conditions of employees in the United States, given the constant threat that, if our workers refuse to work under worse conditions and for less, companies can always find a younger, more disempowered and deregulated labor force to do it. Our decision to tightly control the movement of labor through immigration policy while deregulating the movement of capital in our so-called global economy also has the effect of keeping consumers less and less informed about who produced the goods they consume and under what conditions. Very few of us now make anything that we wear, build anything that we live in, grow anything that we eat, or fix anything we use—or know by name and character the people who do. (The local food movement is the most important counterexample, and the importance of it should not be underestimated.[20]) Ignorance leads to abuse, given the fact that, as Wendell Berry notes, it is easy to abuse that which one does not love, and fail to love that which one cannot know.[21]

---

18. See Pat Garofalo, "Average Fortune 500 CEO Now Paid 380 Times as Much as the Average Worker," accessed 10 August 2015, http://thinkprogress.org/economy/2012/04/19/467516/ceo-pay-gap-2011/.

19. Shell, *Cheap*, 139–41; Wendell Berry, "Conservation Is Good Work," in *Sex, Economy, Freedom and Community*, 27–43; Berry, "The Pleasures of Eating," in *What Are People For?*, 145–52.

20. Michael Pollan, *The Omnivore's Dilemma* (London: Penguin, 2006), 239–60.

Finally, the quick birth and easy death of replaceable products, many of which are built with planned obsolescence, that is, built *in order to be replaced,* rather than maintained and fixed, leads us to become "disburdened of involvement," to use Matthew Crawford's term.[22] We don't expect or even want to have enduring relationships with material goods any more than with particular partnerships. In fact, our high discount culture has been so successful that many of us do not even think we deserve quality.[23]

This admittedly brief sketch of the rise of our culture of cheap traces how we have moved not only from citizen to consumer, but also, to a particular kind of consumer/discarder—one who wants things as cheaply as possible and who is willing to promptly replace them. It also shows that the consumer gets those cheap goods so cheaply largely by remaining removed—geographically, emotionally, and in terms of awareness—from the plights of those who produce them. Finally, it suggests that as prices decline, so do wages and benefits, as well as the value we place on the manufactured goods and the natural resources and "human capital" from which they came.

Where does Christianity come in? It is common within Christian critiques of consumerism to hear the charge that the world is too materialistic, or the plea that people should love the Creator rather than the stuff of creation. Given the above analysis, however, I think it is misleading to suggest that North Americans and other first-world shoppers are "materialistic" or "too attached" to material things. Given how often we return what we have purchased, and how quickly we replace those we keep, it would seem that we are much more addicted to shopping—to looking for the *next* new thing—than we are addicted to the things themselves. If we value anything too highly, it is "the

---

21. Berry, *Life Is a Miracle,* 129–42.
22. Matthew B. Crawford, "Shop Class as Soulcraft," *The New Atlantis* 13 (Summer 2006): 7–24, as cited in Shell, *Cheap,* 143.
23. Shell, *Cheap,* 144. Shell puts the matter like this: "Although almost everyone seeks bargains, most of us make the tacit and often unconscious tradeoff of quality for price: Regardless of what the tag or brand claims, we perceive things bought on sale or at a discount as less desirable or efficacious or durable than things for which we paid full price. The less we pay for something, the less we value it and the less likely we are to take care of it, with the result that cheaper things—even if well made—seem to wear out and break more quickly" (71).

deal"—not the object of the deal.[24] Consumers seem *not nearly attached enough* to the materiality of God's good creation[25]—they are *not nearly materialist enough.*[26] Indeed, Christianity in America has become a largely spiritualized faith where the faithful too readily abandon care for the earth and its "material goods" for the promise of some heaven light years away. Such a spiritualization of the Christian faith only exacerbates our proclivities to buy and discard, while providing a convenient cover of being spiritual, not materialistic. If only we were *more* concerned with the materials of creation! If only we imagined salvation as the restored health (*salus*) *of* the earth, rather than salvation *from* it.[27]

American Christians thus reinforce and defend a neo-gnostic form of Christendom. Like the old Christian heresy of Gnosticism, Christians ostensibly value "spirit" or the afterlife by devaluing the body and this material world. By pitting spirit against flesh, glorifying the first and debasing the second, Christians inadvertently exacerbate the problems of consumerism (what they wrongly call materialism) in the very effort to overcome it. The fetishizing of price and of cheap also leads to the desacralization of the created world. Indeed, to make something sellable it *must* be disenchanted.[28]

I am suggesting that an unnamed but pernicious form of Gnosticism, where materiality is seen as bad and spirituality as good, has become

---

24. Ibid., 118–19, 123.

25. William T. Cavanaugh, *Being Consumed: Economics and Christian Desire* (Grand Rapids, MI: Eerdmans, 2008), 34–35; Vincent J. Miller, *Consuming Religion: Christian Faith and Practice in a Consumer Culture* (New York: Continuum, 2004), 107–45.

26. This might be understood in a Marxist or critical theory sense. Silas Morgan summarizes Marx's critique of religion as "not materialist enough to be politically useful," which in turn, is "good for business." "Ideology and Theology in the Postsecular 'Christendom,'" unpublished paper delivered at the Midwest American Academy of Religion conference (Northern Ohio University, April 5, 2014), 5.

27. Wendell Berry, "Christianity and the Survival of Creation," *CrossCurrents* 43.2 (Summer 1993): 149–64; see also Wirzba, *The Paradise of God*, 48, 83, 129; and Jason Peters, "Wendell Berry's Vindication of the Flesh," *Christianity and Literature* 56.2 (Winter 2007): 317–32.

28. As Harvey Cox points out, in the "mass of the Market," things that have been held sacred—an enchanted forest, holy relic, family heirloom, one's own personhood under the guise of expendable "labor"—get transmuted into appraisable and interchangeable items for sale. Cox, "The Market as God," *The Atlantic* 1999, issue 3, accessed August 10, 2015, http://www.theatlantic.com/magazine/archive/1999/03/the-market-as-god/306397. Compare Metz's description (in *The Emergent Church*, 7–8) of money as the "quasi-sacrament of solidarity and sympathy."

one key characteristic of the overarching civil religion, or "bourgeois religion,"[29] of Western industrial economies. Such a devaluing of materiality ironically spawns and spurs the rabid material*ism* from which we suffer, just as the Gnostics of earlier centuries expressed their disdain for the world hedonistically by indulging their appetites for food, wine, and sex just as readily as they ascetically denied themselves those things. Our situation might be the more dangerous. The Christian consumer today finds herself in a worldwide marketplace. Whereas the scope of earlier Christendoms was limited by an awareness of those outside the fold—other empires or nation-states that did not call themselves Christian—today's Christians so easily confuse the catholicity of their faith with the seemingly endless expansion of international markets.[30] Increasingly evangelical churchgoers disdain the ostensible exclusivism and elitism of denominations and established liturgical forms, seemingly unaware that their particular conversion scripts, worship events, and fellowship opportunities are patterned after motivational speeches, rock concerts, and Starbucks.[31] The church is tempted to collaborate with such powers because they seem so universal. Certainly, the market's formative power is great. Yet, the market excludes plenty of people (and other creatures) on its own—expendable labor, welfare moms, unproductive citizens, those too poor even to be debtors, precious topsoil under the disparaging term "dirt," and other victims of its collateral damage.

As we turn back 500 years from twenty-first-century America to Reformation Germany, we notice a number of theological staples that, if retrieved and reinvigorated, might help resist this trend toward the cheapening of gifts and giftedness. I will flesh out some of these "Lutheran" resources for resisting the cheapening of God's good gifts of creation and salvation. But one Lutheran theme—perhaps *the*

---

29. Metz, *The Emergent Church*, 12, 27, 45–65.
30. Cavanaugh, *Being Consumed*, 59–88.
31. Stewart M. Hoover, "The Cross at Willow Creek: Seeker Religion and the Contemporary Marketplace," in *Religion and Popular Culture in America*, ed. Bruce David Forbes and Jeffrey H. Mahan (Berkeley, CA: University of California Press, 2005), 139–53.

principal Lutheran theme—seems to pull in the opposite direction. Didn't Luther make grace free? Doesn't that devalue it insofar as God's favor and Christian salvation cost exactly nothing? When Kierkegaard and Bonhoeffer subsequently attack Christendom for dispensing grace on the cheap, are they not targeting the very bull's-eye of the Reformation? Certainly, Lutheran understandings of justification by God's free grace through faith and apart from all human work help clear the way for those who want to make discipleship as cost-effective as possible. But, as I will try to show, such developments entail a misunderstanding and misuse of Luther's central proclamation and the Lutheran tradition, not their inevitable product. By my account, Luther, Kierkegaard, and Bonhoeffer foresaw and tried to forestall Christendom's dependence on cheap grace—even if they could not see its connection to cheap labor and cheap oil in America's neo-Christendom.

Economies of Salvation

So far, I have pointed to some instances of the commercialization of society that led to the protraction and persistence of acculturated and accommodated Christianity. I want now to underscore the difference between economic accountings and God's unmerited grace. For Luther, that difference is not primarily between the profane and the sacred, or between the "material" world and the "spiritual" world. Luther's orthodox understanding of Incarnation and the real presence of Jesus's body made available in the Lord's Supper quickly deconstruct such hierarchies. Nor is the difference between that which requires human cost and that which is free in terms of costing or requiring nothing. Rather, God's grace exceeds economic accountings altogether; it is "free" not because it costs zero cents, but because ledgers of costs beside benefits, of human efforts beside God's help, cannot help but distort the reality of that which they are meant to appraise. God's grace becomes properly valued only when all closed economies and systems of exchange fail to appraise that value. At the same time, the removal of grace from accounting sheets allows one to see that it really is valuable—and even costly. Bonhoeffer insists that it will cost us our very lives, as it cost the life of Jesus.

Against the Commodification of Grace

On October 31, 1517, Luther famously offered for debate ninety-five pithy protests against the sale of plenary indulgences, publicly posting the theses (at least by legend) to the door of Wittenberg's Castle Church. The history of offering indulgences—what my Lutheran confirmation class referred to as "get out of jail free cards"—goes back to the Crusades. Christian soldiers marching into battle were extended an indulgence, literally a "leniency" or "generosity," that would free them from making satisfaction for sins incurred in battle. Later, the leniency was broadened to include those who supported the so-called Holy War with money and prayer. In the early sixteenth century, penances became part of a capital campaign to fund the restoration of St. Peter's Basilica in Rome, as well as to pay for the purchase of a second archbishop title by the already appointed Archbishop Albrecht.[32] By this time, indulgences were extracted from the entire process of the sacrament of penance. (Earlier, the buyer of an indulgence still had to be truly penitent and confess his or her sin.) Also, one could now buy them to offset not only penance owed on earth, but that which would continue in purgatory. What is more, the indulgence was made transferable—you could use it for yourself or apply it to the loved one of your designation. Finally, sellers in the sixteenth century now offered an exceptional value as the indulgences hawked cheaply were "plenary"—able to forgive the *entire* debt of the soul.

Having become purchasable, extractable, transferable, and a damn good deal, the indulgences that the Dominican monk Johannes Tetzel sold quickly became a hot commodity, hardly requiring his superior salesmanship, complete with intimidation and fear-mongering. In retrospect, it is easy for us to assume that, if indulgences trafficked in

---

32. Martin Marty, *Martin Luther* (New York: Penguin, 2004), 29–35.

crude commerce, objections to them were by way of spiritual ideals; but this, of course, would only recapitulate the gnostic Christendom explored above. While the reform movement as a whole does tend to spiritualize grace and other gifts from God, Luther himself was a practical "materialist" in many ways.

Indeed, a good many of Luther's ninety-five theological theses instruct us on what to do with our money and other material gifts. Thesis 43 speaks of wise investments: "Christians are to be taught that he who gives to the poor or lends to the needy does a better deed than he who buys indulgences." Thesis 46 speaks against profligacy: "Christians are taught that, unless they have more than they need, they must reserve enough for their family needs and by no means squander it on indulgences." Other theses exemplify what we now call behavioral economics and the psychology of consumer behavior. They probe into the often-hidden motives for why we buy and sell what we do, and into the qualitative evaluations masked by quantitative price. Thesis 40 reads: "A Christian who is truly contrite seeks and loves to pay penalties for his sins; the bounty of indulgences, however, relaxes penalties and causes men to hate them—at least it furnishes occasion for hating them." In Thesis 82, Luther interrogates why the pope "does not empty purgatory for the sake of holy love and the dire need of the souls that are there if he redeems an infinite number of souls for the sake of miserable money with which to build a church." Finally, a number of the protests boil down to straightforward economic justice, for example Thesis 86: "Why does not the pope, whose wealth is today greater than the wealth of the richest Crassus, build this one basilica of St. Peter with his own money rather than with the money of poor believers?"[33]

Luther's objections cannot be called "economic" in any reductionist sense of the term. He is concerned with money as it crisscrosses other endowments, costs, and values within all of creation (God's Great Economy), both "spiritual" and "material." Luther even plays upon the

---

33. Martin Luther, "The Ninety-Five Theses (1517)," in *Martin Luther's Basic Theological Writings*, ed. Timothy F. Lull, 2nd ed. (Minneapolis: Fortress Press, 2005), 40–46.

inextricable intersections of materiality and spirituality to name the present abuses. Theses 65 and 66, for example, read:

> Therefore the treasures of the gospel are nets with which one formerly fished for men of wealth.

> The treasures of indulgences are nets with which one now fishes for the wealth of men.

The charge is not that the sacred has been profaned but that the church currently functions as ideology. It protects the interests of the dominant classes by obfuscating the relation that commoners should have to their labor, the land, the church, and God.

Beyond Balance Sheets of Grace and Work

Many assume that Luther critiqued the institutional church for demanding too much of its parishioners, for confusing simple faith and trust with arduous "works righteousness." While this side of the critique is true, Luther frames these early protests by showing how the penitential system in general and the commodification of indulgences in particular curtail not only God's grace, but also, human striving; they make *both* into quantifiable goods that can be exchanged, transferred, or withdrawn. The first thesis announces, "when our Lord and Master Jesus Christ said, 'Repent' [Matt 4:17, translated in the vulgate as 'do penance'], he willed *the entire life of believers* to be one of repentance" (my emphasis). Uncoupling Christ's command from a codified system of exchange demands more "work" of repentance—not less. In the following two theses, Luther notes that Christ's call to repentance cannot be contained within "the sacrament of penance, that is, confession and satisfaction, as administered by the clergy," but neither can it be contained within the private contrition of individuals or "solely inner repentance," which Luther calls "worthless unless it produces various outward mortifications of the flesh." Luther thus calls for "more" work of repentance, work that spans a person's life and moves freely from inward conviction to outward practice and back again. At an even deeper level, he critiques any closed economy of salvation that presumes to balance countable human works against a treasury of God's graces.[34] Such spiritual book-keeping errs not in valuing human efforts or God's grace too highly or too little, but in the very assumption that they can be measured. Such accountings offer false security—the security of assumed objectivity, of faith as eternal life insurance, of value quantitatively calculated.

The final two theses say as much: "Christians should be exhorted to be diligent in following Christ, their head, *through* penalties, death, and hell; [a]nd thus be confident of entering into heaven through many tribulations *rather than through the false security of peace*."[35] Luther here names the problem that ensues when, as Marx might say, the use-value of discipleship is undercut entirely by its exchange-value. When an indulgence voucher displaces necessary penance and purgation, the monetary cost of the indulgence inevitably eclipses the intrinsic value of repentance and grace. This cheapens salvation and incites false confidence in what is essentially an abstraction. Only by refusing to commodify the painful work of discipleship are Christians able to faithfully "count on" God's promise of new life.

Haggling Heaven

Just as one can read the ninety-five Theses in economic terms, broadly construed, so too can one understand the socio-economic consequences of the Lutheran Reformation as a whole. Luther reacts indignantly to the selling of indulgences, of private Masses, and of bishoprics, as well as to Christian participation in usury—all of which turn the church into a "profit-making business."[36] Luther's ostensibly "spiritual" reforms gained traction at a time when 50 to 65 percent of

---

34. Grace in medieval theology connoted a God-given force, given in the sacraments, that transforms humans so that they can love properly; by the sixteenth century, such grace (otherwise singular) became quantifiable, as one became able to receive more or less *graces* from the church, just as one received an assortment of "sacramentals" (prayers, blessings, making pilgrimages, receiving ashes, crossing oneself, etc.). See Samuel Torvend, *Luther and the Hungry Poor: Gathered Fragments* (Minneapolis: Fortress Press, 2008), 20–21, 142n23.

35. Luther, "Ninety-Five Theses," 46 (theses 94–95), my emphasis.

36. Martin Luther, as cited by Torvend, *Luther and the Hungry Poor*, 21, 68.

the German population lived on the edge of subsistence, but also, when an economic system was emerging whereby people born without land or lineage could prosper by hard work and smart business practices. This rising mercantile economy created opportunities for many, but also, eroded subsistence farming and led to widespread food insecurity.[37] At a more systemic level, Luther critiques late medieval theologians such as Ockham and Biel for placing God's role in justification within a readymade system (or "closed economy"), which makes human and divine work commensurable and exchangeable, and thus, domesticates God's free grace.[38] That *theological* economy remains inextricable from the *material* exchange of gifts, rewards, money, property, and status. For example, according to the social benefaction system that arose hand in hand with late medieval theology, giving to the hungry poor earned a person favor from God and the church. The logic is patterned after an ancient patronage system whereby "God the 'patron' would favor with 'benefits' those who were capable of offering a 'gift.'"[39] Material "gifts" of money or food earned one spiritual reward, and the affluent therefore could acquire acceptability before God in ways that the poor, bound only to receive, could not.

The benefaction system in Luther's day meant that giving material gifts became the means toward receiving spiritual benefits, motivated by the belief that—like Adam Smith's Invisible Hand—acting from such self-interest would inadvertently help the neighbor, since giving to the poor was necessary for reaping the graces of God. Luther turns all of this on its head. For him, God's favor or grace precedes and occasions any and all sacrifice and service, whether "spiritual" (fervent

---

37. Torvend, *Luther and the Hungry Poor*, 17, 41, 110.
38. William C. Placher, *The Domestication of Transcendence: How Modern Thinking about God Went Wrong* (Louisville: Westminster John Knox, 1996), 38–39.
39. Torvend, *Luther and the Hungry Poor*, 134. Luther's critique of this benefaction system is not far from those critiques of religion as ideology, as justifying the position of the favored, that one finds in Freud, Nietzsche, or Marx. See, for example, Karl Marx, "The Social Principles of Christianity," in *Marx on Religion*, ed., John Raines (Philadelphia: Temple University Press, 2002), 185–86, as cited in Morgan, "Ideology and Theology in the Postsecular 'Christendom,'" 6. Guillermo Hansen demonstrates that Luther's attack upon church practices (indulgences), scholasticism (works righteousness), and the emerging capitalist practices are different expressions of the same critique. Hansen, "Money, Religion and Tyranny: God and the Demonic in Luther's Antifragile Theology," *Journal of Lutheran Ethics*, January 2014, para 27, accessed August 10, 2015, http://elca.org/JLE/Articles/35#_ednref42.

prayer, pilgrimage, etc.) or "material" (donations of time or money). Grace itself, God's free gift, becomes the very context, or overarching economy, that governs every other gift. Our human gift-giving as a *means* toward receiving God's gift/reward thus gets recontextualized, interrupted, and reversed. Every gift we give was already received; we "should" now give only from a sense of gratitude, out of abundance, rather than to get the reward we think we need.

But a perennial problem returns, marked by the scare quotes in my last sentence. Once God's gift of grace is extracted from the spiritual/material closed economy—this late medieval theological system and social benefaction arrangement that so cost-effectively motivated Christians to share—what will now provoke Christians to pass on gifts? Some sort of pure, selfless, spontaneous good will? Again: if the "reward" is given originally by grace through faith, why strive toward economic justice and forms of radical hospitality?[40] The typical Lutheran response to such interrogation is, first, to admit that grace costs absolutely nothing, that there is nothing one does to *earn* it and nothing one *must* do after one has received it. Second, Lutherans typically turn at this point from an "imperative" ethic (proposing what one should do) to an "indicative" ethic; they thickly describe all that one does and can do once the quest for reward by benefaction, fueled by enlightened self-interest, has been upended.[41] Luther's frequent metaphor of a good tree producing good fruit (from Matt 7:17) means to honor the works of love that flow from grace while underscoring both the naturalness and the irreversibility of that process. But still, can't we already hear those predictable nagging questions about moral loopholes and the lack of consequences for those who take them? If I'm

40. By radical hospitality, I mean here something different than giving extravagantly, especially when those gifts solidify the distinction between host and guest, patron and beneficiary, those who freely give and others who depend on their generosities. As anthropologists have shown, even (or especially) profligate gift-giving functions to enact and display the distinction between those who are honored by their gift-giving, and so, benefit the most, and those who, in receiving, get left without honor and social standing. The foundational text is Marcel Mauss's 1950 study, *The Gift: The Form and Reason for Exchange in Archaic Societies*, trans. W. D. Halls (New York: W. W. Norton, 1990).

41. See, for example, Carter H. Lindberg, *Beyond Charity: Reformation Initiatives for the Poor* (Minneapolis: Augsburg Fortress Press, 1993), 97, as cited in Torvend, *Luther and the Hungry Poor*, 35, 123.

already saved, can't I simply rest comfortably—even complacently—in that soft bed of grace?

There are two opposing dangers in answering these charges, which reinforce one another and obscure third options. On the one hand, it is tempting to say that, yes, the Christian *must* give freely, perhaps threatening consequences for those who do not. Luther assumed that such law-language would make the promises and gifts of God through Christ contingent on human obedience. It would also lead to resentment, exchanging the joy of Christian service with begrudging compulsory action. In our language: Luther feared it would reinscribe Jesus in another closed economy so that grace becomes an investment in our capabilities, which we then are indebted to pay back.

On the other hand, faced with the problem of moral loopholes and opportunistic complacency, of free grace seemingly cheapened, it is tempting to proclaim all the more loudly that grace is unearned, undeserved, and unconditional. The most passionate defenders of "pure gift" fall into this camp. They distinguish God's gift from every other. Whereas some sort of reciprocity and circulation, even by way of giving thanks, follows every other gift, in the case of grace, the gift is pure. God is pure Giver; a person can only receive. Whereas the first fix is to re-economize grace, the second is to incessantly de-contextualize or de-economize it. Critics will say that this only further cheapens grace, despite—or rather, because—proponents continually remove it from frameworks of assessment and exchange. For them, absolute categorical distinctions between Christ as gift and our everyday giving and receiving hypostasize "grace" and turn it into an abstraction.[42] Beyond all measure, grace also remains beyond all comprehension, and sometimes then, beyond our consideration and concern. The first danger puts grace to work, as Max Weber famously describes in *The Protestant Ethic and the Spirit of Capitalism*.[43] But the

---

42. See here Christina Grenholm, "Grace, Transcendence, and Patience: A Response to Monica Melanchthon," in *The Gift of Grace: The Future of Lutheran Theology*, ed. Niels Henrik Gregersen et al. (Minneapolis: Fortress Press, 2005), 60–66; and Bo Holm, "Luther's Theology of the Gift," in *The Gift of Grace*, 78–86.

43. Max Weber, *The Protestant Ethic and the Spirit of Capitalism*, trans. Talcott Parsons (New York:

second often individualizes and spiritualizes it, removing it from the social concerns of politics and the marketplace and thereby sanctioning the privileged.[44] Christendom's Christians can sell out in either way.

I think it is clear that reactions against the charge of cheap grace can easily reproduce the problem. One must find the middle ground between monetizing grace and abandoning economic justice altogether.[45] Kierkegaard and Bonhoeffer (but Luther too)[46] remain incisive critics of Christendom's dispensation of cheap grace precisely by describing a circulation of divine grace and human work that upholds their noncompetitiveness. More grace cannot mean less discipleship; in fact, it calls discipleship into being.

Free and Expensive versus Cheap

The problem with getting something for free is that it tends to rob us of our reason. We'll stand in line for an hour for a free scoop of Ben and Jerry's ice cream when the more rational, "economic" thing to do would be to save our time and "potential earnings," and instead, buy a whole tub of Chunky Monkey. We'll spend too much on pricey replacement blades for our Gillette Fusion Power Pro-glide Mach 3 Turbo razor because we got it in the mail for free. In some ways, then, we tend to *overvalue* "free," spending too much time and money to get it. At the same time, we tend to *devalue* the object of the free deal and our enjoyment of it.[47] Through experiments in the field of behavioral economics, we know that, when offered Starbursts for a penny, the average customer buys four; when offered them for free, the average

---

Charles Scribner's Sons, 1958), 11–14. See also Kathryn Tanner, *Economy of Grace* (Minneapolis: Fortress Press, 2005), 5.

44. Dorothee Soelle, *Suffering*, trans. Everett R. Kalin (Philadelphia: Fortress Press, 1975), 127-30.

45. This is partly what is at stake when political theologians writing about economics develop complex comparative methods that neither collapse nor consolidate the difference between modern money economies and the grand economy called God's creation and salvation. See M. Douglas Meeks, *God the Economist: The Doctrine of God and Political Economy* (Minneapolis: Fortress Press, 1989), 19–27; Cavanaugh, *Being Consumed*, vii–xii; and Tanner, *Economy of Grace*, 1–29.

46. Compare Nathan Montover, "From Luther to Bonhoeffer: A Clear Line," *Currents in Theology and Mission* 40.5 (October 2013): 351–56.

47. Shell, *Cheap*, 123.

customer takes only one. Thus: "free is unique among price points because it jettisons market-based values and the question of whether the object or service is worth the cost, in favor of social-based values and the question of whether we are worthy of the object or service."[48] Such is the "the paradoxical power of zero."[49]

Luther must have come to realize this in his own way. When, after 1517, he continued to critique penitential systems and sacrifices of the Mass, scholastic theology and the "Babylonian captivity of the church," none of Luther's proposed reforms raised as much vexation as his underlying conception that humans cannot earn or make good on God's incalculable grace. But while Luther is often read as claiming that God does everything and humanity does nothing, that very zero-sum logic would make grace and human work too commensurable insofar as more of one means less of the other.[50] What Luther so vehemently searches and fights for is a way to reckon God's gift and human response in noncompetitive ways.

God's Happy Exchange

We find strong clues for this alternative accounting in Luther's early sermon, "Two Kinds of Righteousness" (1519), and in a treatise he sends to Pope Leo X a year later, "The Freedom of a Christian" (1520).[51] In both, Luther describes God's grace and Christian discipleship as distinctive, and yet, joined together just as intimately as Christ's equality with God coheres with his becoming human and a servant of other humans—a correspondence that is recapitulated whenever Christians are of the same mind with this self-emptying Jesus.

Both the text of the sermon and the resurfacing subtext of the treatise is the "Christ hymn," a bit of verse probably sung or recited by the earliest Christians, which Paul quotes in Philippians 2, and which

---

48. Ibid., 121–22.
49. Ibid., 122.
50. Jason Mahn, "Beyond Synergism: The Dialectic of Grace and Freedom in Luther's 'De Servo Arbitrio,'" *Augustinian Studies* 33.2 (2002): 239–58.
51. Martin Luther, "Two Kinds of Righteousness" (1519), trans. Lowell J. Satre, and "The Freedom of a Christian" (1520), trans. W. A. Lambert. Both in *Luther's Works*, volume 31, ed. Harold J. Grimm (Philadelphia: Muhlenberg, 1957), 297–306 and 333–77, respectively.

becomes the key to Luther's Christology.[52] Paul beckons fellow Christians in Philippi to look to the interests of others above and beyond their own interests, and to "have the same mind in you" that was in Christ Jesus,

> who, though he was in the form of God,
> did not regard equality with God
> as something to be exploited,
> but emptied himself,
> taking the form of a slave,
> being born in human likeness.
> And being found in human form,
> he humbled himself
> and became obedient to the point of death—
> even death on a cross. (Phil 2:6–8)

In this so-called kenotic or self-emptying Christ, Christians have an example of one who resists "capitalizing on" the riches he has through equality with God. Christ chooses instead to humble himself and take on the form of a slave, which in turn, enables others to put on the form of Christ. Luther bases his particular understandings of the work of Christ and the shape of Christian salvation—or what is commonly called his atonement "theory"—on such an interpersonal exchange of qualities that occurs through solidarity and communion. Christ comes as bridegroom and humanity as bride; in consummating the marriage through faith, they become one flesh and hold all things, even their very identities, in common.[53] We thus "get" all that "belongs" to Christ—sinlessness and righteousness in the eyes of God—while Christ takes on our mortality, suffering, and sin. Indeed, that which belongs to Christ and that which belongs to me and to my neighbor in need become difficult to disentangle. Just as it does not make sense to ask whose money is whose in a shared bank account—or, a bit more graphically, to ask whose body "belongs" to whom when lovers lose themselves in ecstatic sex—so too do Christ and the Christian share what they have and are in ways that make ledgers irrelevant.

---

52. Torvend, *Luther and the Hungry Poor*, 30.
53. Luther, "Two Kinds of Righteousness," 297–98; "Freedom of a Christian," 351.

As its title implies, Luther structures his sermon of 1519 according to two kinds of righteousness, or better, two essential dimensions or functions of the righteousness received through grace. First is the righteousness "instilled from without," whereby Christ "is entirely ours with all his benefits."[54] The second is the Christian's "proper righteousness"—or what Samuel Torvend calls her "social righteousness,"[55] which Luther, otherwise ever-so suspect of moral accountings, describes as "that manner of life spent profitably in good works."[56] The order here is supremely important: Without the faith (itself a gift) that Christ's righteousness has become our righteousness and that "all that he has becomes ours; rather he himself becomes ours," we could not seek the welfare of others without keeping one eye open for the merit we were thereby accumulating. As Luther elsewhere puts it, Christ must be received as gift (*donum*) before one can take him as an example (*exemplum*). When the order is reversed, Christ becomes but another Moses; as exemplum alone, Christ's "life remains his own and does not as yet contribute anything to you."[57] Christ is example only as gift. His life must first be received if it is to be repeated. But once God's gift of righteousness becomes "ours" (without ceasing to be God's) in faith, we can and should "work with" it or help extend it as its natural "product," "fruit," and "consequence."[58] Luther emphasizes the naturalness and immediateness of the regifting. Once a person hears Christ the Bridegroom declare "I am yours," and she answers, "I am yours," the marriage is consummated, and then, immediately this: "Then the soul no longer seeks to be righteous in and for itself, but it has Christ as its righteousness *and therefore seeks only the welfare of others*." Having been opened to the self-giving Christ, the Christian almost ineluctably passes on whatever he or she can in order to meet the needs of others.

Unlike what has become the standard theory of atonement, where

---

54. Luther, "Two Kinds of Righteousness," 297–98.

55. Torvend, *Luther and the Hungry Poor*, 50, 85.

56. Luther, "Two Kinds of Righteousness," 299.

57. Luther, "What to Look For and Expect in the Gospels," in *Martin Luther's Basic Theological Writings*, ed. Timothy F. Lull, 2nd ed. (Minneapolis: Fortress Press, 2005), 94–95.

58. Luther, "Two Kinds of Righteousness," 299–300.

Christ takes the place of humanity, receiving God the Father's punishment in our stead (Calvin's substitutionary atonement), or where Christ pays off the debt accrued by a fallen humanity through his perfectly self-sacrificial penance (Anselm's satisfaction atonement), Luther underscores the "happy exchange" (fröhlich Wechsel) between Christ and a person precisely to trouble the very transactional schemes of debt and payment, guilt and punishment, upon which so many atonement theories turn. Christ does not simply "stand in" for humanity to bear our punishment or pay our debt; indeed, there is no clear line distinguishing Christ from his "beneficiaries" in the first place. Luther's model is one of communion through intimate love. If those united in marriage really do share all things, even their flesh, then there is really no transfer and trade *between* them, only a constant circulation of goods *among* them. They simply hold all things in common based on the solidarity and empathy they have with one another. This is what Melanchthon means when he contends that to know Christ is to know his benefits—the gift reveals the giver, Giver and Gift are the same. In the words of one contemporary Lutheran theologian, God's economy coincides with God's own being.[59]

It also follows that the "exchange" (Wechsel) does not constitute a transfer of fungible goods (by which grace becomes a quasi-substantial commodity) or services (by bearing punishment or paying a debt) from one party to another. Rather, the "parties" themselves are transformed. What is more, the exchange is happy or joyous (fröhlich) not because humanity gets the better deal (which would infer that Christ is being "taken"), but because what I bring and what Christ brings each becomes shared—or even reciprocally constitutive, without either party ceasing to be what it earlier was.[60] In fact, through

---

59. Hansen, "Money, Religion and Tyranny," para. 24.
60. Luther thus qualifies that the Christ celebrated in the Christ hymn does not give up "the form of God" in terms of the "essence of God"—"Christ never emptied himself of this" ("Two Kinds of Righteousness," 301). Rather, the form of God means "wisdom, power, righteousness, goodness, and freedom" (ibid.): in other words, those qualities that humans otherwise assign to their ideas of an invulnerable God and to those who aspire to be like "Him." On the other side, humanity too retains its sinful status even when it is clothed in Christ's righteousness, a layering of identities marked by Luther's understanding of being "simultaneously sinner and saint" (simul iustus et peccator). We might say that Christ's "property" of being equal with God and humanity's

the happy exchange, Christ becomes sin but remains one with the Father, and so, "swallows up" sin within the life of God,[61] just as humanity becomes Christ-like and yet still shares in humanity's sin and is thereby able to serve as christs to one another.[62]

Christian Happy Exchanges

One might fruitfully compare the above circulation of goods to the the standard Western system of private property and property rights, which founds our ability to "truck, barter and exchange" one thing for another,[63] and itself rests on the idea that a person essentially owns himself or herself.[64] According to the standard Western narrative, through self-possession, I come to own other things as well; by expending my labor on natural materials, they too become exclusively mine, as does the money I earn by selling or leasing my goods. In theory, my capacities, labor, or "earning potential" is disposable and alienable, but my personhood as such is not. I can sell my labor—in fact, I must sell it if I don't have other assets—without relinquishing the self-possession that enables me to hire myself out in the first place. John Locke, who is usually given credit (or blame) for this theory, emphasizes the distinction between inalienable personhood, which prevents me from selling myself, and alienable labor, which enables me to sell my time, my work, my skills, and anything else I possess.

---

ownership of sin remain inalienable even when those characteristics are taken in by the other. According to a monetary exchange model, this would point to an incomplete transaction, a leasing at best of stuff while keeping the owner unchanged. According to a circulation patterned after Christ's self-emptying, however, the fact that one doesn't cease to be who she or he is even when giving way to and taking on another, ensures that "things" such as grace, virtue, and sin are not confused with commodities that can be transacted without the transformation of the "brokers." It is precisely this commodification of grace that Bonhoeffer resists when he charges Christendom's Christians with trafficking in "cheap grace [that] means the justification of sin but not of the sinner." Dietrich Bonhoeffer, *Discipleship*, trans. Barbara Green and Reinhard Krauss (Minneapolis: Fortress Press, 2003), 43. Ironically, that same charge is leveled at the Lutheran understanding of *simul iustus et peccator* (being simultaneously a saint and a sinner) insofar as it suggests that pronouncements of justification by grace leave the underlying sinner unchanged. See, for example, Karl Rahner, "Justified and Sinner at the Same Time," in *Theological Investigations* (Baltimore: Helicon, 1969), 6:222.

61. Luther, "Freedom of a Christian," 352.
62. Ibid., 368.
63. Smith, *Wealth of Nations*, 14.
64. John Locke, *Treatise of Civil Government and A Letter Concerning Toleration*, ed. Charles L. Sherman (New York: Appleton-Century-Crofts, 1965), 19.

This account of property rights leads to commodity exchanges that remain wholly different from those founded on the kenotic self-giving of Christ. The difference lies not only between goods of which one has exclusive possession (if it is mine, it is not yours, until I transfer ownership) and goods that are nonexclusively shared, public, or even essentially "relational,"[65] although that difference is critical in its own right. The deeper difference is between an understanding of selfhood as self-possession, on the one side, and identity by way of radical self-giving, where Christ is what Christ gives, through which I become what I receive and can share with my neighbor in need, on the other side. If and when Christians "let the same mind be in [them] that was in Christ Jesus" (Phil 2:5), they too become fully themselves by opening themselves to the gifts and needs of others.

Of course, typical circulations of gifts preserve and enhance the cultural, political, and economic disparity between the free giver and obliged recipient. This is true for non-Western and archaic societies as well as for contemporary Western ones.[66] By contrast, a circulation patterned after Christ's self-giving gives away privilege itself—or what Luther calls the "wisdom, power, righteousness, goodness, and freedom" that people assume constitutes the form of God.[67] In the words of Dorothy Day, "If you are voluntarily giving away what you have, giving your coat, don't expect thanks or the reform of the recipient. We don't do it for that motive, with the expectation of reward. We must do it for love of Jesus, in His humanity, for love of our brother, for love of our enemy."[68] Finally, in freely binding oneself to others, thereby freeing them up for similar service, Jesus gives the one

---

65. Whereas the difference between private and public turns on the presence or absence of "interference" in consumption, relational goods are both created and consumed interpersonally. Public goods—say, enjoying my view of Mona Lisa beside others doing the same, are not necessarily shared in this constitutive sense. See Luigino Bruni, *The Wound and the Blessing: Economics, Relationships, and Happiness* (Hyde Park, NY: New City Press, 2012), 85–90.

66. Tanner, *Economy of Grace*, 51.

67. Luther, "Two Kinds of Righteousness," 301. Compare Martin Luther, Heidelberg Disputation (1518), in *Martin Luther's Basic Theological Writings*, ed. Timothy F. Lull, 2nd edition (Minneapolis: Fortress Press, 2005), 57.

68. Dorothy Day, "Reflections During Advent, Part Two: The Meaning of Poverty," *Ave Maria* (December 3, 1966): 21–22, 29, accessed August 10, 2015, www.catholicworker.org/dorothyday/Reprint2.cfm?TextID=560.

gift that destabilizes the hierarchy between the power and freedom of giving and the subjection and humiliation of receiving. Ironically, then, the renunciation of oneself as the benefactor of another and the empowering of the other so that she can accept (or not) the freely bound offering of oneself and so that she is able to give of herself in turn deconstructs the binaries between giver and receiver and between freedom and bondage upon which capitalist economies and archaic gift-economies typically turn. It also makes possible a joyous reception and recirculation of gifts that are genuinely shared.

What would such a countercultural, christological circulation of goods look like? Where in our society do Christians who have received without payment, really give without payment (Matt 10:8) promptly and happily? Certainly, such a grace-filled economy can look like a "pipe dream, deferred until the utopian space of heaven" if it does not just "sound utterly naïve."[69] But there do exist economic arrangements that include gift giving and grateful receiving—that is, those which preserve a place for interdependency, genuinely shared goods, and trust, thereby deconstructing hierarchies that otherwise regulate the movement of capital.

Take, for example, those who participate in social networks primarily used to give informal, no-interest loans to one another. Called *tandas* or *cundinas* in Mexico, *pandeiros* in Brazil, *susus* in West Africa and the Caribbean, and *hui* in Asia, these "rotating savings" or "lending associations" provide alternatives to those predatory payday lenders that punctuate the strip malls of poor urban areas. Typical participants are female; in the United States, they are also typically immigrants from Mexico and often undocumented. The *tanda* works essentially like this: ten or so women introduce themselves to one another, using first and last names, speak about their place of birth, and offer stories about why they are participating. Each then agrees to pay one hundred dollars every two weeks to the organizer who then distributes the collected money, 2000 dollars, at the end of each month to one participant. The process continues ten months until each

---

69. Tanner, *Economy of Grace*, 28; Hansen, "Money, Religion and Tyranny," para. 24.

person has paid 2000 dollars and received 2000 dollars. Essentially, the *tanda* works as a zero percent loan for those who collect early and as a savings plan for those who collect late in the ten-month cycle. It helps many women pay for medical treatment that they would not otherwise be able to afford or raise enough capital to begin a small business.[70] The "collateral" behind such loans is composed entirely of social capital; to fail to follow through with one's commitment breaks community norms and interpersonal connections, rather than a legal contract. In other words, if a participant misses a payment, the consequence is letting down friends—a harsher penalty, says Cuban-American Barb Mayo, than a default notice from a bank.[71] Such small-scale economies are predicated on gift-giving, though without reinforcing the social hierarchies that sustain traditional gift economies. We might call them "kenotic" and or even "Christocentric," so long as that term describes the movement of the gift, rather than the religious affiliation of its participants.

The best example of grace-filled economies, however, is the one found right beneath us. Quite literally, topsoil provides the matrix into which every living thing finally gives itself away (through death) and from which each new germ of creation springs forth (by growing from the soil, or eating what is grown). *Economy* as a term is often taken to mean a monetary (or digital-loan) economy, but the word (from *oikonomia*, the management of a household) applies more directly to that cosmic circulation of energy, nutrients, and life that some know as the biosphere and that Christians (with Jews and Muslims) know as creation. (*Ecology*, in fact, derives from the same Greek root as *ecumenism*, the relationship between Christians within the household called the church.) It follows that, however countercultural and religiously fanciful self-gifting, self-sacrifice, and the radical sharing of goods appear, those christological and cruciform processes are not at all alien to the natural world as God creates it. In fact, they are

70. Shereen Marisol Meraji, "Lending Circles Help Latinas Pay Bills and Invest." National Public Radio, April 1, 2014, accessed August 10, 2015, http://www.npr.org/blogs/codeswitch/2014/04/01/292580644/lending-circles-help-latinas-pay-bills-and-invest.
71. Ibid.

exactly the fundamental principles of nature's great economy. The life of soil, in particular, entails a mysterious process of "profound hospitality" that makes room for manifold creatures to flourish, and then, receives them again into itself as nutrients for the renewal of other life.[72] If we do assume that sharing, hospitality, and self-gifting so that others might live are fanatical ideas, that is probably because our more modern (abstract and exploitative) economies have tried to control the very ecological processes that we should receive as precious gifts and then regift to other human and nonhuman species. Norman Wirzba, perhaps the most theologically astute ecologist/ agrarian working today, writes of creation as a whole, and soil in particular, as the primary sites of God's grace, a grace that we cheapen when we take it as anything other than as gift:

> To live intimately and sympathetically with the earth is to see that we are surrounded and sustained by gifts on every side and to acknowledge that the only proper response to this unfathomable kindness is our own attention, care, and gratitude. . . . Working with the earth and making oneself vulnerable to its mysterious ways is to understand in the fiber of one's bones the difficulty and the hard-fought character of life. Grace is not cheap, nor does life come easily. . . . [And yet] we [often] deprive ourselves of an appreciation for the costliness of God's good gifts, if we see them as gifts at all.[73]

Given the presence of this gift economy on all sides, and even below us, we might even turn the practicality question around and ask: What ever would *impractical* grace look like? If we take the Christ hymn seriously, there is simply no righteousness, no spiritual status, that is not always already emptied out as a response to the other's physical need. In this sense, theology cannot be separated from the economy any more than human culture can be separated from the natural world or the true form of God can be separated from the body that Christ assumes. For Luther's part, both "Two Kinds of Righteousness" and "Freedom of a Christian" underscore this bond between the freedom and new life gifted by God and our immediate, almost simultaneous

---

72. Wirzba, *The Paradise of God*, 21–22, 27–34.
73. Ibid., 72.

sharing of material gifts among one another. And yet, it is often otherwise, as we know from Luther's day, that of Kierkegaard and Bonhoeffer, and again, from our own context.

Christendom and Commodified Grace

Luther's understanding of Christ, grace, creation as gift, and happy exchanges should forestall the commodification and cheapening of gifts and giftedness. Historically, almost the opposite has happened. Over post-Reformation history, grace had been increasingly mistaken (literally: mis-taken or wrongly received) as that which gets one out of the work of gift-giving that constitutes discipleship (see Matt 19:21). In turn, the Christian tradition—especially mainline Protestant churches—have ceased witnessing to a countercultural, creation-centered economy and have begun reproducing the culturally dominant and abstracted one. Such commodification of grace had begun already in Luther's time.

Luther on Smug Christians

Again and again, Luther describes how "the good things we have from God should flow from one to the other and be common to all."[74] But he is not unrealistic about human sin. In "Freedom of a Christian," he unequivocally names the perverse possibility that, after receiving the gift of grace, "we will take our ease and do no works and be content with faith."[75] Luther attributes such obstinacy to the fallenness of our fleshly desires. He thus calls for ascetic training, for fastings, vigils, labors, "and other reasonable discipline" until the body will finally "obey and conform to the inner man."[76]

Luther also glimpses a certain slippage from grace that is inseparable from service and mutual aid to grace that can be capitalized on and that fulfills one's own desires. One might call it a succumbing to a consumerist form of Christendom:

74. Luther, "Freedom of a Christian," 371.
75. Ibid., 358.
76. Ibid.

Who then can comprehend the riches and the glory of the Christian life? It can do all things and has all things and lacks nothing. It is lord over sin, death, and hell, and yet at the same time it serves, ministers to, and benefits all men. But alas in our day this life is unknown throughout the world; it is neither preached about nor sought after; we are altogether ignorant of our own name and do not know why we are Christians. Surely we are named after Christ, not because he is absent from us, but because he dwells in us, that is, because we believe in him and are Christs one to another and do to our neighbors as Christ does to us. But in our day we are taught by the doctrine of men to seek nothing but merits, rewards, and the things that are ours. . . .[77]

If this slippage from serving to self-serving and from free grace to cheap grace began already under Luther's watch, soon, it becomes as smooth as a well-worn coin.

Over the next few hundred years, there emerges the expanding space called the secular realm and a whole era called the secular age with its own formative process—that of "manufacturing the good life."[78] That which is antithetical to Christian formation has multiplied over the past 500 years: the power of unfettered capital, removed from its use-value in helping the poor; private ownership even of ourselves; and the endless acquisitive desire that is so boundlessly created once we accept advertising as neutrally offering us "choices" even as any rigorous religious training is dubbed brainwashing. According to Bradley Gregory, absent the repeated practices and a somewhat unified moral/ecclesial community in which human desires are sculpted and schooled to be drawn toward the *final good*, we seem compelled now to try to satisfy unformed, unbridled desire with any and every *consumer good*.

Certainly, Luther became aware of the "perverse possibility" that, after receiving the gift of grace, bargain-basement Christians might "take [their] ease and do no works and be content with faith."[79] Could he foresee the even more perverse possibility that Lutherans would use "free grace" to condemn those who do no more than hide behind

---

77. Ibid., 368.
78. Gregory, *Unintended Reformation*, 268–72.
79. Luther, "Freedom of a Christian," 358.

it? Both Søren Kierkegaard and Dietrich Bonhoeffer explicitly seek to reconnect Luther's doctrine of grace to his own striving for faithful discipleship as well as to the strivings that their writings provoke in readers. They also find ways of ordering God's gift and human striving, the economy of justification and material exchanges, in ways other than Luther's temporal and developmental models. They do so not to turn away from the Lutheran emphasis on gift and grace, but precisely to prevent their collapse into new law and their commodification within a closed doctrinal economy.

Kierkegaard on "the Lutheran Establishment"

Kierkegaard begins *For Self-Examination* by retelling the story of Luther and Lutheranism. He clarifies that the error of sixteenth-century Christendom was not that Christians performed too many good works, but that they placed trust in them instead of in God.[80] The entire life of Luther, reminds Kierkegaard, "expressed works—let us never forget that."[81] In *Judge for Yourself*, Kierkegaard portrays the meritoriousness protested by Luther as having become commodified. The Middle Ages, according to Kierkegaard, conceived of Christianity "along the lines of action, life, existence-transformation,"[82] and this was in keeping with true Christianity, Christianity as lived. The first error occurs when this legitimate quest for and training for discipleship became privatized, so to speak, through the professionalization of clerics and monastics. But then:

> Something worse than the first error did not fail to appear: they came up with the idea of meritoriousness, thought that they earned merit before God through their good works. And it became worse: they thought they had merit to such a degree through their good works that they thought they benefited not only the person himself but one could, like a capitalist and bondsman, let others benefit. And it grew worse; it became an out-and-out business: people who had never once thought of producing some of these so-called good works themselves now had plenty to do with good

---

80. Kierkegaard, *For Self-Examination* (with *Judge for Yourself*), trans. Howard V. Hong and Edna H. Hong (Princeton, NJ: Princeton University Press, 1990), 15.
81. Ibid., 16.
82. Kierkegaard, *Judge for Yourself*, 192.

works, inasmuch as they were put into business as hucksters who sold the good works of others at fixed but cheap prices.[83]

"Then Luther appears," as Kierkegaard's next sentence has it. Note that in portraying the rise of the sale of indulgences and other practices of sixteenth-century "hucksters" in these terms, Kierkegaard takes pains to disambiguate them from the earlier, faithful quest to live out one's faith and be transformed into the likeness of Christ. The slippage is not from faith to works, but from faith *and* works as inextricably linked to their disassociation and the concomitant privatization and commercialization of each. Only after discipleship has become privatized and commercialized, confined to the monastery, and then, capitalized on by others, regardless of personal transformation, does merit also slide toward a form of meritoriousness that is particularly prone to abuse.

Kierkegaard is also sure to distinguish Luther's corrective from the received opinion that he does away with imitation of Christ. When one takes Luther's life together with his words, he clearly "did not therefore abolish imitation, nor did he do away with the voluntary, as pampered sentimentality would like to have us think about Luther." Rather, Luther "affirmed imitation in the direction of witnessing to the truth and voluntarily exposed himself to dangers enough (yet without deluding himself that this was meritoriousness)."[84] Once he's dead, Christians tended to separate the "truth" of Luther's doctrine from the self-giving life that first made it true. "Already the next generation slackened," writes Kierkegaard.[85] Lutherans beginning then and continuing into Denmark's Christendom

did not turn with horror away from exaggeration with regard to works (in which exaggeration Luther lived) toward faith. No, it made the Lutheran position into doctrine, and in this way faith also diminished in vital power. Then it diminished from generation to generation. Works—well, God knows there was no longer any question about that; it would be a shame to accuse this later age of exaggeration with regard to works, and neither

---

83. Ibid.
84. Ibid., 193.
85. Ibid.

were people so silly that they resumed to want to have merit for what they exempted themselves from doing. But, now, faith—I wonder if it is to be found on earth?[86]

Just as sarcastically, Kierkegaard narrates the slippage from Luther's emphasis on grace as it incites a life of discipleship to grace as ideological cover for our smug self-satisfaction:

But what happened? There is always a secular mentality that no doubt wants to have the name of being Christian but wants to become Christian as cheaply as possible. This secular mentality became aware of Luther. It listened; for safety's sake it listened once again lest it should have heard wrongly; thereupon it said, "Excellent! This is something for us. Luther says: It depends on faith alone. He himself does not say that his life expresses works, and since he is now dead it is no longer an actuality. So we take his words, his doctrine—and we are free from all works—long live Luther!"[87]

Having cut faith loose from works, the first kind of righteousness from the second, freedom *from* from freedom *for*, one so easily loses one with the other. Grace is no longer received as the gift of new life to one struggling to stay afloat—above 70,000 fathoms of water, as Kierkegaard elsewhere puts it.[88] No, grace now becomes almost indistinguishable from privilege, latitude, and ideological self-justification—exactly that which enables one *not* to act in ways distinguishable from the status quo.

Kierkegaard repeatedly describes this "secular mentality" that is so delighted to have found refuge in Luther's doctrine and grace's commodification. He likens the cheapening of grace to a peasant coming to the market with cost-effective calculations ready at hand, bartering thus: "If it is to be *works*—fine, but then I must also ask for the legitimate yield I have in coming from my works, so that they are meritorious. If it is to *grace*—fine, but then I must also ask to be free

---

86. Ibid., 193–94.
87. Kierkegaard, *For Self-Examination*, 16–17.
88. Kierkegaard, *Concluding Unscientific Postscript to the Philosophical Fragments*, trans. Howard V. Hong and Edna H. Hong (Princeton, NJ: Princeton University Press, 1992), 1:204; Kierkegaard, *Stages on Life's Way*, trans. Howard V. Hong and Edna H. Hong (Princeton, NJ: Princeton University Press, 1988), 466–77.

from works—otherwise it surely is not grace. If it is to be works and *nevertheless* grace, that is indeed foolishness."[89] Kierkegaard answers: "Yes, that is indeed foolishness; that would also be true Lutheranism; that would indeed be Christianity."[90] For three hundred years, early Christians witnessed to the truth of redemption in and with their own lives, frequently being martyred for so vividly displaying the hope that was within them. Already in the fourth century, the time of Constantine (which, for Kierkegaard, provides the negative example reduplicated by Lutheran iterations of Christendom), Christians move from *producing* disciples to *consuming* their merits; they begin already to "live off the doctrine," turning it into "an enormous working capital."[91] But by the nineteenth century, the capital has been used up—this is the true financial statement, asserts Kierkegaard.[92] Only by working again, by producing "character-actions"[93] can Christians regain some measure of the grace that sustains that work. While Kierkegaard is writing of spiritual labors and those who capitalize on grace, many contemporary critics of industrial agriculture claim the same with regard to the work of food production and the consumer's unacknowledged dependence on fossil fuels and "cheap" forms of labor. The issues are different, and yet, as Kierkegaard's language suggests, largely intertwined. Indeed, near the end of his life, Kierkegaard came to see the economization of grace and the monetary economy as inextricably linked. He writes in *The Moment*: "But where everything is Christian and all are Christians, even the atheists, the situation is this: calling oneself a Christian is the means by which one protects oneself against all sorts of trouble and inconvenience in life, and the means by which one secures for oneself earthly goods, conveniences, profit, etc. etc."[94]

According to Kierkegaard, Luther's real theological offering, then, is

---

89. Kierkegaard, *For Self-Examination*, 17, my emphasis.
90. Ibid.
91. Kierkegaard, *Judge for Yourself*, 129.
92. Ibid., 130.
93. Ibid., 136.
94. Kierkegaard, *The Moment and Late Writings*, trans. Howard V. Hong and Edna H. Hong (Princeton, NJ: Princeton University Press, 1989), 32.

neither grace nor works taken alone, but this foolish "nevertheless"—a life of radical discipleship and *nevertheless* coming to know that one has been saved by grace alone. So important for Kierkegaard is the dialectic between grace *and* work, between objective doctrine *and* the life that lives it, that he can even argue that were Luther alive in nineteenth-century Denmark, he would certainly push in the opposite direction, drawing forward the Apostle James (who said faith without work is dead—see James 2:17). He would pay a little more attention to the minor premise (works) in relation to the major premise (grace) in order "to cause the need for *grace* to be felt deeply in genuine humble inwardness and, if possible, to prevent *grace*, faith and grace as the only redemption and salvation, from being taken totally in vain, from becoming a camouflage even for a refined worldliness."[95]

Bonhoeffer on Costly Grace

Bonhoeffer thought Kierkegaard was almost alone in recognizing the inextricability, simultaneity, and "dialectic" of grace and discipleship in Luther's thought and life, which themselves are inseparable, according to Kierkegaard.[96] Bonhoeffer had Kierkegaard's critique of Christendom in front of him as he wrote the opening chapter of *Nachfolge* (in English, *Discipleship* or *The Cost of Discipleship*) while leading the intentional community and underground seminary at Finkenwalde. *Discipleship* famously begins with a penetrating critique of cheap grace. Bonhoeffer sharply contrasts the grace that cost Jesus his life and that continues to bid Christians to "come and die,"[97] with "grace" as license and latitude, "grace" as ideological justification for refusing to hear and respond to Jesus's call to radical discipleship. Reminiscent of the four beatitudes and four woes in Luke's sermon on the plain, the opening paragraphs of *Discipleship* pair lament for

---

95. Kierkegaard, *For Self-Examination*, 24.
96. Geffrey B. Kelly and John D. Godsey, "Editor's Introduction to the English Edition," in Bonhoeffer, *Discipleship*, 10.
97. Bonhoeffer, *The Cost of Discipleship*, trans. R. H. Fuller (New York: Touchstone, 1995), 89. Barbara Green and Reinhard Krauss render Bonhoeffer's famous line thus: "Whenever Christ calls us, his call leads us to death." Bonhoeffer, *Discipleship*, 87.

various forms of cheap grace with praise for their costly antitheses. Whereas cheap grace means "bargain-basement goods" and "cut-rate" forgiveness, comfort, and sacrament—each "doled out by careless hands" from the church's "inexhaustible pantry," costly grace is the hidden treasure in the field or the costly pearl, for which people sell all to go and find (Matt 13:44–45). While cheap grace is an idea, doctrine, principle, or system—essentially, an *abstraction* that denies God's intimacy with creation—costly grace "is the incarnation of God." It is costly because it calls a person to leave her prior life behind; it is grace, though, "because it calls us to follow *Jesus Christ*." Whereas cheap grace promises comfort and security to the one "in possession" of it, justifies sin but leaves the sinner untouched, and actually saves him or her *from* the call to leave the ways in the world by becoming Christian, costly grace is "God's holy treasure which must be protected from the world." Finally, whereas cheap grace is forgiveness without repentance, the Lord's Supper and absolution without confession of sin, and baptism without "the discipline of community," costly grace holds each of these together, as well as suffering, death, and cross with the joy and blessedness of new life.[98]

While Bonhoeffer is most concerned with juxtaposing costly grace and its counterfeit double so that their stark differences can be clearly seen, he also briefly suggests how Christians have subtly slipped from the first to the second. His narrative of decline begins with the time following Constantine, which entails both the "expansion of Christianity" (what I have called *acculturation*) and the "increasing secularization of the church" (what I have called *accommodation*), which together "caused the awareness of costly grace to be gradually lost."[99] As with Kierkegaard, however, Bonhoeffer is most interested in the "turn" or "fall" that follows Luther's own proclamation of pure, costly grace. He suggests that the monasticism protested by Luther was not mistaken because it called for strict discipleship, but only insofar as it made that the "extraordinary achievement of a few," thereby

---

98. Bonhoeffer, *Discipleship*, 43–45, 87–89.
99. Ibid., 46.

claiming meritoriousness for itself while releasing the majority from their own radical vocations.[100] Bonhoeffer emphasizes that Luther was called to be a monk, to leave everything and follow Christ in complete obedience.[101] Luther leaves the monastery, according to Bonhoeffer, only because the monk's world-denial eventually became an ironic form of worldliness, or again, insofar as the humble work of discipleship became the meritorious work of the spiritually elite.[102] Luther's return from monastery to world did not therefore constitute a relaxing or reversal of the call to follow Jesus, but rather, its intensification. Christians were now called toward radical Christoform and cruciform obedience—love of enemy, dying to self, even sometimes selling all that you own to give to the poor—in the very midst of a society that offers security and success by amassing money and weapons. On Bonhoeffer's accounting, Luther thus sought to restore the powerful gift and comprehensive task of humbly following Jesus unto death and beyond.

Instead, according to Bonhoeffer, "what emerged victorious from Reformation history was not Luther's recognition of pure, costly grace, but the alert religious instinct of human beings for the place where grace could be had the cheapest."[103] The Reformation resulted in the commodification of grace and the concomitant emergence of spiritual discount shoppers. Bonhoeffer gives three accounts of the slippage.

First, the affirmation of the secular world as the place from which Christian disciples are called becomes affirmed in and of itself.[104] It is as if Luther's profound claim that a shoemaker is called also to discipleship got mistaken to mean that discipleship is exhausted by making shoes. Second, Bonhoeffer (borrowing from Kierkegaard) charges contemporary Christians with abstracting Luther's reliance on grace from his own lifelong obedience to Christ. For Luther, grace is the final word, a "conclusion" to the whole of his lifelong obedience to

100. Ibid., 47.
101. Ibid.
102. Ibid., 47–48.
103. Ibid., 49.
104. Ibid.

Christ (which is also the work of grace). For Luther's followers, grace becomes a starting point, a "principled presupposition on which to base their calculations." The gift of grace for the contrite and penitent becomes an unrestricted endowment, exactly that which permits nominal Christians "to sin on the basis of this grace."[105]

Third and most perversely, grace even becomes that to which Christians point in order to justify their moral laxity and religious indeterminacy. Several times throughout *Discipleship*, Bonhoeffer acknowledges the complete inversion of grace that might be proffered by Lutheran apologists to justify their unwillingness to visibly follow Jesus's countercultural (but earth-centered) ways.[106] In this case, so-called "Christians," "Lutherans," or even "theologians of the cross"[107] go beyond giving a divine rubber stamp on worldly vocations and beyond using grace as down payment for sin. They actually invoke grace to condemn anyone who would visibly follow Christ, against anyone—or any community, such as the *ekklesia*—that would be called-apart (*ek-klesia*) from the ways of the world. It is not an overstatement to call such a perverse use of grace diabolical if we take into account the accommodation to Nazism that German Lutheran churches had nearly completed by 1937, the year that *Discipleship* was published. Too few were Christian communities, such as Finkenwalde, where members shared resources, practiced peacemaking, and otherwise followed the way of the cross, often literally to the point of death, as with Bonhoeffer himself. Too many were Christians and churches who purchased political shelter by condemning such "fanaticism," confusing Luther's condemnation of meritoriousness with a call *away* from the calling of Christ.

Throughout *Discipleship*, Bonhoeffer underscores the compatibility of God's costly grace and human effort more succinctly and emphatically than either Luther or Kierkegaard: good works *are* God's grace; discipleship *is* grace; discipleship *is* joy; grace *is* the call to follow Christ, just as the call to follow *is* grace. The two "belong inseparably

---

105. Ibid., 50.
106. Ibid., 51, 53, 113, 144.
107. Ibid., 113.

together."[108] The two cannot even be chronologically sequenced, as Luther sought to do with his first and second form of righteousness, and as Kierkegaard sometimes suggests when he writes of ethical rigor (and the effort's failure) as the ironic ground of possibility for accepting God's leniency. According to Bonhoeffer, any such sequencing, even one that serves as a corrective, will tear grace and obedience apart, swapping out discipleship for a baptized consumerism.[109]

Calling Theologians of the Cross

Bonhoeffer and Kierkegaard stood at a crossroads that many Christians in America's new Christendom will recognize. They continue and radicalize Luther's critique of meritoriousness and meritocracy, a critique just as pertinent to twenty-first-century America as to twentieth-century Germany or nineteenth-century Denmark. At the same time, Bonhoeffer and Kierkegaard squarely face the fact that, in practice, the Reformation commodified grace, unintentionally licensing Christendom's privileged Christians *not* to follow Jesus.

At one place in *Discipleship*, Bonhoeffer describes how even Luther's "theology of the cross," the lens through which Christians cherish what others scorn and scrap (vulnerability, suffering, abandonment, and death), can also get decorated with the shiny giftwrap of cheap grace. The context is an analysis of Jesus's proclamation that disciples are the salt of the earth and the light of the world (Matt 5:13–16). Bonhoeffer intersperses Matthew's record of the injunctions of Jesus with his own censure of contemporary Lutheranism. He heeds Jesus's warning against intentionally hiding the light under a bushel basket, of explicitly denying the call to follow Jesus away from conformity with the world. But then, he notes that the figurative bushel basket

> may also be—and this is even more dangerous—a so-called Reformation theology, which even dares to call itself theologia crucis [theology of the cross] and whose signature is that it prefers a "humble" invisibility in the

108. Ibid., 40, 45, 46, 51, 279, 284.
109. Ibid., 63.

200

form of total conformity to the world over "Pharisaic" visibility. In that case the identifying mark of the community ceases to be an extraordinary visibility. Instead, it is identified by its fitness to function within the justitia civilis.[110]

The proper scandal—as in the necessary offensiveness—of the Christian gospel is that it calls disciples to a particular and peculiar way of being in the world that will noticeably stand out from other ways. The indignity—as in the real disgrace—accompanying Christendom's addiction to cheap grace is that, in the name of inclusivity, being nonjudgmental, or even adhering to grace, Christians want to blend in, to run smoothly within dominant society (especially the market), and worst of all, to rebuke those who do not. In marketing Christianity as attractive and rewarding, Christians have put their faith in one more item on the market after hunting for the best possible deal.

Recall from earlier chapters that the "theology of the cross" that Bonhoeffer references gets its name from Luther's early Heidelberg Disputation of 1518. There, Luther contends that God can only be known through the suffering and cross of Jesus—and even there, only as a God who is hidden in God's self-disclosure, in God's suffering.[111] No one is drawn to that God on the cross, as we are to our own more marketable projections of "virtue, godliness, wisdom, justice, goodness," and other abstractions.[112] Yet, for those with eyes to see, God is hidden in suffering, and so, recognizable to those who pick up their crosses and follow Christ. As we explore further in the next chapter, Bonhoeffer's ideal Christian community demonstrates the same play of visibility and hiddenness—of being recognized only under "opposite signs"—that characterizes the God that Luther finds hanging on a tree. Here again, Bonhoeffer is deeply Lutheran in his critiques of the Lutheran establishment, just as he otherwise adopts Luther's central image of a kenotic Christ who draws us to take his own shape.[113] Being formed within a community of the cross (which may also include

---

110. Ibid., 113.
111. Martin Luther, Heidelberg Disputation (1518), in *Martin Luther's Basic Theological Writings*, ed. Timothy F. Lull, 2nd ed. (Minneapolis: Fortress Press, 2005), 57 (thesis 20).
112. Ibid., 57 (thesis 19).
113. Bonhoeffer, *Discipleship*, 283–85.

nonhuman species) might very well save us from all our "normal" desires for less work, more leisure, more consumption, less production, more stuff, and certainly less suffering.

And yet, aside from human communities (many of them agrarian) and the ecological community of creation itself, both of which would school us through formation into gospel-centered ways of receiving and giving gifts, is even the discernment of costly/free grace apart from its cheap replica enough to hold consumerism, the strongest formative power today, at bay? According to the Lutheran theologian Ronald Thiemann, "it is certainly the case that the failure of Protestantism to institutionalize those disciplines of seeing, feeling, tasting, and believing the divine undoubtedly contributed to the diminishment of these skills in the modern world."[114] Bonhoeffer wrote *Discipleship* from Finkenwalde, where he not only talked about costly grace, but also, lived it out within an intentional Christian community by praying together, seeking reconciliation, and sharing material resources.[115] The gifts of creation and its salvation are to be received and regifted—without becoming commoditized and thus undercutting their character as gifts. For this to happen, Christians will probably need to gather closely into communities that resist the individualism upon which consumerism preys. The next chapter turns to the heirs of the Radical Reformation and other anti-Constantinian Christians to show how such resistance is both necessary and possible.

114. Ronald F. Thiemann, *The Humble Sublime: Secularity and the Politics of Belief* (London: I. B. Tauris, 2014), 210n96.
115. Geffrey B. Kelly, "Editor's Introduction to the English Edition," in Dietrich Bonhoeffer, *Life Together* and *Prayerbook of the Bible*, trans. Daniel W. Bloesch and James H. Burtness (Minneapolis: Fortress Press, 1996), 18-19.

7

POLITICS: Getting Radical and Staying Ordinary

In this chapter, I turn from economy to the wider issue of politics, church, and Christian community. I also turn from "Lutheran" critiques of Christian accommodations to critiques that begin from a different place. Kierkegaard and Bonhoeffer critiqued their own Lutheran tradition for abstracting grace from lived discipleship and for living too contentedly from its profits. Both wanted to recontextualize grace within committed lives and social contexts that properly valued it. This chapter explores a similar turn from abstract doctrines to social and intentional practices—but we also turn more fully away from Lutheran critiques of Lutheranism to critiques of Christendom that come from without.

I will call them "radical" because they arise within the stream of the Radical Reformation and try to get to the real *root* or *radix* of the problem. These perspectives are also radical in the political sense insofar as they refuse to cordon off the political from the personal and religious; by doing so, they embrace exactly what many mainliners and mainstreamers would regard as the undue politicization of the church.

Yet, despite common misgivings about getting political in church, the leading critics of Christendom or Constantinianism who are influenced by Anabaptism largely reclaim the church as a political entity, that is, as having a distinctive sociological shape and shared, public practices.

A short personal story exemplifies how far I remain from the "ideal" put forth in this chapter. A couple of years ago, I witnessed a woman nonchalantly walking away with my neighbor's bicycle. I stopped her; she was nonthreatening and seemed to be mentally unwell. I let my neighbor know what had happened and asked what we should do. When my neighbor was indecisive, I said that I would call the police. Later, I identified the tinges of self-satisfaction with having made the "responsible" decision even in a moment of ambiguity and uncertainty. The woman was taken to jail, where I doubt she got the help that she obviously needed. What is more, I came to learn that the woman lived hardly any farther from me than the neighbor whose property I was helping to protect.

Although this is a pretty commonplace incident, I regret the ease with which I called the police, essentially mediating what could have been problems between neighbors with police and the law, chief powers of the state. When I tried to confess to a trusted Christian pastor that I failed to act creatively or even Christianly that day, he quickly assured me that I had done nothing wrong. And yet, at the very least, the episode confirms that I have been formed as a citizen in a liberal democracy, whose chief duty is to protect personal freedom and property ownership, much more thoroughly than I have been formed as a Christian, one who, by "radical" accounts, offers shirt to anyone who takes one's coat (Luke 6:29), and who handles wrongdoings in direct, interpersonal ways whenever possible (Matt 18:15). I say all this to name the difference between the world I inhabit and the one that the present chapter tries to imagine with help from Christians more practiced than I. The difference between us is a matter of distinct politics, divergent ways of structuring relationships between members of a community and of serving those "outside."

For and Against Politics

Many Christian critics of America's neo-Christendom or Constantinianism want to renew the political form and function of the church. This may come as a surprise, given that Constantinianism is typically diagnosed as the conflation of those spheres, and the solution as their uncoupling. But really, there are two senses of *political* here.

First, there is politics as the business of the nation-state and other principalities and powers, which the church accommodates or makes common cause with to its own detriment. In this sense, Christendom entails the "politicizing" of Christianity and the church, and the Holy Roman Empire under Constantine remains a chief example. Many are concerned with the politicizing of church in this sense, and with the state of American politics as typically understood. James Davison Hunter, for example, argues that the Christian Right (since the early 1980s) and the Christian Left (since the 1960s and 1970s) have become implicated in politics and remain implicated today. For Hunter, the church cannot spread its understanding of "values" through legislation, lobbying, or other political channels because politics is about efficiency, power, and coercion, and the church should be about the virtues of faith, hope, and love. Any politicization of "Christian values" thus undermines attempts at their very renewal. When voting becomes the leading civic duty, for example, it sloughs off the responsibility and action that the church should be doing more directly: feeding the hungry, clothing the naked, attending to the sick, visiting the imprisoned, and welcoming the stranger (see Matt 25: 34–46).[1]

Second, though, *politics* might also name the proper form and function of the church as a *polis* in its own right (or as a people, race, or nation).[2] The *polis* here names the primary site of Christian allegiances and the sculptor of Christian dispositions. In other words, "politics"

1. James Davison Hunter, *To Change the World: The Irony, Tragedy, and Possibility of Christianity in the Late Modern World* (Oxford: Oxford University Press, 2010), 171–73.
2. See Michael Budde's helpful comments about the limitations of "polis" language to address Christian white privilege in Michael L. Budde, *The Borders of Baptism: Identities, Allegiances, and the Church* (Eugene, OR: Cascade, 2011), 126.

can designate what gets lost when the church gets grafted onto an alien politics of the nation-state. The first sense of being political should be avoided by Christians, but it is only made possible by the de-politicization of the church in this second sense. Or again: Constantinianism as the unwarranted *politicization* of the church ironically suppressed the properly *political* (communal and public) character of early church and its understanding of Christian salvation.[3]

According to leading critics of Constantinianism—not only those influenced by Anabaptism, but radical Catholics such as Dorothy Day, those in the wake of the social gospel movement, such as Cornel West, and many feminist and liberationist theologians—the wish to keep the church out of politics often gives tacit support to the status quo and obscures the Constantinian arrangement of that same church. In this light, the Constantinian church needs to become *more* intentionally and self-consciously political, in the communal and public sense. To add some historical nuance to this, I continue by exploring how mainline or "magisterial" reformers helped create "the political" in the first sense, and then, how radical reformers critique that politicization by returning to the properly political nature of the church itself.

Getting Political (in a Bad Way)

Constantinianism names, in part, the turn from the proper politics of the church to its accommodations to an alien polity. But exactly when, where, and how did that turn arise? The name implies fourth-century Rome, but many Anabaptist anti-Constantinians pay as much attention to Luther and Calvin in sixteenth-century Saxony and Geneva as they do to Constantine and Theodosius in fourth-century Rome. By returning to the Reformation, we can question how *politics*—as we commonly use the term today—became understood as an autonomous realm, which should ostensibly be kept separate from church.

In 1520, Luther distinguishes between the inner and outer domains of Christian life. He distinguishes between justification in terms of

---

3. Stanley Hauerwas, *After Christendom? How the Church Is to Behave if Freedom, Justice, and a Christian Nation Are Bad Ideas* (Nashville: Abingdon, 1991), 36.

freedom *from* obedience to the law as a vehicle to salvation ("the inner") on the one hand and, on the other hand, the outworking of "proper" or "social" righteousness and the renewed freedom *for* a life of disciplined service to others in need ("the outer"). The initial intent and function of such distinctions was not primarily to delimit spheres or disambiguate theological precepts ("justification" in the first spot, "sanctification" in the second), but rather, to hold them inextricably together. There are two kinds or dimensions of one righteousness in Christ and of one freedom of the Christian. Just as there is no soul without body and vice-versa, so too there is no ethical fruit without inner transformation, no indwelling with Christ without having been taken outward as a "little Christ" to the needy neighbor. In Bonhoeffer's pithier terms—no grace without discipleship.

Sometime after 1520, the function of Luther's distinctions between inner and outer, between personal salvation and public works of love, changes in subtle but important ways. First of all, in later works such as "Secular Authority: To What Extent It Should Be Obeyed" (1523) or "Whether Soldiers, Too, Can Be Saved" (1526) Luther continues to distinguish between inner and outer, personal freedom and public duties, but he does so now with the primary concern that the realms *not be confused*. Second and related, the later Luther and early Lutherans begin to consider the public realm as having criteria for judging what counts as justice or responsible action other than those by which Christians *qua* Christian are guided. Third and finally, these criteria or "other lights"[4]—including reason, efficacy, rule of law, national sovereignty, personal rights, and vocations needed for running society—are deemed necessary, given the overwhelming presence of sin and evil in the world. In Luther's later works, especially as they get reified and codified by subsequent Lutheran Orthodoxy, the "realities" of sin and evil justify the designation of a second kingdom, a political realm, with its own relative sovereignty. The citizens of this

---

4. John Howard Yoder, *The Royal Priesthood: Essays Ecclesiastical and Ecumenical* (Scottdale, PA: Herald, 1998), 184. Yoder also calls these other lights "wider wisdom" (*Royal Priesthood*, 110) or simply the "other Realm." Yoder, *The Christian Witness to the State* (Scottdale, PA: Herald, 2002), 79–83. See also Stanley Hauerwas, *Sanctify Them with the Truth: Holiness Exemplified* (Nashville: Abingdon, 1998), 28.

"kingdom of man" or "kingdom of evil"—while purportedly still under the cruciform lordship of Christ—must be prodded and pressured in other ways. One gets quickly to the point where Christ's injunction to love one's enemies, for example, guides only one's inner intentions or private prayers. *Politics* in its everyday sense must be ruled by other standards, which are thought to be more "realistic" or "applicable" than the teachings and example of Jesus. When my pastor friend (who, by the way, is a Lutheran pastor) assured me that I did nothing worth confessing when I called the cops on my neighbor, he did not explicitly evoke Lutheran distinctions between ecclesial matters and "political necessities." And yet, that distinction has become second nature to most American Christians, whether mainline Protestant, Evangelical, or Catholic.

As Luther frequently admits in his later writings on the use of lethal force, the *donum* (gift) and *exemplum* (example) of Christ is all that Christians would need if society were composed of true Christians. As it stands, to turn the other cheek and love one's enemies while performing one's public duties would be a recipe for social anarchy, at best, and the utter eradication of Christians and Christianity, at worst. It follows for post-Reformation state-churches that all the gifts and tasks of Christians *qua* followers of Christ must be circumscribed within an *ecclesial*, if not *interpersonal* and increasingly *private* domain, leaving the more public, political kingdom to be ruled in other ways. When those ruling are purportedly Christian, as were Luther's Elector of Saxony and leaders of "the free world" today, then it is easy to see how capacious and nominal the designation gets. At best, contemporary avowals that a candidate running for public office is a sincere Christian, without which no presidential candidate in the United States has been elected, mean that her or his public policy will be loosely motivated or occasionally enriched by equally capacious, "Christian" principles: a belief in truth, hope, doing what's right, freedom, and "America" itself. At worse, "Christianity" becomes little more than the meaningless password one must pronounce to get keys to the kingdom.

The slippage I am here recounting is subtle, manifold, and not entirely irreversible. Still, the shift from living into a single Reign of God that has two dimensions to living in two autonomous realms, with different norms judging each, has monumental effects on the locus and meaning of Christianity. Today, the term *Christian* can become wholly equivocal and nominal when applied to each. Here again, one notices how Christendom in its inherited form need not be understood as *monolithically* Christian or *too-churchy*. Our dominant religion is often in name only, thereby covering even more under its umbrella.

When Bonhoeffer houses Christian vocation within a second use of the gospel rather than a first or third use of the law, or when he renames Lutheran orders of creation "orders of preservation" to highlight their contingency and later speaks of divine mandates (callings that can always be interrupted again by God), it is precisely to prevent the otherwise proper recognition that God through Christ is at work outside of church and soul from vindicating every power and principality.[5] It is Christ's will that must be discerned again and again from within the vicissitudes of history, and the shape of that will must still conform to the life, death, and resurrection of Jesus. So, too, when Kierkegaard continually retrieves the "nevertheless" that keeps the gifts given by a gracious God from being confused with simple, immediate "givens."[6] He too distinguishes the inner and the outer,[7] underscoring Christianity's "heterogeneity to this world,"[8] only so that they don't *completely* collapse into one another in some blended Christian-bourgeois household. In these ways, we can read these Lutheran critics of the Lutheran establishment as retrieving an earlier, more dialectical or "paradoxical" account of the relation of church and

---

5. See chapter 4 above.
6. See chapter 6 above.
7. Søren Kierkegaard, *Concluding Unscientific Postscript to the Philosophical Fragments*, trans. Howard V. Hong and Edna H. Hong (Princeton, NJ: Princeton University Press, 1992), 1:54, 138, 296–97, 541.
8. Søren Kierkegaard, *The Moment and Late Writings*, trans. Howard V. Hong and Edna H. Hong (Princeton, NJ: Princeton University Press, 1989), 125.

politics, of "Christ and culture."[9] But other, perhaps even more incisive critiques, typically come from without.

Retrieving Politics (in a Good Way)

From a Radical Reformation perspective, the start of the slide toward dichotomous realms is easier to point to but harder to correct from within. John Howard Yoder dates it somewhere between 1522 and 1525, during which time, both Luther and Ulrich Zwingli, forerunner of Calvin and Calvinism, "decided to ally their renewal movements with political conservatism, thereby withdrawing the challenge to the Constantinian compromise."[10] These reformers are called "magisterial" because they act as chaplains to and rely on the military protections of local princes and other magisteria. They "retained both the social backbone of the Constantinian alliance (religious glorification of and submission to the princes of this world) and its sacramental expression (the baptism of all infants)."[11] The Mennonite critique retrieves the second, alternative understanding of *politics* as it relates to the Christian church. If—at least since the split between the kingdom of God and kingdom of man—"politics" has come to designate that autonomous sphere that must be ruled by "different lights," many anti-Constantinians retrieve a positive sense of the inherent *politics* of the church or church as a distinctive *polis*.

Radical reformers, in particular, assume that membership within the dissident grassroots political community called church (*ekklesia*) entails being different, or called (*kleo*) out (*ek*) from the ways of the world, a calling exhibited by voluntary church membership, meal

9. H. Richard Niebuhr, *Christ and Culture* (New York: Harper and Brothers, 1951), 170–79. Niebuhr takes the slippage we are tracing here, in his words, from "Luther's celebration of the faith that works by love, suffering all things in serving the neighbor, to his injunction to the rulers to 'stab, smite, slay, whoever he can'" (170) to be characteristic of the "Christ and Culture in paradox" position in general. I would place the less dialectical, more dualistic form into something like Niebuhr's "Christ of Culture" type, albeit with the qualification that Christianity here comes to endorse culture ironically through their utter separation, an irony for which Niebuhr's spatial categories have difficulty accounting.

10. John Howard Yoder, *Revolutionary Christianity: The 1966 South American Lectures* (Eugene, OR: Cascade, 2011), 111.

11. Ibid.

fellowship, and other visible marks.[12] Yoder retrieves these social practices from Jesus and the early church—in particular, the practices of nonviolent resistance, forgiveness, and peacemaking—as the name of his best-known book, *Politics of Jesus*, suggests. Because the life and death of Jesus provide a pattern of radical service, forgiveness, and nonviolent resistance to the powers of church and state, disciples of the crucified one will necessarily find their politics countercultural and subversive. Statecraft and the church entail *alternative* social arrangements or different and conflicting politics. Christianity cannot be resigned to the interior, spiritual, or private world of individuals. Christians must choose. The power of anti-Constantinian historical work is to force this choice by giving a thick description of the concrete practices and relationships inherent in discipleship, and then, underscoring its incompatibility with other dominant social arrangements.

How has this critique been received by mainline Christians and mainstream Americans? It seems to have been ignored for the most part. The relative inattention to the witness of the historic peace churches and the Radical Reformation largely follows the fact that they are simply not constitutive for most mainline Protestant and Catholic identities. For many if not most, Anabaptist history is easy to write off as "radical" (in the sense of *extreme* or *fanatical*), and pacifist churches are easy to sentimentalize and marginalize as prophetic movements safely positioned at the margins of dominant society, with its real-world politics and resort to "necessary" legal violence. Spokespersons for radical Christian communities (which they simply call "church") such as Hauerwas or members of the Ekklesia Project are equally easy to dismiss as "sectarian," as safely choosing moral purity over social efficacy, as essentially withdrawing from the ambiguities of political responsibility.[13] Luther himself was to annex many different radical reformers in one fell swoop, ranging from the pacifist defenders of

---

12. John Howard Yoder, *Body Politics: Five Practices of the Christian Community Before the Watching World* (Scottdale, PA: Herald, 1992), 14–46.
13. James Gustafson, "The Sectarian Temptation: Reflections on Theology, the Church, and the University," in the *Proceedings of the Catholic Theological Society*, 40 (1985): 83–94.

believer's baptism in the likes of Menno Simmons to the iconoclastic Zwickau prophets to apocalyptic revolutionaries such as Thomas Müntzer. In Luther's imagination, each restorationist represented wholesale spiritual anarchy. Many were made to share the labels of "fanatical," "spiritualizer," and finally—an epithet of reprobation—"re-baptizers" (ana-baptists).[14]

Yoder responds to the marginalization of his tradition by underscoring the *radicalness* (in the sense of *deep-rootedness*) of the Radical Reformation's departure from Catholic and mainline Protestant assumptions alike. Catholics and mainline Protestants mainly dispute doctrinal issues—most notably, the issue of whether God's justification of humanity is necessarily completed by faith made active in love and by a sanctified life, or whether it remains complete unto itself, breaking forth into good works freely, without recourse to "the law." Such is the primary issue at stake in the principal documents marking Lutheran-Roman Catholic conversation, as well as Reformed-Lutheran discussions concerning a "third use of the law." The differences center on whether and how ethical action (or a person's "work") relates to God's grace. What those differences and discussions do *not* highlight, however, is the concrete and communal *shape* of that work or "ethic"—what anti-Constantinians refer to as the concrete sociological pattern or proper politics of the church. In fact, viewing mainline differences from the perspective of the peace churches' witness makes clear just how similar the mainline churches are: "The difference between Lutheran and Calvinist confessions or between Anglican and Roman confessions in the sixteenth century does not focus on any significant ethical differences," whereas "the debates between the Anabaptists and all those others did include ethical differences."[15] Again, the radical reformers assume that membership

---

14. William Cavanaugh, in "The Invention of Fanaticism," *Modern Theology* 27.2 (April 2011): 229, traces the first contemporary (and pejorative) uses of *fanaticism* to Luther's characterization of Thomas Müntzer (leader of the peasant revolt in 1524–25, which Luther advised the princes to crush) as a *Schwärmer*—one who did not properly relativize religious passion to the authority of the prince and emerging German state. Luther's closest collaborator, Philip Melanchthon, uses *fanaticus homo* to caricature even Anabaptist pacifists, since they too wanted the church to act without the permission and protection of the state.

within the dissident grassroots political community called church entails being different, "called out" from the ways of the world, a calling exhibited by visible marks.

Stanley Hauerwas recounts the unwitting convergence of mainline churches, together with mainstream culture, in still more startling terms. Presenting at an ecumenical conference for Lutherans and Catholics, Hauerwas hoped he "would help them see they had much in common—namely, Catholics and Lutherans had always assumed it was a good thing to kill the Anabaptists."[16] Church bodies such as the Evangelical Lutheran Church in America (ELCA), in their declaration on the condemnation of Anabaptists, have confessed their complicity in this violence and have repudiated "the use of governmental authorities to punish individuals or groups."[17] Nevertheless, lessons about the public, political shape of Christian discipleship and community still need to be learned.

A Tale of Two Democracies

As we have seen, the magisterial reformers divided in theory, but coupled in practice, ecclesial and princely powers in ways that reproduced the church's fall into Constantinianism.[18] In some ways, post-Reformation territorial churches proved more dangerous than the unified medieval Christendom they helped to split apart. With the rise of modern nation-states, the "Christianity" of a country continued to function as that which ordains and buttresses the powers of the state (the church as chaplaincy), rather than curb and critique it, as remained possible in the Holy Roman Empire and medieval Europe. Indeed, the emergence of the modern state and the building of confessional identities went hand in hand. That a territory was confessionally Catholic, Lutheran, or Calvinist distinguished it as a

---

15. John Howard Yoder, *The Priestly Kingdom: Social Ethics as Gospel* (Notre Dame, IN: University of Notre Dame Press, 2008), 108.
16. Stanley Hauerwas, *A Better Hope* (Grand Rapids, MI: Brazos, 2000), 134.
17. "Declaration of the Evangelical Lutheran Church in America on the Condemnation of Anabaptists," accessed August 10, 2015, http://download.elca.org/ELCA Resource Repository/ Declaration_Of_The_ELCA_On_The_Condemnation_Of_Anabaptists.pdf.
18. Yoder, *Priestly Kingdom*, 144.

religious *and* political community from neighboring religious-political communities.[19] But Constantinianism got even worse—or at least, increasingly ironic, further obscuring the root of the problem—when the separation of church and state and the privatization of religion became understood as the most "Christian" arrangement.[20] The official disestablishment of religion after the Enlightenment and the rise of modern liberal democracy can preserve and even solidify the moral identification of church and state.[21] Bonhoeffer concurs that democracy in America is "regarded as the Christian form of the state," and he faults American Christians for confusing tolerance and respect for personal rights with the Christian message itself.[22] Thus, liberal democracy, personal freedoms, and even the legal disestablishment of religion in places such as the United States—while seemingly turning in the reverse direction—nonetheless tighten Christendom's screws. At this point, we must ask: How might Christian communities substantially differ from the form of liberal democracies, especially since the second is such a close simulacrum of the first?

To begin to answer, we should distinguish two different kinds of democracy. Democracy can indicate communal self-rule as a *discipline* that each citizen must learn in service of the common good. But it more commonly refers to *liberal* democracy as contemporary United States citizens "practice" it—or don't—because it can ask so little of us. Allow me to explain.

Liberal democracy arises out of the social contract theories of Thomas Hobbes and John Locke. These political theorists imagine humanity as originally born into a nonpolitical, noncooperative "natural" state where (for Hobbes) individuals are constantly at war with one another or (for Locke) individuals have some sense of individual propriety, but not the means to protect it. Out of need to protect themselves and their stuff, people subsequently enter into

---

19. Cavanaugh, "The Invention of Fanaticism," 230.
20. Yoder, *Priestly Kingdom*, 142.
21. Ibid.
22. Dietrich Bonhoeffer, *Ethics*, trans. Reinhard Krauss et al. (Minneapolis: Fortress Press, 2005), 126–27.

political arrangements or contracts. Those of us born after this rise of social contracts buy into them retrospectively through the theory of popular consent and by having the option to participate in periodic elections. At base, these political philosophies reject any native sense of cooperation or political concert in favor of a foundational myth that portrays humans as, first of all, discrete individuals who try to maximize and protect their possessions and power. Politics itself is thus a necessary compromise, according to this myth. Instead of questing for "power after power, that ceaseth only in death" (Hobbes), people choose to limit their otherwise unlimited desires and respect the rights of others in order to secure autonomy over a more limited—but safely guarded—realm of personal rights and liberties. Liberal democracy in this sense is about the liberation of individuals "from constitutive bonds and cultural ties and only secondarily about the core value of democracy, that is, self-government within a shared acknowledgment of constraint and limits."[23]

For many today, this emphasis on personal liberties and the right to vote for candidates promising to maximize those liberties comprises the only democracy they know. According to Patrick Deneen, however, such usage degrades the word *democracy*—"a word that implies self-governance but instead has come to mean unbridled liberty and unrestrained consumption."[24] The earlier, more substantial understanding of democracy comes from the Greek philosophical tradition of Plato, and especially, Aristotle. For Aristotle—and unlike the modern social contract theorists—humanity is political by nature, a "political animal" from the start. Needed is not an *artifice* to get humanity out of constant war and theft, but rather, an ongoing *discipline* or *tradition* that will enable people to flourish as the political animals that they are. As disciplines, self-rule and leadership of and

---

23. Patrick J. Deneen, "Wendell Berry and Democratic Self-Governance," in *The Humane Vision of Wendell Berry*, ed. Mark T. Mitchell and Nathan Schlueter (Wilmington, DE: Intercollegiate Studies Institute, 2011), 65. Deneen examines Berry's understanding of self-rule of and constraint within local communities as the only real solution to the woes of liberal nation-states. I am indebted to Deneen for my analysis of the competing democracies, as well as to Jason Peters, who first introduced me to Deneen's work.

24. Ibid., 84.

care for others *are learned*; for Aristotle, this is best done by first submitting to the rule and care of others. Participating in a democracy, from this point of view, does not turn on tacitly agreeing to limit one's self-seeking ambitions so that they can be more efficiently fulfilled. Rather, it involves learning to shape and sculpt one's desires so that they properly fit with the social fabric or *polis* from which one comes and in which one participates.

Disciplined and liberal democracies are nowhere more different than in the understandings of human nature and human freedom that they assume. According to Deneen:

> Liberal anthropology is based upon an abstract and arguably fictive form of liberty: it begins by imagining that human beings in their natural state are placeless, historyless, timeless, loveless and without governance. They are, by nature, creatures without a past, and a future that can only include a rapacious desire to acquire and increase possessions and power. They possess insatiable desires and calculating reason. Anything short of thorough dominion by individuals is an imposition upon our nature.[25]

Judith Butler calls this anthropology the "ontology of discrete identity." It is presupposed by liberal norms and remains unmindful of the "interlocking networks of power and position in contemporary life."[26] Compare this to an understanding of human nature and disciplined democratic participation that arises out of Aristotle:

> For Aristotle, the human good, above all, consisted in the realization of human nature. Human nature itself was fundamentally political, directed at the good of the city as a whole that superseded the private satisfaction of individuals. The good of the polis allowed for the flourishing of individuals within the city, centrally if not exclusively, in the exercise of citizenship as part of the well-lived life in which we strive to come to a closer understanding of "the whole." . . . The polis is a culture of moderation and self-restraint, devoted to the education and enactment of self-government.[27]

Given that liberalism presupposes this "ontology of discrete identity"

25. Ibid., 66.
26. Judith Butler, *Frames of War: When Is Life Grievable?* (London: Verso, 2009), 31.
27. Deneen, "Wendell Berry and Democratic Self-Governance," 70–71.

(Butler), its democratic citizen is thought to be a dis-embedded, unencumbered self whose right to maximize self-interest is thoroughly protected as long as he or she respects the right of others to do the same.[28] Alternative citizens understand themselves to come from a political body and submit to that body, first to be schooled, cared for, and otherwise governed before learning to properly school, care for, and take leadership of the community. Two very different political bodies correspond: The first democratic body refers to a "society," nation-state, or another large and abstract bureaucracy that can grow indefinitely, given that its cohesiveness depends more on individual protection, tolerance of others, and procedural rule rather than on mutual trust and shared commitment to the common good. The second democratic body must be smaller in scale, but extends across generations, given that education of the young into citizenship is one of the chief undertakings of citizenship itself. What is more, knowing the particularities of a locality and its "locals" is essential for mutual trust and accountability.

Obviously, I have followed Deneen in favoring Aristotelian democracy over liberal democracy. I am also convinced that the political commitments of Christians today should tend toward communitarianism, or what I have here called disciplined democracy, rather than reproducing America's liberal politics. But even stating the matter this way makes it seem as though Christians should simply choose between various political options, none of which was originally their own.[29] It also tends to understate the degree to which Christianity (and other religions) get privatized and de-politicized by the advent of liberal political thought. John Locke, for example, used religious fanatics as the foil for his own case for tolerance. Later, Voltaire associated religion itself with intrinsically irrational, fanatical, and dangerous passions, which must be checked at the door, if not altogether suppressed, when entering the public, political sphere.[30]

---

28. Compare Kierkegaard's critique of spiritlessness in chapter 3 above.
29. Related here is Hauerwas's comment that "the assumption that we must choose between 'liberalism and communitarianism' is a choice determined by liberal presuppositions." Stanley Hauerwas, God, Medicine and Suffering (Grand Rapids, MI: Eerdmans, 1990), 110.

The privatization and de-politicization of religion ensures that the politics of a liberal democracy is kept safe from religious fanaticism and violence—or so this myth has convinced us.[31] Many, if not most, of us have accepted modernity's story of religious violence just as uncritically as we have accepted liberalism's social contract mythology. We thus believe that, if individual rights are to be protected and the nation-state secured, each of us must keep faith out of politics. This benefits the status quo.[32] It also helps reproduce a form of acculturated Christianity that fully accommodates a rather hegemonic politics of our time—one where everyone is forced to be free but few feel as though they belong anywhere or to anyone. Most now regard church as an "option," something some people choose to do in their *personal* time out of *individual* wants or needs.

The Politics of Christian Community

Can church be more and different? How might Christian communities showcase a distinctive politics that provides a real alternative to the cultural effects of liberal democracy that leave many of us disconnected and suspicious—even of immediate neighbors? An even more important question is this: If Christians were to undergo the discipline necessary to participate in a deeper democracy by covenanting with church members, becoming vulnerable to one another, practicing radical hospitality, and otherwise standing-out from dominant political arrangements, would this come at the expense of personal freedoms? Is personal liberty and liberation incompatible with communal living, or something like its other side?

I here turn from theorizing the relationship between Christianity and politics to showcasing some of what I have learned from members

---

30. Cavanaugh, "The Invention of Fanaticism," 231–33.

31. William Cavanaugh, *The Myth of Religious Violence: Secular Ideology and the Roots of Modern Conflict* (Oxford: Oxford University Press, 2009), 151–80.

32. In the words of Metz, "it is precisely the consistently nonpolitical interpretation of Christianity, and the nondialectical interiorizing and individualizing of its doctrines, that have continually led to Christianity taking on an uncritical, as it were, postfactum political form." Johann Baptist Metz, *The Emergent Church: The Future of Christianity in a Postbourgeois World*, trans. Peter Mann (New York: Crossroads, 1981), 27.

of small intentional communities, sometimes called "neo-monastic" communities.[33] Observations of and conversations with these community members have helped me to consider the shape and function of their radical and ordinary politics.[34] But why should one look to small bands of Christian communities, some no larger than a household, in the attempt to display the proper politics of the church as a whole? Would not looking to institutional churches and to ecclesiology—a theology of the church—be more instructive, as well as more realistic? Attention to Christian communities is important for three reasons.

First, there is the matter of scale. Unlike the typical church member, whose political efficacy is often mediated through churchwide or affiliate organizations such as the denomination's social services or Christian-based homeless shelters or disaster relief programs, members of Christian communities often live out their politics directly, both with community members (decision-making by consensus) and with others (housing the homeless or harboring the undocumented, for example). Dorothy Day, founder of the Catholic Worker movement, insists that neither justice nor love can be enacted through the government or national or international agencies. Both depend on individuals in close proximity who enact small acts of hospitality and care for one another, for strangers, and for enemies. Such acts happen all the time within traditional congregations and in the daily lives of everyday Christians; they are simply more pervasive, pronounced, and purposeful in communities whose reason for being is to incarnate the body of Christ directly and deliberately.

Second, I have found Christians living in community to be

---

33. These communities include the Rutba House in Durham, North Carolina; the Simple Way in Philadelphia; New Hope Catholic Worker Farm in Lamotte, Iowa; Mustard Seed Community in Ames, Iowa; Reba Place Fellowship in Evanston, Illinois; the Mennonite Worker in Minneapolis; and Christ Community Church in Des Moines, Iowa. Grace Koleczek and/or I visited and conducted multiple, open-ended interviews with the last five listed, the findings of which are published in Jason A. Mahn and Grace Koleczek, "What Intentional Christian Communities Can Teach the Church," *Word and World* 34.2 (Spring 2014): 178–87.

34. For accounts written by insiders, see the Rutba House, ed., *School(s) for Conversion: 12 Marks of a New Monasticism* (Eugene, OR: Cascade, 2005); Jonathan Wilson Hartgrove, *New Monasticism: What It Has to Say to Today's Church* (Grand Rapids, MI: Brazos, 2008); and David Janzen, *The Intentional Christian Community Handbook* (Brewster, MA: Paraclete, 2013).

inordinately reflective and articulate about why they do what they do. Communities such as these "process" nearly everything—from who should be doing the dishes to which particular political protests follow from or conflict with their Christian commitments. By displaying their own deliberations, I am able to convey not only the political form and practices of Christians, but also, how they understand their identity and purpose, especially as a response to outsiders who often idealize, romanticize, dismiss, or marginalize them.

Finally, I have found that intentional Christian communities directly face and deliberately work through tensions between their calling to submit to the community and a seemingly opposing calling to preserve and perfect each member's "personal" freedoms. The need to balance freedom and submission sometimes arises from challenges from without. Hearing of intentional religious communities, many in mainline denominations picture some sort of free-love utopian communes filled with libertine flower children from the 1960s. Others imagine charismatic but manipulative leaders brainwashing a cult of disciples. Community members overturn such stereotypes by including diverging and dissenting opinions while still bending to the needs of the whole. Yet, even without the stereotypes of outsiders, members of intentional communities are able to reside at the intersection of two different (but not opposed) politics of their own. The first emphasizes the *form* of communal formation; the second, the *function* of individual liberation. I turn now to this form and function of their communities, as well as to their goals and a salient practice.

Form: Communities of Care

Liberal democracies produce a climate in which many find themselves "bowling alone" and otherwise valuing individual, consumer choices over commitment to the common good.[35] By contrast, intentional religious communities, by and large, attempt to school their members into belonging to a whole that is greater than the sum of its parts.

35. Robert D. Putnam, "Bowling Alone: America's Declining Social Capital," *Journal of Democracy* 6.1 (Jan. 1995): 65–78.

Reba Place Fellowship moved to Evanston, Illinois, in 1957 after being founded a few years earlier by members of the Mennonite seminary and college in Goshen, Indiana. It now comprises a large and relatively loose-knit community insofar as its core members (currently about fifty to sixty) live in various places in the northern Chicago neighborhood, including Fellowship households, apartments surrounded by non-members, and individual households. Given its large membership, its clearly defined layers of commitment,[36] and the extensiveness of its civic and financial engagement (owning property, running food co-op and bike shop businesses, etc.), the fact that members note their reliance on clearly demarcated roles and leadership is not surprising. What is more surprising is that even in a large community with formalized structure and paid employees, participants distinguish it from collectives that are more bureaucratic or liberal in the classic sense delineated above.

For example, Becky, a Reba Fellowship novice, speaks of having "shopped around" among congregations where church was "individualized" and "limited to Sundays." She finds Reba Place Fellowship to be much more communal or communitarian, illustrated by the fact that buying a car, for example, becomes a decision handled through open-ended discernment and prayer within a small group. Members use language of *bending* and even *submitting* to the wisdom of any and every community member, whose sense of responsibility and ownership increases with concerns introduced by another. Individual responsibility and deference to the community here rise in tandem, even though negotiating the two is not always simple.

Both Mustard Seed and New Hope Catholic Worker Farms couple individual freedom and yielding to the community in even more compelling ways. Each Iowan farm tries to embody the anarchism

36. Reba Place Community's layers of membership include apprentices (somewhat like interns living in the community and working in the area), practicing members (those who discern whether this community is the right fit), novice members (those who live on the fellowship's budget but keep their own money while also discerning full membership), and covenant members (the innermost layer comprised of members who share a common purse). Compare David Janzen, "Mark 6: Intentional Formation in the Way of Christ and the Rule of the Community Along the Lines of the Old Novitiate," in Rutba House, ed., *School(s) for Conversion*, 80–96.

propounded by the Catholic Worker's original founders, Dorothy Day and Peter Maurin. They intentionally form nonhierarchical relationships and critique the state's coercion. On a typical day at New Hope, one couple might be raking hay in the field while others are preparing lunch in the outdoor kitchen, tending to the "three sisters" garden (a Native American planting practice), or working on the newest housing structure from wood salvaged from an old barn. *Anarchism*, here, certainly cannot suggest that each member goes her or his own way, but only that they strive for relationships with one another, guests, and the soil itself that are nonhierarchical and nondominating. At the same time, there are centers of power that the community acknowledges. For example, one of the four couples, Mary and Rick, started the community, own the land, and often, provide the public face of the farm to neighboring towns. Still, Brenna, a member, notes that they strive to be a grassroots *organism* rather than a top-down *organization*, refraining from paid roles or titles and making all shared decisions by consensus.

Such communities do seem to resist the residual individualism that characterizes most special-interest groups that pass for "community" or church today. But do they have staying power? Can they work to form people in long-lasting ways and not simply form another niche for those who happen to be interested? Admittedly, Christian communities can come and go at a rapid rate, while individuals join and vacate them even more quickly. For every person I talked to in these communities, I heard of many more who discerned that it was not for them, who started a different community, who had changing needs, and so on. Noteworthy, however, is the fact that members *do* speak of them; they remember the marks (sometimes, the wounds) that they leave behind. One would guess, too, that the frequency of departures would be equal or higher at any typical mainline congregation, especially when one includes those who leave a particular church or parish for reasons completely "understandable" —getting a new job and moving away. Being formed within intentional community makes such mobility less reasonable. In fact, the commitments members make to particular people inhabiting particular places, along with the daily practices that further root them there, work to resist the rampant deracination of our upwardly mobile culture.

In different ways, each community resists the proliferation of possibilities and seductions of self-interest out of affection for *these* people and *this* place. Such resistance depends on what Wendell Berry calls the propriety of scale.[37] In short, one can only properly know what one can properly care for and properly care for just so much. The Catholic Worker farms employ this principle deliberately: New Hope has eight adults on the farm because that is what the land can sustain; Mustard Seed recently purchased ten acres because that is what it can care for. Attention to scale characterizes the urban communities as well. Sarah Lynn, a long-term member of the Mennonite Worker, tells of studying international human rights in college while intending to work for the United Nations or another global organization. She later recognized that the simplest way to do no harm is to work for change on a smaller scale.[38] That is also how one develops deep affections, has one's desires "schooled" to love what one should, and so, stays in a place with those whom one loves. Fidelity to a particular place and community also enables communities to resist temptations to Constantinianism—in Sarah Lynn's case, temptation to work on large levels (for the government, international agencies, or multinational corporations) in order to effect change in the world. As Dorothy Day first noticed (and Wendell Berry confirms), working on such massive scale often erects a barrier between the one seeking to be a "world-changer" and those she or he should serve more personally and faithfully.[39]

Finally, while such stability is initially established through the vows

---

37. See, for example, Berry's 2012 NEH Jefferson Lecture, "It All Turns on Affection," accessed August 10, 2015, http://www.neh.gov/about/awards/jefferson-lecture/wendell-e-berry-lecture.

38. Renunciation of political ambitions and other large-scale aspirations characterizes a number of the conversion narratives of community leaders. See Shane Claiborne, *The Irresistible Revolution* (Grand Rapids, MI: Zondervan, 2006), 291–340; Jonathan Wilson-Hartgrove, *To Baghdad and Beyond* (Eugene, OR: Cascade, 2005), 6–24; Chris Haw, *From Willow Creek to Sacred Heart* (Notre Dame, IN: Ave Maria, 2012), 3–30; and Mark Van Steenwyk, *The UNkingdom of God* (Downers Grove, IL: IVP, 2013), 13.

members make upon joining (in Reba Place's case, commitments to "stay unless God calls you elsewhere"), it would seem that the ties that truly bind form through the intentional work and prayer that happens *after* the initiation. Members do not simply perpetually *stick to* their vows, but become *engrafted* into a body that they eventually cannot do without. Jared and Don from the Mennonite Workers suggest that while many members once *chose* to practice *voluntary* poverty, now their poverty is fairly *involuntary*. It is involuntary not because they wish it were different, but because they find themselves wholly depending on the community and accepting such need as who they are. Mutual dependence holds the body politic together.

Function: Liberation from Oppression

The communal form of these Christian communities largely exhibits Aristotelian rather than liberal understandings of self-governance. This is not terribly surprising, given that these small communities self-consciously provide alternatives to our highly individualized and bureaucratized dominant culture. What is surprising is that even as the form of such communities follows a communitarian shape, their function largely fulfills exactly what liberal democracies quest after but find elusive—the emancipation of individuals to resist the stories, scripts, and traditions that are forced on them from without. Ironically, however, the Christian communities often work to liberate individuals from the oppression of liberalism itself—in Hauerwas's words, from the story that there is no story except the story that each of us chooses for ourselves. To resist *that* hegemonic tradition—what Rodney Clapp calls a "liberal cage"[40]—a different sense of emancipation and freedom is required.

Christ Community Church, for instance, looks much like a "normal" church, with Sunday worship in a church building that follows a liturgy, or order of the service, that is similar to Catholic and mainline

---

39. Interview with Dorothy Day (1977), accessed August 10, 2015, https://www.youtube.com/watch?v=oDkv2ULYSXA.

40. Rodney Clapp, *A Peculiar People: The Church as Culture in a Post-Christian Society* (Downers Grove, IL: IVP Academic, 1996), 67.

Protestant worship. Yet, the liturgy serves to position the church as an alternative to America's managerial, therapeutic culture. It includes a confession of sin where members confess their bondage to the myth of redemptive violence and to other allegiances (the nation-state, economic security, and so forth) over the Lordship of Christ. The final blessing during one of my visits announced that Jesus's sacrifice "set[s] us free from the present evil age," an age that the rest of the service described in terms of militarism, consumerism, and uncritical patriotism. Such liturgies directly pit the powers of government and economy with those of God through Christ, continually creating space for a countercultural politic. Of course, any church's liturgical language can function in subversive ways—for example, whenever witnesses to a baptism renounce the ways of Satan, with all his empty promises (think security through the military, or happiness through rapacious consumption). Christ Community Church simply has the advantage of translating what may seem like purely "religious" language back into the properly theo-political language of Paul, Jesus, and the early church. Or again: it demythologizes liberal Christianity, with its assumption that the church and Christian salvation are spiritual realities hovering above the fray of political contention and conquest.

We should pause here and note that many find such stark and seemingly dichotomous descriptions of discipleship versus captivity to empire unproductive at best for the full emancipation of all persons. Since Hauerwas, in part, has popularized such language, he bears the brunt of many critiques. Recall that Hauerwas believes that the myth of liberalism can only be critiqued by a more compelling story, and that the answer to being formed by the market or the state is to be formed more determinatively by the church. Recall also that Gloria Albrecht charges that such understandings of the church as an alternative polis with alternative formative processes tend to reproduce a monolithic political body, a "singular cultural-linguistic tradition" or "false universal" in which individual differences and freedoms are washed out.[41] To perform church as alternative polis, according to Albrecht, risks setting up but another partisan political party, one that homogenizes individuals no less than do domineering nation-states, a global economy, or any other authoritarian regime.[42] Such strong churches render the individual too passive; the member undergoes full formation but loses her appeal to personal experience and freedom in the process.

Albrecht's critique helpfully indicates an oddity of Hauerwas's understanding of church—namely, that he wants to save it from liberal neo-Christendom only to restore an earlier hegemonic form. The key issue is whether ostensibly passive submission to the church's formative processes (*undergoing* baptism, *being* catechized, *submitting* to church discipline, *learning* Christian virtue by *emulating* Jesus and the saints and martyrs) can really be liberating—can set one free—in any meaningful sense. Can one's "personal" identity be thoroughly shaped by the formative and communitarian practices of Christian communities and still be called free? Or is freedom best understood in the plain negative sense of being able to do what one pleases so long as it does not interfere with the freedom of others?

Of the communities I have visited, the Mennonite Worker of Minneapolis looks, on the surface, to tilt most strongly in the nonauthoritarian direction. Located in a section of Minneapolis known for its vegan fare and anarcho-punk scene, the community's Simone Weil House gives shelter to so many short- and long-term guests (many otherwise homeless) that it can feel like a revolving door. A number of members consider themselves Christian anarchists, as did Dorothy Day, the founder of the Catholic Worker movement. Don (a "resident" or "novice" when I met him) was quick to explain that anarchism only means that they strive for nondomination in discourse and practice, exhibited primarily through rule by consensus alone. Pushed as to whether such freedom *from* the authority of another doesn't fit too squarely with individualism and the political liberalism that Mennonite Workers otherwise resist, Jared (a full member) explicitly

---

41. Gloria H. Albrecht, *The Character of Communities: Toward an Ethic of Liberation for the Church* (Nashville: Abingdon, 1995), 64, 76–77, 90.
42. Compare James Davison Hunter, *To Change the World*, 174–75, who critiques neo-Anabaptists for being hyper-partisan.

questioned why we must think of true authority and individual freedoms as a zero-sum game. He insists that "leveling out the playing field [in decision-making] *necessitates* community—it doesn't do away with it—because all of a sudden there is no one person making the decisions [and so] everyone has to make decisions." Individual freedom and commitment to the community here seem one and the same.

Mark Van Steenwyk, co-founder of the Mennonite Worker, puts the relationship in even more contested terms. Commenting on problems with getting branded as part of the New Monastic movement, Van Steenwyk notes that "when youre primary value is community, you almost always stifle dissent." According to Van Steenwyk, the chief mark of a Christian community, therefore, should not be the *form* of community, but rather, its primary *function*—to enable people to resist empire, redistribute wealth, replace anxiety and workaholism with prayer and rest, and otherwise, to recover from "addiction" to the dominant culture. Van Steenwyk wants his community and the many like it to function as "incubator[s] for anti-imperial politics."[43] The point is what the community *does*, not necessarily its shape or the members' fidelity to it as such. This move from form to function also repositions how and where Christ is recognized in the community's midst. By valuing "liberation" over "Anabaptism" (Van Steenwyk's words), the community recognizes the Spirit at work among the poor and oppressed whom the community "serves." Indeed, the term *service* must then be qualified if it normally connotes charity by the rich to those who need their help. We are all implicated in the "shitty system" that makes the poor dependent on the rich's charity in the first place, argues Van Steenwyk. Recognizing that Jesus is with the poor enables the rich to repent from that system, while empowering the poor to gain some leverage against it. Liberation happens in both directions or not at all. The point of radical communities such as the Mennonite Worker is thus to provide training in such recognition, repentance, and resistance. And yet, while the goal of such training is

---

43. Compare Dorothy Day's description of Catholic Worker houses as schools or training grounds for young people to learn how to love and to overcome fear that precipitates violence. Jim Forest, *All Is Grace: A Biography of Dorothy Day* (Maryknoll, NY: Orbis, 2011), 280.

liberation for all, the problem *does require training*. And training must be undergone, as members *submit* themselves to what amounts to a recovery program for addicts whose desires need radical reforming.[44] The function depends on the form, even if the form can occlude the function.

Purpose: Effective Holiness

A central stereotype about intentional Christian communities—one propagated by many in traditional churches—involves the idea that they essentially withdraw from the messy realities of civic duties, political necessities, and institutional churches in the effort to build idealist and self-righteous subgroups.[45] It is true that, for community members, commitments to the intentional community often absorb and displace commitments to broader worshipping communities—a fact that bothers many among them. Eric and Brenna, a married couple from New Hope Catholic Worker Farm, expressed disappointment with fellow Catholic Workers when, at a recent national gathering, most chose to worship within the gathering, rather than attend Mass at the local parish. According to them, this fails to appreciate and display the movement's longtime commitment to Catholicism and the church itself. Brenna claims that it is that inclusion in the universal church—and in God's grace—that keeps the movement thriving in the first place.

Putting aside the various relationships between these grassroots communities and broader Christian church bodies, the charge of sectarianism accuses such communities with being more interested in holiness (which often strikes critics as self-righteousness), rather than in efficacy. Such radical Christians appear to withdraw from the world,

---

44. The Mennonite Worker hosts a "Recovery from the Dominant Culture," twelve-step program modeled after one developed by Seminary of the Street in Oakland, California. Accessed August 10, 2015, http://www.mennoniteworker.com.

45. The assumption includes several charges: *theologically*, it accuses them of overlooking the universality of sin; *sociologically*, it faults them for being "against" culture rather "transforming" it (to use H. Richard Niebuhr's weighted categories); in terms of moral *dispositions* and religious *piety*, it charges them with caring about the purity of their principles over the effectiveness of their commitments.

rather than change it for the better. There is truth to this allegation as far as the categories hold. Many of the members I have gotten to know are more concerned with staying faithful to their collective calling than with focusing on results, especially when bringing them about would compromise their sense of fidelity. In the words of Jim, from Christ Community Church, "I'm not here to succeed, or even to stay alive, but to bear faithful witness." Political theologian Dorothee Soelle defends the "impracticality" of her political protests in largely the same way. Quoting an incisive saying of Martin Buber, she claims that "Success is not a name of God."[46]

Nonetheless, the image of the impractical, unengaged purist seems wholly false. Alternative practices and witness can become effective means of transforming the world. The relationship between fidelity and effectiveness is complex, as Chad from Christ Community Church brought up when he explained the decline in membership since the church's beginnings. In his words, "If you're really succeeding, it doesn't necessarily mean the Lord's on your side. And if you're really failing—or apparently failing—that doesn't necessarily mean that the Lord's against you." (That, in itself, is a counter-Constantinian remark, insofar as Constantinianism reads God's will directly from the so-called upward progress of Western history.)

Alice, the founder of Mustard Seed Catholic Worker farm, adds that what might not look like much—in her community's case, about ten committed individuals running an eight-acre farm, on which a host of other folks work three hours per week in exchange for a box of vegetables—still has the capacity to change the world. "Fundamentally, we are trying to turn the whole structure of the world upside down," she insists. That seems less overblown when one concedes her next point—namely, that much of the world currently runs by rules that are not only immoral or unchristian, but also, *not working*. Politics and economics as usual create poverty and other domination systems in which so many of us are caught. Perhaps aware of the charge of

---

46. Dorothee Soelle, *Dorothee Soelle: Essential Writings*, ed. Dianne L. Oliver (Maryknoll, NY: Orbis, 2006), 73. See also Jacqueline Bussie, "Dorothee Soelle: Lutheran Liberation Theologian of the Cross," in *Radical Lutherans/Lutheran Radicals*, ed. Jason A. Mahn (Eugene, OR: Cascade, forthcoming).

isolationism, she turns the table again. Compared to cooperatives, unions, farmer's markets, or Mustard Seed itself, the nuclear family looks quite isolationist, unable by its very composition to "create the kingdom of God."[47] Nicholas, an early member of Mustard Seed, distinguishes the long-term goal (to *change* the world) from the short-term task (to *witness* to a different way of life). The trick is to not hide from those who might take notice, while also avoiding becoming "overly ostentatious" or "judgmental."

Such members thus think of themselves as inhabiting *counter* or *alternative* cultures and politics, rather than (only) unplugging from predominant ones. This is especially true of their economic practices. Mennonite Workers, for example, offer personal, home-based hospitality in a culture that either outsources or institutionalizes what used to be a central practice of the church.[48] Yet, community members also participate in a much *wider* "economy" (from the Greek *oikonomia*, "household management") than our monetary economy. Mustard Seed member Rachel, for example, speaks of the power of knowing where her community's food comes from and where its waste goes to (the same place, if done right). Her accountings are wider and more sustainable than what normally passes for economics.

A Central Practice: Peacemaking

While the sectarian charge remains prominent, perhaps the easiest way to romanticize, and so, dismiss intentional Christian communities, especially those considered pacifist, is to take them as comprised of naturally peace-loving, harmonious individuals whose dispositions are enviable, but not permitting of emulation by more conflicted types. Yoder and Kierkegaard each remain aware of how personal evasions and outright dismissals can be disguised as admiration.[49] Actually, the

---

47. For an allegedly "sectarian" view that turns the charge of an overly realized eschatology back on Constantinian churches, see John Howard Yoder, *The Priestly Kingdom*, 136–38.

48. See "The Christ Rooms Project," *The Mennonite Worker of Minneapolis* 1.2 (October 1, 2013), accessed August 10, 2015, http://www.mennoniteworker.com/newspaper/.

49. Yoder, *Priestly Kingdom*, 4; Kierkegaard, *Practice in Christianity*, trans. Howard V. Hong and Edna H. Hong (Princeton, NJ: Princeton University Press, 1991), 241–49.

communities showcase tremendous realism about hostility and conflict in the world, their neighborhoods, and their own communities.

Some communities have directly arisen from the ashes of war. Rutba House, for example, is named after the town of Rutba, Iraq, where two injured members of a Christian Peacemaker Team (with Shane Claiborne and Jonathan and Leah Wilson-Hartgrove) were given care in a medical clinic. The Muslim doctor who sewed up the Christian peacekeeper's wounds explained that, although Rutba's main hospital had been bombed by the United States military just three days earlier, "we will take of you because Muslim or Christian, Iraqi or American, we take care of everyone." When Jonathan and Leah returned to the United States and began, with Isaac Villegas, their intentional Christian community, they named it Rutba House in memory of the peacemakers they encountered in the belly of Babylon.[50]

Community members also know that being pacifist has little to do with passivity or merely verbal disavowals of violence. The day I arrived as a guest at the Simple Way in Philadelphia's Kensington neighborhood, a bleary-eyed core member named Brett explained that he was so sleepy because he had been on the street for most of the night during a domestic dispute that escalated to involve many. Brett spoke of having learned—and of still learning—how to put his body between aggressors, of angling it in certain ways and speaking in particular tones in order to divert violence, reconcile neighbors, and sometimes, calm police officers. He said that he had been in the midst of potentially violent situations three or four times in the past couple of weeks. When I asked him if he was scared in such moments, he replied: "Shitless." "But usually only in retrospect, when I'm trying to calm down," he added. "These are neighbors that I know and that I know don't want to hurt me or anyone else." This kind of peacemaking attempts to unleash true, original human nature from beneath its fallen, more brutish state, Hobbes's mythology notwithstanding.

More than anything, what is clear from these Christian communities is that cultivating peaceful dispositions requires regular and strenuous

---

50. Wilson-Hartgrove, *To Baghdad and Beyond*, 77–94.

practice, and that such practice begins within the community. In fact, the only distinctly religious practice that every community I have studied shared was some version of interpersonal confession/sharing of grievances and a ritual of reconciliation. New Hope Catholic Worker Farm appears the most practiced and deliberate here. Mary and Rick, founders of the community, acknowledge how difficult living in community is; according to Rick, "it's the hardest experiment I've ever been engaged in." Much for him hinges on whether they can work through inevitable conflict: "If we [the eight adult members] can't succeed, and we're all white, middle class, similarly educated, of the same faith, then how are the Palestinians and Israelis or the Sunnis or any other group going to be able to do it? If we can't model a way of working through conflict, the worldwide situation becomes dismal."

Mary adds that active peacemaking always risks exacerbating latent conflict. Wanting to treat discord more intentionally than those (that is, most of us) who avoid conflict, New Hope turned to their shared faith background's sacrament of reconciliation, to the practices of a nearby monastic community, and to the work of Jean Vanier, Henri Nouwen, and others, in order to formalize a weekly ritual of reconciliation.[51] Beginning with silent prayer, New Hope's Friday service continues with admission of faults and shortcomings, along with asking for forgiveness. It continues by naming any grievances that haven't yet been acknowledged, while the one committing the offense "listens with an open heart and without defensiveness." The community then shares affirmations followed by the final step, a sharing of the peace. When persons occasionally raise large conflicts that cannot be "contained" in the ritual, they find even more deliberate strategies for working through them, drawing on nonviolent reconciliation training. In small and larger ways, the community understands itself to be "finding connection *through* violence" and even "living *into* conflict." The peace thereby is forged—strategically

---

51. Mustard Seed's most consistent practice, the "sharing of consolations and desolations," is patterned on an old tradition as well, the Ignatian Daily Examen.

and regularly—in order to more securely and habitually become what one "naturally" is.

The (Hidden) Visibility of the Church

I have been showcasing some of the practices and reflections of intentional Christian communities, rather than of broader church bodies, primarily because defining characteristics "show up" within them more clearly and powerfully. Skeptics still might claim that this focuses too much on young, politically progressive, and seemingly idealistic Christians whose social location and lack of family and work responsibilities allow them to relocate to poor urban areas or live on communal farms, to share economic resources, to practice hospitality to strangers and peacemaking in the midst of violence.[52] Just because older, more "established" Christians cannot do any or all of these things does not mean they are less Christian, the objection continues. However, that very objection partly confirms the importance of this witness. By exhibiting these characteristics, making them public and visible, Christians living in community show that communal formation, liberation for all, effective holiness, and active peacemaking are not highfalutin ideals, but a matter of everyday choices, commonplace practices, and ordinary habits or virtues to which every Christian is called. In my observations and conversations, I have found that community members are also incredibly creative when brainstorming ways that average churchgoers could participate in these practices wherever they find themselves. I, for example, live in an old large house with a finished attic that provides more than enough room for visiting family members and the occasional broke college student who asks to stay there. Might my family and I name it a Christ Room, and designate that space as *belonging* to neighbors and strangers who are hungry and need shelter, as my "radical" Christian friends have suggested? Might our congregation have a list of such

---

52. These comprise four of the twelve marks of New Monasticism according to the Rutba House, ed., *School(s) for Conversion*, xii–xiii.

rooms in the neighborhood that they could share with homeless men and women who knock on the church's door?

In his insider's perspective on new monastic communities, Jonathan Wilson-Hartgrove suggests that such communities should be considered "pro-church" and not simply "parachurch." Parachurch groups, filled with special-interest individuals and good at getting things done (responding to disasters, ministering to prisoners, etc.), have the particular liability of leaving less for the church itself to do. Plus, it is the church catholic, not fringe movements, that makes visible the wisdom of God to the powers of this world (see Eph 3:10).[53] The point here is that intentional Christian communities join other church communities in making discipleship recognizable. Such visibility confirms that radical Christian politics are realizable through ordinary methods and means: feeding the sick, visiting the imprisoned, forgiving one another, making decisions in concert, and so forth. It also exposes the pretexts that many give for hiding within the dominant social order all too well. The church's politics should be visible, as radical reformers convincingly argue, but without becoming one more political faction, as Bonhoeffer also adds.

Anabaptists (over Kierkegaard) on Visible Church Politics

As I have said, the primary beef of anti-Constantinians with the established church is that it presumes to be invisible, a "spiritual" reality—as opposed to having a particular, political form. In other words, we in mainline denominations and mainstream American culture tend to "shut [Jesus] up in the monastery of the heart."[54] The primary problem with Christianity's accommodation to dominant social and political culture is the fact that the "true church" becomes an otherworldly (read: invisible) reality, and so, made compatible with any and every sociopolitical arrangement. So, for example, Christians after Constantine can kill in the empire's or a nation's war despite the

---

53. Wilson-Hartgrove, *New Monasticism*, 145–47; compare Ivan Kauffman, "Mark 5: Humble Submission to Christ's Body, the Church," in Reba House, ed., *School(s) for Conversion*, 68–79.
54. John Howard Yoder, *The Original Revolution: Essays on Christian Pacifism* (Scottdale, PA: Herald, 2003), 175.

disarming of Peter, the "hard sayings" of the Sermon on the Mount, and the prototype of Christ's own nonviolent death, insofar as the otherwise visible marks of the visible church (in this case, nonviolence and peacemaking) have become privatized, hidden, and rendered unrecognizable together with the "true church." The corrective to Constantinianism, then and now, is thus for the church to become *distinguishable* from the world, a *visible* polis with its own *distinctive* politic. The power of this anti-Constantinian work is to force a choice between competing politics by giving a thick description of the concrete practices and relationships inherent in discipleship, and then, underscoring its incompatibility with other dominant social arrangements.

Anabaptists emphasize the visibility of the church against those church traditions (Lutheranism is one) that think of the "real church" as a heavenly, invisible reality, and "real Christians" as known only to God's inscrutable judgment. Even Kierkegaard, who critiques his earlier avowal of hidden interiority as the locus for authentic Christianity, gives little indication of what a visible, counter-Christendom *community* of Christians might actually look like. Instead, he largely portrayed real Christians in images of *individual* renunciation, anguish, and martyrdom, which are repeated mantra-like through his latest newspaper articles and attack essays.[55]

For Kierkegaard, then, Christianity is "marked" almost entirely by its inability to get along in the world, its "heterogeneity" with the world; whereas, for Hauerwas or Yoder, the ability of the Christian church to be "free standing," and thus offer an alternative politic provides the very ground of their critique of Christian accommodation. Without a more robust notion of a true and visible church, one wonders whether, for Kierkegaard, *church* and *Christendom* wholly align, and so, whether the only practical advice he can offer true Christians is stop going to church, as indeed he suggests at the end of his life.[56] By contrast, even if the true marks of the church show up most clearly when set in

---

55. Kierkegaard, *The Moment*, 5, 36, 42, 125.
56. Ibid., 73.

relief from politics as usual in "the world,"[57] Hauerwas and Yoder (with other "radical ecclesiologists") do think that the marks of the church are the marks *of the church*, comparisons notwithstanding. Without a distinctive political shape, one that offers a visible alternative to politics as usual, the church ceases to form members who look and act differently than any typical citizen of a liberal democracy.

This helps qualify what I meant when, at the beginning of this chapter, I wrote that it may have been unchristian for me to call the cops on my neighbor. Certainly, that act was not wrong in any legal or universally ethical sense; nor did it directly break a commandment from God as they are normally understood. What I found wrong—what led to my contrition and confession—was the fact that my Christian identity did not show up in any distinctive way as I confronted one neighbor, consulted the other, and offered to do "the responsible thing" by reporting the incident to the police. My failure was a sin of omission and of concealment, the inability to act in ways that manifest my participation in and formation by the church. That responsibility was mine, although the church as a whole is responsible for schooling members of Christ's body to stand out, when appropriate, from the dominant politics of liberalism. But if Christian witness must be visible, with borders between different corporate bodies, will this make the church into a faction of the righteous?

Bonhoeffer (over Anti-Constantinians) on Hidden Church Politics

Bonhoeffer understands church politics in ways indebted to those emphasizing the visible church. For a class lecture Bonhoeffer delivered at the underground seminary in Finkenwalde, he writes, "The present situation in church and theology can be summed up in the form of the following question: Does the church take up a space within the world, and if so, what kind of space is it? That is basically the question around which the whole theological confrontation with the state revolves."[58] In other words, the question of whether the church

---

57. Yoder, *Original Revolution*, 110.

can directly confront the state, merely capitulates to it, or enacts some other option turns on whether church can be clearly seen—identified as what *those* people over *there* are doing at *this* time—and does not simply name an ideal community of true believers known only in the mind of God. Finkenwalde seminary was created to give such space to one such Christian community. It provided space for Christians to pray together, to seek reconciliation, to share material resources and meals, and to offer hospitality. Bonhoeffer also regarded Christ as the only true mediator between people—one who brings them into intimacy through prayer, but also, makes room for even strangers to pass in and out of the community, perfectly balancing the form of communion with the function of liberating all.[59] Recall also from the previous chapter that Bonhoeffer lampoons that so-called Reformation theology that calls itself a theology of the cross but "whose signature is that it prefers a 'humble' invisibility in the form of total conformity to the world."[60] Without a distinctive political shape, one that takes up space in the world, and so, offers a visible alternative to politics as usual, the church quickly becomes indistinguishable from dominant society as such.

As a theologian of the cross, Bonhoeffer will not hide the particular and scandalous manifestation of a suffering God under a bushel basket, nor dress it up to be more attractive, palatable, or politically expedient. He wants God's good news to the poor and persecuted and the church that lives it out to be visible, as off-putting and invasive as that can be for the privileged. At the same time, Bonhoeffer (again, as a theologian of the cross) knows that God *remains hidden* the very moment that God discloses Godself in the cross and among the oppressed. He follows Luther in confessing to God: "Truly, thou art a God who hidest thyself."[61] Bonhoeffer's true church is not invisible, *but it is still hidden,*

58. Dietrich Bonhoeffer, *Theological Education at Finkenwalde: 1935-1937*, ed. Mark Brocker and H. Gaylon Barker (Minneapolis: Fortress Press, 2013), 153.
59. Bonhoeffer, *Life Together* and *Prayerbook of the Bible*, trans. Daniel W. Bloesch and James H. Burtness (Minneapolis: Fortress Press, 1996), 41–44.
60. Bonhoeffer, *Discipleship*, 113.
61. Martin Luther, Heidelberg Disputation (1518), in *Martin Luther's Basic Theological Writings*, ed. Timothy F. Lull, 2nd ed. (Minneapolis: Fortress Press, 2005), 57 (thesis 20), quoting Isa 45:15.

glimpsed only in unlikely places, and some that seem irreligious. The true form of the church might therefore remain hidden within rather religionless, secular forms, as Bonhoeffer mused near the end of his life. More importantly, the true church always takes the form of the crucified Christ, as Bonhoeffer stressed throughout his life. In particular, Christians are formed to be the body of a Christ who has taken on the sin of others, who dies guilty in solidarity with sinners, so that others might live. It follows that the visible form of the true church, this body of the crucified Christ, also hides under an opposite sign—in the form of those gathered in repentance for their sins and for the sins of others.[62]

Bonhoeffer entreats disciples in training to be content with not seeing the value of their works. Our sanctification does and should remain "hidden from us until the day when everything will be revealed."[63] Again, such hiddenness does not dampen the force of Bonhoeffer's call for the church to be a visible community that resists conformity, one that preserves the boundary between its mission and the shape of the wider world.[64] But necessary hiddenness does mean that "in the very midst of the presumably visible progress in our sanctification in which we would like to rejoice, we are most of all called to repent and to recognize our works as thoroughly sinful."[65] According to Bonhoeffer, Christians are called to bold, political works of radical discipleship *and* to repent of them, especially of the pride they might take in them. His own courageous resistance to Nazism threw him into the moral ambiguities of civil disobedience, espionage, and at least the tacit support of a conspiracy to kill Hitler. At the same time, he confesses the sinfulness of such politics and the politics that it opposes—his own sin and the sin of others—trusting that God can and will redeem both sides.

---

62. Bonhoeffer, *Ethics*, 95–98. See also Jennifer McBride's exquisite study of Bonhoeffer's understanding of the church's visibility through the confession of its and others' sins. Jennifer M. McBride, *The Church for the World: A Theology of Public Witness* (Oxford: Oxford University Press, 2012), 119–52.
63. Bonhoeffer, *Discipleship*, 279.
64. Ibid., 46–49, 110–14.
65. Ibid., 279.

Radical Nonpartisanship

Ironically, the most visible distinction between "the church" and "the world" might just distinguish all political partisanship on the one side—distinctions between conservative and liberal, democrat and republican, friend and enemy, right and wrong, white and black, the haves and the have-nots, sinners and saints—and, on the other side, those whose courageous, repentant solidarity with Christ, and with the suffering and sin of others, tears down every other partition. The church inhabits a politic beyond all partisanship, one that provides a visible alternative to the very self-righteous divisions that otherwise rule our world. Its central practice is the confession of all that Christians have done and left undone, the sins of their community and of the wider world. Solidarity in suffering and sin truly sets Christians apart.

In this light, the contrition and conviction that I felt for behaving unchristianly with my neighbor stemmed not, first of all, from something that I did or did not do, but from the way I imagined who she was, who I am, and the boundaries between us. Were I better formed, better churched into an alternative polis, one whose boundaries are erected between solidarity and partisanship, I would have seen my sin in hers, recognized Jesus in her suffering, and envisioned all of us as members of the broken body of Christ. Whatever I could have or should have done, I would have done it more imaginatively, less independently, with less self-righteousness and greater compassion and solidarity.

Although I have indicated some promising aspects of sharing sin here, the invocation of sin and repentance as a defining mark of the church can lead in unhealthy directions. Too often, the ubiquity of sin gets used to justify a "responsible" resort to coercion and power politics, which only sidesteps the prophetic witness by pacifists, Bonhoeffer, Dorothy Day, and numerous intentional Christian communities. Especially when it comes to war, the fact that the world is a fallen place seems all the reason Christians need to get their hands dirty and resort to "necessary" violence. The next chapter attends to the way of the cross as it intersects with and often capitulates to America's ways of war.

8

WAR: Subversions of the Cross

"Today there must be no more war—the cross will not have it."[1] This sentence was written by Dietrich Bonhoeffer in the summer of 1932, five months before Hitler became Chancellor of Germany and three years before Bonhoeffer wrote *Discipleship*, considered to be his most "pacifist" text, from the underground seminary at Finkenwalde. What does Bonhoeffer mean, *the cross* will not have any more war?

Cross Purposes

In the first-century Roman Empire, torture and execution by crucifixion was reserved for political insurrectionists—those whom Rome found subversive of its political sovereignty. Death by crucifixion was also manifestly public and highly symbolic; the cross was meant to reveal Rome's monopoly on the power to kill, at least with such theatrics. Strangely, about three hundred years later, Christians began retrieving the cross as a symbol of their faith. What had been a symbol of Rome's power over life and death became, for Christians, a symbol

---

1. Dietrich Bonhoeffer, *No Rusty Swords: Letters, Lectures and Notes 1928-1936* (New York: Harper & Row, 1965), 187.

of God's power revealed through Christ in the story of Good Friday and Easter. This Christian retrieval of the cross as symbol was strange and somewhat subversive, but perhaps not wholly incongruous given that, according to legend, Constantine saw "the trophy of a cross" bearing the inscription "conquer by this" before heading into battle, and later, commanded Christian soldiers to hold swords upside down, cruciform, when engaging their enemies. The cross in Christendom thereby became a symbol of the military might of the newly christened *Holy* Roman Empire—often wielded to persecute Jews—no less than it had symbolized Rome's domination over Jesus the Jew 300 years earlier.[2] In both cases, the cross permits and sanctions the power of a government to kill, rather than disallowing it, as Bonhoeffer pleads.

For the cross of Jesus to symbolize resistance to war, for it to subvert the sanctioning of legal violence, it must be re-remembered in creative, constructive, and more determinately Christian ways. This could be done by thoroughly demythologizing the cross, seeing it for what it is—a state-sponsored method of execution that violently killed the nonviolent Jesus of Nazareth. The cross would then connote all that Jesus clearly rejects (but rejects nonviolently, that is, by submitting to it) as he witnesses to a different way of life, and thus becomes the pattern for Christian peacemaking. Alternatively, a highly symbolic "theology of the cross" could be allowed but reconceived—representing not merely a *transfer* of unilateral power from emperor to the Christian God, but rather, a *radical reconception* of what ultimate power entails in light of God's self-revelation in Jesus, especially in his suffering and death. Here, the cross would resist war and other forms of legalized violence by exposing the pride and self-justifications below their wide acceptance. If the very power of God is fully revealed in a dead Palestinian Jew, in one who would rather die than kill, then all our other ostensibly normal associations of power with security,

---

2. James Carroll, *Constantine's Sword: The Church and the Jews* (Boston: Mariner Books/Houghton Mifflin, 2001), 172–77. For the earliest account of Constantine's fabled vision of the cross, see Eusebius Pamphilus, "The Life of the Blessed Emperor," in *Nicene and Post-Nicene Fathers*, 2nd ser. Vol. 1, *Eusebius: Church History, Life of Constantine the Great, and Oration in Praise of Constantine*, ed. Philip Schaff and Henry Wace (Peabody, MA: Hendrickson, 1994), 490, as cited by Carroll, *Constantine's Sword*, 175.

invulnerability, and unilateral action get exposed as sinful. Both of these approaches are needed. To become Christian in "Christian" America will entail conversion to a new, countercultural community of peacemakers. It will also entail the interminable confession of one's complicity in violence and of the sin of worshipping a god of dominance instead of the God of Jesus.

Throughout this chapter, I will argue that Christianity, in its most acculturated and accommodated form, essentially conflates military might with the power of God, and that untangling that entanglement is paramount to becoming a Christian in Christendom. All three leading critiques of Christendom (that of Kierkegaard, Bonhoeffer, and anti-Constantinians) are helpful here, although some in less obvious ways than others. Self-proclaimed Christian pacifists (including Bonhoeffer) often maximize the sharp differences between following a nonviolent Jesus and giving allegiance to a militarized nation-state. Witnessing to this difference and to the ways Christian pacifism can be inhabitable and sustainable (underscoring just how "realistic" it is) offers a tremendous gift to more mainstream Christians accustomed to having one kingdom ruled by the gospel while reserving tough foreign policy for the other. To them—that is, to most of us—Christian pacifists force a choice, one we ought not inadvertently make by evading it.

But this chapter will also demonstrate that those in the wake of Luther's theology of the cross (which also includes Bonhoeffer) can also resist the militarization of so-called Christian countries. Focusing especially on how unilateral power, security, and the pursuit of invulnerability get deified in the first place, theologians of the cross see God and God's power fully revealed in the cross of Christ and recognize their thoroughgoing sinfulness in its light. They do not so much force a choice between discipleship and so-called political necessities, but rather, open the would-be Christian to the painful, powerful process of recognizing his or her complicity in violence as a way of dying to sin and being raised to new life in Christ. In many ways, the difference between Anabaptist pacifists and what is yet to emerge as a distinctively "Lutheran" approach to resisting war resides in the "low

Christology" of the first camp (who stress Jesus as a human and discipleship as becoming like Jesus) and the "high Christology" of the second (who stress Christ as the full revelation of God and discipleship as living into the scandal of this "doctrine"). I will thus need to write of the person and work of Jesus the Christ as well as of the nature and mission of our militarized nation. We continue by contrasting the sacrifices of each.

The Ultimate Sacrifice

It is safe to say that the ubiquitous talk of "sacrifice" today has two overlapping cultural-linguistic homes in the United States. First, many of us think of Jesus's cross, especially given the popularity of substitutionary or satisfaction understandings of the atonement, according to which Jesus is sacrificed in our place to bear our punishment or pay our debt with his very life. Second, we think of and honor the sacrifices of military personnel who give their time, allegiance, and sometimes, their limbs and lives so that the rest of us can live safe and secure. That soldiers symbolize sacrifice, and even offer and signify "the ultimate sacrifice," is reinforced by almost every public ceremony, dedication, and sporting event in this country. Not long ago, singing the national anthem—itself a war song—was enough to create a common spirit of *communitas* out of the motley crew of sporting "fans" (short for "fanatics," or those with uncritical enthusiasm and zeal). Today, it is hard to attend a baseball game, much less a national memorial or celebration, without multiple flags, color guards, gun salutes, and ceremonial flyovers, all of which express and reinforce our country's indebtedness to the sacrifice of its soldiers.

Political speeches reinforce with word what we frequently enact with our songs and salutes. On the eve of America's 2003 invasion of Iraq, George W. Bush modeled moral clarity and robust willpower when he addressed the nation about the mission ahead, adding: "Americans understand the costs of conflict because we have paid them in the past. War has no certainty except the certainty of sacrifice."[3] Seven years later, on the anniversary of September 11, Barack Obama made a speech about gathering "at this sacred hour, on hallowed ground" to remember those who were not only killed, but "sacrificed" in the attacks.[4] These examples are pulled almost at random; just about any political speech about war will honor the sacrifices of America's soldiers, their families at home, and even those who, like a tax attorney looking over his spreadsheet in the World Trade Center around 9:00 a.m. on September 11, 2001, seemingly die tragically as victims but quickly get honored as heroes.[5]

The "Christian" and "secular" connotations of *sacrifice* can, and should, pull in opposite directions. Jesus heads surefootedly to Jerusalem with an awareness that the son of man must suffer and die, readying his followers for the same. Soldiers are trained not to die but to kill—talk of their sacrifice notwithstanding. The sacrifice of Jesus is a sacrifice to end all sacrifices (Heb 10:1–18), whereas the sacrifices of soldiers must be constantly reenacted and reproduced.[6] Still, the image of the one who calls followers to love their enemies, who disarms Peter, and who would rather die than kill can get strangely superimposed with images of those who protect us from harm, those whose first and primary sacrifice is of their natural aversion to killing.[7] Ironically, though, compared to the Christian civilian, the soldier seems much more committed to following Jesus's unparalleled love—"to lay down one's life for one's friends" (John 15:13).

It is in this cultural imaginary and in the overlapping meanings of these two sacrifices that we find the most entrenched and ensconced version of Christendom today. Here, cross and flag bleed almost into one. Here, the irony of being willing to kill to protect a nation that was ostensibly founded on the principles of one who would not, quickly

3. "Bush: 'Leave Iraq within 48 hours,'" CNN, March 17, 2003, accessed August 10, 2015, http://www.cnn.com/2003/WORLD/meast/03/17/sprj.irq.bush.transcript/.
4. As cited by William T. Cavanaugh, "The War on Terror: Secular or Sacred?" *Political Theology* 12.5 (2011): 686.
5. Hauerwas goes so far as to suggest that "Americans do not get to die as victims. They have to be heroes." Stanley Hauerwas, "September 11, 2001: A Pacifist Response," in *Performing the Faith: Bonhoeffer and the Practice of Nonviolence* (Grand Rapids, MI: Brazos, 2004), 203.
6. As Hauerwas puts it forcefully: "war is necessary to sustain our belief that we are worthy to be recipients for the sacrifices made on our behalf in past wars." Hauerwas, *War and the American Difference: Theological Reflections on Violence and National Identity* (Grand Rapids, MI: Baker, 2011), 27.
7. Ibid., 56, 61–67.

fades from public consciousness. Here, we become American Christians or citizen-devotees of a Christian America. Indeed, symbols surrounding the sacrifice of soldiers have been exponentially more efficacious than Jesus's sacrifice on the cross in actually moving American bodies into danger. In the words of Carolyn Marvin and David Ingle, "Americans have rarely bled, sacrificed or died for Christianity or any other sectarian faith. Americans have often bled, sacrificed or died for their country. This fact is an important clue to [America's] religious power."[8]

The idea that America's power to conscript its citizens or memorialize their sacrifices amounts to *religious* power remains difficult for many to swallow. Too rigidly distinguishing "religious" liturgy from "secular" baseball games, Memorial Day parades, or enormous flags flapping over Perkins restaurants, we forget that liturgy (from *leitourgia*) simply means "an action by which a group of people become something corporately which they had not been as a mere collection of individuals."[9] Pledging allegiance to the flag or singing the national anthem creates this sense of the whole—one nation under God—despite the fact and especially because without them a country as large as the United States would fly apart into several million directions.

At any rate, Americans are never more united than when they are at war. War redirects focus from the many differences separating Americans from one another—differences of class, race, gender, ethnic origin, geographic and social location, and so forth—fixing our gaze instead on the seemingly decisive difference between domestic friends and foes overseas. Which is to say that war alone, or almost alone, forms a single political body or *nation* out of our diffuse political *state*.[10]

---

8. Carolyn Marvin and David Ingle, *Blood Sacrifice and the Nation* (Cambridge: Cambridge University Press, 1999), 9.

9. Alexander Schmemann, *For the Life of the World* (Crestwood, NY: St. Vladimir's Seminary Press, 1988), 25, as cited in William T. Cavanaugh, "The Liturgies of Church and State," *Liturgy* 20.1 (2005): 25.

10. According to William Cavanaugh, war is also the vehicle through which sovereign states are created in the first place. Overturning well-worn myths that the sovereign state arises as peaceful solution to sectarian religious wars of the sixteenth century, Cavanaugh offers convincing historical evidence that creators of the emerging state wielded tremendous violence against

The United States became a nation-state with a primary myth of origin, felt camaraderie, and unified language only after it was fought for (or even first created) in the Civil War and then again with the colossal armament of World War I.[11] Lincoln's Gettysburg Address plainly evokes the creation and dependence of national unity by and on the sacralization of its fallen soldiers:

> It is for us the living, rather, to be dedicated here to the unfinished work which they who fought here have thus far so nobly advanced. It is rather for us to be here dedicated to the great task remaining before us—that from these honored dead we take increased devotion to that cause for which they gave the last full measure of devotion—that we here highly resolve that these dead shall not have died in vain—that this nation, under God, shall have a new birth of freedom—and that government of the people, by the people, for the people, shall not perish from the earth.[12]

Only "increased devotion" to the national cause transubstantiates the deaths of past soldiers into sacrifices. Without that devotion, heroes and their holy sacrifices are desecrated, literally de-consecrated or made unholy.

Whereas tributes and memorials consecrate those who die in war, some go on to suggest that the deaths complement and conclude that of Christ. Julia Ward Howard's "Battle Hymn of the Republic" remains a favorite in churches on Memorial Day or Independence Day weekends, presumably because neither God nor Country takes back seat to the other. The final verse climaxes in this:

> In the beauty of the lilies Christ was born across the sea,
> With a glory in his bosom that transfigures you and me;
> As he died to make men holy, let us die to make men free,
> While God is marching on.[13]

its would-be citizens (and then also offered protection from this very violence) as the primary vehicle for establishing sovereignty, claiming a monopoly on the means of coercion. See Cavanaugh, "'A Fire Strong Enough to Consume the House': The Wars of Religion and the Rise of the State," *Modern Theology* 11.4 (Oct. 1995): 397–420; and Cavanaugh, "Killing for the Telephone Company: Why the Nation-State Is Not the Keeper of the Common Good," *Modern Theology* 20:2 (April 2004): 243–74.

11. Cavanaugh, "Killing for the Telephone Company," 261.

12. Abraham Lincoln, "The Gettysburg Address" (Gettysburg, Pennsylvania, Nov. 19, 1863), accessed August 10, 2015, http://www.abrahamlincolnonline.org/lincoln/speeches/gettysburg.htm.

13. Julia Ward Howe, "The Battle Hymn of the Republic," in Benjamin R. Tubb, "Civil War Music:

Honoring the sacrifices of soldiers remains the primary vehicle for identifying with our one nation, under God. To withhold or qualify such honor amounts to American apostasy, a fundamental betrayal of We the People.

I have been arguing that the sacrifices of war and pervasive memorials to them function liturgically to create and sustain a religious or quasi-religious community called America. Two qualifications are in order.

First, one might properly qualify that these liturgical gestures to our civic religion *only almost* amount to religion, as the "quasi-" proviso above admits. When Francis Bellamy, author of the Pledge of Allegiance, advised schoolchildren to recite the pledge daily so that it would become second nature, "the same way with the catechism, or the Lord's Prayer," this very patterning of patriotic formation on religious formation suggests that they are not identical.[14] Or again, when Supreme Court Justice Rehnquist described how Americans honor the flag "with *almost* a mystical reverence,"[15] the qualification was important, and was probably judiciously chosen. According to political theologian William Cavanaugh, endorsers of American civil religion carefully avoid charges of idolatry by never directly acknowledging that the veneration of flags, uniforms, and war anthems entails worship. In Cavanaugh's words, "Here liturgical gesture is central, because gesture allows the flag to be treated as a sacred object, while language denies that such is the case."[16]

Second, just because the vast majority of Americans publicly demonstrate allegiance to the United States military does not mean that they are personally involved with or knowledgeable of its operations. A recent essay by James Fallows, "The Tragedy of the American Military," describes how the percentage of the United States

---

The Battle Hymn of the Republic," accessed August 10, 2015, http://www.civilwar.org/education/history/on-the-homefront/culture/music/the-battle-hymn-of-the-republic/the-battle-hymn-of-the.html. I thank Dan Morris for pointing me to these lines.

14. As quoted in Cecilia O'Leary, *To Die For: The Paradox of American Patriotism* (Princeton, NJ: Princeton University Press, 1999), 178, and referenced by Cavanaugh, "The Liturgies of Church and State," 27.

15. As quoted in Marvin and Ingle, *Blood Sacrifice and the Nation*, 30 (my emphasis).

16. Cavanaugh, "Liturgies of Church and State," 27.

population on active military duty has plummeted from nearly 10 percent at the end of World War II to the less than 1 percent who served in Iraq or Afghanistan during continuous combat over the past thirteen years. And yet, average civilians overwhelmingly support the military as an institution. In a 2014 Gallup poll, three-quarters expressed "a great deal" or "quite a lot" of confidence in the military, compared to one-third of Americans who had such confidence in the medical system, and only 7 percent in Congress—both institutions that they know more intimately and track more carefully.[17] Most everyone follows ubiquitous orders on billboards and soda cups to support our troops. And yet, fewer and fewer people know individual soldiers or much of anything about the military as an institution. Precisely so, the support and honor we give to soldiers and the military as a whole is uninformed and uncritical, and yet, remains extremely enthusiastic. Fanatical, one might say.[18]

Both qualifications above suggest a further point about the nature of this civic religion as it relates to Christianity. If the religion named itself as such, it might precipitate a choice between very different sacred liturgies and theological imaginations, with different meanings of sacrifice and understandings of ultimate power. Or if its devotees were more self-critical, giving their endorsement—but never indiscriminate allegiance—to the military if and when it acted without

---

17. James Fallows, "The Tragedy of the American Military," *The Atlantic*, Jan./Feb., 2015, accessed August 10, 2015, http://www.theatlantic.com/features/archive/2014/12/the-tragedy-of-the-american-military/383516/. In Fallows's words, "Through the past two decades, respect for the courts, the schools, the press, Congress, organized religion, Big Business, and virtually every other institution in modern life has plummeted. The one exception is the military. Confidence in the military shot up after 9/11 and has stayed very high."

18. Cavanaugh, "The Invention of Fanaticism," *Modern Theology* 27.2 (April 2011): 229. The first contemporary (and pejorative) use of *fanaticism* was Luther's characterization of Thomas Müntzer as a *Schwärmer*—one who did not properly relativize religious passion to the authority of the prince and emerging German state. Philip Melanchthon uses *fanaticus homo* to caricature Anabaptist pacifists, since they too wanted the church to act without the permission and protection of the state. By calling American patriotism fanatical, I mean to suggest that its support for the military is just as uncritical; indeed, it is more dangerously so, given that criteria needed for critique have been contained within personal consciences and private, "religious" values. Of course, many "critics" of America's militarization are affected by the same uncritical fanaticism. Quoting Charles J. Dunlap Jr., a retired Air Force major general who now teaches at Duke law school, America exhibits its share of "benign antimilitarism," which, adds Fallows, "would be the other side of the reflexive pro-militarism of recent years." Fallows, "The Tragedy of the American Military."

hubris, then our civil religion, too, could incorporate "prophetic" religious strands to balance out its fanaticism and fundamentalism—a distinction central to Cornel West's diagnosis of America's Constantinian Christians.[19] As it stands, America's faith in national security, with its almost-religious gestures and ubiquitous, unquestioning loyalty, is just as widespread and shallow as the nominally Christian tradition it threatens to subsume. Indeed, a nationalistic Christendom is only possible if love of God and of country are rendered vacuous enough to house one another.

The Priority of Pacifism vs. the Sacralization of Violence

Any textbook on Christian responses to war will describe three seemingly incommensurable and airtight options. Pacifists are those convinced that becoming a disciple of Jesus and following his commandment to love one's enemies (Matt 5:44) makes lethal violence, any use of force, or sometimes, even any bodily resistance to an aggressor impermissible. Just war theorists recognize this priority of pacifism as clearly taught and modeled by Jesus. Yet, they also detail particular criteria that, if met, make Christian participation in war permissible, although always regretfully. Finally, there is the Holy War tradition, typically exemplified by the medieval Crusaders (and more recently, by "Muslim extremists"), in which militaristic enterprises are not simply permitted, but sanctioned and sanctified in God's name.[20]

At first glance, the Holy War tradition seems like the odd ball out. Whereas pacifists and just war theorists agree that the primary calling of Christians is to love enemies, pray for those who persecute them, and turn the other cheek (but disagree about whether to permit

19. Cornel West, *Democracy Matters: Winning the Fight Against Imperialism* (New York: Penguin, 2004), 145–72.
20. The typology was first cast thusly by Roland Bainton, *Christian Attitudes Toward War and Peace: A Historical Survey and Critical Re-evaluation* (Nashville: Abingdon, 1960). Dan Morris has pointed out to me that Bainton's categories are disputed, largely because even holy wars, wars fought in God's name, still incorporate proper limits, and so, still fall within the just war tradition. I, too, see the categories as porous, but will emphasize movement in the opposite direction. Just war traditions necessarily incorporate sacralizing symbols and good-versus-evil rhetoric because, while war may be permitted on just war grounds, people are mobilized and support it only when the cause is deemed sacred.

exceptions to this "rule"), holy warriors position the infidel, pagan, or heretic so clearly outside the moral/religious circle of goodness and truth that killing him is the accepted—no, an exalted—way of preserving the faith itself. In other ways, however, the just war tradition is unlike both pacifism and holy war. The latter traditions do not attempt to develop detailed criteria or generalizable rules to judge whether and when a war is permitted and how it must be fought, if at all. Rather, both peacemaking and crusading are ways of life—more like the ethos of particular communities than generalizable ethical principles to be employed by anyone and everyone. Only as thoroughly disciplined into peaceable Christian communities could Jonathan and Leah Wilson-Hartgrove "decide" to join a Christian Peacemaking Team and enter Iraq on the eve of the United States' invasion in order to mourn the dead, ask Iraqis for forgiveness, and grieve with those who were grieving.[21] Similarly, only after being recruited, converted, and thoroughly schooled within the Christian Identity movement did Eric Rudolph set off a bomb at the 1996 Olympics in Atlanta, claiming afterwards: "I have fought the good fight, I have finished my course, I have kept the faith."[22] The just war tradition is about lists of principled criteria that enable anyone to choose whether or not to go to war and how and how long to fight therein. By contrast, both pacifists and holy warriors belong to "concrete, converted, and disciplined communities"[23] that form one so deeply as to make violence unimaginable and uninhabitable (pacifism) or to find it almost irresistible, instilled with sacred meaning (holy war).

There are therefore incongruities in what otherwise looks like a stable continuum from "absolutely no war" to "maybe war" to "hell yeah, war." I point them out here in order to prevent these categories from becoming "options" or "positions" from which any individual, converted or not, might choose. Such a view caters to a de-politicized,

---

21. Jonathan Wilson-Hartgrove, *To Baghdad and Beyond: How I Got Born Again in Babylon* (Eugene, OR: Cascade, 2005), 70.

22. Eboo Patel, *Acts of Faith: The Story of an American Muslim, the Struggle for the Soul of a Generation* (Boston: Beacon, 2007), xi–xii.

23. Lisa Sowle Cahill, *Love Your Enemies: Discipleship, Pacifism, and Just War Theory* (Minneapolis: Fortress Press, 1994), 234.

individualized understanding of Christianity that earlier chapters have critiqued. In fact, no one could choose to be a peacemaker or a holy warrior if by "choose," one means the selection of an option after deliberating with autonomous reason. Both "options" require religious formation—the schooling and sculpting of desire—a practice of discipleship that is so constitutive of the "chooser" that he or she finds other options simply unimaginable. Really, then, there are not three ways in which Christianity might be coordinated with war, but rather, one fundamental conflict between two formative communities: one that blesses peacemakers and another that sanctifies violence. Thus understood, the intermediate just war tradition can be compared to disputed territory over which the other two camps are fighting. I will try to explain this and its importance for America's militarized Christendom by taking each category in turn.

Blessed Are the Peacemakers

Nonviolence (said negatively) or peacemaking (said positively) remains normative for many Christians who take the story and teachings of Jesus seriously. Comprising the longest single address recorded in the New Testament, Jesus's Sermon on the Mount (Matt 5–7) and its parallel, the Sermon on the Plain (Luke 6:17–49) include some of the best-known verses in the Bible, the Beatitudes and Lord's Prayer, as well as some of the most exacting. The "hard sayings" are named appropriately:

> You have heard that it was said, "An eye for an eye and a tooth for a tooth." But I say to you, Do not resist an evildoer. But if anyone strikes you on the right cheek, turn the other also; and if anyone wants to sue you and take your coat, give your cloak as well; and if anyone forces you to go one mile, go also the second mile. Give to everyone who begs from you, and do not refuse anyone who wants to borrow from you.

> You have heard that it was said, "You shall love your neighbor and hate your enemy." But I say to you, Love your enemies and pray for those who persecute you, so that you may be children of your Father in heaven; for he makes his sun rise on the evil and on the good, and sends rain on the righteous and on the unrighteous. For if you love those who love you,

what reward do you have? Do not even the tax collectors do the same? And if you greet only your brothers and sisters, what more are you doing than others? Do not even the Gentiles do the same? Be perfect, therefore, as your heavenly Father is perfect. (Matt 5:38–48)

Christological pacifists[24]—that is, pacifists schooled by the non-violence of Jesus—make clear that such injunctions carry weight because Jesus himself embodies them. Jesus famously disarms Peter (Matt 26:52), which, for Tertullian, entails a disarming of all Christians, presumably even those with second amendment rights. More importantly, the climax of each gospel involves the direct confrontation between Pontius Pilate, Herod, and Jewish elites in collaboration with them, each of whom *wields* the cross or defers to those authorized to do so, on the one hand, and Jesus and the band of disciples whom he repeatedly calls to *undergo* the cross, on the other. Finally, the gospel writers underscore the primacy of Jesus's nonviolent, self-giving love by portraying every temptation he faces as seduction away from it. Jesus could have incited the crowds to rise up against Rome after the feeding of the multitudes, after his triumphant entry into Jerusalem, and during the trial at Gethsemane.[25] He repeatedly faced and resisted the particular temptation to participate in a justified revolution through violent methods.[26] Lisa Cahill sides with the vast majority of Christians over 2000 years when she concludes that, "Although certain ambiguous or qualifying biblical texts can be cited (for example, Luke 3:14; Matt 8:5-13; Rom 13:1-4; 1

---

24. I have and will continue to use "pacifism" as shorthand for christological pacifism, that is, the renunciation of violence and sometimes any form of resistance after the example and teaching of Jesus. There are many other forms of pacifism, including an idealist, Enlightenment pacifism that structures peace on the inviolability of the human person and reason's ability to stand above the tribal loyalties of particular religions or nation-states. See Immanuel Kant, "Perpetual Peace," in Kant, *On History*, ed. Lewis White Beck (New York: Macmillan, 1963), 85–135. Catholic pacifists such as Dorothy Day, Thomas Merton, Philip Berrigan, and others focus on developing empathy and service to common humanity, sometimes mystically felt, as in Merton's case (see Cahill, *Love Your Enemies*, 213–23). Yet, the Sermon on the Mount and Jesus's example remains primary. The Anabaptist Yoder, and the self-proclaimed "high church Anabaptist" Hauerwas, most emphatically distinguish their christological pacifism over-and-against idealist types, a distinction they think not adequately made by Reinhold Niebuhr in dismissing the helplessly idealistic, inadequately realistic pacifism of the liberal church that he earlier inhabited. Reinhold Niebuhr, *An Interpretation of Christian Ethics* (New York: Seabury, 1979), 108.

25. Yoder, *The Politics of Jesus*, 39–55.

26. Ibid., 98.

Tim 2:1-2; 1 Peter 2:13-17), nothing is clearer in the moral message of Jesus than his exhortations to and example of forgiveness, mercy, and meekness in the face of abuse and assault."[27] Given this Christian presumption against violence, how could exceptions to "the rule" ever be entertained?

Embattled Is the Just War Tradition

Architects of the just war tradition, from St. Augustine to Reinhold Niebuhr, could not and would not abandon the centrality of Jesus's nonviolence. Rather, they preserve the centrality of the Christian calling to love even enemies (even sometimes idealizing it), and yet, delimit the sphere in which it might be enacted.[28] In Paul Ramsey's words, "understanding of the validity of Jesus' strenuous teachings must involve putting a limitation upon the area of their intended application."[29] Augustine and Ambrose argue that love for enemies should characterize the inner intentions of Christians, but it need not manifest itself directly in outward works. A Christian can and sometimes should kill an enemy, but must always do so out of love. In a major strand of this tradition, such love is directed at the vulnerable victim of the enemy's aggression; one uses force, lethal force if necessary, to lovingly protect the neighbor. With this comes an additional distinction between self-protection and neighbor love. While a Christian should not use lethal force to protect herself, she might do so—indeed, should do so—when the neighbor's life is at stake. But for Augustine, Christian love should also be directed at the one being killed; the Christian can kill out of love. This might seem like a recipe for hypocrisy, the overwrought distinctions of which can be exposed with little more than a bumper sticker: "When Jesus said love your enemies, I'm pretty sure he meant don't kill them." But to Augustine, it really does matter whether violence is wielded out of love

---

27. Cahill, *Love Your Enemies*, 3.
28. James F. Childress, "Moral Discourse about War in the Early Church," *Journal of Religious Ethics* 12 (Spring 1984): 12. Cahill mentions Childress's distinctions (*Love Your Enemies*, 56), and draws on them periodically, but also complicates them appropriately.
29. Paul Ramsey, *Basic Christian Ethics* (New York: Scribner's, 1951), 39.

for the neighbor and even for the killed—whether it is "for their own good," as it were.[30]

Throughout the Middle Ages, the church permitted the lethal violence of some by distinguishing between the precepts of the gospel, commandments that are obligatory for all Christians, and councils of perfection, those voluntary vows that priests, nuns, and monks take on in living out a higher calling. For much of Christian history, nonviolence was thus given due priority, but it was also deemed unrealizable for those individuals who cannot devote themselves entirely to chastity, perfect charity, and unreserved obedience to the church. The reformers democratized religious "calling," and so, all but erased the medieval distinction, only to redraw it between one's personal affairs and one's public office. A Christian should never kill out of personal vengeance or even self-protection, though he or she may be called to do so when upholding a public office.[31] Reinhold Niebuhr builds on this distinction, redrawing it according to detailed investigations into modern social structures, characterized by collective egoism. Isolated individuals or small intentional communities might (and should) aspire to the gospel's "ideal," but doing so will also reveal what an "impossible possibility" that ideal is, given that individuals are always already engrafted into social structures and institutions that do not have singular wills, and so, cannot love perfectly. Distinguishing then moral man from immoral society, or pure Christian love from approximations of justice, Niebuhr calls for a more "realistic" social ethic than the one he saw fancied by the politically idealistic and religiously naïve pacifism of the liberal church.[32]

---

30. Cahill, *Love Your Enemies*, 55–80. The distinction between intention and action or what a later philosophical tradition will call the principle of double effect stems for Augustine from his more primary distinction between the peace of the heavenly city and the more limited peace that can be enjoyed on earth, along with the problem of sin that both necessitates and characterizes earthly justice. See Cahill, *Love Your Enemies*, 61–65, 78–80, and Michael Kirwin, *Political Theology: An Introduction* (Minneapolis: Fortress Press, 2009), 55–87.

31. Cahill, *Love Your Enemies*, 97–118.

32. Reinhold Niebuhr, *Moral Man and Immoral Society: A Study in Ethics and Politics* (New York: Scribner's, 1932, 1960); Niebuhr, *An Interpretation of Christian Ethics* (New York: Seabury, 1979), 108; Cahill, *Love Your Enemies*, 186–96.

Each theologian and church tradition thereby makes certain distinctions—between inner intention and outer action, between priests and laity, between an individual's self-defense and more public protection of the neighbor, and so on—that relegate the applicability of Jesus's nonviolent ethic to the delimited sphere of primary intentions, higher callings, personal priorities, inspiring but impossible ideals, and so forth. To put it this way distorts the matter insofar as it suggests that, once Christians occupy a zone outside the one regulated by gospel, they are free to do as they please. The just war tradition, in fact, includes a number of rigorous criteria that must be fulfilled before a Christian is permitted to enter war. An early sketch of these criteria came from Cicero; Christian jurisprudence took them over after Constantine, and church bodies have used evolving versions of the list to assess whether modern warfare, too, is considered just.[33] Called *jus ad bellum*, or the right to go to war, criteria such as proper authority, just cause, right intention, reasonable hope of success, proportionality, and last resort must *all* be demonstrably met before Christ's commandment to love enemies can allow for exceptions.[34] Added to criteria concerning if and when to go to war are equally strict, sometimes overlapping criteria for deciding how combatants must act therein. Lists of *jus in bello*, or right conduct in war, typically include noncombatant immunity, proportionality (not doing more harm than the threat of harm from the enemy), and fair treatment of prisoners of war. At best, then, the just war tradition or just war doctrine assumes Christianity's priority of peace[35] and develops careful distinctions and

---

33. See paragraphs 2307–17 of the Catechism of the Catholic Church, accessed August 10, 2015, http://www.vatican.va/archive/ccc_css/archive/catechism/p3s2c2a5.htm.

34. Language of "exceptions" misleads insofar as it portrays pacifism as a principle or rule rather than communal formation presupposing conversion into a countercultural Christian community. See Yoder, *The War of the Lamb: The Ethics of Nonviolence and Peacemaking*, ed. Glen Stassen, Mark Thiessen Nation, and Matt Hamsher (Grand Rapids, MI: Brazos, 2009), 117–21.

35. I am here reading just war theory through the lens of pacifism, underscoring the priority of peace (or presumption against violence) as their shared starting point, as does Yoder and nearly every pacifist as well as some just war theorists, for example Daniel M. Bell, *Just War as Christian Discipleship: Recentering the Tradition in the Church rather than the State* (Grand Rapids, MI: Brazos, 2009), 23–25. Others, including authors of recent Roman Catholic social teachings, argue that justice and natural law rather than Jesus's peace ethic properly name the starting point of just war thinking. See Cahill, *Love Your Enemies*, 205–13. Paul Ramsey argues for just war's presumption against injustice (located in the criteria of just cause and right intention) as more encompassing

rigorous criteria that make war unlikely. Has it worked? No, and this for two reasons.

First, many assume that some criteria within *jus ad bellum* and (especially) within *jus in bello* are outdated and now inappropriate for modern warfare. Noncombatant immunity, the commitment that our side will take every measure possible to restrict its killing to combatants, seems especially anachronistic. The rise of urban warfare, technological advances making airstrikes incredibly effective, and seemingly omnipresent "new enemies" comprising embedded terrorists and insurgents fighting on behalf of underground movements and networks, can make noncombatant immunity seem outdated at best. Can the United States clearly distinguish combatant from informant or sympathizer or bystander under the new conditions of modern warfare? If not, then it has not met a chief criterion of the just war tradition and should not enter into or remain in such a conflict. What most will say, however, is that it is the criterion of noncombatant immunity that must evolve to match modern warfare, that to appeal to it as is would put America at the mercy of terrorists who do not play by most, if any, of the same rules. But that is precisely the point. The just war tradition has developed over 2000 years of Christian history not as a contract between international bodies, the breach of which necessitates a change of tactics on the other side. Rather, just war criteria dictate whether *we*, the moral community employing the criteria, can enter or remain in war *regardless of what the other side does*. The stockpiling of nuclear weapons (the use of which can *never* distinguish between warriors and civilians) was ostensibly done by our government and approved by most civilians (embodied through their own fallout rituals[36]) for a single reason—to deter Russia from using its own. The removal, hyperbolizing, or relativizing of

and logically prior to a presumption against violence, which is included, but not prioritized, in the last-resort criterion. See Ramsey's response to the United Methodist Bishops' Pastoral Letter "In Defense of Creation" in Ramsey, *Speak Up for Just War or Pacifism* (University Park: Pennsylvania State University Press, 1988), 54.

36. Dorothy Day and fellow Catholic Workers refused to participate in such nuclear fallout drills, understanding that they were not primarily civil emergency training but rituals that idolized the sovereignty of the state. Jim Forest, *All Is Grace: A Biography of Dorothy Day* (Maryknoll, NY: Orbis, 2011), 202–10.

noncombatant immunity (for example, incurring as little "collateral damage" as is "necessary") by those who find its strict espousal imprudent shows that nonviolence no longer serves as the norm presupposed by possible just war exceptions to it. Rather, "we" selectively employ the criteria, if at all, with safety and security as "our" chief concerns. National security and christological nonviolence comprise very different starting points of very different moral communities, as my scare quotes around "we" and "our" try to suggest. This brings us to a second, more encompassing reason for the failure of the just war tradition.

Second, then, the just war tradition has lost its ability to deem some or most wars unjust because it is no longer practiced as moral formation in a church with moral authority. When just war criteria are used by church bodies, the result is, at most, an open letter published to a website about the church's stance on a war. In recent history, these have had little to no practical effect as to whether the war will be waged and (more to the point) whether those who worship in the churches will enlist and be deployed. Nearly every Catholic and mainline Protestant church body declared America's invasion of Iraq in 2003 to be unjust, almost always employing just war criteria to make their cases. These church bodies include the Episcopal Church, the Evangelical Lutheran Church in America, the Presbyterian Church (U.S.A.), the Orthodox Church in America, the African Methodist Episcopal Church, the Christian Church (Disciples of Christ), and the United Church of Christ, not to mention ecumenical associations such as the National Council of Churches and the United States Conference of Catholic Bishops, as well as various international bodies such as the World Council of Churches, the Anglican Consultative Council, the Lutheran World Federation, the Archbishop of Canterbury, and the Vatican itself.[37] The result was next to nothing. Popes and bishops condemned the war, parishioners took little notice, and citizens of the

---

37. Peter Steinfels, "Churches and ethicists loudly oppose the proposed war on Iraq, but deaf ears are many," *The New York Times*, September 28, 2002, accessed August 10, 2015, http://www.nytimes.com/2002/09/28/us/beliefs-churches-ethicists-loudly-oppose-proposed-war-iraq-but-deaf-ears-are.html.

United States—80 percent who reported to be Christian in 2003—went on sending their sons and daughters overseas.[38]

I noted above that the just war tradition had roots in ancient philosophy, but was taken over by post-Constantine Christians as a way of retaining the priority of peace while recognizing regretful exceptions. Some pacifist critics of Constantinianism interpret this timing as proof positive that the whole just war tradition compromises Christianity from the start. Surprisingly, Yoder, Hauerwas, and other christological pacifists have spent much more time and energy encouraging just war theorists to take their tradition more seriously. In order to do this it is essential to reconceive the tradition as belonging squarely in the church—as being their territory, to return to my earlier metaphor. According to Daniel Bell, just war deliberation is best conceived as embedded and embodied in the life and practice of the church, comprising part of the moral training through which Christians come to sacrifice their bodies for a just cause or refuse to do so.[39] As it stands, the just war tradition more often than not gets deployed to *justify* war, rather than to limit it. This explains why commanders-in-chief refer to it as often as church leaders. Given how religion has been privatized and how the nation-state is assumed to be the keeper of the common good, when church leaders do apply the criteria more rigorously or with different conclusions, their deliberations are easily racked up as religious, that is, personal, opinions. The just war tradition may have once been deployed (and might still be?) as a deliberative practice capable of producing churches who refuse to let their members fight or who do so extremely prudently and with contrition because their very faithfulness to Jesus is at stake. Instead, most defer to the state as the only political body that can really put our bodies on the line. Regardless of dissenting "opinions," Christians in "Christian" America follow their Commander-in-Chief's orders rather religiously. Absent the presence of a church capable of mobilizing Christians, language of peace and just war

---

38. Jonathan Wilson-Hartgrove, *To Baghdad and Beyond: How I Got Born Again in Babylon* (Eugene, OR: Cascade, 2005), 87–88.
39. Bell, *Just War as Christian Discipleship*, 71–100.

become little more than "hollow abstractions inviting casuistical games at best and ideological perversions at worst."[40]

Mobilizing Is Sacred Violence

My last several sentences above suggest that the real disagreement over just war is not whether a particular war is just, but whether the political bodies behind those decisions have the institutional power to mobilize individual bodies toward or away from battlefields. More decisive than any distinction between inner and outer, personal and public, for oneself or for the neighbor, is that between the authority of the church and the authority of the nation-state to decide who, when, and how one goes to war. The church has been thoroughly *de-politicized* in this regard. At the same time, the authority of our so-called secular state has been progressively *sanctified*. Witness the fact that even those raising verbal objections still obey the state with their bodies and revere Her with their symbols and songs.[41] Even just war deliberations by Christians on Christian grounds sometimes suggest that because the President of the United States represents the proper authority to declare war and is uniquely positioned to know whether it is the last resort or not, all other just war criteria are rendered toothless, as if the right to deliberate about war were reserved for the one with authority to declare it. It may be that war is never really decided on after rational scrutiny, the analytic categories and exception/rule modalities of the just war tradition notwithstanding.[42] Rather, the cause of war must be inspiring and hallowed, if Americans are to sacrifice for it.[43] Only holy wars can mobilize people. Wars must be imbued with ultimate meaning

---

40. Hauerwas, "Epilogue: A Pacifist Response to the Bishops," in Ramsey, *Speak Up for Just War or Pacifism*, 152.

41. By far the most tenacious chronicler of the migration of religious power, that is, the power to shape dispositions and move bodies, from the church catholic to the modern "secular" state, is William T. Cavanaugh. In addition to the essays cited above, see Cavanaugh, *Migrations of the Holy: God, State, and the Political Meaning of the Church* (Grand Rapids, MI: Eerdmans, 2011); and Cavanaugh, *The Myth of Religious Violence: Sacred Ideology and the Roots of Modern Conflict* (Oxford: Oxford University Press, 2009).

42. Yoder, *The War of the Lamb*, 117–21.

43. Hauerwas, *War and the American Difference*, 32–34. Hauerwas goes so far as to suggest that just war criteria, dis-embedded from the practices of a church that has already been de-politicized, often become mere "ideological mystifications" (33).

and fought for salvific reasons. According to Hauerwas's probing analysis,

> Wars, American wars, must be wars in which the sacrifices of those doing the dying and the killing have redemptive purpose and justification. . . . How do you get people who are taught they are free to follow their own interest to sacrifice themselves and their children in war? Democracies by their very nature seem to require that wars be fought in the name of ideals, which makes war self-justifying. Realists in the State Department and Pentagon may have no illusions about why American self-interest requires that a war be fought, but Americans cannot fight a war as cynics.[44]

Hauerwas's evocative language unsettles many. Still, it works to turn our attention to all the ways that war gets sanctified in the United States. While *Holy War* normally entails a special designation marking only those wars fought for explicitly ecclesial causes and with the official sanction of the church (and therefore, is not possible in a democracy with the disestablishment of religion), careful attention to political rhetoric surrounding recent wars shows that it almost always functions to *justify* and even *sacralize* legal violence. Almost every war is a holy war from this perspective. It is difficult to wage a war that is not.

The blending of political rhetoric with religious sanction affects the way American Christians understand and use the just war tradition. I here name three aspects to this blending and repurposing:

First, references to just wars no longer function to introduce criteria that lead to moral deliberation and, after rigorous debate, collective decisions as to whether a war is just. Rather, wars are pronounced to be just according to the authorities who announce them. What is more, such pronouncements are surrounded on all sides by language that underscores America's moral-religious superiority. George W. Bush's speech on the eve of America's invasion of Iraq is a case in point. He plainly addresses just war criteria such as proper authority and just cause. But these are peppered with language that vindicates, validates,

---

44. Ibid., 32, 34.

and arouses support for the war. Speaking of the justness of the cause, for example, Bush preemptively counters the objection that America's invasion is preventative, and so, not in self-defense, by claiming that "responding to such enemies only after they have struck first is not self-defense. It is suicide. The security of the world requires disarming Saddam Hussein now."[45] Just war criteria of just cause and last resort here give way to justifying the imminent war by invoking the irrationality of containment. Likewise, whereas one classic just war criterion demands proportionality of force, Bush asserts that "the *only* way to reduce the harm and duration of war is to apply the *full* force and might of our military, and we are prepared to do so." Or again, "The United States and other nations did *nothing* to deserve or invite this threat, but we will do *everything* to defeat it."[46] Throughout the speech, Manicheist-like, good-versus-evil rhetoric describing Americans as "peaceful people" and Iraqi leaders as "thugs and killers" and "the violent" who have a "deep hatred of America" colors the otherwise more balanced, discerning articulations of just cause, proper authority, and last resort. Positioned as such, language about a war's *justness* cannot help but to further *justify* the war, bestowing on it ultimate meaning and importance.

Second and related, certain just war criteria tend to dominate what little deliberation Americans give to war, and these criteria include those most susceptible to religious sanctification. For example, proper authority has become predominant, and *authority* has come to connote not just legal sanction but moral certainty. Bush follows his claim that the United States "has the sovereign authority to use force in assuring its own national security" with numerous articulations of accepting this vow on behalf of America with perfect moral certitude and resolute willpower; for example: "No act of [Iraqi leaders] can alter the course or shake the resolve of this country." He even suggests that proper authority itself rests on America's unbending will: "This is not a question of authority, it is a question of will."[47] Chris Hedges draws

---

45. "Bush: 'Leave Iraq within 48 hours,'" CNN, March 17, 2003, accessed August 10, 2015, http://www.cnn.com/2003/WORLD/meast/03/17/sprj.irq.bush.transcript/.
46. Ibid., my emphases.

on decades of experience as a war correspondent to suggest that such moral certainty in wartime has become "a kind of fundamentalism," a "dangerous messianic brand of religion, one where self-doubt is minimal."[48] Whenever being properly authorized to declare war comes to mean having perfect clarity, no doubts, and an absolute will, all other just war criteria—meant to question and carefully discern—become rather irrelevant.

The justness of a cause has also become disproportionately important within political rhetoric and civic practices that sacralize war. Almost always, the justness of a cause turns on the ability of a country to hold up victims of the enemy's prior attack. This, in turn, transubstantiates the *just* cause into a *holy* one. The attack on Pearl Harbor was absolutely essential for America's entrance into World War II. Attempts to connect the victims of the 9/11 attacks to Saddam Hussein were equally necessary, just as their demythologization directly diminished support for the Iraqi war. Hedges quotes Elias Canetti in claiming that "it is impossible to overrate the part played by the first dead man in the kindling of wars. Rulers who want to unleash war know very well that they must procure or invent a first victim."[49] The effect of such procurement is nothing less than the deification of war itself, as Hedges's own religious language so vividly suggests: "The cause, sanctified by the dead, cannot be questioned without dishonoring those who gave up their lives. We become enmeshed in the imposed language. When any contradiction is raised or there is a sense that the cause is not just in an absolute sense, the doubts are attacked as apostasy."[50]

Finally, the very language of *war* that one uses when deliberating about its justness tends to sanction it preemptively, consciously or unconsciously. After all, *war*—as opposed to *violence, terrorism,* or *murder*—is understandable, rational, internationally recognized, and widely acceptable as appropriate and necessary. Thus, to discuss

---

47. Ibid.
48. Chris Hedges, *War Is a Force That Gives Us Meaning* (New York: Anchor, 2002), 147.
49. Ibid., 145.
50. Ibid.

whether a *war* is just or not already skews toward a positive answer, given that *war* is the very name we use to name legalized, understandable violence. Hauerwas underscores this point by asking rhetorically: Is an unjustified war *war*? Or is it simply murder? If the latter, shouldn't we be talking about whether murder can ever be justified?[51] In other words, framing the debate in terms of the justifiability of war may subtly confuse an exception (killing may be permitted in unusual circumstances) with a rule (war is understandable and acceptable). A very different conversation would transpire were Christians consistently to begin with Jesus's call to love one's enemies, and then, to ask whether in some contexts one might still kill them.

Judith Butler concurs that the language of *war* always already sidesteps the deepest reservations about it.[52] Words that seem to be descriptive actually establish the kinds of violence that can be justifiable, and by extension, which lives can be properly lamentable. This is not a matter of misrepresenting the issue at hand, since there is never a neutral description prior to normative assessments. But noticing the self-justifying function of *war* does enable people to deconstruct categories that presume to be neutral, to notice how easily terms can be exchanged for alternative purposes (when a *terrorist* becomes a *freedom fighter*, for example),[53] as well as to more carefully choose whether to enter into a debate whose terms are already loaded. Talal Asad agrees that "complacent public discourse" that bandies about terms such as *war, terrorism, Islamic militants, religious violence,* and a host of other value-laden words already makes the war America wages understandable—while also making other forms of violence utterly nonsensical.[54]

Apostasy and Idolatry

Above, I have tried to reexamine the categories of pacifism, just war,

---

51. Hauerwas, *War and the American Difference*, 42–46.
52. Judith Butler, *Frames of War: When Is Life Grievable?* (London: Verso, 2009), 152–56.
53. Ibid., 158.
54. Talal Asad, *On Suicide Bombing*, as quoted in Butler, *Frames of War*, 157.

and holy war to illuminate a central conflict between formation in Christian discipleship on the one hand, and Christendom's sacralization of war as making ultimate meaning, securing peace, saving democracy, and preserving Western civilization on the other. According to this analysis, the just war tradition is less like an unallied third option and more like disputed territory that is employed by Christian pacifists and American militarists toward opposing ends. The problem is not that Christians in the United States sometimes decide to go to war, but that they often do so having been thoroughly schooled in an alternative religion—a religion whose ultimate goal is security, rather than faithfulness, and that sanctifies the unilateral power promising to protect Americans from enemies.

Notwithstanding typologies that position just war theory as an autonomous enterprise between pacifism and holy war, in practice, questions about whether a war is just are always already framed in certain ways that lead to certain right answers. When a policymaker deliberates about just cause or proper authority while invoking moral certitude and categorically distinguishing war from the threat of religious radicals, the language functions not primarily to name and sustain deliberation, but to motivate, mobilize, and bless. The just war tradition has become somewhat toothless not only because the church has lost or forfeited its moral authority, but also, due to the religiously-laden self-justifications of allegedly secular governments. In other words, it is not only that churches are not "political" enough, that they do not inhabit an alternative *polis*, as anti-Constantinians repeatedly suggest. It is also that the secular state is *too religious*, almost never *secular enough* to deliberate judiciously about whether a war should be waged, given the priority of nonviolence and according to stringent criteria.

This problem seems almost intractable, largely because it appears unproblematic. By this, I mean that Christian capitulation to American militarism not only involves: (1) a betrayal of the distinctive peace ethic of Jesus (a process of accommodation), but also, (2) the thorough co-optation of sacrifice, the cross, innocent suffering, redemptive power, and other Christian matters to the point where the militarized faith easily passes itself off as Christianity itself (a process of acculturation). While I can only be suggestive at this point, I think that most pacifist critics of American Christianity, including Yoder, have attended more carefully to acculturation than to accommodation. Yoder, for example, often uses the "blunt names"[55] of apostasy and heresy to describe the "fall" from early church faithfulness into Constantinian accommodations. Such language highlights the essential incompatibility between Christian discipleship and dominant assumptions and practices, including those extended by American patriotic militarism. Moreover, Yoder denounces war and apostasy (and war *as* apostasy) from the position of one outside the compromised (apostatized) situation. Yet, what condemnations of apostasy do not do—perhaps cannot adequately do—is attend to the way that accommodations always already involve acculturations as well. "Falling" into Christendom or Constantinianism involves not only a compromised state, a clear departure from Jesus's example or the peace ethic of the early church; it also entails the repurposing of Christian terms, practices, and even images of God to cover over the difference, essentially baptizing power politics and portraying soldiers in the image of Christ. Such erasure of the difference between Christianity and militarism tends to undercut the privileged epistemological position that critics such as Yoder try to adopt in their condemnations. What is more, the merging of what would be distinctive cultures/religions into an all-encompassing "Christian America" effectively makes even dissenting voices complicit in the capitulations they denounce.[56]

Comparing Yoder's or Hauerwas's pacifism to the recent work of Judith Butler highlights the difference between these construals of our

---

55. Peter J. Leithart, *Defending Constantine: The Twilight of an Empire and the Dawn of Christendom* (Downers Grove, IL: InterVarsity, 2010), 316.

56. I cannot develop these criticisms of Yoder's approach at length here. They overlap with the strident criticisms of Leithart (*Defending Constantine*, 303–6, 316–21), which accuse Yoder's anti-Constantinian Fall narrative of falling victim to the same "monological" historical ideology as the Constantinianism it opposes. While Leithart's criticisms are incisive, more nuanced and constructive are those of Alex Sider, *To See History Doxologically: History and Holiness in John Howard Yoder's Ecclesiology* (Grand Rapids, MI: Eerdmans, 2011), 97–132.

militarized Christendom. All three figures remain keenly perceptive of the ways that seemingly neutral, descriptive categories (for Hauerwas, even the use of the pronoun "we"[57]) serve to frame matters of life and death in ways that uncritically hallow America's war-making while demonizing enemies abroad and dissidents at home. Butler thus understands that "violence and non-violence are not only strategies or tactics, but form the subject and become its constitutive possibilities,"[58] no less than these theologians interested in deep religious formation. But while Yoder suggests that the world's violence is best diagnosed and held at bay from the alternative, presumably less violent place called church, Butler assumes that nonviolence itself "denotes the mired and conflicted position of a subject who is injured, rageful, disposed to violent retribution and nevertheless struggles against that action."[59] Or again, she claims that "the struggle against violence accepts that violence is one's own possibility."[60] In other words, only those constantly vigilant of their own inclinations toward violence are capable of offering genuine resistance and subversion.[61] Butler seems to have in mind someone like Yoder—or at least Yoder when he wields the blunt names of heresy and apostasy—when she warns about the "moralization of the subject that disavows the violence it inflicts."[62]

I am trying to suggest that proclamations of apostasy do not fully get at the complexity of America's Christendom in its principal contemporary form, nor to complex negotiations with power,

---

57. Of the many articulations, see Hauerwas, "September 11, 2001," 203: "I am a pacifist, so the American 'we' cannot be my 'me.' But to be alienated from the American 'we' is not easy."

58. Butler, Frames of War, 165.

59. Ibid., 171.

60. Ibid.

61. Hauerwas may be closer to Butler than is Yoder here. In particular, Hauerwas's frequent testimonial that he is a pacifist because he is "too damn violent not to be a pacifist," might comprise his own confessional version of Butler's insight that there are always "regimes of power that produce and constrain certain ways of being" and that nonviolence provides a strategy for working through (never apart from) one's participation in these regimes. Butler, Frames of War, 169.

62. Ibid., 172. That Yoder sexually abused women might exemplify this criticism of his work, but the criticism remains relevant even to those who do not egregiously abrogate their own commitments to nonviolence. I leave it to members of Yoder's Mennonite church to consider how Yoder's own sins qualify or disqualify his case for Christian peacemaking. See chapter 5, footnote 19 above.

privilege, and complicity that point the way out. Christian militarism is a matter of idolatry just as much as apostasy. Yoder is certainly correct when he charges the majority of us with abandoning the particular ethos of the church, increasingly guiding our ways by "other lights."[63] But it is also true that those other moral norms are charged with religious significance. They function to ordain and sanctify political power. Their pantheon of gods—security, sovereignty, unilateral power—have so thoroughly adopted the Christian God within popular imaginations that becoming a Christian in America's militarized Christendom must entail not only resounding condemnations of what apostates "over there" have done, but also, the interminable confession of one's own complicity in Christendom—a complicity that colors even the disavowals of countercultural Christians.

While someone such as Butler (following Foucault) will write of regimes of power, for would-be Christians, the language of *idolatry* remains promising; there are three reasons for its value. First, it signals that Christian war-waging is always already religiously imbued, that people need ideologies and idols to go to war, and that war itself transfigures tragedy and death into mission, sacrifice, and redemption. Second, whereas charges of apostasy are cast from without (by those who often assume a position of moral clarity and superiority), idolatry can only be named by the person or group confessing it. (Of course, religious people of all stripes also call outsiders idolaters, but the language only really "sticks" for one who realizes—however inchoately—that the image or idol she worships fails to point to the God she should be worshipping.[64]) Finally, idolatry (the worship of surrogate gods such as national security) and ideology (the use of those gods to immunize oneself from critique) are ongoing risks for Christians facing accommodation and acculturation—that is, for Christians in America today. The confession of these sins, therefore, must be interminable as well. In this sense, one cannot really be *anti-*

---

63. Yoder, *Royal Priesthood,* 184.
64. Diana L. Eck makes a related point about how idolatry can only be self-diagnosed—never used to name those outside a tradition—in *Encountering God: A Spiritual Journey from Bozeman to Banaras* (Boston: Beacon, 2003), 78–79.

Constantinian or *post*-Christendom if that means refusing to acculturate to dominant culture or disavowing it unambiguously. One becomes Christian by facing one's complicity, while also undergoing the *askesis* (the reformation of desire) necessary for proper worship and discipleship of Jesus.

Highlighting the religious justifications that necessarily accompany war helps indicate that the solution entails not only more faithful discipleship of a political Jesus, but also, the confession of sin for having portrayed God in Caesar's image. The first comes from critics of Constantinianism, but the second appears in those in the wake of Luther's theology of the cross. The latter theological tradition includes the idea that humans idolize unilateral power and imagine God in its image rather than glimpse God in suffering and weakness, as symbolized by Christ.

Having said this, we should note that linking Christian peacemaking with an awareness of the ubiquity of sin seems to many to be at cross-purposes from the start. Christological pacifists, in particular, typically remain suspicious of the invocation of the ubiquity of sin insofar as it is often used to justify the necessity of "getting one's hands dirty" (i.e., participating in lethal violence). But are there other ways to combine the gospel's priority of peace with recognition of ubiquitous sin—even the sin of the peacemaker? We quickly get to the salient issues by turning to recent controversies about how to interpret Dietrich Bonhoeffer.

Pacifism and/or Realism: Bonhoeffer as Case Study

The question of how one interprets Bonhoeffer's life and writings has become a litmus test for where one stands on Christian pacifism and political realism, or the idea that a sinful and dangerous world requires Christians to suspend the priority of pacifism in order to responsibly and forcefully curb and contain evil. In no other single figure do we have a coherent avowal (see Bonhoeffer's *Discipleship*) and practiced embodiment (*Life Together*) of Christocentric pacifism *as well as* his own later suggestions (in *Ethics*) that Christian responsibility might accrue guilt, not to mention the standard portrayal of Bonhoeffer's involvement in a plot to kill Hitler, for which, ostensibly, he was hung in retribution. A recent book entitled *Bonhoeffer the Assassin?* goes to this issue directly. According to the authors, the realist interpretation has all but won the battle over Bonhoeffer. That Bonhoeffer sought to kill Hitler, and that he bravely bore the guilt of doing so, has been raised to the status of myth—a story taken as supremely true and so preemptively disarming the pacifist side. Much like the question, "What would you do if a gunman was attacking your daughter?," the rejoinder, "What about Dietrich Bonhoeffer?" has been almost enough to silence those with their finger on Matthew 5:44.[65]

In the first part of the book, the authors examine evidence thought to connect Bonhoeffer to the July 1944 plot to kill Hitler and find it circumstantial at best. They warn that "we need first to gain clarity about the facts" and assert that there is "not a shred of evidence"[66] directly linking Bonhoeffer to any assassination plot.[67] But while the book is about how to interpret Bonhoeffer's life and writing, the burning question is whether and how one can apply Jesus's teaching and example to a sinful, dangerous, violent world.[68] Preventing us from making knee-jerk and well-worn inferences, the first half of the book

65. Mark Nation, Anthony G. Siegrist, and Daniel P. Umbel, *Bonhoeffer the Assassin? Challenging the Myth, Recovering His Call to Peacemaking* (Grand Rapids, MI: Baker, 2013), xiii.

66. Nation et al., *Bonhoeffer the Assassin?*, 82, 86.

67. Ibid., 71–97. Evidence against the historicity of the received myth of Bonhoeffer as assassin include: (1) the fact that Bonhoeffer self-consciously worked for the *Abwehr* (a German military intelligence agency) in order to gain "uk" status—that is, exemption from military conscription—and he used the position to help at least fourteen Jews escape Germany and to prepare for postwar reconstruction. (2) There is no evidence to suggest that Bonhoeffer supported or helped to advance plans to kill Hitler, although we know he knew of them. (3) Only approximately 50 of the 13,000 working for the *Abwehr* were connected to the "resistance," which included sabotage, aiding escapees, and informing international contacts of German war crimes. That Bonhoeffer was involved in this resistance does not infer participation in the even smaller subset of resisters involved in assassination plots. Finally, and most demystifying, (4) the final failed plot on July 20, 1944 that precipitated the imprisonment of 7000 and the execution of 4500 was both planned and carried out after Bonhoeffer was imprisoned. The fact that he was executed after the famous failed assassination attempt means only that Hitler sought vengeance on *anyone* suspected of resisting his regime, directly or by association. The Nazis were not interested in finding and punishing those and only those directly involved; that Bonhoeffer was executed says nothing about whether he was guilty of tyrannicide—even in the eyes of the Nazis.

68. Ibid., 15.

evens the playing field between realists and pacifists. What if Bonhoeffer was pacifist to the end?

The onus of the second part of the book is to show that there are no major politico-theological reversals from the pacifist book *Discipleship* (1937) to Bonhoeffer's musings about acting responsibly and becoming guilty in the *Ethics* manuscript. Although Bonhoeffer famously wrote in 1944 that "today I clearly see the dangers of [*Discipleship*]," he also adds, "I still stand by it."[69] If there is any significant transformation in Bonhoeffer's views about Jesus and violence, it comes between 1928, when he argues that even murder can be justified,[70] and 1933, when he comes to see Christian pacifism as "self-evident"—a conversion that Bonhoeffer, in his words, "previously fought against with passion."[71]

Bonhoeffer the Assassin? tries to show how Bonhoeffer's later comments about accruing guilt and acting responsibly *are not incompatible* with his peace ethic by showing that the latter is not principled or perfectionistic, but christological. The authors suggest that being called to follow a nonviolent Christ might also include the bearing of guilt and confession of sin.[72] But the book does not tell us how. Why and how would Bonhoeffer confess his guilt for involvement in the sins of war if, indeed, he remained a pacifist to the end?

Beyond questions about how to interpret Bonhoeffer, the central theological question is whether recognizing the ubiquity of sin in this violent world and even confessing one's own sinful complicity in it must necessarily function as justification for becoming a "realist" by adopting violence to root out violence. Might not talk of sin actually advance Christian peacemaking? Must it pull one away?

We can take cues from Bonhoeffer himself here. According to him, both sin and salvation are communal. They characterize the church as a whole, rather than individuals (much less individual "souls") within it. What is more, because the church follows the radically incarnate

---

69. Bonhoeffer, *Letters and Papers from Prison*, trans. Isabel Best et al. (Minneapolis: Fortress Press, 2009), 485; Nation et al., *Bonhoeffer the Assassin?*, 161.

70. Nation et al., *Bonhoeffer the Assassin?*, 104–23, 221.

71. Ibid., 223, 225.

72. Ibid., 210–11.

Christ by becoming eminently worldly and identifying with the seemingly godforsaken (including forsaken Jews in 1930s Germany), there is never an airtight boundary or rigid border between "the church" and "the world." Or rather, the border between world and church demarcates between all those other boundaries that try clearly to distinguish between sinners and saints, between lives that are grievable and lives that are expendable, and (in Bonhoeffer's case) between Aryans and Jews, on the one side, and a community where each identifies with the suffering and sin of all others, on the other side.[73] So determinative is such solidarity in suffering and sin that Bonhoeffer coins a word to name the calling of Christians into it. *Stellvertretung*, or "vicarious representative action," describes the way Jesus identifies with even the darkest aspects of human existence—with suffering, sin, and death—to the point where he makes each his own. Christians are called toward vicarious representative action as well. They should associate with—and even "take on"—the sins and sufferings of others in order to bear Christ's healing and forgiving presence to those who need it most. In this light, Bonhoeffer may have been *both* a pacifist *and* complicit in the sin of violence when, in his final days, he remained in solidarity with suffering Jews *and* with Christians who attempted to assassinate Hitler. Just as there was no final line distinguishing his "personal" redemption for the well-being of his Jewish sisters and brothers, so too was there no final line between Christians who loved their enemies and those who—utterly stripped of every justification and sacralization—also sought to kill them.

I recognize that Bonhoeffer's complex case study also muddies clear distinctions between Christianity's peace ethic and America's legal violence, which this chapter otherwise tries to keep straight. What Bonhoeffer helps us to do is imagine how Christians living in America might *recognize* their unavoidable complicity in violence and war and even *accept* this fact without also *justifying* it—making it "right"—by invoking God's name. According to Butler, such recognition that "we

73. See the end of chapter 7 above.

are at least partially formed through violence" or even "mired in violence" through and through provides the ground of possibility for an "aggressive vigilance over aggression's tendency to emerge as violence."[74] The broader point here is that recognizing the ubiquity of (and one's complicity in) the sin of war and violence need not justify war, as Christian realists assume and which Christian pacifists resist. Oddly, Bonhoeffer's confession of sin functions in nearly the opposite way. It deconstructs any and every claim to moral purity and validation, whether proffered by holy pacifists or by holy warriors. It thus clears a space for the Christian to both acknowledge and embody a holiness premised on solidarity (even in sin) rather than on spotlessness. The goal of Christianity is not to be pure but to be Christ-like, like the one who "had no sin" but became "sin for us"—so that "in him we might become the righteousness of God" (2 Cor 5:21).

The Way of the Cross and of Peace

Bonhoeffer attempts to develop a "realism" about the sin of war (and his complicity in it) without thereby justifying violence or glibly accepting the "necessity" of getting one's hands dirty. To do so, he uses a cruciform hermeneutic—a way of viewing the world through the cross of Jesus—that is able to recognize as idolatrous any invocation of God's name over an unjust war or even over seemingly necessary violent resistance. Here again, he owes much to Luther's theology of the cross. Almost all of the Heidelberg Disputation, in fact, constitutes a diatribe against the presumption that what one thinks is just is also pleasing in the eyes of God. Such attempts at religious justifications merely add "sin to sin," making one "doubly guilty," according to Luther.[75] Luther also traces such need for justification and sanction to the "evil" need for self-security.[76] Both this pursuit after security and the use of religious language to justify it can seem natural, unavoidable, pious, and worthy. But according to Luther, accepting

---

74. Butler, *Frames of War*, 167–71.
75. Martin Luther, Heidelberg Disputation (1518), in *Martin Luther's Basic Theological Writings*, ed. Timothy F. Lull, 2nd ed. (Minneapolis: Fortress Press, 2005), 56 (thesis 16).
76. Ibid., 53 (thesis 8).

them amounts to calling evil good and good evil.[77] Seen from the perspective of the cross of Christ, which reveals the paradoxical power of God hidden in suffering, unilateral power, the ultimate goal of security, and the religious sanction often given to it are revealed as ideological and idolatrous.

Admittedly, Luther himself does not directly link religious justifications to those used to justify war. Nor does he link the sinful quest for self-security to broader obsessions with national security, or connect the peculiar power revealed on the cross to the peculiar (but potent) power of Christian nonviolent resistance. Indeed, Luther can be blamed for failing to make those connections, for not living into his own theological vision when he eventually pronounced God's blessing on the violent suppression of rebelling peasants.[78] Still, there are many in his wake that can help us connect the way of the cross with the way of nonviolence and peacemaking.

Kierkegaard and Bonhoeffer help us to recognize that the real scandal (and importance) of the Christian vision has centrally to do with its understanding of what constitutes ultimate power. In *Philosophical Fragments*, Kierkegaard offers a little story called the "god poem," whose title intimates the "Christ hymn" of Philippians 2. He imagines there a king who falls in love with a lowly maiden and wants desperately to win the maiden's love. The king knows that he cannot just show up in all his riches and glory; that might "wow" the girl, but not actually win her love. Likewise, if the king sends his entourage to bring the girl to his castle and dress her up in the finest things so that they could meet as equals, she would always suspect that the king loved something that she was not. The king decides to take the only course open to him; he puts on the garb of a poor servant boy and meets the maiden on her own terms.

So far, this is a fairly predictable allegory for the Incarnation, for

---

77. Ibid., 58 (thesis 21).

78. Martin Luther, "Against the Robbing and Murdering Hordes of Peasants (1525)," *Luther's Works*, volume 46, ed. Harold J. Grimm (Philadelphia: Muhlenberg, 1967). See also chapter 7 above. H. Richard Niebuhr attends to this slippage from "Luther's celebration of the faith that works by love, suffering all things in serving the neighbor, to his injunction to the rulers to 'stab, smite, slay, whoever he can.'" Niebuhr, *Christ and Culture* (New York: HarperCollins, 2001), 170.

God's willingness to "put on" flesh to win humanity's love. Less predictably, however, Kierkegaard immediately notes how the analogy breaks down. The human king-turned-servant could always "go back" once he has won the maiden's love; after some time, he could tell her that they are actually royalty and they could ride (on a white horse, of course!) back to the castle and live happily ever after. By comparison, once God has become human, there remains no possibility of "going back." Kierkegaard explains:

> [When God] from the hour when by the omnipotent resolution of his omnipotent love . . . became a servant, he has himself become captive, so to speak, in his resolution and is now obliged to continue (to go on talking loosely) whether he wants to or not. He cannot betray his identity; unlike that [human] noble king, he does not have the possibility of suddenly disclosing that he is, after all, the king—which is no perfection in the king (to have this possibility) but merely manifests his impotence and the impotence of his resolution, that he actually is incapable of becoming what he wanted to become.[79]

In other words, what appears to be true power in the human king—his "ability" to go back to the castle—is really a sign of his *impotence* insofar as it discloses that he has not actually *become* the servant he wanted to become. Inversely, God's very "inability" to go back, to shed the form of a servant, reveals that God *is supremely able* to become that which God desires to become. God is just *that* powerful. Or better: the distinctive nature of God's power is found (without recourse or reserve) in totally vulnerable, self-giving love. God has no power other than the power of love.[80] Any other so-called power—the power to control, manipulate, or force—is not the power that lies at the center of the universe. God's power, real power, is the power of vulnerable love.

Bonhoeffer agrees from within the eye of the storm of war. Having been imprisoned for his resistance to Nazism, having clearly perceived

---

79. Søren Kierkegaard, *Philosophical Fragments*, ed. Howard V. Hong and Edna H. Hong (Princeton, NJ: Princeton University Press, 1985), 55.
80. While I think this view represents Kierkegaard, it should be distinguished from that of Luther, for whom God does have "recourse" to the traditional understandings of omnipotence. See Oswald Bayer, *Martin Luther's Theology: A Contemporary Interpretation*, trans. Thomas H. Trapp (Grand Rapids, MI: Eerdmans, 2008), 201.

how both "German Christians" and the resistance movement were tempted to justify violence by invoking God's name, Bonhoeffer testified to everyone's idolatrous complicity in the power of war and then could only utter: "Only a suffering God can help."[81] The resort to any power and the invocation of any god other than the seemingly weak God disclosed on the cross will only tempt one toward idolatry. By contrast, to become a disciple of Jesus will entail picking up one's own cross, submitting to violent powers as a way of revealing the true power of God, as Bonhoeffer chose to do.

Yoder would likely raise two closely related objections to this idea that the cross of Christ reveals God's true power, and thus distinguishes it from the "power" of war and violence.[82] First, this emphasis on reasoning about *who God is* in light of Jesus's cross might bypass the more practical and pressing task of actually living like the human Jesus. In other words, this focus on the paradoxical power of God might very well lead to "theologizing" about or worshipping power as uniquely revealed in the cross. But can it also lead to imitation? Can disciples tap into it? Or is it so paradoxical, so otherworldly that one can *only* contemplate it or *only* express awe over it, as Kierkegaard's parable might suggest? Second and related, Yoder would question whether focusing on God's apparent "weakness," which Paul calls a "stumbling block to Jews and foolishness to Gentiles" (1 Cor 1:23-25) can make *any* sense to those outside the church. If not, would Christians have to renounce the public witness to which they are called?[83] In other words, is the idea that war and violence are weak and that suffering love is quite powerful something to be wistfully believed on Sunday mornings,

---

81. Bonhoeffer, *Letters and Papers from Prison*, trans. Isabel Best et al. (Minneapolis: Fortress Press, 2009), 479.

82. According to Hannah Arendt, violence, including the violence of war, does not constitute "power" at all. Rather, "power and violence are opposites; where the one rules absolutely, the other is absent." Hannah Arendt, *On Violence* (San Diego: Harvest/Harcourt Brace Jovanovich, 1970), 56.

83. Yoder, *For the Nations: Essays Evangelical and Public* (Grand Rapids, MI: Eerdmans, 1997; reprinted Eugene, OR: Wipf & Stock, 2002), 33-36. Yoder concludes the essay, "The Paradigmatic Public Role of God's People," by admitting that: "After having accentuated the breadth of applicability of the faith community's being connatural with the wider society . . . we do well to take account of the challenge of one point at which it has been held that this claim is the least credible, namely, 'the words of the cross'" (34). Yoder goes on to name Paul, Luther, and Kierkegaard, as well as contemporary theologians of the cross, including Jürgen Moltmann and Douglas John Hall, as lifting up the scandal of the cross in ways that at least seem "opaque to the outsider" (ibid.).

but never exemplified publicly on the streets, much less in the alleys of Sarajevo or Fallujah? Yoder thinks that there is, in fact, public and historical evidence to support Christianity's case that "weakness wins":

> When Paul wrote that the word of the cross is weak to those who look for signs, but God's saving power to those who believe, he was promoting not otherworldly mysticism but the kind of political reality which brought down Bull Connor in 1963, Ferdinand Marcos in 1986, and Erich Honecker in 1989. . . . That suffering is powerful, and that weakness wins, is true not only in heaven but on earth. That is a statement about the destiny not only of the faith community but also of all creation.[84]

Anti-Constantinians would call Christians who follow Paul in contemplating the cross of Christ to also follow Jesus in picking it up. If God's power is fully revealed in the power of nonviolent love, and if that power is the *real* one, one that exposes war and other violence as *false* power, then Christians should be able to embody the "weakness of God" in very practical, powerful, and political ways and then carefully track how it "works."

There are, in fact, a number of self-proclaimed theologians of the cross who link the paradoxical power of God that they find in Christ (a "high Christology") with a strategic practice of peacemaking patterned after Jesus (a "low Christology"). The post-Shoah (or post-Holocaust) German political theologian Dorothee Soelle is but one example. As Jacqueline Bussie shows, throughout her life, Soelle reworked and radicalized traditional ideas about a theology of the cross, "making them not only her own but revivifying them for relevance and liberative praxis in the twenty-first century."[85] Soelle differs from Luther in that, for her, "*every* theological statement has to be at the same time a political one."[86] She participates in war-resistance and creative peacemaking throughout Cold War America and Germany, convinced that it is only by following the very human Jesus, who

---

84. Ibid., 35.
85. Jacqueline Bussie, "Dorothee Soelle: Lutheran Liberation Theologian of the Cross," in *Radical Lutherans/Lutheran Radicals*, ed. Jason A. Mahn (Eugene, OR: Cascade, forthcoming).
86. Dorothee Soelle, *Against the Wind: Memoir of a Radical Christian*, trans. Barbara Rumscheidt and Martin Rumscheidt (Minneapolis: Fortress Press, 1999), 38, as referenced by Bussie, "Dorothee Soelle."

resisted the powers of Rome, that one has the right to be called a Christian.[87] At the same time, she believes that the nonviolent death of Jesus and all those who die as victims of the state reveal who and where the Ruler of the Universe actually is: "God is not in heaven; he is hanging on the cross. Love is not an otherworldly, intruding, self-asserting power—and to meditate on the cross is to take leave of that dream."[88]

God through Jesus calls Christians to peacemaking. This vocation can be discerned by reading the gospels, seeing who Jesus was and what he did, and then, patterning one's life after the prototype. The call to peacemaking can also be discerned by looking to the cross, marveling over (if never completely understanding) the scandalous idea that God is here known, or that the power of God turns out to be the power of vulnerable, noncoercive love. Living out that vocation will put Christians in conflict with any culture that confuses the "power" of unilateral force, which promises security and protects national interests, with *real* power, and that uses religious language to try to cover over that difference. Christians will thus stand out from the ways of dominant society and central components of its civic religion.

87. Dorothee Soelle, *Suffering*, trans. Everett R. Kalin (Philadelphia: Fortress Press, 1975), 127–34.
88. Ibid., 148.

9

RELIGION: Guests in the House of Israel

This book as a whole seeks to retrieve the uniqueness of Christianity over and against its acculturation into and accommodation by dominant American society. According to earlier chapters in part 3, the particular form of Christendom infecting this time and place essentially confuses Christian accountings of grace with the free market economy, the *polis* called church with a privatized religion, and the power of Jesus's sacrifice with unilateral power and the sacrifices of war. To become a Christian in Christendom is to be called away from consumer choice, from the individualism attendant to political liberalism, and from those forms of patriotism that venerate and necessitate violence.

Does the call to authentic Christianity also call one away from other religions? Does becoming determinately Christian amount to accentuating the superiority of Christian discipleship over and against the lives of faithful Jews and Muslims, of Sikhs, seekers, and secular humanists? If so, wouldn't this lead one right back into a more obvious and egregious iteration of Christendom? Even to mark Christianity as *unique*—as this book has tried to do—would appear to lead to Christian exclusivism, triumphalism, and privilege.

Alternatively, what if what made Christians faithful, and Christianity unique, was not certainty about the status of their salvation or the truth of their tradition over-and-against the wayward wanderings of others, but rather, a certain humility about how Christians come to know God and God's grace, which is taught by the central story of Jesus, and then, also through their encounters with non-Christians? What if they learned how to be hospitable to non-Christians by first understanding themselves to be the cherished guests of others—as humbling as that training would be (see the Parable of the Good Samaritan, Luke 10:25–37)? Or, switching to one of Paul's metaphors, what if those who confess Jesus as Lord came to understand themselves as new branches grafted onto an older olive tree called Israel, the people of God (Rom 11:16–24)? What if they understood Muslims as comprising an additional shoot? Could Christians become *both* deeply, uniquely Christian *and* open to, conversant with, and even reliant on the faiths of others?

This chapter argues that Christians should question widespread cultural assumptions that pit Christian commitment against openness to dialogue and cooperation with those of other religious traditions. It also argues against some leading proponents of religious pluralism who ask Christians and others to "balance" religious commitment and interfaith openness, a sentiment that subtly continues to oppose the two and that is closely linked to America's liberalized Christendom. The problem of Christian supremacy is not resolved by tempering Christian voices in the public sphere or by mediating and moderating them in order to make them more tolerant. This can lead to more subtle forms of imperialism, as Christians understand themselves to have a supremely privatized faith while stereotyping those religions that are not adequately privatized—especially Islam. The trick to overcoming Christian supremacy vis-à-vis other religions is rather to reclaim one's robust identity, allowing others to do the same. Christians may, in fact, learn from Jews, Muslims, and others how to do exactly this.

I here explore ways that Christians might become more

determinately Christian *by* engaging others, as well as how such commitments to interfaith cooperation arise *not despite, but because* one is a committed Christian.[1] In the process, I try to rethink dominant assumptions, paradigms, conundrums, proposals, and crises related to interfaith engagement today. We begin with an assumption that drives much of America's concern with religion itself.

Dominant Assumption: Religions Lead to Conflict

Although it might sound strange, those outside the faith, including academics and politicians, invented religion. By this, I mean that classifying beliefs and practices within the category called *religion* and giving them a single name (Judaism, Hinduism, Buddhism, etc.) is usually done by those outside the tradition.[2] With the possible exception of Islam, most major religious traditions did not think of themselves or call themselves religions when they first arose. Rather, *religion* was invented from without in order to categorize and often to control. Only by naming can an outsider assume understanding, and thus reify (essentialize or "thing-ify"). The classic example is Hinduism, or rather, how the richly diverse practices of the subcontinent of India came to be known as Hinduism. Expanding their empire from the northwest, Muslims in the second millennium witnessed so many unfamiliar and seemingly exotic rituals that they needed some way to name and contain them. They coined the word *Hindu*—a rough and ready Persian term meaning little more than those non-Muslims on the other side of the *Sindhu River*. Muslims—who already thought of themselves as adhering to a kind of religion[3]—could thereby try to make sense of and relate to people who were both

---

1. Eboo Patel insists that one best comes to interfaith cooperation not despite, but because one is deeply rooted in one's own religious tradition. Patel, *Acts of Faith: The Story of an American Muslim, the Struggle for the Soul of a Generation* (Boston: Beacon, 2007), 179. See also Patel, "Toward a Field of Interfaith Studies," *Liberal Education* 99.4 (Fall 2013), accessed August 10, 2015, http://www.aacu.org/liberaleducation/2013/fall/patel.
2. Wilfred Cantwell Smith, *The Meaning and End of Religion* (Minneapolis: Fortress Press, 1991), 51–63.
3. Ibid., 80–87; but see Ramón Grosfoguel, "The Multiple Faces of Islamophobia," *Islamophobia Studies Journal* 1.1 (Spring 2012): 29: "Islam does not consider itself a 'religion' in the Westernized, Christianized sense of a sphere separated from politics, economics, etc." More on this below.

like and unlike them. Both groups had "religion," and only thus could Muslims try to convince Hindus that they had the right one.[4]

Some comparative theologians, such as Wilfred Cantwell Smith, prefer to speak of *faiths*—diverse modes of relating interpersonally to the transcendent—rather than *religions*, precisely because the latter term connotes a single system, and is often used to essentialize "the other."[5] Yet, the trend in religious studies since Smith's classic *The Meaning and End of Religion* has been to give up on categorizing religions or treating them as subsets of the class called *religion* altogether. It just seems too difficult to develop criteria by which the nontheistic tradition of Buddhism can be called a religion, while zealous Marxists or committed materialists would be categorized as secular. It is better—so the trend goes—to stay anthropological and ethnographic, to merely describe each particular community or individual's belief and practice. The same focus on particularity and on personal faith rather than reified systems has influenced those now doing *interfaith* work (note the deliberate change from *interreligious* dialogue). Their newest language for religious diversity is to speak of individuals who "orient around religion differently."[6] Yet, this whole trend constitutes a failure of scholarly analysis, according to others. Jonathan Z. Smith, one of today's leading theorists of religion, argues that understanding religion depends on categories and taxonomies, on having to decide what counts as a religion and to explain why. To give up on this admittedly ambiguous project is "to run the risk of losing that very partiality, that casting of particular features into bold relief, those tensions of similarity and difference that give rise to thought."[7]

The debate over the name and use of *religion* can seem more than a little pedantic. The stakes rise considerably when we note that the category of religion and the categorizing of traditions arose not simply

---

4. Smith, *The Meaning and End*, 63–66.
5. Ibid., 170–92.
6. In particular, this is the consistent messaging of the Interfaith Youth Core, a Chicago-based nonprofit, founded by Eboo Patel, that partners with colleges and universities to foster interfaith cooperation. Accessed 10 August 2015, www.ifyc.org.
7. Jonathan Z. Smith, "A Matter of Class: Taxonomies of Religion," *Harvard Theological Review* 89.4 (1996): 397.

from imperialist outsiders or by academics who needed something to debate. Instead, religions arose from those with a vested interest in *privatizing* religion, those who want to make religion compatible with allegiance to nation-states and the smooth functioning of the market.

Many if not most believe in what William Cavanaugh calls the myth of religious violence. We in the West assume that nation-states were established and that democracies are necessary because, without them, religious factions and fanatics would forever war with one another and tear civilization apart. This deep association of nonprivatized religion with violence helps the "secular nation-state appear as necessary to tame the inherently volatile effects of religion in public life."[8] The invention of religion—that is, of an essential, interior, transcultural, and apolitical set of beliefs that can be separated from public loyalty—stems directly from the dominant myth that without it we would have only warring tribal factions. To construe Christianity and other traditions as "expressions" of an interior urge called religiosity or spirituality itself helps to separate loyalty to God from the devotion demanded by nations and the global economy. Religions become sentiments or personal beliefs that can be safely tucked away in our hearts. This presents a number of problems for America's new Christendom and the difficulty of becoming Christian within it.

Christianity as (the Best) Religion

First, insofar as different religions are said to be expressions of an essential and interior religiosity, they come to be understood as functionally equivalent and thus mutually exclusive. In other words, by demarcating a line between deep, timeless religion itself and its various expressions in everyday life, many understand the essence of religion to be the same but their expressions to be in competition. Just as one can love baseball itself and be a fan of the New York Yankees or the Boston Red Sox, but never (ever!) both, so too it seems that one

---

8. William Cavanaugh, "The Invention of Fanaticism," *Modern Theology* 27.2 (April 2011): 228; compare Cavanaugh, *The Myth of Religious Violence: Secular Ideology and the Roots of Modern Conflict* (Oxford: Oxford University Press, 2009), 123–80.

can be religiously Jewish or religiously Christian, but never a Jew *and* a Christian.[9] Christians thus define themselves over-and-against other religions ("I'm Christian, not Jewish"), but seldom, if ever, against other loyalties and politics ("I'm a Christian, not a patriot or a capitalist"). Because we call these other spheres *economics* and *politics* and discipleship *religion*, we presuppose that they do not compete; each seems to remain in its respective domain. It follows that the primary way we understand religion closely guards against syncretism (the blending of religious identities) while actually inviting their cultural or political co-optation.

Second, among the different religions in North America, Christianity seems the most easily privatized, and so, the most susceptible to standing in for religion itself. I'm reminded here of Kierkegaard's playful story of the woman who admonishes her husband for wondering whether he is Christian.[10] It is clear that her husband is not Jewish or a Muslim, so, she pleads, what else could he be but Christian? However caricatured, the assumptions behind such conjectures are real. They stem from the way Christianity, especially Protestant Christianity, gets refashioned within both Enlightenment and Romantic strands of modernity.

On the Enlightenment side, Immanuel Kant has convinced many that Protestant Christianity is the "pure moral religion," or at least, the "germ of true religious faith" that might provide the "foundation of a universal world religion."[11] By contrast, other revealed religions do not stay within the limits of reason, and thus remain less "evolved," more prone to getting stuck on or "fetishizing" particularistic rules and regulations.[12] Given this bifurcation between real, rational religion

---

9. Much of Yoder's work on Judaism and early Christianity aims to challenge the inevitability of the split between Judaism and Christianity and to highlight the "Jewishness of the free church vision." John Howard Yoder, *The Jewish-Christian Schism Revisited*, ed. Michael G. Cartwright and Peter Ochs (Scottdale, PA: Herald, 2008), 105. For a Jewish response, see Daniel Boyarin, "Judaism as a Free Church: Footnotes to John Howard Yoder's *The Jewish-Christian Schism Revisited*," *CrossCurrents* (Winter 2007): 6–21.

10. See Introduction above and Søren Kierkegaard, *Concluding Unscientific Postscript to the Philosophical Fragments*, trans. Howard V. Hong and Edna H. Hong (Princeton, NJ: Princeton University Press, 1992), 1:50–51.

11. Immanuel Kant, *Religion within the Bounds of Bare Reason*, trans. Werner S. Pluhar (Indianapolis: Hackett, 2009), 139–45.

and its many irrational, subethical substitutes, Judaism weighs in as "not a religion at all."[13] Contemporary tropes about Islam as a primitive, underdeveloped, authoritarian, and essentially violent tradition likewise function to make it supremely irrational, and thus unethical in Kant's sense.[14]

At the spring of modernity's more Romantic stream, Friedrich Schleiermacher argued that every determinate religion expresses a pre-linguistic awareness of ultimate dependence, or what he called the *Gefühl*, a feeling for God or original piety. All religious and nonreligious people—Hindu, Jew, and atheist—have, according to Schleiermacher, "the consciousness of being absolutely dependent, or, which is the same thing, of being in relation with God."[15] It is monotheists, however, who "express" this feeling of ultimate dependence most transparently, and Protestantism expresses it best of all. Judaism is too nationalistic and exclusive; Islam too sensual and emotional. Protestant Christianity alone expresses true religion without additive or remainder; it is thus "the most perfect of the most highly developed forms of religion."[16]

What Kant and Schleiermacher argued, many of us now simply assume. We take it that religion is something innately in us, and that Christianity (especially Protestant Christianity) describes not only a particular manifestation of religion, but the whole of religion in its purest, most rational, or expressivist form. Jonathan Z. Smith confirms these assumptions by reflecting on problems he encountered while editing the HarperCollins Dictionary of Religion. While entries on non-Christian "world religions" devoted considerable space to issues of definition and classification, Smith noted "the persistence of an easy, unarticulated assumption of the universality of Christianity" in entries devoted to it. As editor, he found himself having to insert "Christian"

---

12. Ibid., 135. See the helpful discussion in G. A. Lipton, "Secular Sufism: Neoliberalism, Ethnoracism, and the Reformation of the Muslim Other," *The Muslim World* 101 (July 2011): 429–30.

13. Kant, *Religion within the Bounds*, 21; Lipton, "Secular Sufism," 430.

14. Grosfoguel, "Multiple Faces of Islamophobia," 13.

15. Friedrich Schleiermacher, *The Christian Faith*, trans. H. R. Mackintosh and J. S. Stewart (Edinburgh: T&T Clark, 1928), 12.

16. Ibid., 38.

to properly qualify what was written from Christian points of view. No other tradition posed that sort of editorial problem.[17]

The Specter of Religious Violence

The very quest to find or invent an essence of religion largely arises from deeply seated assumptions that religious difference easily leads to religious violence. Cavanaugh convincingly argues that the specter of religious fanaticism and violence often functions to legitimize the containment and confinement of religion—violently, if necessary.[18] But even those who strive to end violence, whether state-sponsored or "religious," often portray religious difference as a problem to be solved or a threat to be contained. Huston Smith, author of the classic *The World's Religions*, unapologetically sifts through a motley crew of religious histories and institutions for the great and enduring wisdom beneath. Why? He explains that, whereas a "more balanced view of religion would include human sacrifice and scapegoating, fanaticism and persecution, the Christian Crusades and the holy wars of Islam," the search for essential religion or wisdom might inspire us to nobler, more enlightened ideals.[19] In other words, without an understanding of the essence of religion beneath their messier actualizations, we would be left with histories and politics that would be too irrational and aggressive to restrain.

The idea that religious difference breeds violence is held even by those who hold those differences up. Stephen Prothero critiques the idealizing and de-historicizing work of authors such as Huston Smith. At the same time, he continues to associate the idealized unity with peace and his more careful attention to lived religion with the possibility of conflict. "Unfortunately," Prothero writes, "we live in a world where religion seems as likely to detonate a bomb as to defuse one." Unlike Smith, who uses such associations to justify his attention

17. Smith, "A Matter of Class," 397.
18. Cavanaugh, "Invention of Fanaticism," 235. Cavanaugh quotes from new atheist writer Sam Harris, *The End of Faith: Religion, Terror, and the Future of Reason* (New York: W. W. Norton, 2004), 52–53.
19. Huston Smith, *The World's Religions: Our Great Wisdom Traditions* (New York: HarperCollins, 1991), 4.

to religion's higher ideals, Prothero argues that the very deadliness of religion necessitates studying it with all the realism one can muster.[20] The subtitle of his book *God Is Not One* asserts that the eight religious traditions studied in all their specificity are "rivals." He thus agrees with Smith that religious difference breeds competitiveness and enmity; he differs only in his willingness to examine this "fact" more candidly.

At first glance, the association of religious difference with rivalry and latent conflict seems to characterize even the leading proponent of interfaith engagement today. Eboo Patel's first book, *Acts of Faith*, begins with Eric Rudolph, the member of the Christian Identity white supremacy group that set off the bomb at the 1996 Atlanta Olympics. It juxtaposes Rudolph with middle school students in Whitwell, Tennessee, Protestant kids who came to stand up for the religious freedoms of others after they met with Holocaust survivors and learned about contemporary Judaism. Patel concludes that the deepest and darkest "faith line" is not between different religions, but between "religious totalitarians" such as Rudolph and "religious pluralists" such as the middle school students.[21] He emphasizes that neither the totalitarians nor the pluralists act on their own or directly from some deep religious feeling. Each group is taught to be that way—"produced by a movement and encouraged by a culture"—from an early age.[22] But for all Patel's nuance, a book arguing for interfaith cooperation that begins with religious violence can easily lead readers to assume that religions need to cooperate because violence is the only alternative. Readers might assume that unmediated religion leads to conflict. Patel's later work makes clear that interfaith understanding and cooperation should not do away with religious distinctiveness; in fact, they presuppose and preserve it.[23] Yet, I fear that anxiety over religious

20. Stephen Prothero, *God Is Not One: The Eight Rival Religions That Run the World—and Why Their Differences Matter* (New York: HarperOne, 2010), 7.
21. Patel, *Acts of Faith*, xi–xv. In "Toward a Field of Interfaith Studies," Patel also frames the need for interfaith cooperation in terms of the threat of violence by recommending starting an interfaith course by reading Samuel Huntington's *Clash of Civilizations*, and then, inquiring into situations that lead diverse communities that coexist and cooperate rather than clash and kill.
22. Patel, *Acts of Faith*, xii.

conflict runs so deep that appeals for interfaith understanding are often heeded primarily to make religions safe.

Certainly, religious difference can—and does—occasion violence. Christian supremacy groups kill Jews. So-called Christian nations go to war against "militant Islamic extremists." Neocolonial divisions between Sunnis and Shiites wreak havoc on the geopolitics of the Middle East. Buddhists and Hindus continue to fight in Sri Lanka. It matters whether such violence is named "religious" (or "extremist," "fanatical," or "Jihadist") or not, and the use or absence of that language is never innocent. My primary concern here is that when religious difference is assumed to lead to conflict, we are tempted to elide differences in the name of peace. Out of the understandable desire to find some core religious sentiment or common commitment to ethics or justice that would bring different religions together, some interfaith advocates undercut the very diversity that they otherwise want to affirm. A similar irony marks dominant paradigms for understanding religious diversity. By turning to these, we can question whether typecasting or "othering" people of other religions— accentuating their differences from one's own—is really the most pressing problem. Thinking that all religions are the same might stereotype and lead to conflict just as easily.

Dominant Paradigm: Exclusivism, Inclusivism, and Pluralism

There are at hand some fairly well-worn categories to describe how persons of faith might interpret and regard the faiths of others. These categories were invented, or at least formalized and popularized, with the publication of *The Myth of Christian Uniqueness* in 1987. In the Introduction, the editors John Hick and Paul Knitter lay out a typology that has structured interfaith understanding since. They write of the "exclusivist" position, the understanding that one's own religion has a monopoly on truth or is the only road to salvation. According to exclusivist interpretations, the line between my way of true faith and

---

23. Eboo Patel, *Sacred Ground: Pluralism, Prejudice, and the Promise of America* (Boston: Beacon, 2012), 139–41.

devotion and those heretical and idolatrous beliefs and practices *over there* is clear and stark. The editors then describe a second, "inclusivist" position, comprising the idea that while my religion has the fullest manifestation of truth or gives its proper name, other traditions also glimpse this truth and designate it with their own analogous terms. In many ways, this mindset remains more open to listening to and learning from others. Still, it remains supremely confident that Christ, as one example, or the revelation of the Qur'an to Mohammed, as another, comprises the *full* and *final* revelation of God. Other traditions are affirmed only insofar as they resonate with that final truth.

Third and finally, we get the position called "pluralism." Diana Eck helpfully argues that pluralism is distinct from the sheer fact of religious plurality or diversity.[24] It entails an interpretation of that diversity and an affirmation of multiple religions for contributing to an understanding of God (or "the Ultimate," or "the Real") or for joining in efforts for social justice. The editors of *The Myth of Christian Uniqueness* describe the passage from inclusivism to pluralism as a crossing the Rubicon toward recognizing the independent validity of other religions.[25] Even more suggestive is this earlier imagery: Going from inclusivism (where it is still *my* tradition that provides the norms and sets the terms of inclusivity) to pluralism is like going from a Ptolemaic understanding of the universe to a Copernican model, where each religious tradition is but circling around an Ultimate that is beyond the sphere of each.[26]

This typology of exclusivism, inclusivism, and pluralism can be incredibly helpful for reminding Christians and other religious people that God is not contained within any of their traditions. God (or Buddha-nature, or Dharma, or "the Real") always transcends the terms and stories that we have for Him (or Her, or It). According to a famous Jataka Tale of Buddhism, we should not confuse the finger that points

---

24. Eck, *Encountering God: A Spiritual Journey from Bozeman to Banaras* (Boston: Beacon, 2003), 191.
25. Paul Knitter, "Preface," in John Hick and Paul F. Knitter, eds., *The Myth of Christian Uniqueness: Toward a Pluralist Theology of Religions* (Maryknoll, NY: Orbis, 1987), viii.
26. John Hick, *God and the Universe of Faiths* (Oxford: Oneworld, 1973), 133–47.

to the moon for the moon itself. Each tradition points to the truth, but none of them contains it.

At the same time, however, the categories are limited and sometimes unhelpful.[27] To start with, notice the way that the account of plurality that you find in the pluralist position subtly relegates religions into different versions *of the same thing.* Once one understands that all religions are like planets circling around the same sun, or are like different paths leading up the same mountain, one has just portrayed them as essentially or functionally equivalent, as versions of the same kind of thing. *Salvation, enlightenment, moksha,* and *paradise* get relegated to specific versions of a more abstract and overarching final end. *Yahweh,* the *Triune God, Allah,* and *Dharma* all become different ways to describe "the Ultimate" or "the Real." At worst, then, differences can appear so shallow and unimportant that the traditions begin to resemble brand names—one person prefers her New Age iPhone and another is still clinging to his Doctrinal Blackberry, but either gets the job done and the wiring is about the same, once we peel off the plastic.

Ironically, then, pluralism *as a final position* can undercut the plurality it is meant to affirm. Related to this problem is this: many self-proclaimed pluralists end up introducing a philosophical framework that is meant to mediate differences between religious "frameworks," but simply add an additional framework in need of mediation. To return to our earlier metaphor, we could say that the Ptolemaic model of the universe is also just a model of, an earthly perspective on, the universe—*itself* no more geocentric than other perspectives. Or again: seeing that each tradition's finger only points to the moon gets one no closer to standing on the moon. In fact, you can only indicate *that* truth with yet another finger that points to the fingers pointing, and so on.

27. The following is informed by S. Mark Heim, *Salvations: Truth and Difference in Religion* (Maryknoll, NY: Orbis, 1995); compare the similar account by the scholar of Islam, Muhammad Legenhausen, in *Islam and Religious Pluralism* (London: Al-Hoda, 1999).

Is Exclusivism the Pressing Problem?

Let me go at the difficulty related to pluralism as a category in a different way by suggesting that it answers a problem that may not, in fact, be our most pressing one. Certainly, the tactics of "othering" employed by the exclusivist—her proclivity to stereotype, scapegoat, and even demonize those outside her own fold—have been and are a major concern of Christianity, in particular, with its too-long history of baptism under duress, of pogroms, and of holy wars, and with current essentialist representations of Islam. But does that too-clear understanding that I possess absolute truth and you do not characterize the majority of Christians in this time and place? Recall that, according to the National Study of Youth and Religion (NSYR), the vast majority of teenagers who call themselves Christian actually have little to no idea what Christianity entails, aside from the idea that they are supposed to be nice and that God will protect them if they are. Propounding a religion more accurately called Moralistic Therapeutic Deism, these "Christian" kids believe in a pretty hands-off God, an ethereal Big Daddy in the sky, who just wants them to be good (which often means nonjudgmental) and, most of all, to be happy.[28] Tolerance is not lacking here; in fact, it is something of the confessional creed of this new religion. Speaking of how to regard non-Christians, one teenager represented the majority with this: "There isn't a wrong answer. 'Cause it's God, you can't prove [any religion], it's just what you believe."[29]

Perhaps then an overly stark separation of me and my tradition from you and yours is not the primary obstacle to interfaith understanding today. Perhaps the primary challenge is the problem of Christian majoritarianism and Christian privilege and the concomitant inability to see religious difference (and especially Christianity as *different*) because Christianity is taken as normal and normative. In an almost off-handed comment, Diana Eck, Director of Harvard's Pluralist Project

---

28. Christian Smith with Melinda Lundquist Denton, *Soul Searching: The Religious and Spiritual Lives of American Teenagers* (New York: Oxford University Press, 2005), 118–71.
29. Ibid., 145.

and leading scholar of comparative religion, notes that whereas exclusivism is the typical posture of religious minorities, those in the majority typically espouse inclusivism.[30] From a perspective that is normalized to the point of invisibility, other religions appear as closer or more distant versions of the same.

The vast majority of Christian teens who say that religion is important to them still have trouble articulating in any meaningful way how religion is important, what it means to them, or where in their daily lives it matters. These same teens tend to be incredibly nonjudgmental about differing religious commitments and traditions; in fact, they seem vehemently resistant to the thought of assessing or otherwise negotiating competing religious truth claims at all. Everybody gets to decide what feels right to them; nobody gets to tell another person what to believe, or so our teens profess. Even more reflective forms of inclusivism or distinct respect for other faiths get lost within this capacious form of what Gregory Bradley calls "whateverism,"[31] with its own pithy taglines: "To each his own." "Whatever floats your boat." "It's all good."[32]

This is not to say that exclusion, stereotyping, and essentializing are no longer problems. According to the NSYR, outspoken exclusivists do comprise a "minor fringe of dissenters"[33] from the relativistic, anti-judgmental "Christianity" present in so many American teens. Their intolerance is no less tolerable for its rarity. In fact, however saddened I am when reading of teenagers' accommodation of God to their subjective preferences, I all but cringe when reading how a minority of dissenters regard faiths other than their own: "If you're practicing another religion, it's pretty pointless, it doesn't matter what religion

30. Eck, *Encountering God*, 176–77, 185.

31. Gregory Bradley, *The Unintended Reformation: How a Religious Revolution Secularized Society* (Cambridge, MA: Harvard University Press, 2012), 77: "In Western society at large, the early twenty-first-century basis for most secular answers to the Life Questions seems to be some combination of personal preferences, inclinations, and desires: in principle truth is whatever is true for you, values are whatever you value, priorities are whatever you prioritize, and what you should live for is whatever you decide to live for. In short: whatever."

32. Recall from chapter 2 that such sentiments are not contained on one side of a generation gap. The tolerant and accommodating but also dissolute and borderless faith of American teenagers largely reflects the faith of their parents and the rest of us. Smith and Denton, *Soul Searching*, 191.

33. Ibid., 146.

you're believing if you don't believe in Jesus and the cross." More dismissive still are comments such as this: "I know this is completely against PC, but you know people like Muslims and stuff, they're not all about peace and love. Completely ridiculous. Their scripture tells them to kill Jews! If you want people to believe in a faith, you want them to believe in a particular faith, not any old faith. The best would be to be a Christian."[34]

Can Christians believe and practice a particular faith, not any old borderless, culturally accommodated one, without relegating other faith traditions to a debased foil for their own, to an "other" by which the superiority of Christianity is bolstered? Or from the other side: Can one remain open to and actively appreciate divergent faith traditions without one's own perspective becoming so accommodating, wide, and meaningless that *Christian* subtly slides toward *whatever*?

One reasonable way forward would be to concentrate *first* on cultivating one's native religious identity, and *then*—after one's own religious identity is firmly established—move on to encountering difference. In his book *Acts of Faith*, Patel raises serious concerns about this order of priority. He writes of trying to get interfaith cooperation among youth off the ground in Chicago by meeting with synagogue, mosque, and church leaders. The repeated response he heard was this: "We barely have enough time to teach our kids about their *own* religion. . . . It's just not a high enough priority to spend that precious time exposing them to others."[35] That is the sort of zero-sum thinking that understands difference as a threat to identity rather than that which arises with it. Patel's Interfaith Youth Core gracefully cuts through this perceived dilemma of priorities by showing how engaging other religions and reflecting on one's own strengthen one another. What I am trying to warn against here is that "pluralism," when made an "-ism," when regarded as a final position and answer, might enable nominal Christians in America's new Christendom to settle too quickly

34. Ibid., 145–46.
35. Patel, *Acts of Faith*, 164.

for shallow relativism, skirting the difficult and rewarding work of interfaith exchange and action.

Inclusivism as Uniquely Problematic

Notice the way that positioning *inclusivism* along a spectrum spanning from the narrowest forms of *exclusivism* to the widest embrace of *pluralism* tends to reduce it to a kind of halfway-house position. To the pluralist, it looks not as good as pluralism, but a whole lot better than exclusion. To the critic of pluralism, inclusivism seems like a happy medium—not as closed-minded as the exclusivists, but also, not as abstract and all-accommodating as the pluralist. (Inclusivists prefer their category for the same reasons Goldilocks prefers the middle bed—it is not too hard, not too soft.) But describing inclusivism in these ways actually obscures the *unique* set of challenges that arise when people understand other religions as being analogues or shadows of their own. These challenges are especially prevalent in traditions that share histories and texts—as when Christianity interprets Judaism as having part of its full truth, or when Islam thinks in a similar way about the other "religions of the book."

This is the specific problem of supersessionism—the idea that one's faith, as newer and more complete, surpasses and supplants that which has gone before.[36] Eck rightly locates the danger of supersessionism within the category of inclusivism.[37] While it would seem to be more affirming, the understanding that other faiths approximate or mirror limited dimensions of my own can actually be more degrading than their outright rejection.

Christian supersessionism—or a Christian "theology of displacement"—suggests that God's election of the Jewish people is replaced by Christ and the Christian church.[38] For two millennia, implicit or

36. R. Kendall Soulen, *The God of Israel and Christian Theology* (Minneapolis: Fortress Press, 1996), 1–12; Michael Wyschogrod, *Abraham's Promise: Judaism and Jewish-Christian Relations*, ed. R. Kendall Soulen (Grand Rapids, MI: Eerdmans, 2004), 183–84.

37. Eck, *Encountering God*, 178–80.

38. O'Hare, in *The Enduring Covenant: The Education of Christians and the End of Antisemitism* (Valley Forge, PA: Trinity Press International, 1997), 7, offers eight tenets of supersessionism: "(1) revelation in Jesus Christ supersedes the revelation to Israel; (2) the New Testament fulfills the Old Testament;

explicit supersessionism has taught that God chose the Jewish people to prepare the world for Christ, and that, after his coming, the role of God's chosen people *comes to end* and its place is taken by the church, the new Israel.[39] Accordingly, the legitimacy of Judaism ends where Christianity begins; a carnal "chosen people" is displaced by a spiritual church; exclusivity is replaced by inclusivity; law gives way to love.

Notice that the problem of supersessionism is not the problem of relegating the other as completely "other," as strange and utterly unknown, but rather, the temptation to include her under terms that are really my own. If this kind of inclusivism can be toxic, and history shows that it can, then the remedy must come by underscoring differences and by keeping them from becoming divisive by cultivating gratitude and even holy wonder for them. Later, I want to show how Christians in light of the cross help cultivate such gratitude and wonder for the particularity and uniqueness of theirs and other religious traditions. But first, we must come to terms with the depth and durability of Christendom's supersessionism.

Dominant Conundrum: "The Jewish Question"

In *Constantine's Sword: The Church and the* Jews, James Carroll argues that supersessionism and anti-Judaism in general, that is, subtle and not-so-subtle denigrations of Judaism as a way of underscoring Christian triumphalism, provide the soil from which racist anti-Semitism naturally sprouts.[40] Others will argue that the causality is less linear, but no one argues with the fact that Hitler had a long history of

---

(3) the church replaces the Jews as God's people; (4) Judaism is obsolete, its covenant abrogated; (5) post-exilic Judaism was legalistic; (6) the Jews did not heed the warning of the prophets; (7) the Jews did not understand the prophesies about Jesus; (8) the Jews were Christ killers."

39. Soulen, *God of Israel*, 1–2.

40. James Carroll, *Constantine's Sword: The Church and the Jews* (Boston: Houghton Mifflin, 2001), 476: "However modern Nazism was, it planted its roots in the soil of age-old Church attitudes and a nearly unbroken chain of Church-sponsored acts of Jew hatred. However pagan Nazism was, it drew its sustenance from groundwater poisoned by the Church's most solemnly held theology—its *theology*." Note that, despite this close association, Carroll makes the common distinction between anti-Judaism, a theological position by which "the Jew" provides the negative other for Christian self-understanding, and anti-Semitism, a racist ideology that first emerges in the fifteenth century and climaxes in National Socialism's pseudoscience (22, 346, 382, and 475–78). While naming this distinction, Carroll contends that it ought not to prevent one from seeing the "narrative arc" that begins with anti-Judaism and ends in anti-Semitism. I find myself

Christian anti-Judaism at his disposal when stereotyping, scapegoating, and almost systematically eliminating European Jewry. Connections between the church's more subtle triumphalist postures and explicit demonization of Jews are so subtle that sometimes, the first is propagated in the very effort to resist the latter.

Take, for example, Bonhoeffer's earliest resistance to Nazi ideology. Responding to the Aryan clauses of 1933, which sought to expel everyone with "Jewish blood" from public office, including offices of the church, Bonhoeffer insisted that, "from the point of view of the church of Christ, Judaism is never a racial concept but a religious one."[41] He also claimed that the church "has an unconditional obligation to the victims of any . . . society, even if they do not belong to the Christian community."[42] Yet, Bonhoeffer also admits that "the Jewish question" is something with which Germany must deal, and "the state is justified in adopting new methods in dealing with it."[43] Most ambiguous is Bonhoeffer's use of Christian anti-Judaism as a tool for resisting Nazi anti-Semitism. He refuses to let the state define what it means to be a Jew or a Christian, and yet, his own definitions portray Jews by what they *lack*—as those who have refused to embark on their rightful "homecoming" to God by accepting Christ. Whereas Bonhoeffer vigilantly resists Hitler's anti-Semitism, his earliest resistance thereby perpetuates forms of Christian supersessionism. While some understand this as the brave endeavor of fighting fire with fire, others liken it to driving out the devil with the help of the devil.

As we saw in chapter 4, Bonhoeffer first defended Jews primarily because their persecution by the Nazis overstepped the church's right to define who is Christian and who is Jewish on theological grounds—that is, according to who has been baptized. This willingness to defend non-Christians for reasons that seem self-serving may not always be all bad. Recall from chapter 2 that Tim Wise urges other

among those who have been moved by the force of Carroll's book but who have reservations about the linearity and cohesiveness of this narrative arc.

41. Dietrich Bonhoeffer, *No Rusty Swords: Letters, Lectures and Notes 1928-1936* (New York: Harper & Row, 1965), 227.

42. Ibid., 225.

43. Ibid., 223.

whites to get involved in matters of racial justice for reasons that also look, at first glance, to be self-serving. White people should come to terms with white privilege because privilege and racism are their problems—they hurt them.[44] Similarly, Christian theologian Kendall Soulen argues that the problem of Christian supersessionism is *a Christian problem*, a problem of Christian identity. That is, if Christians believe that God could revoke an earlier covenant, replacing it with a new, allegedly more inclusive one, what prevents them from fearing that the hope they find in Jesus will not also be replaced?[45] Put positively, for Christians to fully trust the second testament, the new promises of God through Christ, they must also believe that God would not revoke the first covenant with the people of Israel.

Germany in 1933 is not the only time when Christian self-understandings turn, for good or ill, on Christian interpretations of "the Jews." Often, the denigration of Judaism in the self-refuting posture of Christian triumphalism takes subtle and seemingly harmless forms. I remember singing "Oh You Can't Get to Heaven" at Camp Omega as a young Missouri Synod Lutheran kid. Most verses were harmless enough:

Oh You can't get to heaven
In a Kleenex box [...]
The Lord don't want no little snots.

But a particular verse confirmed what I thought I knew about the difference between Christians and those who do not see Jesus as Lord:

Oh you can't get to heaven
As a Pharisee [...]
The Lord don't want no hypocrisy.

In my third-grade mind, "Pharisee" did not name particular authorities of Second Temple Judaism with whom Jesus—also a Jew—had a number of intra-religious debates. Rather, it stood in for all Jews, whose

---

44. Tim Wise, *White Like Me: Reflections on Race from a Privileged Son*, rev. ed. (Berkeley, CA: Soft Skull Press / Counterpoint, 2011), 179–82.
45. Soulen, *God of Israel*, 4.

hypocrisy provided a foil for my anticipated Christian salvation. The alleged legalism of Judaism (and for some Protestants, of Catholicism) often functions to bolster Christian understandings of themselves as knowing grace rather than judgment, love rather than law. At times, this elusive logic shows itself fairly clearly, for those with eyes to see. Such was the case—or should have been the case—in 2004 with the release of the controversial film, *The Passion of the Christ.*[46]

Once More with Passion

Mel Gibson's film helpfully marks popular assumptions about early-twenty-first-century Christians as they subconsciously position themselves over-and-against Jews, rather than over-and-against consumerism, individualism, or—the most obvious other candidate, given the date of its release in 2004—the war-making of political empires. The film invites this discussion about Christianity's proper foil insofar as it focuses on three representative biblical characters: Pontius Pilate and his Roman Empire, the high priest Caiaphas and the sacerdotal authority of Judaism, and Jesus and his followers.

Tracing the supersessionistic elements of *The Passion of the Christ* is more fruitful than debating the historical accuracy or alleged anti-Semitism. This is partly because, as Soulen has noted, Christians have their own reason for rethinking their relationship to Judaism.[47] Again, if it is the God *of Israel* who is revealed in Jesus of Nazareth, then Christian trust in that revelation depends on God's continued fidelity to the first covenant. *The Passion of the Christ* can be accused of perpetuating Christian supersessionism on several accounts.

First, by using a narrative framework that links Jesus to the universal story of Genesis, rather than to Judaism and the God of Israel, the film makes the Sanhedrin's (the Jewish high court's) conviction of Jesus as inexplicable as possible. In the opening scene of the movie, Jesus resists Satan and crushes the head of a serpent—imagery that beckons back to

---

46. *The Passion of the Christ*, DVD, directed by Mel Gibson (2004; Beverly Hills, CA: Twentieth Century Fox Home Entertainment, 2004).

47. Soulen, *God of Israel*, 4.

Genesis 3. Later, when Mary the Mother of Jesus exclaims at the foot of the cross, "Flesh of my flesh, heart of my heart," her words again remind the viewer of Adam's assessment of Eve: "This at last is bone of my bones and flesh of my flesh" (Gen 2:23). The story the movie tells begins in Eden, and then, skips immediately to Golgotha. The time between—including the years of Jesus's public ministry—are left out of the framing of the story. Without a context that would make religious resistance to Jesus understandable, the film makes the condemnation of Jesus appear incomprehensibly perverse.

Second, the Jewish setting is not only omitted by the movie's framing, but also, reinterpreted by it. The first glimpse we are given of Mary the Mother of Jesus, for instance, has her awakening with a premonition that something has happened to her son. She desperately exclaims to Mary Magdalene: "Why is this night different from every other night?" Magdalene answers: "Because once we were slaves and we are slaves no longer." The lines are paraphrases of the first and last lines of the *Haggadah* from the Jewish Seder meal. But here, words that are otherwise spoken in a highly *scripted* way ("Seder" literally means "order") now convey spontaneous and personal expectation, rather than a commemorative ritual. By eliding the *Haggadah's* narration of Exodus, Mary Magdalene's answer sounds more like a spontaneous evangelical confession of faith, rather than scripted lines from the Passover. *The Passion* minimizes or even anachronistically "Christianizes" the Jewish historical setting that would otherwise frame the last fifteen hours of Jesus's life.

Third, and most telling, a highly symbolic portrayal of the scribes and elders consistently associates them with a rigid and artificial clericalism. These Jewish religious leaders appear more like richly textured images than like characters of a story. They are painted with broad strokes and provide the "backdrop" for those individuals who care for Jesus. At no time in the film are the high priests portrayed individually. More often than not they appear shoulder to shoulder—almost as replicas of one another. Rarely do we see their profiles and never do we see any of their skin besides their heavily bearded faces. As such they appear as two-dimensional figures—the personification of a hierarchical clericalism, mere officers of an impersonal establishment. The symmetry of their vestments, which are heavily clad in metal and which arch over their faces, makes the figures resemble actual buildings. Collectively, they connote an edifice—a cold and impersonal structure.

Comparing them to the other characters proves interesting. The Roman soldiers are depicted as street thugs. They laugh while torturing Jesus and are whimsically and stupidly cruel. Their evil is the naughtiness of children; it is tremendously violent, but also, stupid and even pathetic. Next to them, the Jewish leaders appear refined and constrained, but also calculating, manipulative, and shrewd. Thus, while the film does present the Roman military as merciless, its cruelty is the maddening horror of pure malice rather than the bureaucratic, systemic evil that one would expect from an occupying regime. Next to the soldiers, the Jewish leaders are seen as dispassionate and overly judgmental. Even if both groups are depicted as evil, only the *dispassion* of the latter diametrically opposes the *passion* of the Christ. Paralleling the logic of supersessionism, the movie pits hypocrisy, legalism, and judgment against truthfulness, forgiveness, and love.

The disparity between Roman tomfoolery and Jewish slavishness is made even starker through the characters of Pilate (the Roman governor) and Caiaphas (the high priest). From extra-biblical records, we know that Pilate was particularly ruthless in dealing with Jews of Second Temple Israel.[48] Biblically, he is portrayed more favorably, most likely in the effort by nascent Christians to win tolerance from the Roman Empire. The movie, however, sympathizes with Pilate in a noteworthy way. Pilate looks and talks like an upper-middle-class businessman caught in a middle management position between the mandates of Caesar and an unhappy labor force. If Caiaphas personifies the evils of a heartless system, Pilate is among those victims caught in its machinations. Indeed, if there is a character with whom American

48. Amy-Jill Levine, *The Misunderstood Jew: The Church and the Scandal of the Jewish Jesus* (New York: HarperOne, 2006), 99; Marcus Borg and John Dominic Crossan, *The Last Week: What the Gospels Really Teach about Jesus's Final Days in Jerusalem* (New York: HarperCollins, 2006), 41, 144–47.

upper-middle-class Christians might easily identify, it is with this clean-shaven, physically fit, soul-searching leader who is bound by the tragic circumstances of his day. To us, the Jewish leaders appear antiquated in a way that Pilate and Rome do not.

At the climax of the film, Cassius, one of the Roman centurions, gets baptized by water and blood from Jesus's pierced side while the Jewish leaders are thrown about as the temple is rent asunder. The scene starkly juxtaposes love to law, living faith to ritualized obedience, and earnest confession to hopeless despair. As Cassius kneels, gazing in wonder at Jesus, Caiaphas cowers at the sight of his broken building. Whereas Jesus can withstand tremendous suffering out of love for humanity, and individuals like Cassius can withstand the pain of contrition out of love for Christ, Caiaphas is portrayed as so desperately clinging to the wooden entrapments of organized religion that the destruction of stone sends him reeling. The film continually pits spiritual belief in Jesus against a contrived fidelity to custom, structure, and law.

What would *The Passion* look like if it were more thoroughly edited to show the Jewishness of Jesus and the structural evil perpetuated by the Roman regime? Would the American audience continue to identify with a Pontius Pilate who crucifies Jesus not because his tragic circumstances force him to, but because an empire that honors Caesar as lord will crush any competing lordships? How would this new film be viewed by those of us whose Christian identities are regularly formed in relation to other religions ("I'm Christian, not Jewish"), but rarely in relation to national commitments ("I'm a Christian, not a nationalist")? Would the new film be able to call into question those unreflective commitments through which we often find ourselves conformed to this world (Rom 12:2)?

Dominant Proposal: Moderating Religion

Many, if not most, Americans associate religious fanaticism and extremism with religious exclusivism and religious violence. The new atheists are unique largely for assuming that religion in and of itself is extremist, exclusivist, and death-dealing. In *The End of Faith*, atheist author Sam Harris insists that religion is so *inherently* irrational and perilous that moderating religion with liberal openness, assuring others that one is not *too* religious, would be almost worse. "While moderation in religion may seem like a reasonable position to stake out," writes Harris, it actually "offers no bulwark against religious extremism and religious violence."[49] Moderation might keep religion in check with a dose of Enlightenment reason, but in doing exactly that, it covers over the most pernicious aspects of religion and makes it seem as though it—religion—were not as inherently irrational and fanatical as it is.[50]

This critique of efforts to moderate religion is about the only thing about which I agree with Harris, but for almost opposite reasons. To suggest that religion needs to be moderated by more enlightened, rational, or liberal sentiments confirms the assumption that, left to their own, religions will prove violent—an assumption shared by Harris and the liberal Christians he takes to task. Diana Eck inadvertently perpetuates similar assumptions about the relationship between deep religious commitments and openness to the faiths of others. In *Encountering God*, she describes progression from exclusivism through inclusivism to pluralism as developing a "wider sense of we"—that is, of opening the boundaries of one's tradition out to include respect for all. This universal embrace of others is honorable; I join Eck in wishing more would aspire to it. The question is where the motivation for it comes from. Do particular religions pull believers into sectarian enclaves and exclusionary claims, which need to be balanced and tempered by openness that comes from elsewhere? Or can one imagine being extremely and fanatically Christian (or extremely and fanatically Jewish or Muslim or Buddhist) *and thus,* being supremely open to the religious claims of others?[51]

---

49. Harris, *End of Faith*, 20.
50. Ibid., 16–23.
51. See Stanley Hauerwas's compelling retrieval of "fanaticism" in "The Nonviolent Terrorist: In Defense of Christian Fanaticism," in *The Church as Counterculture*, ed. Michael L. Budde and Robert W. Brimlow (Albany: State University of New York Press, 2000), 89–104.

As Patel persuasively argues, there are histories, stories, and other "theologies of interfaith cooperation"[52] within each tradition that point outward toward interfaith work. Yoder ends an essay on Christian foundations for interfaith dialogue by describing repentance as the posture necessary for true interfaith engagement. Repentance is necessary not because Christians have held their faith too tightly or exclusively, but rather, because the faith that they *should* hold tightly *itself* calls them toward repentance (*metanoia*), and also, because the long history of Constantinianism in relation to that central calling gives them much to confess.[53]

Confession of Sin as a Foundation for Interfaith Engagement

Taking these cues from Patel and Yoder, I think my own tradition of Lutheranism should come to interfaith dialogue and cooperation first by confessing Luther's own dramatic shortcomings when it comes to understanding and working with people of other religions. The sixteenth-century reformer had only a cursory knowledge of "the Turks" (as he called Muslims south and east of Saxony), and he displayed a good deal of ambivalence about them. On the one hand, the expanding Ottoman Empire extended much more religious tolerance than did the church against which Luther was dissenting, and Luther knew it; he wondered whether the Sultan might not become a tactical ally. He also quips, in a sort of double-critique, that "a smart Turk makes a better ruler than a dumb Christian."[54] On the other hand, Luther could describe a clash of civilizations between the Christian West and Turks from the East with enough good-versus-evil imagery as to make Samuel Huntington blush. When Luther pens his famous "A Mighty Fortress Is Our God" around 1527, it was probably first used as a battle song to inspire soldiers to rise up against encroaching Muslims.[55]

---

52. Patel, *Sacred Ground*, 95–103, 142–45.
53. John Howard Yoder, "The Disavowal of Constantine: An Alternative Perspective on Interfaith Dialogue," in *The Royal Priesthood: Essays Ecclesiastical and Ecumenical* (Scottdale, PA: Herald, 1998), 242–61.
54. Lewis W. Spitz, *The Protestant Reformation 1517-1559* (New York: Harper & Row, 1985), 330.
55. John Merriman, *A History of Modern Europe: From the Renaissance to the Age of Napoleon 1*, 3rd ed. (New York: W. W. Norton, 2010), 101.

When in the fourth verse, Luther writes, "Were they to take our house, goods, honor, child, or spouse, though life be wrenched away, they cannot win the day. The kingdom's ours forever," the "they" may, in fact, be Muslims and the "kingdom" over which they battle may, in fact, be Western Europe, even if the song also refers to other forces and powers, both visible and invisible, then and today.

Luther's anxieties about and caricatures of other traditions get more treacherous when it comes to Judaism. As is well known, Luther had hoped that once his own evangelical reforms did away with "papist" distortions, Jewish people would finally see that their own Hebrew scriptures pointed toward their fulfillment in the gospel, and thus would start lining up for Christian baptism. Early in his career, he writes "That Jesus Was Born a Jew" (1523), condemning the fear-tactics and baptism by sword used by earlier Christians and encouraging his contemporaries to "treat the Jews in a brotherly manner." They are the "blood relatives" of Jesus, insists Luther; we Gentile Christians are only "aliens and in-laws."

When, despite Luther's soft-sell, most Jews continued to politely decline the invitation to convert, Luther became outraged. Writing "On the Jews and Their Lies" twenty years later (1543), Luther mounts a violent invective. Where he once called Jews the blood relatives of Jesus, he now calls them poisoners, ritual murderers, and parasites. In his last sermon, delivered just days before his death, Luther calls for the expulsion of Jews from Germany altogether. Luckily, the influence of these tirades was not very great in Luther's time. Yet, twentieth-century German Jews did not need such texts waiting to be picked up and used for ideological justification 400 years after the fact. Luther's writings have not only led to supersessionism and anti-Judaism, the defamation of Jews on theological grounds, but have also been appropriated in support of anti-Semitic racist ideology, scapegoating, fear-mongering, and murder.

The confession of Lutheran complicity in the stereotyping and scapegoating of others must be the starting place for any candid commitment to interfaith understanding and cooperation. In this regard, one of the most significant contributions Lutherans have made to interfaith is the statement on Lutheran–Jewish relations that the Church Council of the Evangelical Lutheran Church in America adopted in 1994. This document underscores the importance of Luther's central confession of faith:

> Honoring [Luther's] name in our own, we recall his bold stand for truth, his earthy and sublime words of wisdom, and above all his witness to God's saving Word. Luther proclaimed a gospel for people as we really are. . . .[56]

But at this point, as Lutherans confess God's saving word and sufficient grace, they also confess their sin, how that "grace [must reach] our deepest shames and address the most tragic truths." The document continues:

> In the spirit of that truth-telling, we who bear his name and heritage must with pain acknowledge also Luther's anti-Judaic diatribes and the violent recommendations of his later writings against the Jews. . . . [W]e reject this violent invective, and yet more do we express our deep and abiding sorrow over its tragic effects on subsequent generations. . . .
>
> Grieving the complicity of our own tradition within this history of hatred, moreover, we express our urgent desire to live out our faith in Jesus Christ with love and respect for the Jewish people. We recognize in anti-Semitism a contradiction and an affront to the Gospel, a violation of our hope and calling.[57]

Confession of sin is central to Lutheran identity—Lutherans (like many other Christians) typically do not start worship without it. As earlier analyses of Luther's Heidelberg Disputation make clear, confession of sin is also part and parcel of reforming Christians' reception of grace. So, too, with interfaith encounter. Such confession—of what Christians have done badly and failed to do altogether—is one of the gifts that they bring to the table when meeting brothers and sisters from other traditions. To confess the sins of one's church is not to moderate

---

56. ELCA (Evangelical Lutheran Church in America), "Declaration of the Evangelical Lutheran Church in North America to the Jewish Community," 1994. Accessed August 10, 2015, http://download.elca.org/ELCAResourceRepository/Declaration_Of_The_ELCA_To_The_Jewish_Community.pdf.
57. Ibid.

religion, becoming half-Christian and half-liberal or tolerant or enlightened. To confess sin is rather to become deeply Christian. Christians best enter into interfaith cooperation as fanatical, extremist penitents.

The Dominant Crisis: Muslims, Christendom, and the Scandal of the Cross

When I teach my undergraduate students the logic and history of Christian supersessionism, the first question that smart, Christian students ask goes something like this: "Isn't Islam guilty of supersessionism as well?" The question can sometimes sound like the charge of reverse discrimination from a person confronting white privilege for the first time. But it is a fair question. Muslims understand themselves to have the full and final revelation from God in the Qur'an, a revelation that references and supplements, but also, corrects and supplants, scriptures first revealed to Jews and Christians, which have since become corrupted, according to Muslims. I tell the students that I concentrate on the problem of *Christian* supersessionism because that is the tradition that I know and love the most; thus, I am most critical of it. What I am usually unable to suggest is that, while Muslims might be charged with a supersessionistic logic of their own, Christian supersessionism has run so deep, has penetrated America's secular neo-Christendom so fully, that it colors and caricatures Muslims just as easily as Jews—however anachronistic that logic might be. I will try to explain what I mean by this.

Neo-Christendom versus the Muslim World

Islam arose as a religion in the seventh century. Technically, it cannot be historically superseded by Christianity, which arose roughly six centuries beforehand. But the deep logic of supersessionism pits a pure, progressivist faith against its retrograde and legalistic foil—and Islam (especially sharī'a, or Islamic law) plays that role rather nicely in the popular imaginations of American Christians. In those same imaginings, supersessionism also pits a tolerant, peaceful faith against a thoroughly violent one. What is more, Christianity has been so thoroughly confused with the private, internal, secularized, and ostensibly peace-loving faith of modernity—whether through Kantian awe for the universal moral law or a Romantic feeling of absolute dependence—that Islam, which for many in the West amounts to an antisecular, antimodernist fundamentalism, cannot but seem unevolved and therefore violent by nature. Christians of America's neo-Christendom thereby see themselves as having spiritually progressed beyond the retrograde, all-too-political, dangerous form of religion that Islam chiefly exemplifies.

Bernard Lewis, in the 1990 essay "The Roots of Muslim Rage," used exactly this logic to explain "why so many Muslims deeply resent the West, and why their bitterness is not easily mollified."[58] Lewis traces heightening tensions between "the Muslim world" and "the West" back to the fact that Islam permits no separation of religion from politics while Western democracies originated and thrive on the legal separation of church and state. Lewis might have portrayed the rivalry in terms of fundamentalist Muslims versus a thoroughly secular democracy and Western capitalism. For him, however, both sides of the conflict are religious. Lewis argues that democracy and secularism are compatible with Christianity; indeed, they have purified and perfected the faith. I quote a pivotal paragraph in full:

> The origins of secularism in the west may be found in two circumstances—in the early Christian teachings and, still more, experience, which created two institutions, Church and State; and in later Christian conflicts, which drove the two apart. Muslims, too, had their religious disagreements, but there was nothing remotely approaching the ferocity of the Christian struggles between Protestants and Catholics, which devastated Christian Europe in the sixteenth and seventeenth centuries and finally drove Christians in desperation to evolve a doctrine of the separation of religion from the state. Only by depriving religious institutions of coercive power, it seemed, could Christendom restrain the

58. Bernard Lewis, "The Roots of Muslim Rage: Why So Many Muslims Deeply Resent the West, and Why Their Bitterness Is Not Easily Mollified," *Policy* 7.4 (Summer 2001-02): 17–26. [Originally published in *The Atlantic*, September 1990, accessed August 10, 2015, http://www.theatlantic.com/magazine/archive/1990/09/the-roots-of-muslim-rage/304643/.]

murderous intolerance and persecution that Christians had visited on followers of other religions and, most of all, on those who professed other forms of their own.[59]

Notice here how Christianity itself—or "early Christian teachings"— sows the seeds for the separation of religion from politics. (Lewis earlier traced that separation back to Christian scriptures that enjoin Christians to "render unto Caesar the things which are Caesar's"—Mark 12:17; Matt 22:21.[60]) At the same time, the disestablishment of religion is purified and perfected only after Christians realize that, without it, they are unable to "restrain the murderous intolerance and persecution" characterizing Europe's so-called wars of religion.

Lewis suggests that without a Reformation and, thus, without warring religious factions *within* their own faith tradition, Muslims have not had to overcome the threat of murderous intolerance that older forms of Christendom have had to confront. While Christians have weaned themselves from the violence of political religion, Muslims are yet to do so, or so the logic goes. Christianity accordingly becomes most itself when it is re-formed into its essentially privatized, safe, and original form. That Islam has not been so secularized proves that it has not yet fully evolved as a religion, and thus, still sanctions religious violence. Some Christians of neo-Christendom point to this as the reason that Muslim extremists must be killed.[61]

"The Roots of Muslim Rage" rehearses the same logic that would later appear in the "Clash of Civilizations" theory made popular by Samuel Huntington. Huntington, too, portrays Western Christianity as the foundation for Western secularism, and Islam as the negative foil for each.[62] Were two equally political or equally religious ideologies at war with one another, it would be hard to show why one deserves one's allegiance while the other can be demonized. As it stands, a supersessionistic logic pitting a tolerant religion of choice against an

---

59. Ibid., 24.
60. Ibid., 17.
61. Harris, *End of Faith*, 52–53.
62. Samuel P. Huntington, *The Clash of Civilizations and the Remaking of World Order* (New York: Simon & Schuster, 2003), 70.

intolerant religion of force[63] has become the most pervasive ideology infecting nearly every popular discussion of global Islam.[64]

Given the ubiquity of this logic, Eboo Patel takes pains to show how American Muslims can contribute just as much to the flourishing of American democracy and the common good as can Christians, Jews, or secular humanists. He compares sharī'a law to canon law; if American Catholics have been able to follow Catholic teachings while still obeying the law of the land (including America's disestablishment of religion), then American Muslims certainly can do the same.[65] A future Muslim candidate running for the presidency of the United States would only need to give the same assurances that John F. Kennedy gave when he ran for president—namely, that her or his religion would provide the moral basis for leadership but never directly influence policy. Patel convincingly argues that Muslims are equally capable of separating religion from politics in this way.[66] It is supremely understandable that Patel, an American Muslim and advocate for interfaith cooperation, would want to emphasize Islam's compatibility with the secular state over and against many stereotypes and inferences to the contrary. Still, regrettable are the supersessionistic assumptions that demand such defenses, and the way that the defenses might subtly confirm assumptions that the purest, most peaceable religions are also the most privatized.[67]

The Narrow Way of the Cross ... Opening to Others

It is true that American Protestants often define themselves in contrast to Islam, at least to an imagined Islam. But as my colleague Cyrus Zargar reminds me, European secularism has not done much better when it comes to Islamophobia; in fact, many of the advocates of the

63. Amina Wadud helpfully reverses the assumed categories in "American by Force, Muslim by Choice," *Political Theology* 12.5 (2011): 699–705.
64. Saba Mahmood, "Religious Reason and Secular Affect: An Incommensurable Divide?" in Talal Asad, Wendy Brown, Judith Butler, and Saba Mahmood, *Is Critique Secular? Blasphemy, Injury, and Free Speech* (New York: Fordham University Press, 2013), 73–77.
65. Patel, *Sacred Ground*, 49–53.
66. Ibid., 41–47.
67. See especially, Lipton, "Secular Sufism."

hijab ban in France, or the minaret ban in Switzerland, are staunchly secular.[68] How then do Christians in a secularized Christendom best retrieve their tradition as a source for interfaith action? At risk of invoking Luther's theology of the cross one too many times, I want to offer it as an example of the ways that Christians might become more deeply, determinately Christian, and *thus*, become open to non-Christians in all their own particularities. Luther's understanding of the gospel—as carried out by Kierkegaard, Bonhoeffer, Soelle, and others—might offer a way of coupling seemingly narrow claims with openness to honest dialogue and cooperation.

As I have noted, early in his career, Luther distinguished theologians of glory, whom he critiqued for having all-too-cozy understandings of God, from theologians of the cross—those who rightly know and serve the God revealed through the suffering of Jesus. In his famous Heidelberg Disputation (1518), Luther puts it this way: "A theologian of glory calls evil good and good evil. A theologian of the cross calls the thing what it actually is." Luther then explains:

> This is clear: He [the theologian of glory] who does not know Christ does not know God hidden in suffering. Therefore he prefers works to suffering, glory to the cross, strength to weakness, wisdom to folly, and, in general, good to evil. These [however] are the people whom the apostle calls "enemies of the cross of Christ" [Phil 3:18], for they hate the cross and suffering and love works and the glory of works. . . . [But] *God can be found only in suffering and the cross. . . .*[69]

Certainly, these are exclusivist claims, including a clear distinction between "the friends of the cross" and "enemies of the cross of Christ." To claim that God can be found *only* in suffering and the cross is enough to make almost any non-Christian uncomfortable. (Muslims and others with an understanding of the absolute indivisibility and impassibility

---

68. Cyrus Zargar made such comments in a question to Stanley Hauerwas when Hauerwas recently visited Augustana College. Stanley Hauerwas, Interview: "The State of College and Christianity: A Conversation with 'America's Best Theologian.'" Fall Symposium Day, Sept. 17, 2015, accessed September 29, 2015, https://www.youtube.com/watch?v=makm-BAvirA.
69. Martin Luther, Heidelberg Disputation (1518), in *Martin Luther's Basic Theological Writings*, ed. Timothy F. Lull, 2nd ed. (Minneapolis: Fortress Press, 2005), 58 (explanation to thesis 21), my emphasis.

of God may here downright cringe.) But we should be careful to note what exactly Luther's exclusivist claims exclude. The theologian of glory is one who looks around to whatever has value in our dominant society and projects them onto God: God is like the power of domination—only stronger. God is like a kingly authority—only more unquestionable. God is like the Unmoved Mover—only more invulnerable. It is over-and-against these seemingly obvious, self-assured, and typically ideological understandings of "the divine" (in other words, ones that function to secure our own power and authority) that Luther posits the God who freely discloses Godself in the most unusual places—in a barn in Bethlehem and on a cross outside Jerusalem. Luther thus underscores the *particularity* of a God who fully reveals Godself in such unlikely places and the necessary *peculiarity* of Christians who follow this God. Kierkegaard repeatedly underscores the particularity of God's revelation by calling it a scandal, but a necessary one. He helps make Christianity strange by emphasizing the intellectual paradox and affective indignity of the gospel in the face of the many attempts, then and now, to hem in God's unbounded love.

How might particular and seemingly exclusivist claims such as these help foster authentic interfaith encounter? First, theologians of the cross—if they take this peculiar self-revelation of God seriously—are formed to see God in unlikely places. The One revealed "outside the camp" (Heb 13:13) is utterly free to be revealed outside Christian circles as well. Christians will be ready to find God in unusual places, and so enter into interfaith exchange with eyes wide open.

Second, embracing their own scandalous particularity, Christians allow space for others to inhabit their own stubborn particularity. Without a sense of the tradition's particularity and limits, without ample witness to a God who eludes its own grasp, theologians of glory are bound to mistake their particular glimpse of God with full and final comprehension. When others cannot or will not see it the same way, they will get exasperated, as Luther himself became with the unconverted Jews around him. A theologian of the cross, by contrast, knows the limits of her sight of God. Or, to put it positively:

appreciating the fact that God is strangely, wonderfully revealed in this peculiar way, the Christian allows space for other revelations, each of which are no more graspable and incontestable—and no less wonderful—than one's own.

Christians are called to resist the idolization of their own tradition so that they can better inhabit it. Conversations with people of other religions provide the primary vehicle for such reflective critique. Unlike empty skepticism or something that we assume to be "pure secular reason," the differing beliefs, practices, and virtues of other faiths provide the footing, so to speak, as Christians step back to examine their own, just as the committed Christian provides the opportunity for the Hindu or Jew to reconsider and reinhabit her or his own faith. Learning about Avalokitesvara, the Bodhisattva of Compassion, from the committed Mahayana Buddhist might help a Christian consider whether his own self-sacrificial love has not been too self-serving, a round-about strategy to get into heaven. Listening to the committed Muslim speak of God's radical oneness and transcendence might help the Christian consider whether her Christ doesn't look too much like the Buddy Christ from the satirical film *Dogma*. Even listening to the atheist who has read his first bit of Nietzsche and goes around proclaiming to his churchy friends that "God is dead" might help the Christian consider how her own tradition repeats the same truth in a different register. Yes, God is dead—fully revealed in the cross of Christ—and yet, still ruling the world with that vulnerable, suffering love.

Finally, while Christians come to humble service because their Lord humbly serves, they should not be surprised to find Jews engaged in the same service, who come in the spirit of the Jewish prayer *tikkun olam*—from the hope that by doing small acts that contribute to God's ongoing creation, humans can "heal the world."[70] And they shouldn't be surprised to find Muslims so engaged, perhaps responding to the Qur'an's exhortation to believers to "strive in the way of God with a

---

70. Kristin Johnston Largen, *Finding God Among Our Neighbors: An Interfaith Systematic Theology* (Minneapolis: Fortress Press, 2013), 235–37.

service worthy of Him" (Qur'an 22:78). When Buddhists participate in shared service with the Heart Sutra on their lips, or when lovers of the Bhagavad Gita come with intentions to act for good simply and purely, "without attachment to the fruits of their actions,"[71] Christians, again, should not be surprised. They are not surprised because they already believe in a God of surprises, a God who shows up in such unexpected places—even Golgotha—that Christians find themselves attending especially to those beyond Christian borders.

On Truth and Relativity

The leading neo-orthodox theologian of the twentieth century, Karl Barth, was once pushed to compare his own Protestant Christianity to Pure Land Schools of Buddhism, given their similar understandings of salvation "only by grace" and "only by faith." Shockingly to some, Barth rejected a priori the idea that Buddhists had a valuable perspective on or even a portion of religious truth. Why are they wrong? Because, for Barth, there is only one criterion distinguishing ultimate truth from error, and "that one thing is the name of Jesus Christ . . . which alone constitutes the truth of our religion."[72] Such avowals of Christian uniqueness typically tout that "salvation is found in no one else, for there is no other name under heaven given to mankind by which we must be saved" (Acts 4:12). They are often interpreted—wrongly, I think—as the strut and swagger of Christians who have a monopoly on the cultural and social capital of Western Europe and the United States. By contrast, Barth claimed that God's specific, special election of Jesus (as with God's election of Israel) calls Christians to hope that all might be saved. Yet, the grounds of that hope are always specific. It is because of the truth of Christ and of

71. *The Bhagavad-Gita*, trans. Barbara Stoler Miller (New York: Bantam, 1986), II.44–47: "Be intent on action, / not on the fruit of actions; / avoid attraction to the fruits / and attachment to inaction!"
72. Karl Barth, *Church Dogmatics*, Vol. 1 Part 2: Doctrine of the Word of God (London: T&T Clark, 2004), 343. See discussions in Paul Knitter, *No Other Name: A Critical Survey of Christian Attitudes Toward the World Religions* (Maryknoll, NY: Orbis, 1985), 82–84, and Diana Eck, *Encountering God*, 87. For a more nuanced retrieval of Barth's theology for encountering non-Christians, especially Jews, see Chris Boesel, *Risking Proclamation, Respecting Difference: Christian Faith, Imperialistic Discourse, and Abraham* (Eugene, OR: Cascade, 2008).

Christ alone that Christians know the expansive stretch of God's unlimited love.

I have wanted in this chapter to reconceive the deep convictions of Christians as not necessarily narrow or exclusionary and therefore needing to be balanced by more tolerant, liberal, or secularized standpoints. Rather, it is that very assured faith—what Luther describes as a living, daring confidence in God's grace—that enables Christians to humbly recognize the God of Jesus in people of other faiths. To many, this can seem like a sleight of hand. Being open to truth as revealed outside Christian quarters, am I not here abandoning the very truth claims that make confessional Christians such as Barth so particular and faithful? Stanley Hauerwas (himself a Barthian and no lover of pluralism[73]) also finds little so maddening as the knee-jerk relativizing of the claim that "Jesus is the only way to salvation," with appeals to subjective feelings: ". . . according to my personal opinion."[74]

I admit that I often want to add "according to my Christian perspective" to my own truth claims, especially when talking to persons of other faiths. Does this relativize what ought to be a daring and confident proclamation? How should one speak about Christianity as something particular—as something, but not everything—without relativizing and compartmentalizing religious belief as *merely* belief or personal opinion? This is no easy feat; it would seem as though particularity infers relativity; if something is true in this way rather than that, then it is not absolutely true and thus not worthy of our unqualified devotion.

In part, the ability to underscore the particularity (and peculiarity) of Christianity without sliding into wholesale relativism depends on distinguishing the relativity of religious communities from the "object" of their devotion. God is absolute (at least in some senses), but the God of Jews, Muslims, and Christians also reveals Godself in

---

73. Hauerwas asserts that "pluralism" as a position plays into the assumptions of American Constantinianism. Stanley Hauerwas, *The State of the University: Academic Knowledges and the Knowledge of God* (Malden, MA: Blackwell, 2007), 60: "From my perspective, 'pluralism' is the ideology used by Protestant liberals to give themselves the illusion they are still in control of, or at least have the responsibility for, the future of America."

74. Hauerwas, Interview, "The State of College."

scandalously particular and peculiar ways. In believing that God is three-in-one, Christians also believe that God is relational and relative insofar as each person of the Trinity (Father, Son, and Holy Spirit) is who He or She is according to how He/She relates to the other persons of the Trinity and to the created, redeemable world. In short, the God who is revealed through the relativities of salvation history is who God truly is. God is thus relational through and through—a Relative Absolute—or so the doctrine of the Trinity assuredly claims. Knowing God as relative and knowing relatively thus provides the appropriate way to be with the One who is with us. Put differently, if one knows God through Christ, then one necessarily knows through story, song, scripture, and all the other particularities of historical communities and traditions. There is no other way to know a God who makes Godself known.

The ability to claim particularity without capitulating to bottomless relativism also depends on owning up to relativity at the level of communities and historically extended traditions while refusing relativism at the level of individual preferences and personal values. In fact, when we fail to mark the difference between the *relativity* of Christian historically extended communities and traditions[75] and the *relativism* of each individual, then the professed relativism easily passes over into a certain sort of absolutism.[76] Take, for example, how unbending—how absolutist—is the claim that everyone can have his or her own truth in contemporary American society. When Christians accommodate such dominant culture, they lose the particularity of their faith tradition. In the language of Prothero, this is the quickest way that "the ideal of religious tolerance" can morph "into the straightjacket of religious agreement."[77]

Finally, to keep the relativity of the Christian tradition from becoming relativistic, Christians must distinguish *truth claims* from

---

75. Alasdair MacIntyre, *Whose Justice? Which Rationality?* (Notre Dame, IN: University of Notre Dame Press, 1988), 349–403.
76. Compare Catherine Keller, *On the Mystery: Discerning God in Process* (Minneapolis: Fortress Press, 2008), 1–22.
77. Prothero, *God Is Not One*, 4.

how they are *justified*. Throughout *Unapologetic Theology: A Christian Voice in a Pluralistic Conversation*, William Placher repudiates a modernist foundational epistemology (or any absolutely certain way of knowing) that presumes to possess an indubitable truth upon which everything else is built. But after spending the greater part of the book underscoring the appropriateness of Christian relativity, Placher surprisingly claims that Christians can and must continue to make robust truth claims. He faces the apparent discrepancy head on:

> I have repeatedly emphasized that all argument operates within some particular tradition, that there is no universal standard of rationality. . . . [At the same time,] as a Christian I believe that the central claims of the Christian faith are true—not merely "true for Christians" or "true within the context of the Christian tradition" but in a strong sense just plain true.[78]

Borrowing from Jeffery Stout, Placher's solution involves an important distinction between the truth one confidently knows and the relative manner by which one can justify it:

> As Stout says, a big part of the solution to the puzzle lies in distinguishing claims about *truth* and claims about *justification*. To use his example: he believes that slavery is wrong—not just in some times and places but everywhere and always. Maybe he is wrong to make that claim across all cultures, but that is really what he believes. On the other hand, he does not know of any way to *argue* for that belief except in the context of some particular tradition. The way we can go about justifying a belief is always context dependent, but the truth claimed for that belief is not.[79]

Following Placher and Stout, I want to suggest that one path toward interfaith engagement would be to recognize that all justifications for Christian truth claims necessarily come from within the tradition. There is simply no neutral, knock-down evidence that would necessarily convince outsiders that Christian truth claims are true. Christians can only witness—largely by giving thick descriptions of the

---

78. William Placher, *Unapologetic Theology: A Christian Voice in a Pluralistic Conversation* (Louisville: Westminster John Knox, 1989), 123.
79. Ibid. Placher here works with Jeffrey Stout, *Ethics After Babel* (Boston: Beacon, 1988), 24–28. See also George A. Lindbeck, *The Nature of Doctrine: Religion and Theology in a Postliberal Age*, 25th anniversary ed. (Louisville: Westminster John Knox, 2009), 134.

world as created by God and redeemable by Christ, relying on the work of the Spirit to enable others to see as they see. Such *witness*, precisely because it differs from *disputing* and even more so from *proving*, invites others also to witness to their own peculiar, particular vision of our shared world.

But Christians also come with a stronger, more paradoxical truth claim—namely, that the Christ in whom Christians see God and to whom they commit themselves and bear witness himself models radical openness to others. Answering the question, "Who is my neighbor?" Jesus tells the "expert in the law" (who already knows that he is to love his neighbor as himself) a story about one outside their own Jewish quarters who aided and abetted a wounded Jew when insiders and authorities would not. It turns out that the answer to a question about how far one's affections and responsibilities should go turns on the example of an "outsider" treating an "insider" as a neighbor (Luke 11:25–37). Even the ministry of Jesus was pried open by the Syrophoenician woman, from whom he learns that non-Jews are worthy of being fed and healed and made whole (Mark 7:25–30; Matt 15:21–28). When Paul describes non-Jewish Christians as new shoots grafted onto an older tree, as guests in the house of Israel, he likewise teaches what being good guests entails: "But if some of the branches were broken off, and you, a wild olive shoot, were grafted in their place to share the rich root of the olive tree, do not boast over the branches. If you do boast, remember that it is not you that support the root, but the root that supports you" (Rom 11:17–18). Those who want to be good hosts must first learn to be good guests. Christians encounter those of other faith traditions and no faith tradition with humility, awe, and graciousness because they understand themselves to be adopted into God's own family.

PART IV

RE-FORMATION

10

Conclusion: Becoming (a) Christian in Christendom

The epigraph of this book quotes Kierkegaard in asking "Where are we? What is the situation in Christendom?" Kierkegaard immediately responds: "It is not difficult to say what the situation is; it is more difficult to change it."[1]

The book as a whole has described "Christian" America, or what I have called our newest form of Christendom. According to Kierkegaard, this is the easy part. The difficult step is to try to change it, or (again in Kierkegaard's terms) to become a Christian in Christendom. In this concluding chapter, I will briefly return to predominant themes introduced in the prior three parts of the book, but with special attention to how one actually becomes more particularly and faithfully Christian among the perils and pitfalls of Christendom.

---

1. Søren Kierkegaard, *For Self-Examination. Judge for Yourself*, trans. Howard V. Hong and Edna H. Hong (Princeton, NJ: Princeton University Press, 1990), 123.

The Tenacity of Christendom

Although I have tried to describe the new set of problems facing Christians in America in the first quarter of the twenty-first century, the problem of Christian identity and discipleship in a culture that renders them normal and innocuous resurfaces throughout the ages. In fact, the problem of cultured Christianity may be—like the poor according to Jesus (Mark 14:7)—one that we will always have among us. Part 1 of this book thus criticized those so-called "post-Christendom" spokespersons who assume that it is easier to be authentically Christian today, now that the cultural-political status of Christianity has dwindled or dropped away. Of course, I share with them the hope that would-be Christians will learn to embody their faith without the kickbacks and trappings of accommodated and acculturated Christianity. However, this book has suggested that we "still" live squarely in Christendom—in a dominant culture that largely presumes to be Christian or where Christianity explicitly or implicitly remains the social norm. It follows that we also "still" live with the difficult task of learning to become Christian *in* (not after) Christendom. Indeed, I doubt whether "Christendom"—for me, a theological concept—is the right word for any historical arrangement that will, by its own momentum, give way to a new and more opportune time. I have departed from post-Christendom writers in three ways:

First, proclaimers of so-called post-Christendom do not take our entanglements in that which we are "post-ing" seriously enough. Unlike the best work on postmodernity, which understands how postmodern culture reproduces and exacerbates the fantasies of modernity, leading to hyper-modern quests for mastery and control, many who celebrate the imminent arrival of a post-Christendom era seem almost glibly optimistic. Besides a view of history more indebted to Enlightenment progress than to the God of scripture, this optimism reflects what Charles Taylor calls a simple subtraction theory. It assumes that Christianity once existed in some uncompromised, nonpolitical form and will again so exist once the shroud of cultured

Christianity drops away. This makes the task of becoming "authentically" Christian seem much easier than it actually is. The danger of Christian accommodation to ill-fitting politics and cultures is perpetual. To become Christian in the face of this danger demands vigilance and ongoing negotiations, rather than the good luck of being born at this time, followed by the straightforward selection of an untarnished tradition.

Second, I believe that the problem of cultured Christianity is a theological problem deeply intertwined with how Christians understand God's providence and human history, the nature of the church, human sin, who Jesus is, and what his cross reveals. And so, unlike some post-Christendom writers who take their cues from the rapidly shifting landscape of American religion, I have taken mine from theologians such as Kierkegaard, Bonhoeffer, and a number of anti-Constantinians, all of whom have addressed the more enduring theological issues of Christian faithfulness and the countercultural witness of the church. Writing in different times and places and diagnosing different sociopolitical compromises, these theologians nonetheless orbit around a perennial theological problem—the problem of how to live out the Christian faith within a culture that idealizes and privileges that tradition while also rendering it redundant and innocuous.

Third, I find the assumption that one can more easily or authentically "choose" to become Christian once Christianity has dropped its cultural trappings and political baggage to be naïve at best, and perhaps off the mark, theologically speaking. The assumption misses what I take to be the most ironic and threatening form of Christendom facing us today. North American dominant society, with its roots in political liberalism and now nearly consumed by consumerist culture, is nothing if not the leading purveyor of free choice. Christianity gets entwined with this allegiance to the right of individuals to decide everything for themselves no less than with pre-canned liturgies or America's militarism or exceptionalism. I find no indication that the call to discipleship by Jesus is any more aligned with an unencumbered freedom to choose than with rote repetition or violent force. Thus when post-Christendom celebrants associate Christendom exclusively with hierarchical church structures, unchosen baptism, and formalistic rituals, celebrating instead the right and freedom of individuals to forge their own way, it can look a bit like a red herring—if not a red, white, and blue one. By my account, the unformed preferences of isolated individuals are part of what gets christened in the latest form of Christendom. To think otherwise confuses an intractable problem with easy escape from it. Celebrations of choice thereby bypass without solving theological issues related to religious formation—namely, how human freedom complements and couples with God's grace, but never really "selects" it, since God first chooses the chooser.

How might one intentionally and determinately become Christian without putting faith in one's choice rather than in the God that summons it? That is a challenge I first introduced when mentioning the difficult decision of whether to allow my oldest son to be baptized. I'll return to baptism and other church practices here, all of which provide paths (when properly reconceived) away from cultured Christianity and into faithful discipleship. And yet, going to church cannot capture all that the task of becoming a Christian entails. *How* one does so depends on—but also, surpasses—*what* Christianity even means.

The What and the How

As part 3 of this book described, the pervasive dangers of America's neo-Christendom include (but are not limited to): its exploitative economy that cheapens human giftedness; its political liberalism, within which the church becomes indistinguishable from coteries of people with similar "interests"; its justification of war; and its self-defeating lip-service to religious inclusivity. I have tried to imagine alternatives to conventional, Constantinian Christendom—ones whereby the church has, or rather *is*, a distinctive and alternative social politic, where it commits to cruciform nonviolence, appreciates gifts by giving them away, and knows its boundaries well enough to acknowledge and learn from those on the other side. I hope to have convincingly portrayed the broad contours of Christian accommodations, of faithful forms of discipleship and community, and the difference between them.

That might sound conclusive, but a book that takes its bearings from Kierkegaard simply cannot get away with portraying the *what* of conventional and countercultural Christianities without further considering *how* a person gets from one to the other. This being said, many "Kierkegaardians" today are sure to emphasize that even Kierkegaard's highly extolled "how" depends in part on the "what." They insist that the most passionate subjective questing does in fact quest after something that, while often paradoxical, is not indeterminate. Or again: they emphasize that there is no formation apart from discernible prototypes whose power pulls us and whose contours steer us toward the good. So, you need a "what," a description of discipleship, after which "the how" patterns itself. Yet, the whole of Kierkegaard's writings battle for the *how*, for the *becoming*, and against the assumption that true Christianity is a faith properly positioned, adequately explained, or correctly administered. For Kierkegaard, faith cannot be true without being truly lived. Indeed, the particular iteration of Christendom he encountered was one where the "what" had almost totally eclipsed the "how," where Christianity was affirmed by cultural guardians and systematized by theological eggheads but inhabited by next to no one. In this situation, Kierkegaard could only emphasize passionate risk and decisive action. Almost any leap would seem to do: "Venture a decisive act; then we can begin."[2]

The Christendom of twenty-first-century North America is both different and similar to that of Kierkegaard. Both lack shape, borders, and attention to "existential" matters. But for Kierkegaard, the amorphous "Christianity" was largely the result of those speculative systematic theologians and other intelligentsia who wanted to read, think, and reflect rather than to act.[3] To find some shape and get

2. Kierkegaard, *Judge for Yourself*, 191.

some existential traction, one had to venture an act of the will, had to passionately *choose* to become Christian. Otherwise, it was as though one kept on sewing and sewing with no real results because one hadn't first tied a knot in the thread.[4]

The assumed Christianity of the United States no longer comprises an overly objective system that almost everyone comprehends, but nearly no one embodies. In fact, American "Christianity" can remain so ambivalent, if not dismissive, of anything that smacks of highbrow comprehension that the knot may need to be tied on the other end, so to speak. Becoming Christian in Christendom may require much more training in *reflection*, intellectual and otherwise, exactly because a self-refuting "whateverism" and general lack of specificity characterizes faith in our public square.

These comments help explain why the present project needed to spend a good deal of time on the *what* of Christianity before fully considering *how* a would-be Christian might live it out. Yoder's writings (despite his own grave inability to live them out consistently) remain valuable in this light. Beside the emphasis he gives to believer's baptism and to "personal" choice as the only access to the faith, Yoder, more than Kierkegaard, equally accentuates that which must inform the believer's choice; he offers a thick description of the concrete political practices of Jesus and the church. Just as idealist descriptions are worthless without a resolution of the will, as Kierkegaard urges, so too are "authentic," passionate choices spurious so long as the social space and political practices of the church go unimagined and unrecognized. Hauerwas, broadly following Yoder but with added reservations about voluntarism and liberal individualism, remains critical of the false separation between belief and practice, or theology and ethics, in the first place. According to him, it is ingenuous to assume "that if we get our 'beliefs' right, we will then know how to

---

3. Søren Kierkegaard, *Concluding Unscientific Postscript to the Philosophical Fragments*, trans. Howard V. Hong and Edna H. Hong (Princeton, NJ: Princeton University Press, 1992), 1:131–33.

4. Søren Kierkegaard, *Sickness unto Death*, trans. Howard V. Hong and Edna H. Hong (Princeton, NJ: Princeton University Press, 1980), 80. I borrow this apt metaphor although Kierkegaard makes a different point with it.

act right."[5] This hits close to home for me. Those, like me, who find themselves captivated by a vision of radical church, but have been so (de)formed by the inadvertent practices of cultured Christianity, need some help on how to move forward. Luckily, the churches have a couple thousand years of practice in helping folks like me become more fully Christian. We turn now to the place and practices of church.

Centering the Church at the Margins

I do not think one could understate the importance of recognizing the pitfalls of cultured Christianity from the perspective of those on the margins, of those who do not benefit from Christianity's presumed "success." Theologians of the cross join liberation theologians, feminists, and neo-monastic communities in intentionally inhabiting that space. Having glimpsed God as fully revealed in the suffering and cross of Jesus, they recognize how ideological (Luther says *sinful*) are our typical understandings of God. Almost inevitably, we *project* onto God our own desires for supremacy, invulnerability, and mastery. In turn, seemingly devout understandings of God as All-Powerful, Supreme, and Impenetrable get used to *justify* our own quests after power and control. But for those who come to know God through Jesus—Jesus the Servant, the Peacemaker, the Crucified—faith can come to function in a different way. It does not prop up social, cultural, or political power but comes to speak truthfully about a God who dispossesses us, who literally frees us to be with those who have little.

But how do Christians—especially relatively affluent, white, "first-world" Christians—best position themselves to come to know such a God? Can individual congregations or the church as a whole occupy a different kind of cultural space? Recall that many post-Christendom writers call on the church to "disestablish" itself, to shed its residual politico-cultural status as a way of making ideological self-justifications less likely. For some, the disestablishment of the established church promises to return us to pre-Constantinian models

---

5. Stanley Hauerwas, *Sanctify Them with the Truth: Holiness Exemplified* (Edinburgh: T&T Clark), 157.

of the Christian "movement."[6] As I have already suggested, I tend to doubt that pleas for disestablishment properly account for the tenacity of Christendom. The desire to restore a primitive, noninstitutional church can also seem quixotic; and exactly because it is quixotic, it is in danger of getting repackaged and resold as the newest form of cultural (and commodified) Christianity. Would not something resembling "relocation"—rather than disestablishment—provide the alternative perspective and *metanoia*, the conversion, needed to see and know God, as well as true discipleship, rightly?

The first "mark" of the new monasticism movement is the church's relocation to abandoned places of empire.[7] As feminists and liberation theologians also suggest, it is at the margins of the dominant society that one is afforded the clarity of vision necessary to discern and follow the will of God. Radical intentional Christian communities literally renounce social and ecclesial power by relocating to poor communities. But it should also be noted that members of the movement are interested in revitalizing the entire church, rather than righteously distinguishing themselves from it. In the words of Jonathan Wilson-Hartgrove, New Monasticism is a pro-church as well as a para-church movement.[8] While relocation might happen by permanently moving to the margins of society, Wilson-Hartgrove suggests that congregations can "experiment" with (I would say "practice") relocation by moving some forms of Christian ministry, such as adult education, to local prisons, centers for troubled teens, group homes, and so forth. The purpose of leaving the church building for such programs would not be service but formation. We would repeatedly enter abandoned places (if only for an afternoon at a time), in order to come to see and know as its residents do.[9] I would add

6. Douglas John Hall, *The End of Christendom and the Future of Christianity* (Harrisburg, PA: Trinity, 1997), 51–66. In *The Cross in Our Context: Jesus and the Suffering of the World* (Minneapolis: Fortress Press, 2003), 169 (and elsewhere), Hall suggests that "the end of Christendom could become a new beginning for the Christian Movement."

7. The Rutba House, ed., *School(s) for Conversion: 12 Marks of a New Monasticism* (Eugene, OR: Cascade, 2005), 10–25.

8. Jonathan Wilson-Hartgrove, *New Monasticism: What It Has to Say to Today's Church* (Grand Rapids, MI: Brazos, 2008), 145–47.

9. Ibid., 86.

that such relocation and re-vision will be quite painful, as parishioners undoubtedly will come to understand themselves as complicit with forces that marginalize those from whom they are learning. Such pain may comprise the communal, affective correlate of the "scandal of particularity" (Kierkegaard) to which Luther's Heidelberg Disputation also so graphically points.

Churches within dominant society can, with the help of those outside their doors, provide the very practices and training that are necessary for them to see their own complicity with unjust powers. Ironic to some, we need to preserve the institutional church in order to rethink its social captivity. There is great risk in such a venture, of course. Even if institutions are needed to sustain the practices that lead us to rightly discern God in the world, those institutions qua institutions will also be concerned with acquiring and distributing money, power, and status. (Luther might say that they necessarily "institutionalize" our proclivity for calling evil good and good evil.[10]) But even Alasdair MacIntyre, who is famous for distinguishing the "internal goods" and virtues accomplished through the disciplines of lived traditions from the "external goods" sought by institutions, will concede that you cannot have one without the other.[11] Without a church of the cross, we can produce no theologians of the cross—no persons capable of knowing things as they actually are.

Familiar Practices Made Strange

Nominal, cultural "Christians" become disciples by reimagining God and faithfulness beside those who have less status and power to lose from such discipleship. By relocating, Christian churches learn how to cultivate persons who can "comprehend the visible and manifest things of God seen through suffering and the cross."[12] But this training happens inside the church as well, even and especially on Sunday

10. Martin Luther, Heidelberg Disputation (1518), in *Martin Luther's Basic Theological Writings*, ed. Timothy F. Lull, 2nd ed. (Minneapolis: Fortress Press, 2005), 58 (thesis 21).
11. Alasdair MacIntyre, *After Virtue*, 2nd ed. (Notre Dame, IN: University of Notre Dame Press, 1984), 194.
12. Luther, Heidelberg Disputation, 57 (thesis 20).

morning. While we could argue about the proper proportion between traditional worship and discipleship out in the world, I resist Hartgrove-Wilson's appeal for more service and fewer church services.[13] Through the sacraments and other church practices, Christians can come to see the presence of God where others simply cannot—in the cross of Jesus and the faces of addicts and prisoners, the poor and forgotten. Could then a church that is composed of—or better, a church that produces—theologians of the cross come to know not only God, but also itself, as both fully visible and still hidden? If so, perhaps the church of the cross becomes a visible alternative to the ways of the world *in and through* its immersion into it.

Three central church practices might develop the attentiveness necessary to see God and the "true church" as each is revealed in its hiding.

Communion: Seeing God in a Godless World

First, the sacrament of the Lord's Supper, especially within those traditions that adhere to "real presence," may train congregants to *see* the hidden God in addition to bestowing God's grace and forgiveness. Luther fought so vehemently against Zwingli about the mode of Christ's presence in the Eucharist not only to emphasize the ostensible passivity involved in receiving grace, but also, to underscore the subtle but vital difference between remembering a Christ who is absent from us (because seated at the right hand of the Father) and recognizing Christ as fully present, although hidden, in the elements.[14] It is not even as if Christ becomes "spiritually" present in the "material" sign. Rather, for Luther, when Christians take in the elements, they consume Christ, body and soul, although as hidden "in, with, and under" the bread and the wine. By saying "Amen" to the words of institution and after the receiving of the meal, communicants not only *proclaim* the mystery of faith, but also, come to *see and know* God where God

---

13. Wilson-Hartgrove, *New Monasticism*, 130–33.
14. Martin Luther, "Confession Concerning Christ's Supper—From Part I (1528)," in *Martin Luther's Basic Theological Writings*, ed. Timothy F. Lull, 2nd ed. (Minneapolis: Fortress Press, 2005), 259–76.

chooses to hide. At best, communion becomes an ongoing *discipline* that gradually redirects our lines of vision from where we think God resides ("spiritually" up in heaven) to the bread and people whose brokenness both mask and disclose a crucified God.

Confession of Sin: Revealing the "True Church"

Whereas communion thus might entail "practice" in recognizing a present, hidden God, the order of confession and forgiveness might help Christians to recognize themselves and the church as a whole. In other words, turning from the center of the liturgy to its necessary beginning incorporates ecclesiology, understandings of church, into the ecclesia itself. Through the confession of sin, church comes to see itself rightly. Given that the practice of confession is best positioned before the entrance hymn but after any opening announcements, it is simultaneously worship already underway and the necessary precursor to its beginning. Confession thus comprises a kind of internal "relocation" of the church, a turning outside-in, as well as the "re-visioning" necessary to see itself rightly. In this sense, it is the practice necessary to and corresponding with the final sending and benediction, by which parishioners are (again) turned out to remember the poor.

Certainly confession, like communion, is the "means" by which Christians come to receive the graces of God. Yet, in this reading, it is also a *practice* that redirects them to the will and ways of God. Note, for example, that the pastor's invocation asks God to "cleanse the thoughts of our hearts" so that all present might perfectly love God and magnify God's name.[15] Or stronger still: the leader petitions the power of the Spirit so that the assembly can begin confessing its sins at all. The assembly then asks for forgiveness, renewal, and guidance not as ends to themselves but "so that [it] may delight in [God's] will and walk in [God's] ways."[16] Confession does not primarily constitute

---

15. "Holy Communion, Setting One," in *Evangelical Lutheran Worship*, Pew Edition (Minneapolis: Augsburg Fortress Press, 2006), 94–96.
16. Ibid.

the relinquishing of some misdeeds so that we might come to God "unburdened." It is a matter of becoming aligned with God's knowing ("to whom all hearts are open, all desires known, and from whom no secrets are hid") so that we might see ourselves as God sees us: as simultaneously sinners and saints—more deeply fallen than we could otherwise know, more deeply loved than we could otherwise bear.

The fact that for most churches, this entire practice is communal should be more than a matter of expediency. Just as we are deeply implicated in the social nature of sin (and so, responsible not only for what we have done but for what we have left undone), so too do members of the community need one another to know themselves truthfully. We are both sinful and saved not as a collection of individuals but as the one body of Christ. Indeed, knowing ourselves as such requires communal practices of the church, whereby all of us are convicted for our failures to be the true church.[17]

We have seen that theologians who emphasize the invisibility of the church often do so out of a realism about sin. If a visible, holy church means that it is virtuous and without blemish, then certainly the awareness of sin makes the true church unrecognizable, at least at first glance. And yet, whether we only "glance" or if we might otherwise come to recognize the church makes all the difference. As the eminent Catholic theologian Karl Rahner has shown, the tendency in Catholicism since Vatican I (1868–70) (according to anti-Constantinians, it has been since the fourth century), has been to be "realistic" about the institutional church's sin by positing an abstract or "spiritual" church that stands as a separate entity over-and-against real churches and real people.[18] Theologians of the cross and other

---

17. See the last chapter of *Life Together* (with *Prayerbook of the Bible*), trans. Daniel W. Bloesch and James H. Burtness (Minneapolis: Fortress Press, 1996), where Bonhoeffer describes confession of sin as constituting a breakthrough to new life (112), or as conversion itself and thus central to becoming a Christian (112–13).

18. Karl Rahner, "The Sinful Church in the Decrees of Vatican II," in *Theological Investigations VI: Concerning Vatican Council II* (New York: Seabury, 1974), 288–89, as cited by William T. Cavanaugh, *Migrations of the Holy: God, State, and the Political Meaning of the Church* (Grand Rapids, MI: Eerdmans, 2011), 153. The idea that I am exploring here about using the confession of sin to mediate between the visibility and invisibility of the church largely follows Cavanaugh's essay, "The Sinfulness and Visibility of the Church: A Christological Exploration," in *Migrations of the Holy*, 141–69.

critics of Christendom show us how the cross trains us to see otherwise. For them, the opposite of smugly identifying the true church "as though [it] were clearly perceptible" in the world[19] is to insist not on the church's invisibility, but on its hiddenness. The holiness of the church is made visible—obscurely and compellingly—in its very repentance of sin. Indeed, the church's corporate confession comprises the very training that is needed to see this.

Baptism: Resisting Conventions and/of Choice

Confessing sin and becoming the body of Christ by partaking in the supper are practices in which all, or almost all, churchgoing Christians partake. I have tried to suggest that confession of sin is not only a rite that Christians instinctively recite, and that communion is not only a sacrament that they passively receive; rather, both might constitute *intentional practices* that help reform the desires and refocus the vision of would-be Christians so that they can come to see God's presence in the world and so love the "highest good," especially as found in the weak and oppressed. A third central practice—that of baptism—is equally important for Christian training, perhaps most important. But here, certain arguments arise, especially from those who explicitly interpret baptism as a way of resisting Christian accommodation and acculturation. In chapter 2, I mentioned one very personal instance of this concerning whether to have our first child baptized as an infant. I here return to the broader ecumenical discussion.

Mennonites and others deemed "Anabaptist" (literally, rebaptizers) have largely associated the rise of the Constantinian church with the ascendancy, if not the invention, of infant baptism. Historically, the two certainly line up. It was not until Christianity became permitted and then sanctioned by the Roman Empire that the boundaries of church became aligned with Western civilization, that creeds were written and used to distinguish orthodoxy from heresy, that sin was understood to be a state into which babies were born, and (related to

---

19. Luther, Heidelberg Disputation, thesis 20.

each of the above) that infant baptism became the widely accepted, often almost compulsory, rite of passage into *both* political citizenship *and* the realm of God's grace. By maintaining the practice of infant baptism (rather unreflectively, according to its critics), the sixteenth-century magisterial reformers seemed simply to relocate Christendom from Empire to smaller and various ecclesial-political bodies. In the Peace of Augsburg (1555), reformers allowed the prince of each region to decide the official Christianity of his territory (*cuius regio, eius religio*; "whose realm, his religion"). Later, the Peace of Westphalia (1648) reaffirmed this commitment while establishing state sovereignty, essentially aligning nation-states with different confessional identities. Throughout all of this, babies regularly became simultaneously citizens of a particular region or state and Christians of a particular stripe long before they knew what they were getting into. Infant baptism thereby *reproduced* assumptions about established Christendom while also quite literally *repopulating* it—almost step-by-step with reproduction itself.

For many contemporary Anabaptists, the ongoing and mainstream practice of baptizing babies still signals complicity to, and the perpetuation of, Constantinianism or established Christendom. Of course, baptism is no longer regarded as entrance into citizenship for most of the Western world, and has never been so regarded in the United States. But if "Christendom" now entails the alignment of Christianity with dominant American values and culture and not simply the mechanisms of the state, then certainly, baptism of babies is one primary way that "Christian" families carry forth a cultural-religious tradition simply because it seems to be expected, normal, or "the right thing to do."

This charge is often dead-on, and I return briefly to my own family as an example. My father (a lifelong Lutheran) expressed consternation when my spouse and I let him know that we were waiting to baptize Asa (and later, his younger brother Gabriel) until they were older and could voluntarily submit to the practice (or not). On some level, I'm sure my father was concerned about the state of his grandchildren's salvation. At another level (and perhaps primarily), I think he suspected that his son and daughter-in-law were intentionally standing apart from cultural-religious-familial traditions that he regarded as good and customary and that need not be broken; he was simply bothered by my/our unwillingness to conform. Critics of infant baptism could easily point to his consternation as evidence that infant baptism has at least as much to do with cultural expectations as with God's grace, forgiveness of sin, or the call to radical discipleship.

The Anabaptist critique of infant baptism largely turns on the fact that babies do not knowingly and voluntarily submit to it. Discipleship for such (pacifist) Christians entails accepting the possibility of martyrdom, however remote. A Christian is one who vows to follow Jesus's countercultural way of the cross, which entails the willingness to suffer rather than protect oneself by resorting to means that Jesus clearly rejected. The seriousness and potentially dangerousness of this call means that no other agent—not the state, not the church, not even parents—has the right to answer it on behalf of another. Because they associate baptism with dying to the ways of the world and freely choosing a life of discipleship, even unto a literal death, radical Christians want each would-be Christian to undergo the waters if and when they are ready to do so.

I take these criticisms of infant baptism to heart. At the same time, however, they too can lead into their own self-justification and capitulations to non-Christian norms. Interestingly, there are a number of Mennonites who now question whether they should continue to link Christendom with infant baptism; indeed, they ask whether the newest forms of Christendom are not reproduced by churches that put too much stock in believers' choices.

Chad Mason, one of the members of Christ Community Church that I cited in chapter 7, raises these concerns in an essay called "Mennonite but not Anabaptist."[20] Mason argues that believer's baptism—and especially, the (rare) practice of literally rebaptizing a person who had been baptized as an infant—can capitulate to American dominant society just as easily as indiscriminate infant baptisms capitulated to

20. Chad. S. Mason, "Mennonite but not Anabaptist," *The Mennonite*, January 8, 2006, 8–10.

European society in the sixteenth century. What resisted Christendom then may inadvertently bolster it today. Mason explains how believer's baptism, and especially rebaptism, once functioned:

> In rebaptizing their converts, radical reformers publicly rejected the indiscriminate practice of infant baptism in medieval Europe and its entanglement with the machinations of state power. . . . In the context of 16th-century Europe, rebaptism served as a clarion call for Christians to reconnect baptism with discipleship and to disconnect baptism from state control.[21]

Yet, for Mason, the context that required rebaptism 500 years ago has changed considerably. Here and now, a different set of cultural entanglements can repackage and reabsorb rebaptism, making it into a practice that unwittingly complies with America's neo-Christendom:

> Today our willingness to rebaptize is most often rationalized in ways that seem to owe more to the Declaration of Independence than the Schleitheim Confession. We justify rebaptism by arguing that the individual did not choose her infant baptism and cannot remember it, so it somehow lacks "meaning" or "personal importance" for her. . . . In 21st–century America, rebaptism may serve to underwrite individualism, which is as perilous to Mennonites as to Catholics [or mainline Protestants].[22]

Mason is largely concerned with the willingness to rebaptize those adults who were already baptized as infants and then converted to the Mennonite Church. But his incisive critique can be extended to any understanding of the sacraments—or in general, of becoming Christian—that would focus exclusively on an individual's intentions and choices and neglect the equally countercultural understanding that God is working through God's people (infants included) and the sacraments of the church long before an individual understands, submits to, and responds to these. In the words of Bonhoeffer, baptism

---

21. Ibid., 9.
22. Ibid. For examples of the way the Schleitheim Confession (1527), a defining Anabaptist confession of faith, linked believer's baptism with conscientious withdrawal from political involvement, see articles I, IV, and VI of "The Schleitheim Confession: Adopted by a Swiss Brethren Conference, February 24, 1527" (Crockett, KY: Rod and Staff, 1985). Accessed August 10, 2015, http://www.anabaptists.org/history/schleith.html.

at full stretch entails a "paradoxically passive action; it means *being* baptized, *suffering* Christ's call."[23]

Clearly, paths that led away from older forms of Christendom can become the point of entry into new forms. Luther and mainline reformers accentuated the utter gratuitousness of God's grace made tangible in communion and in baptism in order to break apart the closed spiritual economy of late medieval Christendom. And yet, the very emphasis on the wonder of free grace easily gets cheapened; it becomes the excuse that "spiritual discount shoppers" need to avoid the work of discipleship. The emphasis within the Radical Reformation on commitment, choice, and the dangerous work of discipleship provides a corrective to this cheapening of grace and of baptism as its "dispenser." At the same time, when the fact of having chosen itself becomes venerated, choices and the unencumbered individuals who make them also can get in the way of authentic discipleship and rightful witness to God's grace. Put positively, conversion, baptism, and any other entry point into Christianity must entail a curious blend of intentionality and volition, on the one hand, and receptivity and witness to God's grace, on the other.

Reforming Christians, Inside and Outside of Church

What is true for the sacraments is also true for the gift and work of discipleship itself. Both Bonhoeffer and Kierkegaard emphasize the indispensability of personal appropriation and responsibility for becoming Christian. Yet, both also understand that free assent to comprise the ground of possibility for faith rather than the whole kit and caboodle of faith itself. Kierkegaard urges readers to venture a decisive act, to make a "leap of faith," but he repeatedly explains that such an act provides only the ground of possibility for the faithful reception of grace, which is itself a grace. Analyzing Jesus's calling to the first disciples, Bonhoeffer notes what the person can and should do: "Peter can leave his nets."[24] Yet, note that this "merely" puts Peter

23. Dietrich Bonhoeffer, *Discipleship*, trans. Barbara Green and Reinhard Krauss (Minneapolis: Fortress Press, 2003), 207.

in a position where faith becomes possible; it neither guarantees nor exhausts the life of faith itself. The same is true for contemporary would-be Christians, as Bonhoeffer advises directly:

> You can leave your home on Sunday and go to hear the preaching. If you do not do it, then you willfully exclude yourself from the place where faith is possible. In this the Lutheran confessions show that they know there is a situation which enables faith and one in which faith is possible. To be sure this knowledge is very hidden here, almost as if they now were ashamed of it, but it is present as one and the same knowledge of the significance of the first step as an external deed.[25]

Something must be done that positively contributes to making faith possible. And yet, Bonhoeffer's very next sentence is this: "Once this knowledge is ascertained, then something else must be acknowledged, namely, that this first step as an external deed is and remains a dead work of the law, which can by itself never lead to Christ."[26]

The call to discipleship demands that one act decisively when answering it without misdirecting one's trust and hope from the God who calls to one's own decisive response. But there is another element of Bonhoeffer's description of discipleship that will strike modern readers as strange. In order not to exclude ourselves "from the place where faith is possible," Bonhoeffer would have us go to church. Indeed, while the calling to discipleship is an individual summons, the community called church is absolutely essential to the substance of discipleship: "Everyone enters discipleship alone, but no one remains alone in discipleship."[27] Hauerwas concurs: "To be Christian is not something you do alone."[28]

I resist weighing in on the question of whether there is salvation outside the church. Yet, I am absolutely convinced that there is no radical discipleship outside a community of believers that can help each "individual" become the faithful follower that she or he is called to become. In the words of Dorothy Day, such communities make it

24. Bonhoeffer, Discipleship, 64.
25. Ibid., 65.
26. Ibid.
27. Ibid., 99.
28. Stanley Hauerwas, Hannah's Child: A Theologian's Memoir (Grand Rapids, MI: Eerdmans, 2010), 247.

easier to be good. They do so not by making Christianity popular or by "leveling" its radical ideals (Kierkegaard's worry), but by giving each of us something to give ourselves over to and so enabling the process of formation. However, I admit that my convictions about the importance of church are largely intellectual in nature. More "existentially," and like so many others today, I find myself pulling back from Christian community, *especially* when considering the various pitfalls of acculturated and accommodated Christianity. I have *felt* the absence of a robust tradition or communal fellowship just as acutely as I have *known* that I need it.

Whatever my own hopes and hang-ups might be, it is certainly true that American Christians today no longer live under the authority and formative power of a deep and abiding tradition called church. Very few of us have been formed by church practices so determinatively that we find ourselves belonging to the church even before we consciously choose it. Many post-Christendom writers celebrate this dis-embedding of the individual for shoring up her power of choice. But others only desperately hope that free commitment might now do for individuals what the tradition once did for all of us:

> In the past religious integration was handed down by a tradition. But that tradition itself has lost its authority in the eyes of our contemporaries, including most believers. What then ought the Christian to do to survive as a genuine religious believer? I see no alternative but that he or she must now personally integrate what tradition did in the past. Nothing in culture today compels our contemporaries to embrace a religious faith. If they do, they alone are responsible for allowing their faith to incorporate all aspects of their existence. Hence the vital importance of the spiritual life.[29]

These lines, written by Catholic philosopher Louis Dupré, emphasize the responsibility that individuals must now take for their own religious "formation." The conscious change of individual hearts is no easy thing "because it implies confronting each person with his or her unique responsibility to *decide* on a personal attitude toward

---

29. Louis Dupré, "Seeking Christian Interiority: An Interview with Louis Dupré," *The Christian Century*, July 16–23, 1997, 655.

existence." According to Dupré, "Each person must find his or her own way in the world"—becoming a Christian "from within"—which Dupré admits is a daunting task. Yet, he calls for decision as our only authentic action, even if he also maintains that Christianity is "a faith that is not a 'choice' but, for those chosen to it, an absolute summons."[30]

The fact that we no longer find ourselves securely embedded in the tradition called church means that the task of forging a spirituality largely on our own cannot be bypassed, even for faithful churchgoers. Yet, I think the intentionality and creativity and exertion needed today even goes beyond what Dupré suggests. It is not only that we are no longer embedded in an ecclesial tradition that would teach us what is worth desiring "from without." It is also that we have been born into Christendom—a tradition that misshapes our desires, one that misleads us into wanting normalcy and niceties more than the love of Christ and his church. As Judith Butler reminds us, we are always already formed into "regimes of power that produce and constrain certain ways of being."[31] No complete break is possible; what is needed is constant vigilance and resistance to paths that are all-too-well trodden so that new paths might slowly open up. In this sense, the formation that is necessary—inside and outside of church—will always entail re-formation. Acculturated and accommodated Christianity has become such a normal state of affairs that more faithfully inhabiting the faith will entail as much unlearning and resistance as it takes avowals, commitments, and decisions. It will be less like learning to ride a new, tricky bike and more like unlearning to ride a "normal" one.[32]

Reformulating Radicals: Theologians of the Cross

Finally, while this book has focused on Christendom and its critics, rather than the ways these critics relate to one another, allow me to say a final word about the weight of their combined witness when

---

30. Dupré, "Seeking," 655, 659.
31. Judith Butler, *Frames of War: When Is Life Grievable?* (London: Verso), 169.
32. One can, in fact, unlearn to ride a bike; see https://www.youtube.com/watch?v=MFzDaBzBlL0 (accessed August 10, 2015) for certain proof.

viewed together. I have suggested that Christendom has seen its sharpest critics not only among the peace churches, who typically call it *Constantinianism*, but also within a notable strand of Lutheran theologians, beginning with Martin Luther, made famous by Søren Kierkegaard, and popularized (with all the inherent risks of being glamorized and pigeonholed) by Dietrich Bonhoeffer. The targets of their criticisms are not the same, of course. Yoder's or Hauerwas's American Constantinianism and the church's witness to the state are not quite Kierkegaard's Danish "establishment" and his call for passionate commitment, which are not exactly Bonhoeffer's German-Christian church and his vision of religionless Christianity or the renewal of discipleship as a response to costly grace.

At the same time, I have tried to suggest that we would do well to consider these famous critics of Christendom in relation to one another. Certainly, there are broad influences, direct and indirect: Kierkegaard and Bonhoeffer together anticipate the marks of a visible church and can be read as influenced by the sixteenth-century Radical Reformation.[33] Kierkegaard shares an emphasis on Christian volition and critique of infant baptism with anti-Constantinians. Bonhoeffer connects through his pacifist rejection of state-sponsored warfare, which gets complicated, but not undone, in his participation (to whatever degree) in a plot to overthrow Hitler. Literature from the new monastic movement draws substantially on Bonhoeffer, and especially on the communitarian and pacifist Bonhoeffer of *Discipleship* and *Life Together*. Hauerwas, too, writes of Bonhoeffer as an exemplar, even a saint, of the pacifist tradition.[34] Less predictably, he credits Kierkegaard with first focusing his attention on the how, rather than the what, of Christianity.[35]

---

33. For Kierkegaard, this was primarily through his participation with the Moravians and his relation with the free church "awakenings" of his day. See Jørgen Bukdahl, *Søren Kierkegaard and the Common Man* (Grand Rapids, MI: Eerdmans, 2001). For even deeper connections between Kierkegaard and radical Christianity, see Vernard Eller, *Kierkegaard and Radical Discipleship: A New Perspective* (Princeton, NJ: Princeton University Press, 1968). Recall also that Bonhoeffer was "introduced" to pacifist convictions and practices through Jean Lasserre, a Huguenot and pacifist.

34. Hauerwas, *Performing the Faith: Bonhoeffer and the Practice of Nonviolence* (Grand Rapids, MI: Brazos, 2004), 33–72.

35. Hauerwas, *Hannah's Child*, xi. See also Hauerwas's comments about taking Paul Holmer's course on

Without dissolving the differences, I might even suggest that each of these leading critics of Christendom might fruitfully be called a theologian of the cross. Luther critiques "theologians of glory" for assuming that God is best reflected in what is most powerful, idealized, and invulnerable in mainstream society. Against this assumed continuity between the greatness of God and that of our cultural achievements and political sovereignties, Luther witnesses to a rather strange God made known in unlikely places: through Jesus of Nazareth, in the Bethlehem barn where he was born, and, especially, on the cross where he was tortured and killed as a religious-political insurrectionist.

God's revelation through the rejection and suffering of Jesus is disturbing. For Luther, Jesus's death *should* remain scandalous because it turns our everyday notions of dominion, divinity, and discipleship upside-down. Who is God if a dead Palestinian Jew fully reveals "Him"? Can following this peculiar God and the way of the cross ever really *work* among social, cultural, and political norms that inevitably underwrite idols and ideologies? The pressure to domesticate Christianity, to siphon from its full-bodied and suffering God a thinner, more spiritualized, and palatable deity—one that falls in line with our other gods—seems almost inevitable.[36] The God of Jesus predictably gives way to our abstractions, and discipleship becomes innocuous.

Kierkegaard can be called a theologian of the cross when he underscores the particularity and peculiarity of "eternity's entrance into time," which should remain an intellectual paradox and an affective scandal. Rather than skirt the possibility of offense that the scandal of Christ introduces, Christians ought to face it head on, and so claim their own eccentricity. Bonhoeffer can be called a theologian of the cross when he underscores the fact that disciples "follow after" one who is rejected and despised. In *Discipleship*, he adds that "when Christ calls a man, he bids him come and die."[37] His famous late musing

---

Kierkegaard in 1962 in his foreword to Paul L. Holmer, *On Kierkegaard and the Truth*, ed. David J. Gouwens and Lee C. Barrett (Eugene, OR: Cascade, 2012), ix.

36. "Just try once to apply this *ne quid nimis* [nothing too much] to the god who allows himself to be crucified." Kierkegaard, *Concluding Unscientific Postscript*, 404.

from prison that "only a suffering God can help" likewise points to a scandalous God whose particular help ceases to be offensive only to those abiding in the abandoned places of empire (prisons, urban ghettos, the rural poor, concentration or refugee camps) or others who learn to see empathically from their perspective. Finally, anti-Constantinian pacifists can be called theologians of the cross when they remind us that the cross itself was not firstly a free-floating symbol of Christian atonement but an instrument of political torture wielded by an occupying regime. Whatever it might mean to Christians today, it should not get wrapped in the flag and made to endorse the very powers that Jesus nonviolently confronted. Lifting it high, Christians instead witness to a particular, peculiar, and wholly countercultural way of living in a world that remains determined by war in the name of security. With their emphasis on the distinctive shape of the church, anti-Constantinians also push other theologians of the cross to live out their scandalous knowledge of God in concrete, communal ways.

I am not suggesting that the "thin theological tradition"[38] known as the theology of the cross was invented by Martin Luther, that the critiques of Lutheranism by Kierkegaard and Bonhoeffer are overshadowed by their place therein, or that anti-Constantinians and other radicals can simply be grafted onto a theological tradition that has roots in different ecclesial soil. Nor am I suggesting that we are not helped by attending to the abiding and generative tensions between divergent descriptions of Jesus Christ, grace, sin, church, and discipleship. What I am suggesting is that many of the sharpest critiques of cultured Christianity arise from a shared witness to a God whose majesty takes the form of servant-hood, a God who is revealed in the depths of human suffering, a God who would rather die than kill. The church's peculiarity stems from its worship and discipleship of a peculiar God. The church is strange because it is a church of the cross,

---

37. Bonhoeffer, *The Cost of Discipleship*, trans. R. H. Fuller (New York: Touchstone, 1995), 89. See chapter 6, footnote 97 above.

38. This is the designation used by Douglas John Hall in many of his works. See, for example, Hall, *Cross in Our Context*, 13–16.

and the cross is strange because it is the cross of God. Christians can become something new and strange only and always as they imitate and worship *that* God.

For Further Reading

On Christendom, Secularism, and American "Christian" Culture

Baldwin, James. *The Fire Next Time*. New York: Vintage, 1993.

Bellah, Robert N., Richard Madsen, William M. Sullivan, Ann Swidler, and Steven M. Tipton. *Habits of the Heart: Individualism and Commitment in American Life*. New York: Harper & Row, 1985.

Clapp, Rodney. *A Peculiar People: The Church as Culture in a Post-Christian Society*. Downers Grove, IL: IVP Academic, 1996.

Cox, Harvey. *The Secular City: Secularization and Urbanization in Theological Perspective*. New York: Macmillan, 1965.

Dean, Kendra Creasy. *Almost Christian: What the Faith of Our Teenagers Is Telling the American Church*. New York: Oxford University Press, 2010.

Gregory, Bradley. *The Unintended Reformation: How a Religious Revolution Secularized Society*. Cambridge, MA: Harvard University Press, 2012.

Hall, Douglas John. *The End of Christendom and the Future of Christianity*. Harrisburg, PA: Trinity, 1997.

Niebuhr, H. Richard. *Christ and Culture*. New York: HarperCollins, 2001.

Percy, Walker. *Love in the Ruins: The Adventures of a Bad Catholic at a Time Near the End of the World*. New York: Avon, 1971.

Smith, Christian, and Melinda Lundquist Denton. *Soul Searching: The Religious and Spiritual Lives of American Teenagers*. New York: Oxford University Press, 2005.

Taylor, Charles. *Ethics of Authenticity*. Cambridge, MA: Harvard University Press, 1991.

_____. *A Secular Age*. Cambridge, MA: Harvard University Press, 2007.

West, Cornel. *Democracy Matters: Winning the Fight Against Imperialism*. New York: Penguin, 2004.

Wise, Tim. *White Like Me: Reflections on Race from a Privileged Son*. Revised and Updated Edition. Berkeley, CA: Counterpoint, 2011.

Selected Works by/about Søren Kierkegaard

Barrett III, Lee C. *Kierkegaard*. Nashville: Abingdon, 2010.

Kierkegaard, Søren. *Concluding Unscientific Postscript to the Philosophical Fragments*. Translated by Howard V. Hong and Edna H. Hong. Princeton, NJ: Princeton University Press, 1992.

_____. *Fear and Trembling. Repetition*. Translated by Howard V. Hong and Edna H. Hong. Princeton, NJ: Princeton University Press, 1983.

_____. *For Self-Examination. Judge for Yourself*. Translated by Howard V. Hong and Edna H. Hong. Princeton, NJ: Princeton University Press, 1990.

_____. *The Moment and Late Writings*. Translated by Howard V. Hong and Edna H. Hong. Princeton, NJ: Princeton University Press, 1989.

_____. *Practice in Christianity*. Translated by Howard V. Hong and Edna H. Hong. Princeton, NJ: Princeton University Press, 1991.

Kirkpatrick, Matthew D. *Attacks on Christendom in a World Come of Age: Kierkegaard, Bonhoeffer, and the Question of "Religionless Christianity."* Eugene, OR: Wipf & Stock, 2011.

Walsh, Sylvia. *Kierkegaard: Thinking Christianly in an Existential Mode*. Oxford: Oxford University Press, 2009.

Selected Works by/about Dietrich Bonhoeffer

Bonhoeffer, Dietrich. *Discipleship*. Translated by Barbara Green and Reinhard Krauss. Minneapolis: Fortress Press, 2003.

_____. *Ethics*. Translated by Reinhard Krauss, Charles C. West, and Douglas W. Scott. Minneapolis: Fortress Press, 2005.

____. *Life Together. Prayerbook of the Bible.* Translated by Daniel W. Bloesch and James H. Burtness. Minneapolis: Fortress Press, 1996.

____. *Letters and Papers from Prison.* Translated by Isabel Best, Lisa E. Dahill, Reinhard Krauss, and Nancy Lukens. Minneapolis: Fortress Press, 2009.

____. *No Rusty Swords: Letters, Lectures, and Notes, 1928-1936.* New York: Harper & Row, 1965.

____. *Sanctorum Communio: A Theological Study of the Sociology of the Church.* Translated by Reinhard Krauss and Nancy Lukens. Minneapolis: Fortress Press, 1998.

Bonhoeffer: Pastor, Pacifist, Nazi Resister. Directed by Martin Doblmeier. 2004. New York: First Run Features, 2004. DVD.

Kirkpatrick, Matthew D. *Attacks on Christendom in a World Come of Age: Kierkegaard, Bonhoeffer, and the Question of "Religionless Christianity."* Eugene, OR: Wipf & Stock, 2011.

Marsh, Charles. *Strange Glory: A Life of Dietrich Bonhoeffer.* New York: Knopf, 2014.

McBride, Jennifer M. *The Church for the World: A Theology of Public Witness.* Oxford: Oxford University Press, 2012.

Nation, Mark, Anthony G. Siegrist, and Daniel P. Umbel. *Bonhoeffer the Assassin? Challenging the Myth, Recovering His Call to Peacemaking.* Grand Rapids, MI: Baker, 2013.

Constantinianism and Its Critics

Guth, Karen V. *Christian Ethics at the Boundary: Feminisms and Theologies of Public Life.* Minneapolis: Fortress Press, 2015.

Hauerwas, Stanley. *After Christendom? How the Church Is to Behave if Freedom, Justice, and a Christian Nation Are Bad Ideas.* Nashville: Abingdon, 1991.

____. *God, Medicine and Suffering.* Grand Rapids, MI: Eerdmans, 1990.

____. *Performing the Faith: Bonhoeffer and the Practice of Nonviolence.* Grand Rapids, MI: Brazos, 2004.

Hauerwas, Stanley, and William H. Willimon, *Resident Aliens: A Provocative Christian Assessment of Culture and Ministry for People Who Know That Something Is Wrong.* Nashville: Abingdon, 1989.

Leithart, Peter J. *Defending Constantine: The Twilight of an Empire and the Dawn of Christendom*. Downers Grove, IL: InterVarsity, 2010.

Schüssler Fiorenza, Elisabeth. *In Memory of Her: A Feminist Theological Reconstruction of Christian Origins*. Tenth Anniversary Edition. New York: Crossroad, 1994.

Sider, Alex. *To See History Doxologically: History and Holiness in John Howard Yoder's Ecclesiology*. Grand Rapids, MI: Eerdmans, 2011.

West, Cornel. *Democracy Matters: Winning the Fight Against Imperialism*. New York: Penguin, 2004.

Yoder, John Howard. *The Politics of Jesus*. Grand Rapids, MI: Eerdmans, 1994.

_____. *The Priestly Kingdom: Social Ethics as Gospel*. Notre Dame, IN: University of Notre Dame Press, 2001.

_____. *The Royal Priesthood: Essays Ecclesiastical and Ecumenical*. Scottdale, PA: Herald, 1998.

Economy, Ecology, and Grace

Berry, Wendell. "Christianity and the Survival of Creation." In *Sex, Economy, Freedom, and Community: Eight Essays*, 93–116. New York: Pantheon, 1993.

_____. *Life Is a Miracle: An Essay Against Modern Superstition*. New York: Counterpoint, 2000.

Cavanaugh, William T. *Being Consumed: Economics and Christian Desire*. Grand Rapids, MI: Eerdmans, 2008.

Luther, Martin. "The Freedom of a Christian" (1520). Translated by W. A. Lambert. In *Luther's Works*, volume 31, edited by Harold J. Grimm, 333–77. Philadelphia: Fortress Press, 1957.

_____. "The Ninety-Five Theses (1517)." In *Martin Luther's Basic Theological Writings*, edited by Timothy F. Lull, 40–46. Minneapolis: Fortress Press, 2005.

_____. "Two Kinds of Righteousness" (1519). Translated by Lowell J. Satre. In *Luther's Works*, volume 31, edited by Harold J. Grimm, 297–306. Philadelphia: Fortress Press, 1957.

Sandel, Michael J. *What Money Can't Buy: The Moral Limits of Markets*. New York: Farrar, Straus & Giroux, 2012.

Tanner, Kathryn. *Economy of Grace*. Minneapolis: Fortress Press, 2005.

Torvend, Samuel. *Luther and the Hungry Poor: Gathered Fragments*. Minneapolis: Fortress Press, 2008.

Weber, Max. *The Protestant Ethic and the Spirit of Capitalism*. Translated by Talcott Parsons. New York: Charles Scribner's Sons, 1958.

Wirzba, Norman. *The Paradise of God: Renewing Religion in an Ecological Age*. Oxford: Oxford University Press, 2003.

Politics, Church, and Intentional Christian Communities

Budde, Michael. *The Borders of Baptism: Identities, Allegiances, and the Church*. Eugene, OR: Cascade, 2011.

Cavanaugh, William. *Migrations of the Holy: God, State, and the Political Meaning of the Church*. Grand Rapids, MI: Eerdmans, 2011.

Claiborne, Shane. *The Irresistible Revolution*. Grand Rapids, MI: Zondervan, 2006.

Forest, Jim. *All Is Grace: A Biography of Dorothy Day*. Maryknoll, NY: Orbis, 2011.

Hall, Douglas John. *Has the Church a Future?* Louisville: Westminster John Knox, 1980.

Haw, Chris. *From Willow Creek to Sacred Heart: Rekindling My Love for Catholicism*. Notre Dame, IN: Ave Maria, 2012.

McClintock Fulkerson, Mary. "A Place to Appear: Ecclesiology as if Bodies Mattered." *Theology Today* 64 (2007): 159–71.

Metz, Johann Baptist. *The Emergent Church: The Future of Christianity in a Postbourgeois World*. Translated by Peter Mann. New York: Crossroad, 1981.

Rutba House, ed. *School(s) for Conversion: 12 Marks of a New Monasticism*. Eugene, OR: Cascade, 2005.

Schlabach, Gerald W. *Unlearning Protestantism: Sustaining Christian Community in an Unstable Age*. Grand Rapids, MI: Brazos, 2010.

Wilson-Hartgrove, Jonathan. *New Monasticism: What It Has to Say to Today's Church*. Grand Rapids, MI: Brazos, 2008.

_____. *To Baghdad and Beyond: How I Got Born Again in Babylon*. Eugene, OR: Cascade, 2005.

Violence, War, and Peacemaking

Arendt, Hannah. *On Violence.* San Diego: Harvest/Harcourt Brace Jovanovich, 1970.

Bell, Daniel M. *Just War as Christian Discipleship: Recentering the Tradition in the Church rather than the State.* Grand Rapids, MI: Brazos, 2009.

Butler, Judith. *Frames of War: When Is Life Grievable?* London: Verso, 2009.

Cahill, Lisa Sowle. *Love Your Enemies: Discipleship, Pacifism, and Just War Theory.* Minneapolis: Fortress Press, 1994.

Cavanaugh, William. *The Myth of Religious Violence: Secular Ideology and the Roots of Modern Conflict.* Oxford: Oxford University Press, 2009.

Hedges, Chris. *War Is a Force That Gives Us Meaning.* New York: Anchor, 2002.

Kant, Immanuel. "Perpetual Peace." *On History.* Edited by Lewis White Beck. New York: Macmillan, 1963.

Luther, Martin. "Whether Soldiers, Too, Can be Saved" (1526). Translated by Charles M. Jacobs. *Luther's Works,* vol. 46, edited by Robert C. Schultz. Philadelphia: Fortress Press, 1967.

Hauerwas, Stanley. *War and the American Difference: Theological Reflections on Violence and National Identity.* Grand Rapids, MI: Baker, 2011.

Hauerwas, Stanley, and Jean Vanier. *Living Gently in a Violent World: The Prophetic Witness of Weakness.* Downers Grove, IL: InterVarsity, 2008.

Yoder, John Howard. *The War of the Lamb: The Ethics of Nonviolence and Peacemaking.* Edited by Glen Stassen, Mark Thiessen Nation, and Matt Hamsher. Grand Rapids, MI: Brazos, 2009.

Religious Plurality and Interfaith Cooperation

Asad, Talal, Wendy Brown, Judith Butler, and Saba Mahmood. *Is Critique Secular? Blasphemy, Injury, and Free Speech.* New York: Fordham University Press, 2013.

Carroll, James. *Constantine's Sword: The Church and the Jews.* Boston: Houghton Mifflin, 2001.

Eck, Diana. *Encountering God: A Spiritual Journey from Bozeman to Banaras.* Boston: Beacon, 2003.

Heim, S. Mark. *Salvations: Truth and Difference in Religion*. Maryknoll, NY: Orbis, 1995.

Largen, Kristin Johnston. *Finding God Among Our Neighbors: An Interfaith Systematic Theology*. Minneapolis: Fortress Press, 2013.

Levine, Amy-Jill. *The Misunderstood Jew: The Church and the Scandal of the Jewish Jesus*. New York: HarperOne, 2006.

Lindbeck, George A. *The Nature of Doctrine: Religion and Theology in a Postliberal Age*. 25th Anniversary Edition. Louisville: Westminster John Knox, 2009.

Patel, Eboo. *Acts of Faith: The Story of an American Muslim, the Struggle for the Soul of a Generation*. Boston: Beacon, 2007.

____. *Sacred Ground: Pluralism, Prejudice, and the Promise of America*. Boston: Beacon, 2012.

Placher, William. *Unapologetic Theology: A Christian Voice in a Pluralistic Conversation*. Louisville: Westminster John Knox, 1989.

Wyschogrod, Michael. *Abraham's Promise: Judaism and Jewish-Christian Relations*. Edited by R. Kendall Soulen. Grand Rapids, MI: Eerdmans, 2004.

Yoder, John Howard. *The Jewish-Christian Schism Revisited*. Edited by Michael G. Cartwright and Peter Ochs. Scottdale, PA: Herald, 2008.

Jesus, Empire, and the Cross

Borg, Marcus J., and John Dominic Crossan. *The Last Week: What the Gospels Really Teach about Jesus's Final Days in Jerusalem*. New York: HarperOne, 2006.

Crossan, John Dominic. *God and Empire: Jesus Against Rome, Then and Now*. New York: HarperCollins, 2007.

Hall, Douglas John. *The Cross in Our Context: Jesus and the Suffering of the World*. Minneapolis: Fortress Press, 2003.

Howard-Brook, Wes. *"Come Out, My People": God's Call out of Empire in the Bible and Beyond*. Maryknoll, NY: Orbis, 2010.

Luther, Martin. Heidelberg Disputation (1518). *Martin Luther's Basic Theological Writings*. Edited by Timothy F. Lull, 47–61. Minneapolis: Fortress Press, 2005.

Moltmann, Jürgen. *The Crucified God*. 40th Anniversary Edition. Minneapolis: Fortress Press, 2014.

Soelle, Dorothee. *Suffering*. Translated by Everett R. Kalin. Philadelphia: Fortress Press, 1975.

Solberg, Mary M. *Compelling Knowledge: A Feminist Proposal for an Epistemology of the Cross*. Albany, NY: State University of New York Press, 1997.

Trelstad, Marit, ed. *Cross Examinations: Meanings of the Cross Today*. Minneapolis: Fortress Press, 2006.

Westhelle, Vítor. *The Scandalous God: The Use and Abuse of the Cross*. Minneapolis: Fortress Press, 2006.

Index

0

and vicarious representative action, 272–73; life of, 96–100; on cheap grace vs. costly grace, 196–200; on Lutheranism, 97, 100–101, 197–202, 209; on peace and war, 241–42, 269–76; on visible but hidden church, 236–38; sacramentality according to, 108–9, 336–37; Western history according to, 109–16

Borg, Marcus, 135

Bruce, Steve, 63

Buber, Martin, 229

Budde, Michael, 20n28, 49–50, 205n2

Buddhism, 282, 289–90, 313

Bush, George W., 244, 261–63

Bussie, Jacqueline, 277

Butler, Judith, 139n37, 216, 264, 266–68, 272, 340

Caiaphas (high priest), 298, 300–301

calling. *See* vocation

Carroll, James, 295, 295–96n40

Catholic Workers, 226, 228, 257n36

Cavanaugh, William, 62n17, 90–91, 212n14, 246–47n10, 248, 260n41, 283, 286

chaplaincy, 123–26, 127–28

choice, 29–32, 323–24, 326, 339–40; and baptism, 31, 333–37; and neo-Christendom, 29–32, 309

Christ Community Church (Des Moines, IA), xiv, 218n33, 224–25, 229, 335

Christ hymn (Phil 2), 181–82, 184n60, 189, 274

Christendom: and baptism, 30–32, 333–34; and civil religion, 11–12, 63, 73–74, 137–40, 150, 171, 248–50; and consumerism, 167–72; and contemporary culture, 7–12, 20–27; and Islam, 280, 306–9; and nationalism, 85–88, 90–92, 245–46; liberalized versions of, 18–24, 280, 307–8; traditional definitions of, xvii, xix, xxvi, 11–12; versus post-Christendom assumptions, x, xvii, 13–15, 119, 269, 322–24, 339

Christian culture: as chaplaincy, 123–28; as patriotic citizenship 85–92; as purveying comfort, 56–60

Christianity: accommodation of, x–xi, 8, 10–11, 14, 23, 39, 51, 118–19, 123, 132, 153, 155, 197, 265–66, 293; acculturation of, x–xi, 8, 10–11, 17, 39, 82, 132, 153, 197, 265–66, 269; and other religions, 279–317; as all-inclusive, xxii–xxiii, 285–86 (*see also* supersessionism); as assumed, xx–xxiii, 291; as normal, xxiii–xxvi, 291; borders of, 17–18, 20–21, 132, 236–38, 313; Catholic and Protestant,